CREATION IMAGERY IN THE GOSPEL OF JOHN

Carlos Raúl Sosa Siliezar

LONDON · NEW YORK · OXFORD · NEW DELHI · SYDNEY

T&T CLARK
Bloomsbury Publishing Plc
50 Bedford Square, London, WC1B 3DP, UK

BLOOMSBURY, T&T CLARK and the T&T Clark logo
are trademarks of Bloomsbury Publishing Plc

First published in Great Britain 2015
Paperback edition first published 2018

A catalogue record for this book is available from the British Library.

ISBN: HB: 978-0-56766-424-2
PB: 978-0-56768-165-2
ePDF: 978-0-56766-425-9

Library of Congress Cataloging-in-Publication Data
Sosa Siliezar, Carlos Raúl.
Creation imagery in the gospel of John / by Carlos Raúl Sosa Siliezar.
pages cm. – (Library of New Testament studies; volume 546)
Includes bibliographical references and index.
ISBN 978-0-567-66424-2 (hardback)
1. Bible. John–Criticism, interpretation, etc. 2. Creation–Biblical teaching. 3. Bible. John–
Language, style. I. Title.
BS2615.52.S657 2015
226.5'06–dc23
                    2015018728

Series: Library of New Test ament Studies, volume 546

Typeset by Forthcoming Publications Ltd (www.forthpub.com)

To find out more about our authors and books visit
www.bloomsbury.com and sign up for our newsletters.

To
Gabriela

ἡ γυνὴ ὅταν τίκτῃ λύπην ἔχει, ὅτι ἦλθεν ἡ ὥρα αὐτῆς·
ὅταν δὲ γεννήσῃ τὸ παιδίον, οὐκέτι μνημονεύει τῆς θλίψεως
διὰ τὴν χαρὰν ὅτι ἐγεννήθη ἄνθρωπος εἰς τὸν κόσμον
(John 16.21)

CONTENTS

ABBREVIATIONS

1. Bibliographical

AB	Anchor Bible
ABR	*Australian Biblical Review*
ABRL	Anchor Bible Reference Library
AcT	*Acta theologica*
AGJU	Arbeiten zur Geschichte des antiken Judentums und des Urchristentums
AnBib	Analecta biblica
ANF	*Ante-Nicene Fathers*
AsTJ	*Asbury Theological Journal*
ATANT	Abhandlungen zur Theologie des Alten und Neuen Testaments
ATR	*Anglican Theological Review*
BAR	*Biblical Archaeology Review*
BBB	Bonner biblische Beiträge
BBR	*Bulletin for Biblical Research*
BBRSup	Bulletin for Biblical Research Supplements
BDAG	W. F. Bauer, F. W. Danker, W. F. Arndt, and F. W. Gingrich, *Greek–English Lexicon of the New Testament*
BDF	F. Blass, A. Debrunner, and R. W. Funk, *A Greek Grammar of the New Testament and Other Early Christian Literature*
BeO	*Bibbia e oriente*
BETL	Bibliotheca ephemeridum theologicarum lovaniensium
BHS	*Biblia Hebraica Stuttgartensia*
Bib	*Biblica*
BibRes	*Biblical Research*
BiPa	Biblia Patristica: Index des citations et allusions bibliques dans la littérature
BIS	Biblical Interpretation Series
BJS	Brown Judaic Studies
BK	*Bibel und Kirche*
BNTC	Black's New Testament Commentaries
BTNT	Biblical Theology of the New Testament
BZAW	Beihefte zur Zeitschrift für die alttestamentliche Wissenschaft
BZNW	Beihefte zur Zeitschrift für die neutestamentliche Wissenschaft
CahRB	Cahiers de la Revue biblique
CBET	Contributions to Biblical Exegesis and Theology
CBQ	*Catholic Biblical Quarterly*

CJT	*Canadian Journal of Theology*
CQR	*Church Quarterly Review*
CRINT	Compendia rerum iudaicarum ad Novum Testamentum
CS	Collezione Storica
CSCO	Corpus scriptorium christianorum orientalium
CSEL	Corpus scriptorium ecclesiasticorum latinorum
DCLS	Deuterocanonical and Cognate Literature Studies
DJD	Discoveries in the Judaean Desert
DRev	*Downside Review*
EBib	Etudes bibliques
ECC	Eerdmans Critical Commentary
ECS	Early Christian Studies
EstBíb	*Estudios bíblicos*
EstEcl	*Estudios eclesiásticos*
ETL	*Ephemerides theologicae lovanienses*
EvQ	*Evangelical Quarterly*
ExAud	*Ex auditu*
ExpTim	*Expository Times*
FAT	Forschungen zum Alten Testament
FC	Fathers of the Church
FCB	Feminist Companion to the Bible
FN	*Filología neotestamentaria*
GOTR	*Greek Orthodox Theological Review*
Greg	*Gregorianum*
GRM	Graeco-Roman Memoirs
GsAP	Guides to Apocrypha and Pseudepigrapha
HBT	*Horizons in Biblical Theology*
HR	*History of Religions*
HSTE	HochschulSammlung Theologie, Exegese
HTKNT	Herders theologischer Kommentar zum Neuen Testament
HTR	*Harvard Theological Review*
Int	*Interpretation*
JAJSup	Journal of Ancient Judaism Supplements
JBL	*Journal of Biblical Literature*
JCSD	Jewish and Christian Self-definition
JCTCRS	Jewish and Christian Texts in Contexts and Related Studies
JJS	*Journal of Jewish Studies*
JSem	*Journal of Semitics*
JSJ	*Journal for the Study of Judaism in the Persian, Hellenistic, and Roman Periods*
JSNT	*Journal for the Study of the New Testament*
JSNTSup	Journal for the Study of the New Testament: Supplement
JSPSup	Journal for the Study of the Pseudepigrapha: Supplement Series
JSSSup	Journal of Semitic Studies Supplements
JTS	*Journal of Theological Studies*
KJV	King James Version

KTU	*Die keilalphabetischen Texte aus Ugarit.* Edited by M. Dietrich, O. Loretz, and J. Sanmartín. Neukirchen–Vluyn, 1976. 2nd enlarged ed. of *KTU*: *The Cuneiform Alphabetic Texts from Ugarit, Ras Ibn Hani, and Other Places.* Edited by M. Dietrich, O. Loretz, and J. Sanmartín. Münster, 1995
LCL	Loeb Classical Library
LD	Lectio divina
LFC	Library of the Fathers of the Church
LHBOTS	Library of Hebrew Bible / Old Testament Studies
LNTS	Library of New Testament Studies
LPT	Le Point théologique
LSJ	H. G. Liddell, R. Scott, and H. S. Jones, *A Greek–English Lexicon*
LumVie	*Lumière et vie*
L&N	J. P. Louw and E. A. Nida (eds.), *Greek–English Lexicon*
MH	*Museum helveticum*
MM	J. H. Moulton and G. Milligan, *The Vocabulary of the Greek Testament*
NAWG	Nachrichten (von) der Akademie der Wissenschaften in Göttingen
NA^{28}	*Novum Testamentum Graece*, 28th edn
NCB	New Century Bible
Neot	*Neotestamentica*
NETS	New English Translation of the Septuagint
NICNT	New International Commentary on the New Testament
NIGTC	New International Greek Testament Commentary
NKGWG	Nachrichten von der Königlichen Gesellschaft der Wissenschaft zu Göttingen: Philologisch-historische Klasse
NovT	*Novum Testamentum*
NovTSup	Novum Testamentum Supplements
NPNF[1]	*Nicene and Post-Nicene Fathers*, Series 1
NPNF[2]	*Nicene and Post-Nicene Fathers*, Series 2
NTAbh	Neutestamentliche Abhandlungen
NTL	New Testament Library
NTOA	Novum Testamentum et Orbis Antiquus
NTS	*New Testament Studies*
NTTS	New Testament Tools and Studies
OBO	Orbis biblicus et orientalis
OTP	J. H. Charlesworth (ed.), *Old Testament Pseudepigrapha* (2 vols.)
PD	Presencia y diálogo
PDD	Parole de Dieu
PGL	G. W. H. Lampe, *Patristic Greek Lexicon*
PL	J.-P. Migne (ed.), *Patrologiae cursus completus: Series latina*
ProEccl	*Pro ecclesia*
PRSt	*Perspectives in Religious Studies*
PTL	*PTL: A Journal for Descriptive Poetics and Theory of Literature*
PVTG	Pseudepigrapha Veteris Testamenti graece
RB	*Revue biblique*
RechBib	Recherches bibliques
RefR	*Reformed Review*

RevBL	*Review of Biblical Literature*
RevScRel	*Revue des sciences religieuses*
RHPR	*Revue d'histoire et de philosophie religieuses*
RSR	*Recherches de science religieuse*
RST	Regensburger Studien zur Theologie
RSV	Revised Standard Version
SBE	Semana bíblica española
SBF	Studium Biblicum Franciscanum
SBFLA	*Studii biblici Franciscani liber annus*
SBLDS	Society of Biblical Literature Dissertation Series
SBLECL	Society of Biblical Literature: Early Christianity and Its Literature
SBLEJL	Society of Biblical Literature Early Judaism and Its Literature
SBLMS	Society of Biblical Literature Monograph Series
SBLRBS	Society of Biblical Literature Resources for Biblical Study
SBLSBS	Society of Biblical Literature Sources for Biblical Study
SBLSCS	Society of Biblical Literature Septuagint and Cognate Studies
SBLSymS	Society of Biblical Literature Symposium Series
SBLTT	Society of Biblical Literature Texts and Translations
SBT	Studies in Biblical Theology
SC	Sources chrétiennes
ScrTh	*Scripta Theologica*
SCS	Septuagint Commentary Series
SE	*Studia evangelica*
SFSHJ	South Florida Studies in the History of Judaism
SJT	*Scottish Journal of Theology*
SNTSMS	Society for New Testament Studies Monograph Series
SP	Sacra Pagina
SPAW	Sitzungsberichte der preussischen Akademie der Wissenschaften
SQEF	Synopse des quatre évangiles en français
SR	*Studies in Religion*
SScEJC	Studies in Scripture in Early Judaism and Christianity
STDJ	Studies on the Texts of the Desert of Judah
Str-B	H. L. Strack and P. Billerbeck, *Kommentar zum Neuen Testament aus Talmud und Midrasch*
SVTP	Studia in Veteris Testamenti pseudepigraphica
SVTQ	*St. Vladimir's Theological Quarterly*
TBN	Themes in Biblical Narrative
TDNT	G. Kittel and G. Friedrich (eds.), *Theological Dictionary of the New Testament*
ThSt	*Theological Studies*
TLG	*Thesaurus linguae graecae*
TS	Texts and Studies
TSAJ	Texte und Studien zum antiken Judentum
TSt	Textos y estudios
TTod	*Theology Today*
TU	Texte und Untersuchungen
TUGAL	Texte und Untersuchungen zur Geschichte der altchristlichen Literatur

TynBul	*Tyndale Bulletin*
UniSt	Unitrel Studieserie
UUÅ	Uppsala universitetsårsskrift
VC	*Vigiliae christianae*
VE	*Vox evangelica*
VerEc	*Verbum et Ecclesia*
VTSup	Supplements to Vetus Testamentum
WBC	Word Biblical Commentary
WUNT	Wissenschaftliche Untersuchungen zum Neuen Testament
YJS	Yale Judaica Series
ZAC	*Zeitschrift für Antikes Christentum / Journal of Ancient Christianity*
ZNW	*Zeitschrift für die neutestamentliche Wissenschaft und die Kunde der älteren Kirche*
ZRGG	*Zeitschrift für Religions- und Geistesgeschichte*
ZTK	*Zeitschrift für Theologie und Kirche*

2. Biblical

1 Chron.	1 Chronicles
1 Cor.	1 Corinthians
1 Esd.	1 Esdras
1 Kgs	1 Kings
1 Macc.	1 Maccabees
1 Pet.	1 Peter
1 Sam.	1 Samuel
1 Tim.	1 Timothy
2 Chron.	2 Chronicles
2 Cor.	2 Corinthians
2 Esd.	2 Esdras
2 Kgdms	2 Kingdoms
2 Kgs	2 Kings
2 Macc.	2 Maccabees
2 Pet.	2 Peter
2 Sam.	2 Samuel
3 Kgdms	3 Kingdoms
4 Kgdms	4 Kingdoms
Bel	Bel and the Dragon
Col.	Colossians
Dan.	Daniel
Deut.	Deuteronomy
Eccl.	Ecclesiastes
Eph.	Ephesians
Ep. Jer.	Epistle of Jeremiah
Est.	Esther
Exod.	Exodus
Ezek.	Ezekiel
Gen.	Genesis
GJohn	The Gospel of John

GLuke	The Gospel of Luke
GMark	The Gospel of Mark
GMatthew	The Gospel of Matthew
Hab.	Habakkuk
Hag.	Haggai
Heb.	Hebrews
Hos.	Hosea
Isa.	Isaiah
Jer.	Jeremiah
Jn	John
Judg.	Judges
Lk.	Luke
Mal.	Malachi
Mic.	Micah
Mk	Mark
Mt.	Matthew
Nah.	Nahum
Neh.	Nehemiah
Num.	Numbers
Phil.	Philippians
Prov.	Proverbs
Ps., Pss.	Psalm, Psalms
Rev.	Revelation
Rom.	Romans
Sir.	Sirach
Song	Song of Songs
Sus.	Susanna
Tit.	Titus
Tob.	Tobit
Wis.	Wisdom
Zech.	Zechariah

3. Pseudepigrapha

1 En.	*1 (Ethiopic) Enoch*
2 Bar.	*2 (Syriac) Baruch* [= *Apocalypse of Baruch*]
2 En.	*2 (Slavonic) Enoch*
3 Bar.	*3 (Greek) Baruch*
4 Ezra	*4 Ezra* [= 2 Esd 3–14]
4 Macc.	*4 Maccabees*
Apoc. Abr.	*Apocalypse of Abraham*
Apoc. Adam	*Apocalypse of Adam*
Apoc. Elij.	*Apocalypse of Elijah*
Apoc. Sedr.	*Apocalypse of Sedrach*
Ep. Arist.	*Letter of Aristeas*
Fr. Ps.-Gr. Poets	*Fragments of Pseudo-Greek Poets*
Hell. Syn. Pr.	*Hellenistic Synagogal Prayers*
Jos. Asen.	*Joseph and Aseneth*

Jub.	*Jubilees*
LAB	*Liber Antiquitatum Biblicarum*
LAE	*Life of Adam and Eve*
Liv. Proph.	*Lives of the Prophets*
Mart. Isa.	*Martyrdom of Isaiah*
Odes	*Odes of Solomon*
Pr. Man.	*Prayer of Manasseh*
Pss. Sol.	*Psalms of Solomon*
Sib. Or.	*Sibylline Oracles*
T. Adam	*Testament of Adam*
T. Ash.	*Testament of Asher*
T. Benj.	*Testament of Benjamin*
T. Dan	*Testament of Dan*
T. Levi	*Testament of Levi*
T. Mos.	*Testament of Moses*
T. Naph.	*Testament of Naphtali*
T. Sol.	*Testament of Solomon*

4. Other Early Jewish and Christian Literature

1 Apol.	Justin, *First Apology*
1 Clem.	*1 Clement*
Acts Paul	*Acts of Paul*
Aristob.	*Aristobulus*
Autol.	Theophilus, *Ad Autolycum*
Barn.	*Barnabas*
C. Ar.	Athanasius, *Orationes contra Arianos*
Catech.	Augustine, *De catechizandis rudibus*
Comm. Jo.	Origen, *Commentarii in evangelium Joannis*
Dial.	Justin Martyr, *Dialogus cum Tryphone*
Ep. Apos.	*Epistle to the Apostles*
Epid.	Irenaeus, *Epideixis tou apostolikou kērygmatos*
Gos. Pet.	*Gospel of Peter*
Haer.	Irenaeus, *Adversus haereses* (*Against Heresies*)
Herm.	Tertullian, *Adversus Hermogenem*
Hom. Jo.	Chrysostom, *Homiliae in Joannem*
Ign. *Magn.*	Ignatius, *To the Magnesians*
Inc.	Athanasius, *De incarnatione*
Inf. Gos. Thom.	*Infancy Gospel of Thomas*
Marc.	Tertullian, *Adversus Marcionem*
Pasc.	Melito, *Peri Pascha* (*On the Pascha*)
Praep. ev.	Eusebius, *Praeparatio evangelica*
Prax.	Tertullian, *Adversus Praxean*
Spect.	Tertullian, *De spectaculis*
Trim. Prot.	Nag Hammadi Codex XIII,1 *Trimorphic Protennoia*
Vit. Ant.	Athanasius, *Vita Antonii*

5. Philo

Abr.	*De Abrahamo*
Cher.	*De cherubim*
Conf. Ling.	*De confusion linguarum*
Congr.	*De congress eruditionis gratia*
Dec.	*De decalogo*
Det. Pot. Ins.	*Quod deterius potiori insidiari soleat*
Ebr.	*De ebrietate*
Fug.	*De fuga et inventione*
Leg. All.	*Legum allegoriae*
Leg. Gai.	*Legatio ad Gaium*
Migr. Abr.	*De migration Abrahami*
Mut. Nom.	*De mutatione nominum*
Op. Mund.	*De opificio mundi*
Plant.	*De plantatione*
Poster. C.	*De posteritate Caini*
Praem. Poen.	*De praemiis et poenis*
Quaest. in Gen.	*Quaestiones et Solutiones in Genesin*
Rer. Div. Her.	*Quis rerum divinarum heres sit*
Sacr.	*De sacrificiis Abelis et Caini*
Sobr.	*De sobrietate*
Somn.	*De sommiis*
Spec. Leg.	*De specialibus legibus*
Virt.	*De virtutibus*
Vit. Mos.	*De vita Mosis*

6. Josephus

Apion	*Against Apion*
Ant.	*Jewish Antiquities*
War	*The Jewish War*

7. Dead Sea Scrolls and Related Texts

1QH[a]	The first copy of *Hymns / Hodayot*
1QM	*War Scroll*
1QS	*Community Rule / Manual of Discipline*
3Q15	3QTr (*Copper Scroll*)
4Q176	4QTan (*Consolations*)
4Q265	4QSD (*Community Rule + Damascus Document*)
4Q266	*Damascus Document*[a]
4Q271	4QD[f] (*Damascus Document*[f])
4Q305	*Meditation on Creation B*
4Q381	4QapPs[b] (Non-Canonical Psalms B)
4Q385	4QpsEzek[a] (*Pseudo-Ezekiel*)
4Q392	liturgical
4Q422	*Treatise on Genesis and Exodus*
4Q423	*Sapiential Works A*[e]
4Q440	Qumran document, hymnic
r 4Q504	recto 4QDibHam[a] (*Words of the Luminaries*)

4Q511	4QShir^b (*Songs of the Sage*)
4Q530	4QEnGiants^b ar (*4QBook of Giants^b ar*)
11Q5	11QPs^a
11Q19	11QT (*Temple Scroll*)

8. Mishnah, Talmud, Targumic Texts, and Related Literature

b. B. Bat.	Babylonian Talmud Baba Batra
Gen. Rab.	Genesis Rabbah
Lev. Rab.	Leviticus Rabbah
Midr. Ps.	Midrash Psalm
m. Meg.	Mishnah, *Megillah*
m. Taʿan	Mishnah, *Taʿanit*
Pesiq. Rab.	Pesiqta Rabbati
Pesiq. Rab Kah.	Pesiqta de Rab Kahana
Tg. Neof. Gen.	*Targum Neofiti* Genesis
Tg. Onq. Gen.	*Targum Onqelos* Genesis
Tg. Ps.-J Gen.	*Targum Pseudo-Jonathan* Genesis
t. Taʿan.	Tosefta, *Taʿanit*

9. Non-Christian Greek and Latin Works

Aen.	Virgil, *Aeneid*
Argon.	Apollonius of Rhodes, *Argonautica*
Fac.	Plutarch, *De facie in orbe lunae*
Herc. fur.	Seneca, *Hercules furens*
Hist.	Herodotus, *Historiae*
Il.	Homer, *Iliad*
PGM	*Greek Magical Papyri*
Symp.	Plato, *Symposium*

10. Textual Criticism

1 … 527	Cursive manuscripts
046 … 0303	Uncial manuscripts
a … f	Old Latin manuscripts
A … Z	Uncial manuscripts
Bo^k	Bohairic manuscript
C''	Some manuscripts of the Catena
f	The minuscule family
L'`	Lucianic witnesses
LA^A	Jerome's Latin translation
O''	Hexaplaric witnesses
POxy	Oxyrhynchus papyri
S	Codex Sinaiticus (Septuagint)
Syr^{cur}	Old Syriac Curetonianus version
א	Codex Sinaiticus, IV century
Γ … Ψ	Majuscule manuscripts
κτλ.	καὶ τὰ ἕτερα (and the other things)

11. Others

2nd	second
3rd	third
B.C.E.	before the Common Era
c.	*contra*
ca.	*circa*
C.E.	Common Era
cf.	*confer* (*compare*)
d.	died
ed.	edition, edited by
edn	edition
eds.	editors
e.g.	*exempli gratia* (for example)
ET	English translation
et al.	*et alii* (and others)
frgs.	fragments
idem	the same
i.e.	*id est* (that is)
LXX	Septuagint (the Greek Old Testament)
MT	Masoretic text (of the Old Testament)
n., nn.	footnote, footnotes
NT	New Testament
OT	Old Testament
p., pp.	page, pages
rev.	revised
trans.	translator
v., vv.	verse, verses
vol., vols.	volume, volumes
§	paragraph

INTRODUCTION

The Gospel of John (hereafter GJohn) opens with exactly the same phrase as the book of Genesis in the Septuagint: ἐν ἀρχῇ (Jn 1.1; Gen. 1.1). Furthermore, Jn 1.3-10 contains clear references (vv. 3, 10) to the creation of the world and imagery (vv. 4-5) that arguably evokes the story of creation in Genesis, the first book of the Pentateuch and the first book of what it is now known as the Old Testament (OT). Unlike the other three canonical gospels, John[1] begins his account with creation. This inevitably leads to the question: 'What is the place and significance of creation imagery in GJohn as a whole?' This work seeks to answer that question by mapping out the extent of creation imagery in GJohn, by assessing instances that other scholars have proposed, and by explaining the role that valid instances play in their immediate literary contexts and in the context of GJohn as a whole. By answering that question, I try to elucidate how creation imagery contributes to the overall message of GJohn. I will begin in the following sections by reviewing the major conclusions of previous investigations, explaining their limitations and clarifying how this project advances the discussion.

I. Previous Discussions

Sir Edwin Clement Hoskyns was the first to argue for the place and significance of creation imagery in GJohn. While he is best known for his commentary on GJohn,[2] he also published an article in 1920 in which

---

1. Following Church tradition (e.g. Irenaeus, *Haer.* 3.1.1), I refer to the author or final editor of GJohn as 'John' without making any claim about the authorship of this text.

2. E. C. Hoskyns, *The Fourth Gospel* (ed. F. N. Davey; 2 vols.; London: Faber & Faber, 1940). The following discussion of previous research on creation in GJohn closely follows C. R. Sosa Siliezar, 'La creación en el Evangelio de Juan: Una revisión bibliográfica de autores anglófonos', *ScrTh* 45 (2013), pp. 445–63. Permission to reprint here a substantial part of this article was kindly granted by *Scripta Theologica*, Universidad de Navarra.

he contended that John drew extensively from Gen. 1–3 in the composition of his Gospel, especially in the passion and resurrection narratives.[3] Hoskyns claimed that there were more than a dozen instances of creation imagery in GJohn, including the woman in 16.21 (Gen. 2.23), the account of Jesus reclining his head in sleep in 19.30 (Gen. 2.21-22), and the mention of a garden in 18.1, 26; 19.41 and the misunderstanding of Jesus as the gardener in 20.15 (considered to be allusions to the garden of Eden, Gen. 2–3).

In light of John's apparent use of Gen. 1–3 to this extent, Hoskyns drew two basic conclusions. First, John insists 'on the importance…of Christianity as the new creation, and the return to the presence of God, which had been lost by the sin of Adam and Eve'.[4] Second, John 'suggests that the events which caused the original fall are…reversed, and once again the Garden of Eden is open to men'.[5]

However, many of the instances Hoskyns claims of creation imagery can be questioned on methodological grounds. He did not state specifically what criteria he used to identify links to Gen. 1–3 in GJohn, but he seems, for one thing, to have regarded verbal parallels and similar concepts as evidence that John was borrowing from Gen. 1–3. Therefore, he felt justified in drawing a parallel between the woman (γυνή) in Jn 16.21 and Eve, who is called woman (γυνή) in Gen. 2.23. Hoskyns also used the history of interpretation in order to support the credibility of links he suggested to Gen. 1–3 in GJohn. For example, he claimed that quotations from the Fathers in Corderio's catena on Jn 19.31-34 and Ephraem's commentary on the Diatessaron 'shew that…traditional exegesis apparently naturally compared and contrasted Adam and Christ'.[6] Another implicit criterion in Hoskyns' analysis has to do with Johannine language itself. He claimed that GJohn 'contains many words and phrases which bear two or even three meanings, and each different meaning carries with it further allusion and suggestion'.[7] In light of this, Hoskyns proposed that when Mary mistakes Jesus for the gardener in Jn 20.15, this is an instance of double meaning in which the reader may find an allusion.[8]

---

3. E. C. Hoskyns, 'Genesis I—III and St John's Gospel', *JTS* 21 (1920), pp. 210–18.
4. Hoskyns, 'Genesis', p. 217.
5. Hoskyns, 'Genesis', p. 215.
6. Hoskyns, 'Genesis', p. 210. Cf. B. Corderio, *Catena Patrum Graecorum in Sanctum Ioannem ex Antiquissimo Graeco Codice Ms. Nunc Primum in Lucem Edita* (Belgium: Ex Officina Plantiniana Balthasaris Moreti, 1630).
7. Hoskyns, 'Genesis', p. 210.
8. Hoskyns, 'Genesis', p. 210.

Upon closer examination, however, Hoskyns seems not to have applied these criteria completely rigorously or consistently. A reader who assumes that conceptual parallels are evidence of John's dependence on Gen. 1–3 can find allusions to the Genesis story of creation virtually anywhere in the Gospel. There are a few limits to one's imagination once words that are commonplace and even concepts that lack verbal parallels are admitted as evidence of literary dependence. As for the criterion of history of interpretation, Hoskyns seems to have applied it inconsistently. He failed to show how this criterion applied to all of his suggested instances of creation imagery. On the other hand, he tended to extrapolate patristic interpretations of other New Testament (NT) books into the interpretation of GJohn. For instance, he observed that Justin Martyr, commenting on Lk. 1.35 (*Dial.* 100), drew a parallel between Eve and Mary.[9] He offered this observation to support his claim that Mary also is the new Eve in Jn 19.26-27.

During the rest of the twentieth century, five more essays and one thesis appeared in which scholars argued for the place and significance of creation imagery in GJohn. In the first of these essays, written in 1947, W. J. Phythian-Adams endeavoured to prove that John confirms and completes Paul's ideas about new creation.[10] He proposed several links to Gen. 1–3 in GJohn, claiming, for instance, that Jn 4.13-14 and 7.37-39 were each an 'allusion to the waters of the abyss, stored at the Creation beneath the "navel" ("belly") of the earth'.[11] This author posited a new creation theme in GJohn (the removal of sin and evil from the world) and concluded that both John and Paul share the same perspective about the new creation.[12] Nevertheless, Phythian-Adams' work was once again hampered by a lack of criteria for the identification of putative instances of creation imagery in GJohn. For example, he argued that in GJohn those who acknowledge the signs of Jesus are a new creation 'fashioned in his Maker's image', and that this acknowledgment indicates the 'consummation of the Six Days' Work'.[13] In support of this conclusion, he quoted Augustine, who considers in *Catech.* 39 that Christ

9. Hoskyns, 'Genesis', p. 212. Cf. P. Bobichon, *Justin Martyr: Dialogue avec Tryphon. Édition critique, traduction et commentaire* (Paradosis, 47; 2 vols.; Fribourg: Academic Press Fribourg, 2003), vol. 1, pp. 454–7.

10. W. J. Phythian-Adams, 'The New Creation in St. John', *CQR* 144 (1947), pp. 52–75. He even recognized that his suggestions about GJohn 'have emerged from [his] study of St. Paul' (p. 53).

11. Phythian-Adams, 'Creation', p. 69.

12. Phythian-Adams, 'Creation', p. 69.

13. Phythian-Adams, 'Creation', pp. 74–5.

came to inaugurate the 'sixth age' in God's plan. The difficulty with Phythian-Adams' use of Augustine is that this church father was making general comments about the 'ages of the world' as he saw them in several passages of the whole Christian canon without restricting his observations to GJohn. Therefore, using Augustine as evidence that John was intending creation imagery is hardly legitimate.

Without claiming any conceptual relationship between GJohn and Paul, Raymond Thomas Stamm studied the theme of creation in GJohn in an article published in 1969.[14] Stamm concluded that in GJohn God's work of creation is unfinished and that Jesus came to continue God's creative work through the forgiveness of sins, bringing humanity into a right relationship with God. Stamm also claimed that Jesus called his disciples to continue God's creative work. Stamm indicated that the 'command in the book of Genesis to be fruitful and multiply and fill the earth and till and keep the garden [Gen. 1.28; 2.15] continues in force' in Jesus' statement that his disciples ought to bear much fruit (Jn 15.5).[15] Stamm based his larger conclusions on six proposed conceptual parallels between GJohn and Genesis.[16] All six alleged conceptual parallels, however, lack significant word agreements. Furthermore, Stamm has omitted (without any explicit justification) any detailed treatment of the Johannine prologue, in which creation imagery is actually clearer and more evident.

Two Spanish scholars also worked on the theme of creation in GJohn.[17] They argued that creation is one of the most important topics in the theology of GJohn. They proposed that John's use of chronology was intended as a pointer to the theme of creation: the sequence of days in Jn 1.19–2.1 was arranged in light of the six days of creation in Gen. 1. They also concluded that John intends to portray Jesus as Adam when

14. R. T. Stamm, 'Creation and Revelation in the Gospel of John', in *Search the Scripture: New Testament Studies in Honor of Raymond T. Stamm* (ed. J. M. Myers; Leiden: Brill, 1969), pp. 13–32.

15. Stamm, 'Creation', p. 14.

16. As an example of Stamm's 'conceptual parallels', see his following remark: 'This intimate relationship between the Creator and his human creatures in the Gospel of John [13.23] overcomes man's alienation and realizes God's original intention as expressed in the story of his walking in the garden of Eden ready at any time to converse with Adam' ('Creation', p. 19).

17. J. Mateos and J. Barreto, *Vocabulario Teológico del Evangelio de Juan* (Madrid: Cristiandad, 1980), pp. 16, 46, 52–3. See also their commentary *El Evangelio de Juan: Análisis lingüístico y comentario exegético* (Madrid: Cristiandad, 3rd edn, 1992).

referring to him as man and son of man.[18] They even posited a number of commonplace words as indicators of 'creation vocabulary': ζωή, ζάω, ζωοποιέω, γεννάω, πατήρ, υἱός, and φῶς.[19] Mateos and Barreto asserted that John's 'extremely free' (*extremadamente libre*) use of the OT allows them to find creation imagery in the Gospel.[20] Again, however, without explicit criteria for the identification of creation imagery in GJohn, the possibilities to see creation in this Gospel seem unlimited.

A far more moderate proposal is found in the work of Abraham Terian, who sees creation imagery in the Johannine prologue and in the two healing narratives performed by Jesus on the Sabbath (Jn 5 and 9).[21] Yet, Terian also posits in passing that the darkness in Jn 6.17 could be related to Gen. 1.2, that the light in Jn 9.5; 11.9; 12.35 recalls the creation of light in Gen. 1.3-5, and that Jn 20.22 is an instance of creation imagery.[22] These three suggestions require more defence, but Terian does not provide a full argumentation to sustain them. Furthermore, Terian does not fully develop how Jn 20.22 functions as an instance of creation imagery in GJohn. Terian also fails to explain how Jn 17.5 and 17.24 function in the Gospel as instances of creation imagery. Notwithstanding these limitations, Terian's suggestion that the prologue is somehow related to the two healing narratives performed on the Sabbath is valuable.

The last essay devoted to creation in GJohn produced in the twentieth century was offered by Paul Sevier Minear. He proposed more than a dozen instances of creation imagery scattered through the prologue and the account of Jesus' ministry, including: (1) the phrase 'grace and truth' (Jn 1.14, 17) as evidence that Jesus came in order to open the way to return to the situation of Gen. 1; (2) the negations in Jn 1.13 as evidence that God had lifted the curse of the first woman; (3) the designation of Jesus as lamb that takes away the sin of the world (1.29) as an echo of Gen. 3; (4) the pasture in Jn 10.9 as a reminder of the good earth in Gen. 1.[23] He was careful to assign varying degrees of probability to his

18. Mateos and Barreto, *Vocabulario*, pp. 15, 47–8. An Adam Christology in GJohn has also been suggested by J. Ronning, *The Jewish Targums and John's Logos Theology* (Peabody: Hendrickson, 2010), pp. 99–100, 105.

19. Mateos and Barreto, *Vocabulario*, pp. 14, 46.

20. Mateos and Barreto, *Vocabulario*, pp. 10, 17–18, 57.

21. A. Terian, 'Creation in Johannine Theology', in *Good News in History: Essays in Honor of Bo Reicke* (ed. Ed. L. Miller; Atlanta: Scholars Press, 1993), pp. 45–61.

22. Terian, 'Creation', pp. 51, 55, 58.

23. P. S. Minear, *Christians and the New Creation: Genesis Motifs in the New Testament* (Louisville: Westminster John Knox, 1994), pp. 83–5, 92–3, 95, 100–101. See also Minear's two articles: 'Logos Affiliations in Johannine Thought', in

suggestions. For example, he indicated that 'it remains uncertain whether the narrator consciously referred to the Genesis curses [in Jn. 1.13]'.[24] But he remarked that Jn 1.29 is 'surely an echo' of Gen. 3.[25] According to Minear, Jesus in GJohn came in order to eliminate the curse over Adam and Eve and to re-create people by taking away the sin of the world. The same critique that I have made of previous proposals can be made of Minear's suggestion: there is a lack of methodological clarity about the links to Gen. 1–3 that have occurred to him.

The only full-scale treatment of creation in GJohn during this period is the thesis of Terence Craig Voortman.[26] His main purpose is to read GJohn 'with the creation theme constantly in mind'.[27] He argues that 'the creation perspective is *only one* perspective (point of view) with which to understand the Gospel'.[28] Voortman's approach allows him to see the creation theme everywhere in the Gospel: e.g. (1) Jesus creates by his word alone in 4.50 and (2) Jesus, as the Creator, transcends the natural and physical laws in 2.9.[29] However, it seems that Voortman has imposed the creation theme onto the text, since he has attempted to read GJohn with this topic constantly in mind.

This description of previous discussions on creation imagery in GJohn in the twentieth century invites several observations. First, there are limited attempts to provide a detailed investigation of this topic. There are merely six articles and one thesis specifically dealing with this topic in GJohn as a whole that have appeared in a period of eighty years (1920–2000) that I have been able to identify.[30] Second, there are significant disagreements over the full number of instances of creation imagery in

---

Christology in Dialogue (ed. R. F. Berkey and S. A. Edwards; Cleveland: Pilgrim, 1993), pp. 142–56 (144); 'The Promise of Life in the Gospel of John', *TTod* 49 (1993), pp. 485–99 (488).

24. Minear, *Christians*, p. 100.

25. Minear, *Christians*, p. 85.

26. T. C. Voortman, 'Understanding the Fourth Gospel from the Perspective of the Creation Theme' (D.Litt. et Phil. diss., Rand Afrikaans University, 1998).

27. Voortman, 'Creation', p. 1.

28. Voortman, 'Creation', pp. 2, 7 (his emphasis).

29. Voortman, 'Creation', pp. 84–7, 152–3.

30. One cumulative and classified bibliography of books and periodical literature on GJohn covering a period from 1920 to 1965 does not even have the entry 'creation'. The other compilation covering a period from 1965 to 1985 does have the heading 'The Creation' but under it there is only one entry, a book devoted to the Greek philosophical approach to the concept of creation that includes a brief treatment of the Johannine prologue. E. Malatesta, *St. John's Gospel 1920–1965: A Cumulative and Classified Bibliography of Books and Periodical Literature on the*

GJohn. Third, there is by no means a consensus concerning the import of creation imagery for the interpretation of GJohn. Fourth, it is difficult to discern which criteria each scholar has used in order to posit instances of creation imagery. As we will see in the following paragraphs, these issues are not fully resolved in our present century.

The interest in creation in GJohn seems far more prominent in twenty-first-century scholarship. In the last thirteen years no fewer than eight relevant works have been produced. One of those studies is the recent thesis by Anthony Moore.[31] He proposes that creation is 'the underlying theme running through John's gospel'[32] and argues that John consciously 'uses Gen. 1:1–2:4a as the model for the first part of his gospel (Jn 1:1–17:26) and Gen. 2:4b ff for the second part [Jn 18–21]'.[33] Specifically, he claims that 'the sequence of the days of creation [Gen. 1.1–2.4a], may be seen as the "groundmap" of the Book of Signs (Jn 2–12), the High Priestly Prayer (Jn 17) and have connection with Jn 21'.[34] In his view, only a special group of readers that have become very familiar with the text of GJohn may have detected what Moore deems is the ever-present theme of creation running through GJohn.[35]

Moore provides a long list of what he terms creation indicators in GJohn as the basis for his conclusion that creation imagery is the main theme in the Gospel.[36] The list includes thirty-nine commonplace verbs, nouns, adjectives, and adverbs. Furthermore, he claims that the Johannine signs are a 're-presentation of the days of creation in the Genesis sequence'.[37] According to him, his thesis has two major implications for the interpretation of GJohn: Jesus is revealed as the Creator who has divine sovereignty and Jesus brings the restoration of paradise.

Moore's thesis has at least two major problems. First, GJohn has been the subject of study, discussion, meditation, and reflection over the centuries, but extant early Christian interpretations of this text do not

Fourth Gospel (AnBib, 32; Rome: Pontificio Istituto Biblico, 1967), pp. xii–xiv; G. Van Belle, *Johannine Bibliography 1966–1985: A Cumulative Bibliography on the Fourth Gospel* (BETL, 82; Leuven: Leuven University Press, 1988), pp. 336–7.

31. A. M. Moore, 'The Theme of Creation in the Fourth Gospel' (Ph.D. diss., University of Leeds, 2010). The thesis has been recently published as *Signs of Salvation: The Theme of Creation in John's Gospel* (Cambridge: James Clarke, 2013). Here, however, I use the dissertation form of Moore's work.

32. Moore, 'Creation', p. 55; cf. p. 15.

33. Moore, 'Creation', p. 64.

34. Moore, 'Creation', p. 37.

35. Moore, 'Creation', p. 9; cf. pp. 10, 276.

36. Moore, 'Creation', p. iii.

37. Moore, 'Creation', pp. iii, 184–271.

reflect Moore's reading of creation in this Gospel. Second, he only considers the Johannine references to a garden (Jn 18.1, 26; 19.41; cf. 20.15) as a 'case study of John's literary device of intentional allusion to earlier texts'.[38] Moore fails to establish the case for the numerous other suggested allusions to Gen. 1–2 (some of them lacking even verbal correspondences). Allusions should be demonstrated, not assumed. To argue, as Moore does, that Gen. 1–2 has been the most important OT influence in the composition of GJohn is to build a tall thesis on a narrow base.

Unlike Moore's thesis, which lacks a defence of the numerous proposed allusions to Gen. 1–2, Jeannine Brown attempts to establish the case for her suggested allusions and echoes.[39] She proposes more than ten instances of creation imagery in GJohn, including the seven Johannine signs as following the structure of the seven days of creation, and the presentation of Jesus as man in Jn 19.5 as an allusion to Adam. According to her, John alludes to Gen. 1–3 in order to signal that the completion and renewal of God's creative work has arrived with Jesus' ministry and resurrection.[40] She also claims that GJohn presents God as inaugurating creation's renewal through Jesus, the new Adam.[41] Jeannine Brown concludes, 'If John is emphasizing creation...then the Gospel contributes to the NT theme of renewed creation, already evident in Paul and Revelation'.[42] However, her application of criteria seems to lack enough rigour. How, for instance, does a putative Adam Christology cohere with John's explicit presentation of the Word as the agent of creation in Jn 1.1-5? How, to cite another example, is the healing of the royal official's son in Jn 4.46-54 (day two of new creation in Jeannine Brown's proposal) an echo of Gen. 1.6-8 when God created the expanse and separated the waters?

In several publications John Painter has given attention to creation in GJohn.[43] He posits several instances of creation imagery, such as the

---

38. Moore, 'Creation', p. 63 (see also p. 273).

39. J. K. Brown, 'Creation's Renewal in the Gospel of John', *CBQ* 72 (2010), pp. 275–90. A. J. Köstenberger, *A Theology of John's Gospel and Letters: The Word, the Christ, the Son of God* (BTNT; Grand Rapids: Zondervan, 2009), pp. 336–54, follows closely Brown's article.

40. J. K. Brown, 'Creation', pp. 275 n. 2, 277, 290.

41. J. K. Brown, 'Creation', p. 281.

42. J. K. Brown, 'Creation', p. 290.

43. J. Painter, 'The Signs of the Messiah and the Quest for Eternal Life', in *What We Have Heard from the Beginning: The Past, Present, and Future of Johannine Studies* (ed. T. Thatcher; Waco, Tex.: Baylor University Press, 2007), pp. 233–56 (236). Painter's publications on the topic include: 'Earth Made Whole: John's

noun 'good' (καλός) in Jn 10.32 as related to Gen. 1–2,[44] and the scenes between Mary and Jesus in the garden (20.11-17) as reminiscent of Gen. 3.8.[45] The criteria used by Painter for the identification of creation imagery in GJohn seem implicit. Painter concludes that John depicts the unfinished state of creation that Jesus and his disciples bring to completion.[46] He contends that the signs performed by Jesus make people whole and, therefore, his ministry points toward the wholeness of the material world.[47]

Following a narratological methodology, Jan A. du Rand provides a theological reading of GJohn, proposing that creation is its major theme. He contends that his reading 'is but one possibility for reading and understanding its story'.[48] Therefore, it is not always clear whether du Rand proposes his reading as one probably intended by John or one of many possibilities. Du Rand suggests to divide GJohn into three parts: (1) 1.1-51, the new creation incarnated; (2) 2.1–17.26, the new creation unfolds; (3) 18.1–21.25, the ultimate proof of the new creation.[49] If, however, John's primary theological purpose in every part of his Gospel was the portrayal of new creation through Jesus, he might be expected to have made the connection much more explicit.

In a recent article Hans Ulrich Weidemann attempts to identify 'the *function* of the creation statements in the *establishment of the identity of the Johannine communities*'.[50] Weidemann posits several allusions to

Rereading of Genesis', in *Word, Theology, and Community in John* (ed. J. Painter, R. A. Culpepper, and F. F. Segovia; St. Louis, Miss.: Chalice, 2002), pp. 65–84; '"The Light Shines in the Darkness…": Creation, Incarnation, and Resurrection in John', in *The Resurrection of Jesus in the Gospel of John* (ed. C. R. Koester and R. Bieringer; Tübingen: Mohr Siebeck, 2008), pp. 21–46.

44. Painter, 'Earth', pp. 70, 77–8. Cf. J. Painter, 'Inclined to God: The Quest for Eternal Life—Bultmannian Hermeneutics and Theology of the Fourth Gospel', in *Exploring the Gospel of John: In Honor of D. Moody Smith* (ed. R. A. Culpepper and C. C. Black; Louisville: Westminster John Knox, 1996), pp. 346–68 (349).

45. Painter, 'Light', p. 44.

46. Similar ideas are found in S. M. McDonough, *Christ as Creator: Origins of a New Testament Doctrine* (Oxford: Oxford University Press, 2009), pp. 213–34.

47. Painter, 'Earth', pp. 66, 83.

48. J. A. du Rand, 'The Creation Motif in the Fourth Gospel: Perspectives on Its Narratological Function within a Judaistic Background', in *Theology and Christology in the Fourth Gospel* (ed. G. Van Belle, J. G. van der Watt, and P. Maritz; BETL, 184; Leuven: Leuven University Press, 2005), pp. 21–46 (21).

49. Du Rand, 'Creation', p. 24.

50. H. U. Weidemann, 'The Victory of Protology Over Eschatology? Creation in the Gospel of John', in *Theologies of Creation in Early Judaism and Ancient Christianity* (ed. T. Nicklas and K. Zamfir; DCLS, 6; Berlin: W. de Gruyter, 2010), pp. 299–334 (302, original emphasis).

Gen. 1–3 in GJohn, but without establishing the case for each of them. For example, he thinks that the words τελειοῦν, ποιεῖν, and ἔργα are linked to Gen. 2.1-3. He also suggests a parallel between Jn 3.31 and Gen. 2.7.[51] Since his primary interest lies in explaining the role of the creation motif in the *Sitz im Leben* ('setting in life') of the putative Johannine communities, he gives little attention to the role each alleged instance of creation imagery plays in its particular literary context.

Best known for her work on temple symbolism in GJohn,[52] Mary Coloe has recently argued that 'the Fourth Gospel begins and ends with the theme of Creation' and that creation is 'one of the major themes' in GJohn.[53] She thinks that Gen. 1–3 had a pervasive influence on the composition of GJohn. Coloe deems, for instance, that the structure of Jn 1.1-18 is 'closely modelled on the first chapter of Genesis',[54] that the phrase about Jesus being 'in the middle' (Jn 19.18) 'echoes the phrase in Genesis where God plants "the tree of life in the middle of the garden"' (Gen. 2.9),[55] and that Jesus' mother in Jn 19.25-26 is a 'deliberate evocation' of Eve (Gen. 2.23).[56] Coloe concludes, among other things, that Mary plays the role of the new Eve in GJohn who 'reverses the actions and consequences of the woman in the garden of Genesis'.[57]

Several scholars have tried to understand the function of creation imagery in GJohn. However, the many proposals are unsatisfactory, since they are limited either by a lack of explicit criteria for the identification of links between GJohn and Genesis or by a lack of rigour in the application of some suggested criteria. There is yet the need for a full-scale study with a comprehensive treatment of the data in order to arrive at a properly nuanced estimate of the place and significance of creation imagery in this Gospel.

II. Methodological Remarks

In this investigation I will use an explicit set of questions to interrogate the evidence in order to assess creation imagery in GJohn. I develop

51. Weidemann, 'Protology', pp. 315, 327.
52. M. L. Coloe, *God Dwells with Us: Temple Symbolism in the Fourth Gospel* (Collegeville: Liturgical, 2001).
53. M. L. Coloe, 'Theological Reflexions on Creation in the Gospel of John', *Pacifica* 24 (2011), pp. 1–12 (1).
54. Coloe, 'Creation', p. 1. Cf. M. L. Coloe, 'The Structure of the Johannine Prologue and Genesis 1', *ABR* 45 (1997), pp. 40–55.
55. Coloe, 'Creation', p. 5.
56. Coloe, 'Creation', p. 5.
57. Coloe, 'Creation', p. 8.

these questions in dialogue with a set of tests that scholars have proposed for the identification of oblique references to the OT in the NT.[58] These tests have already been successfully applied and verified in the study of the impact and influence of the OT in GJohn.[59] But before establishing those criteria, a definition of 'creation imagery' is in order.

There is consensus in Johannine scholarship that John uses earlier traditions about creation. However, as has been noted in the previous section, there is disagreement about the extent of John's use of such traditions. Some have argued that John closely follows the structure of the days of creation in the Genesis account. Others have suggested that John has borrowed language from Gen. 1–3 at various points in his Gospel. Previous scholars have used a number of labels to represent what they consider to be John's dependence on earlier traditions about creation. For instance, when they observe similarities between Jn 1.1 and Gen. 1.1, they assert that in Jn 1.1 the Evangelist is 'alluding to', 'echoing', or 'making a reference' to Gen. 1.1.

In this inquiry I will use a general label to encapsulate what seem to be literary links between GJohn and OT traditions about creation. For example, instead of suggesting that Jn 1.1 is an allusion to, an echo of, or a reference to Gen. 1.1, I will state that Jn 1.1 is an instance of 'creation imagery'. The reasons for using this label are twofold. The first reason is the symbolic nature of GJohn. Although John uses earlier traditions about creation in his Gospel, it is clear that he has adapted and infused

58. R. B. Hays, *Echoes of Scripture in the Letters of Paul* (New Heaven: Yale University Press, 1989), pp. 29–32. Hays himself has revisited these criteria in *The Conversion of the Imagination: Paul as Interpreter of Israel's Scripture* (Grand Rapids: Eerdmans, 2005), pp. 34–45. Cf. also the collection of essays in C. A. Evans and J. A. Sanders (eds.), *Paul and the Scriptures of Israel* (JSNTSup, 83; SScEJC, 1; Sheffield: JSOT Press, 1992).

59. S. Mihalios, *The Danielic Eschatological Hour in the Johannine Literature* (LNTS, 436; London: T&T Clark International, 2011), pp. 8–10; J. McWhirter, *The Bridegroom Messiah and the People of God: Marriage in the Fourth Gospel* (New York: Cambridge University Press, 2006), pp. 23–31; S. Hylen, *Allusion and Meaning in John 6* (BZNW, 137; Berlin: W. de Gruyter, 2005), pp. 53–9; G. T. Manning, Jr., *Echoes of a Prophet: The Use of Ezekiel in the Gospel of John and in Literature of the Second Temple Period* (JSNTSup, 270; London: T&T Clark International, 2004), pp. 3–19; A. C. Brunson, *Psalm 118 in the Gospel of John: An Intertextual Study on the New Exodus Pattern in the Theology of John* (WUNT, 2/158; Tübingen: Mohr Siebeck, 2003), pp. 7–16; M. Daly-Denton, *David in the Fourth Gospel: The Johannine Reception of the Psalms* (AGJU, 47; Leiden: Brill, 2000), p. 11; E. Little, *Echoes of the Old Testament in the Wine at Cana in Galilee (John 2:1-11) and the Multiplication of the Loaves and Fish (6:1-15): Towards an Appreciation* (CahRB, 41; Paris: Gabalda, 1998), p. 4.

them with symbolic meaning. A case in point is John's use of 'light' and 'life' in Jn 1.4-5. As I will show in the next chapter, this language ('light' and 'life') is used in Gen. 1 to indicate that God created 'light' (1.3) and that he breathed into man the breath of 'life' (2.7). However, John uses these nouns to represent the Word, who in the beginning took an active role in the creation of the world (1.3, 10). Elsewhere in his Gospel, John uses these nouns in contexts where Jesus is portrayed as bringing salvation, revelation, and judgement (e.g. 8.12-19).

The second reason is the peculiar 'sensorial' character of GJohn. John uses rich language that appeals to the senses of his readers. In particular, there is an abundance of language about 'seeing' in GJohn. As was observed long ago by Edwin Abbott, 'It is a remarkable fact that John does not relate a single instance of the cure of the deaf'.[60] Instead, John included an extensive narrative about the healing of a man born blind (Jn 9.1-41).

Since 'imagery' entails 'visually descriptive or figurative language',[61] it seems appropriate to use 'creation imagery' here to label those places where John uses earlier traditions about creation. This label ('creation imagery') has already been employed by Matthew Gordley in his study of creation in Qumran Hymns and Prayers.[62] He proposes the use of 'creation imagery' as a general label that encapsulates Qumranic 'terms or concepts found in the canonical creation accounts'.[63] Gordley also suggests four 'distinct yet interconnected ideas' that 'can carry the designation "creation imagery"'.[64]

In this study I will also use 'creation imagery' as a general label. Two phenomena can carry the designation 'creation imagery' in GJohn, the first of which are direct assertions about the creation of the world that are not dependent upon a particular OT text. John refers to the creation of the world three times, albeit without making a link to OT texts: 'the world

---

60. E. A. Abbott, *Johannine Vocabulary: A Comparison of the Words of the Fourth Gospel with Those of the Three* (London: Adam & Charles Black, 1905), p. 116.

61. A. Stevenson (ed.), *Oxford Dictionary of English* (New York: Oxford University Press, 3rd edn, 2010).

62. M. E. Gordley, 'Creation Imagery in Qumran Hymns and Prayers', *JJS* 59 (2008), pp. 252–72.

63. Gordley, 'Creation Imagery', p. 256.

64. Gordley, 'Creation Imagery', pp. 256–7. The four ideas that can carry the designation 'creation imagery' are: (1) explicit references to God as creator, (2) statements that 'show [the Lord] to be superior in comparison with his creation', (3) aspects of creation such as earth, stars, creatures, rain, and (4) creation images used in a metaphorical sense.

was made through him' (1.10), 'the world was made' (17.5), and 'the foundation of the world' (17.24). The second phenomenon involves instances where John could have more subtly drawn on and creatively deployed terms, images, or concepts stemming from earlier biblical traditions about creation. In this case I understand 'creation' in GJohn as occasions on which Jesus performs acts that resemble those of the Creator God and those instances where Jesus is portrayed as showing his power over the created order. As I will show in Chapter 6, Jesus performs an act that resembles that of the Creator God in Gen. 2.7 when he breathes on his disciples after his resurrection in Jn 20.22. Moreover, as I will show in Chapter 4, Jesus shows his power over the created order in Jn 6.19 when he walks on the sea, just as the Creator God is described as walking on the sea as on dry ground in Job 9.8.

Therefore, I will not delineate strictly between 'allusion' and 'echo'. Scholars often distinguish between allusions and echoes as two distinctive modes of reference to previous texts in the NT.[65] This distinction often refers to whether the *author* was using a precursor text consciously (allusion) or unconsciously (echo), or whether the intended *audience* had the capacity to hear the precursor text (allusion) or not (echo).[66] However, I will characterise oblique references to creation as instances where John could have more subtly drawn on and creatively deployed terms, images, or concepts stemming from earlier biblical traditions about creation. Competent readers (those acquainted with the LXX) may be expected to detect John's instances of creation imagery.[67]

65. Daly-Denton, *David*, pp. 9, 11; McWhirter, *Bridegroom*, pp. 21–2, 29; Hays, *Echoes*, p. 29; Brunson, *Psalm 118*, p. 13. Cf. C. A. Beetham, *Echoes of Scripture in the Letter of Paul to the Colossians* (BIS, 96; Leiden: Brill, 2008), pp. 17–19, 24; S. E. Porter, 'Allusions and Echoes', in *As It Is Written: Studying Paul's Use of Scripture* (ed. S. E. Porter and C. D. Stanley; SBLSymS, 50; Atlanta: Society of Biblical Literature, 2008), pp. 29–40; D. C. Allison, Jr., *The Intertextual Jesus: Scripture in Q* (Harrisburg: Trinity University Press, 2000), p. ix.

66. As for the distinctions between author- and audience-centred approaches in the study of references to the OT in the NT, see C. D. Stanley, *Arguing with Scripture: The Rhetoric of Quotation in the Letters of Paul* (London: T&T Clark International, 2004), pp. 38–61.

67. For a critique of these labels ('allusion' and 'echo'), see A. Kubiś, *The Book of Zechariah in the Gospel of John* (EBib, 64; Pendé, France: Gabalda, 2012), pp. 21–5; J. C. Edwards, *The Ransom Logion in Mark and Matthew: Its Reception and Its Significance for the Study of the Gospels* (WUNT, 2/327; Tübingen: Mohr Siebeck, 2012), p. 16. Edwards abandons these labels and uses 'degrees of similarity' that the modern reader is able to observe when comparing ancient texts.

Although there is a range of views about intertextuality as a literary-critical approach in biblical studies,[68] here I will attempt to discern as best as I can whether John probably intended links to earlier biblical traditions about creation. On the one hand, it is impossible to be totally certain whether John indeed intended creation imagery at various points in his Gospel. Authorial intent of ancient texts is a problematic notion nowadays.[69] On the other hand, we need to use all the tools that are available to us to interrogate the limited extant evidence in order to arrive at a plausible explanation of an observable literary phenomenon in GJohn. Responding to Robert Kysar's observations about the influence of postmodernism in the historical task, John Ashton comments: 'swimming as strongly as I can against the tide of postmodernism, I still believe that it makes sense to look for the meaning that the first readers of a text would have found in it'.[70] It makes sense to look for the intended meaning of GJohn because it is evident that John wanted to be understood. There are many parentheses in this text in which the narrator provides clarification to the reader and further information about his narrative (e.g. 1.41; 4.2; 20.16), and there is also a clear statement about the purpose for writing this text (20.31).

Having provided a definition of 'creation imagery' and a justification for its use in this investigation, I will explain, in the following paragraphs, the set of questions that I will use to assess instances of that imagery in GJohn.

The first criterion to aid in determining what counts as an oblique reference to the OT has been traditionally named 'availability'. The vast majority of instances of creation imagery suggested by scholars that I will assess here are related to Gen. 1–2. Therefore, we should ask whether it is plausible that the first book of the Pentateuch was available to John. There is evidence in the Gospel itself that John almost certainly knew the book of Genesis. There are straightforward references to Gen. 48.22 (Jn 4.5) and Gen. 17.10-12 (Jn 7.22), a quotation from Gen. 28.12 in Jn 1.51, and detectable oblique references to the first book of the OT: e.g. Jn 2.5 (Gen. 41.55) and 8.44 (Gen. 3).[71]

68. S. Moyise, 'Intertextuality and Biblical Studies: A Review', *VerEc* 23 (2002), pp. 418–31, offers a survey of five different 'types' of intertextuality.

69. See J. Ashton, 'Second Thoughts on the Fourth Gospel', in Thatcher (ed.), *What We Have Heard*, pp. 1–18 (10).

70. Ashton, 'Second Thoughts', p. 10.

71. M. J. J. Menken, 'Genesis in John's Gospel and 1 John', in *Genesis in the New Testament* (ed. M. J. J. Menken and S. Moyise; LNTS, 466; London: Bloomsbury T&T Clark, 2012), pp. 83–98 (84–95). However, John's favourites are Isaiah and Psalms. Cf. J. Zumstein, 'Intratextuality and Intertextuality in the Gospel of

Genesis circulated widely in ancient times. For example, Genesis was a popular writing in the Qumran community: 'Both the number of biblical manuscripts and the collection of scrolls involved with retelling its compelling stories attest to this fact'.[72] Jewish literature of the Second-Temple period reflects exegesis of Gen. 1–3[73] or follows the seven-day structure of God's creation (e.g. *Jub.* 2; Josephus, *Ant.* 1.29-32; *2 En.* 30; *4 Ezra* 6; Philo, *Op. Mund.* 13, 29, 37, 45). In other books of the NT the Genesis creation account is quoted several times: Gen. 1.27 (Mt. 19.4; Mk 10.6); Gen. 2.2 (Heb. 4.4); Gen. 2.7 (1 Cor. 15.45); Gen. 2.24 (Mt. 19.5; Mk 10.7-8; 1 Cor. 6.16; Eph. 5.31).[74] Another example of the circulation of Genesis in ancient times is found in the early fourth-century POxy 4365, 'To my dearest lady sister, greetings in the Lord. Lend the Ezra, since I lent you the little Genesis. Farewell in God from us.'[75]

John' (trans. M. Gray), in *Anatomies of Narrative Criticism: The Past, Present, and Futures of the Fourth Gospel as Literature* (ed. T. Thatcher and S. D. Moore; SBLRBS, 55; Atlanta: Society of Biblical Literature, 2008), pp. 121–35 (133).

72. M. Abegg, Jr., P. Flint, and E. Ulrich, *The Dead Sea Scrolls Bible* (Edinburgh: T. & T. Clark, 1999), p. 3. Cf. K. Berthelot, T. Legrand, and A. Paul, *La Bibliothèque de Qumrân: Torah. Genèse* (vol. 1; Paris: Cerf, 2008); E. Ulrich (ed.), *The Biblical Qumran Scrolls: Transcriptions and Textual Variants* (VTSup, 134; Leiden: Brill, 2010), pp. 1–7.

73. M. Goff, 'Genesis 1–3 and Conceptions of Humankind in 4QInstruction, Philo and Paul', in *Early Christian Literature and Intertextuality* (ed. C. A. Evans and H. D. Zacharias; LNTS, 392; London: T&T Clark International, 2009), pp. 114–19; J. T. A. G. M. van Rutten, 'The Creation of Man and Woman in Early Jewish Literature', in *The Creation of Man and Woman: Interpretations of the Biblical Narratives in Jewish and Christian Traditions* (ed. G. P. Luttikhuizen; TBN, 3; Leiden: Brill, 2000), pp. 34–62; F. García-Martínez, 'Creation in the Dead Sea Scrolls,' in *The Creation of Heaven and Earth: Re-interpretations of Genesis I in the Context of Judaism, Ancient Philosophy, Christianity, and Modern Physics* (ed. G. H. van Kooten; TBN, 8; Leiden: Brill, 2005), pp. 53–70; B. G. Wold, *Women, Men, and Angels: The Qumran Wisdom Document* Musar leMevin *and Its Allusions to Genesis Creation Traditions* (WUNT, 2/201; Tübingen: Mohr Siebeck, 2005).

74. D. M. Turpie, *The Old Testament in the New: A Contribution to Biblical Criticism and Interpretation* (London: Williams and Norgate, 1868), p. 271; M. D. Goulder, 'Exegesis of Genesis 1–3 in the New Testament', *JJS* 43 (1992), pp. 226–9. There is also evidence in rabbinic material that the account of creation was recited in synagogues (*m. Ta'an.* 4.2-3; *m. Meg.* 3.3-6; *t. Ta'an.* 3.3-4), according to C. R. Koester, *Symbolism in the Fourth Gospel: Meaning, Mystery, Community* (Minneapolis: Fortress, 2nd edn, 2003), p. 144.

75. J. R. Rea (ed.), *The Oxyrhynchus Papyri* (GRM, 83; London: Egypt Exploration Society, 1996), p. 45. See also POxy 2785, R. A. Coles et al. (eds.), *The Oxyrhynchus Papyri* (GRM, 51; London: Egypt Exploration Society, 1970), pp. 83–4, 'Receive in peace our sister…and receive for edification a man who is being instructed in Genesis'.

Nevertheless, it is impossible for us to know which text or texts of Genesis were available to John. Previous investigations on the use of the OT in GJohn have concluded that the critically reconstructed text of the LXX is probably the closest we get to John's *Vorlage* in most of his quotations.[76] John preferred a Greek version of the OT because his intended audience might have used it as their OT text.[77] In my assessment of instances of creation imagery in GJohn I will use the critically reconstructed text of the LXX as found in the Göttingen LXX edition with attention to its critical apparatus.[78]

The second criterion for evaluating suggested instances of creation imagery will be significant similarities. The minimum requirement for a valid instance of creation imagery should be verbal parallels between the two texts. The word agreement should be a group of words or, at least, a single significant word.[79] Once one has identified word agreement, other similarities can be observed: common syntactical patterns, common

---

76. B. G. Schuchard, *Scripture within Scripture: The Interrelationship of Form and Function in the Explicit Old Testament Citations in the Gospel of John* (SBLDS, 133; Atlanta: Scholars Press, 1992), pp. xvii, 151. Cf. M. J. J. Menken, *Old Testament Quotations in the Fourth Gospel: Studies in Textual Form* (CBET, 15; Kampen: Pharos, 1996), p. 205. Schuchard clarifies that only in Jn 19.37 is it unclear whether or not John used an alternative textual tradition (pp. 151–2). E. D. Freed, *Old Testament Quotations in the Gospel of John* (NovTSup, 11; Leiden: Brill, 1965), pp. 117–30, provided nuanced judgements about John's dependence on the Hebrew or Greek in his quotations. Freed concluded: 'Where Jn agrees exactly with an O. T. text it is always with the LXX, and we can be certain of this in only four places: 2:17; 10:34; 12:38; 19:24… For all other quotations [except Jn 19.37]…a stronger case can be made for the use of the Gr. than for the Heb.' (p. 126).

77. Schuchard, *Scripture*, p. 154 n. 11; M. Cimosa, 'La traduzione greca dei Settanta nel Vangelo di Giovanni', *BeO* 39 (1997), pp. 41–55 (54). Cf. McWhirter, *Bridegroom*, p. 25; A. D. Myers, *Characterizing Jesus: A Rhetorical Analysis on the Fourth Gospel's Use of Scripture in Its Presentation of Jesus* (LNTS, 458; London: T&T Clark International, 2012), p. 20. As for Christian adoption of the LXX as a translation of the OT, see E. Tov, 'The Septuagint', in *Mikra: Text, Translation, Reading and Interpretation of the Hebrew Bible in Ancient Judaism and Early Christianity* (ed. M. J. Mulder; CRINT, 2; Philadelphia: Fortress, 1988), pp. 161–88 (163); M. Harl, *La Bible d'Alexandrie: La Genèse* (Paris: Cerf, 2nd edn, 1986), pp. 44–9.

78. If there is no Göttingen LXX edition for a particular OT book, I will use Rahlfs' edition. The reconstructed Greek text of GJohn will be taken from NA[28]. I will also consult the Hebrew text (*BHS*) when appropriate.

79. Hays, *Echoes*, p. 30; Beetham, *Echoes*, pp. 17, 29; Manning, *Echoes*, pp. 9–10. Mihalios, *Hour*, p. 9 n. 32, offers some examples of one-word oblique references to the OT in GJohn.

themes, similar imagery, similar structure,[80] and similar contexts and circumstances.[81] Word agreement and other similarities should be significant not commonplace: the greater the rarity of a word or words (both in GJohn and in the OT), the higher the probability that John intended a connection. I will ask: (1) Are the common words identical or cognates? (2) Does John use the vocabulary in question in other parts of his Gospel? (3) 'Should we have expected something different?' (4) 'Is there a unique combination of significant words?'[82] In order to answer some of these questions I will compare GJohn with the other canonical Gospels. Without accepting the so-called Leuven Hypothesis, which proposes that GJohn has a direct literary relationship to the Synoptic Gospels,[83] it is reasonable to think that John may have known traditions that also shaped the other three canonical gospels.

Once similar vocabulary can be confirmed, other criteria can be brought into the process of assessment. The third criterion that I will use is prominence: OT books, stories, or verses that are foundational, prominent, or well-known in ancient Jewish communities are more likely to be evoked than stories, passages, or verses that are not so famous or popular in ancient Jewish circles.[84] In using this criterion, I should ask also how often John refers to the same scriptural passage or book elsewhere in his Gospel.[85]

The following question will be asked in order to determine the historical plausibility of a proposed instance of creation imagery: Taking account of all factors, could John have intended the suggested instance of

80. Hays, *Conversion*, p. 35; E. Waaler, *The* Shema *and The First Commandment in First Corinthians: An Intertextual Approach to Paul's Re-reading of Deuteronomy* (WUNT, 2/253; Tübingen: Mohr Siebeck, 2008), p. 37 n. 190; D. C. Allison, Jr., *The New Moses: A Matthean Typology* (Edinburgh: T. & T. Clark, 1993), p. 20.

81. Allison, *Moses*, p. 19; McWhirter, *Bridegroom*, pp. 25–6.

82. M. Thompson, *Clothed with Christ: The Example and Teaching of Jesus in Romans 12.1–15.13* (JSNTSup, 59; Sheffield: JSOT Press, 1991), p. 31.

83. G. Van Belle, 'Tradition, Exegetical Formation, and the Leuven Hypothesis', in Thatcher (ed.), *What We Have Heard*, pp. 325–37 (333–6).

84. Two tools that I will use to identify the prominence of an OT text are: A. Lange and M. Weigold, *Biblical Quotations and Allusions in Second Temple Jewish Literature* (JAJSup, 5; Göttingen: Vandenhoeck & Ruprecht, 2011), and B. H. McLean, *Citations and Allusions to Jewish Scripture in Early Christian and Jewish Writings through 180 C.E.* (Lewiston, New York: Edwin Mellen, 1992).

85. Hays, *Conversion*, pp. 36–7; Hays, *Echoes*, p. 30; McWhirter, *Bridegroom*, p. 28; Brunson, *Psalm 118*, p. 14; Beetham, *Echoes*, p. 34; Allison, *Jesus*, p. 12. I have combined what Hays, *Conversion*, pp. 36–7, calls 'volume' and 'multiple attestation' into one single criterion called 'prominence'.

creation imagery, and could his competent first-century readers have understood it?[86] John's explicit handling of OT texts and traditions suggests that he comes from a Jewish environment and now has become a follower of the early Christian movement.[87] Therefore, we should ask whether creation imagery was used and referred to in extant Second-Temple[88] Jewish texts in ways that resemble what scholars propose is going on in GJohn. Along with Second-Temple Jewish texts, I will also consider Christian literature of the first century (and first decades of the second century) in order to determine whether early Christian communities dealt with creation imagery in ways that resemble suggested instances in GJohn.[89]

Recent research has shown that early Johannine Christians mostly received the Gospel orally and in groups (i.e. gathered worship-circles), since they depended upon a person (or group of people) who might have read and explained it to them.[90] The many parentheses in the text of

86. Hays, *Conversion*, p. 41.
87. W. D. Davies, 'Reflexions on Aspects of the Jewish Background of the Gospel of John', in Culpepper and Black (eds.), *Exploring the Gospel of John*, pp. 41–64; É. Cothenet, 'L'arrière-plan vétéro-testamentaire du IVe Évangile', in *Origine et postérité de L'évangile de Jean* (LD, 143; Paris: Cerf, 1990), pp. 43–69 (50–60). Cf. R. Bauckham, 'The Relevance of Extra-Canonical Jewish Texts to New Testament Study', in *Hearing the New Testament: Strategies for Interpretation* (ed. J. B. Green; Grand Rapids: Eerdmans, 1995), pp. 90–108.
88. 'Second Temple' generally denotes a period between the second century B.C.E and the first century C.E. Cf. J. Ashton, *Understanding the Fourth Gospel* (Oxford: Oxford University Press, 2nd edn, 2007), p. 58 n. 1.
89. Tools that I will use while applying the criterion of 'historical plausibility' include: McLean, *Citations*; S. Delamarter, *A Scripture Index to Charlesworth's The Old Testament Pseudepigrapha* (London: Sheffield Academic Press, 2002); M. G. Abegg, Jr., J. E. Bowley, and E. M. Cook (eds.), *The Dead Sea Scrolls Concordance* (3 vols.; Leiden: Brill, 2003–2010); P. Borgen, K. Fuglseth, and R. Skarsten, *The Philo Index: A Complete Greek Word Index to the Writings of Philo of Alexandria Lemmatised & Computer–Generated* (UniSt, 25; Trondheim: University of Trondheim, 1997); K. H. Rengstorf, *A Complete Concordance to Flavius Josephus* (4 vols.; Leiden: Brill, 1973–1983); A. M. Denis, *Concordance grecque des pseudépigraphes d'Ancien Testament* (Louvain: Université catholique de Louvain, 1987).
90. See Justin, *1 Apol.* 67; H. Y. Gamble, *Books and Readers in the Early Church: A History of Early Christian Texts* (New Haven: Yale University Press, 1995), pp. 204–5; M. Hengel, 'Eye-Witness Memory and the Writing of the Gospels', in *The Written Gospel* (ed. M. Bockmuehl and D. A. Hagner; Cambridge: Cambridge University Press, 2005), pp. 70–96 (92–3). Cf. H. J. de Jonge, 'The Use of the Old Testament in Scripture Readings in Early Christian Assemblies', in *The Scriptures of Israel in Jewish and Christian Tradition* (ed. B. J. Koet, S. Moyise, and J. Verheyden; NovTSup, 148; Leiden: Brill, 2013), pp. 377–92. For a description of

GJohn[91] might indicate that a full understanding of the intended message of the Gospel required an acceptable level of knowledge of the OT scriptures.[92] Two pertinent examples are Jn 20.9 (where the author says that the disciples 'did not yet understand the scripture', cf. 2.22) and Jesus' indication that the 'scriptures testify about' him in 5.39. However, we do not have access to the supposed verbal explanations of the Gospel that intended readers might have given for the benefit of their audience. The best that we can do is to investigate extant written interpretations of GJohn in order to determine whether early readers detected creation imagery. The criterion associated with this inquiry is history of interpretation.[93]

The most ancient Johannine commentaries are not fully available to us; e.g. Heracleon's (ca. 160–180 C.E.)[94] or Hippolytus' (ca. 170–236 C.E.). But there is evidence that GJohn was quoted and alluded to in several early Christian texts.[95] Early quotations from and allusions to GJohn are a rich source in order to determine whether ancient readers detected creation imagery.[96] Once I have determined that ancient readers of GJohn detected creation imagery in the Gospel, the next questions would be these: Are they claiming that John intended that instance of creation imagery? Or are they making allegorical or typological interpretations of GJohn? If the latter, the evidence provided by the history of interpretation carries very little weight for present purposes.

---

features which indicate that a specific unit of material in GJohn was designed for oral delivery, see C. H. Williams, 'Abraham as a Figure of Memory in John 8.31-59', in *The Fourth Gospel in First-Century Media Culture* (ed. A. Le Donne and T. Thatcher; LNTS, 426; London: T&T Clark International, 2011), pp. 205–22.

91. G. Van Belle, *Les parenthèses dans l'évangile de Jean: Aperçu historique et classification, texte grec de Jean* (Leuven: Leuven University Press, 1985).

92. Cf. Menken, *Quotations*, p. 208.

93. Hays, *Conversion*, pp. 43–4; Hays, *Echoes*, p. 31; McWhirter, *Bridegroom*, p. 30; Waaler, *Shema*, pp. 44–5; Allison, *Jesus*, p. 10.

94. E. Pagels, *The Johannine Gospel in Gnostic Exegesis: Heracleon's Commentary on John* (SBLMS, 17; Nashville: Abingdon, 1973).

95. Cf. T. Rasimus (ed.), *The Legacy of John: Second-Century Reception of the Fourth Gospel* (NovTSup, 132; Leiden: Brill, 2010); C. E. Hill, *The Johannine Corpus in the Early Church* (Oxford: Oxford University Press, 2004); R. A. Culpepper, *John, the Son of Zebedee: The Life of a Legend* (Edinburgh: T. & T. Clark, 2000), pp. 114–19.

96. The main tool used here for locating quotations from and allusions to GJohn in extant early Christian texts is BiPa. I will also benefit from *ANF* 9; J. Reuss, *Johannes-Kommentare aus der griechischen Kirche* (TUGAL, 89; Berlin: Akademie Verlag, 1966); and J. C. Elowsky (ed.), *Ancient Christian Commentary on Scripture* (vols. 4a–4b; Downers Grove, Ill.: InterVarsity, 2006–2007).

The other criteria for the assessment of creation imagery in GJohn are thematic coherence and satisfaction.[97] Since both criteria are closely related, here I place both under the heading thematic coherence. The set of questions that I will ask in order to satisfy this criterion are: How well does the supposed oblique reference to the OT fit into the line of argument that John is developing? Does the proposed precursor text fit together with the point that John is making? Is John's use of the precursor texts consonant with his overall argument and/or use made of other texts? Does the proposed reading illuminate the surrounding discourse and make some larger sense of John's argument as a whole?[98] Some studies on GJohn hypothesized about incongruences in the redaction of the Gospel.[99] Their observations about possible layers of tradition or conflicts in the putative sources led them to conclude that it is not possible to trace a coherent line of argumentation in GJohn. If that were the case, our criterion of thematic coherence would be inappropriate or unworkable. Nevertheless, there has been a growing interest in the study of GJohn as a whole, trying to show how the different parts and sections of the Gospel cohere with one another.[100] Here I benefit from the results of those studies when asserting that it is possible to find thematic coherence in John's line of argumentation in his Gospel.

The criteria discussed above provide an explicit set of questions for assessing creation imagery in GJohn. Such criteria will serve to achieve what Ziva Ben-Porat calls the 'process of actualization' of oblique references to independent texts.[101] The process involves three stages. The first stage entails the recognition of a marker in the text (here GJohn) that might hint at an independent text (here an OT book). Such a marker

97. Hays, *Conversion*, p. 44.

98. I have reproduced almost *verbatim* Hays' questions found in *Conversion*, pp. 38, 44. See also Hays, *Echoes*, p. 30; McWhirter, *Bridegroom*, p. 29; Daly-Denton, *David*, p. 11; Brunson, *Psalm 118*, pp. 139–40; Beetham, *Echoes*, p. 34; Thompson, *Christ*, p. 32; Allison, *Jesus*, pp. 13–14; Waaler, *Shema*, p. 44.

99. The classical example is R. Bultmann, *The Gospel of John: A Commentary* (trans. G. R. Beasley-Murray, R. W. N. Hoare, and J. K. Riches; Philadelphia: Westminster, 1971). See now U. C. von Wahlde, *The Gospel and Letters of John* (ECC; 3 vols.; Grand Rapids: Eerdmans, 2010).

100. T. Thatcher, 'Anatomies of the Fourth Gospel: Past, Present, and Future Probes', in Thatcher and Moore (eds.), *Anatomies of Narrative Criticism*, pp. 1–37. Cf. Ashton's conclusion that GJohn is 'predominantly the work of one man' who altered and adapted his sources to suit his own purposes (*Understanding*, p. 53).

101. Z. Ben-Porat, 'The Poetics of Literary Allusion', *PTL* 1 (1976), pp. 105–28 (110).

indicates that there is a relationship between the text (GJohn) and the referent (OT), and it can include 'a unique noun in a new declension'.[102] The second stage is an obvious one: the identification of the evoked text.[103] The first five criteria explained above will help me complete these two stages.

The third stage I will achieve by using the sixth criterion explained above. Ben-Porat proposes that once a marker and the evoked text have been identified, the interpreter needs to explain the 'modification of the initial local interpretation of the signal'.[104] The modification is 'the result of the interaction between the two texts', the signal is a 'sign' that activates a relationship between the text (GJohn) and the referent (OT), and the local interpretation is the meaning that a word (or words) acquires in its own literary context.[105]

In other words, an oblique reference to the OT in GJohn may activate further and richer meaning, bringing fresh perspectives for the interpretation of the latter text.[106] Although Ben-Porat argues that oblique references to independent texts produce 'free' patterns of relationship between the texts,[107] some control is needed in order to assess whether some relationships were or were not plausibly intended by John. In this case I will ask whether John's use of the precursor text is consonant with his overall argument. Thus, GJohn as a whole (the wider literary context) will dictate whether the 'free' patterns of relationship evoked in the reader were plausibly intended by the Evangelist.

An example may be helpful here. Some scholars have argued that Jesus' encounter with Judas in Jn 18 evokes the battle between Adam and the serpent in Gen. 2–3.[108] Among the arguments in favour of such a

102.   Ben-Porat, 'Allusion', p. 110.

103.   Ben-Porat, 'Allusion', p. 110.

104.   Ben-Porat, 'Allusion', pp. 110–11.

105.   Ben-Porat, 'Allusion', pp. 107–11.

106.   The successful completion of the three stages might 'stimulate the search for more possible links [between the texts]' (Ben-Porat, 'Allusion', p. 115). However, Ben-Porat recognizes that this fourth stage (i.e. the formation of further links between the texts) is optional in the process of interpretation (p. 113).

107.   Ben-Porat, 'Allusion', p. 108 n. 6.

108.   More recently S. A. Hunt, 'The Roman Soldiers at Jesus' Arrest: "You Are Dust, and to Dust You Shall Return"', in *Character Studies in the Fourth Gospel: Narrative Approaches to Seventy Figures in John* (ed. S. A. Hunt, D. F. Tolmie, and R. Zimmermann; WUNT, 1/314; Tübingen: Mohr Siebeck, 2013), pp. 554–67; see, in the same volume, C. N. Revell and S. A. Hunt, 'The Co-Crucified Men: Shadows by His Cross', pp. 607–17.

pattern of relationship between the texts are: (1) the reference to a 'garden' in 18.1 as the place where a struggle took place, (2) the previous identification of Judas as εἷς διάβολός (6.70; cf. 13.2), and (3) the very struggle between Jesus and Judas (18.3). The link between Jn 18 and Gen. 2–3 provides fresh perspectives for the interpretation of GJohn because Jesus is then seen as the 'new Adam' who opens the way back to paradise.

However, a more careful consideration of Jn 18 and of GJohn as a whole makes us conclude that it is unlikely that John intended such activation of meaning. First, it is doubtful that the events narrated in Jn 18.1-12 took place *inside* the garden. Jesus and his disciples did enter (εἰσῆλθεν) a garden in 18.1, but once Judas and the soldiers approach the place, Jesus is said to have gone out (ἐξῆλθεν) (18.4). At least, it is not clear that Jesus' encounter with Judas took place inside the garden. Second, there is not actually a struggle between Jesus and Judas. Jesus even prevents Peter from starting a fight with the soldiers in 18.10-12. Third, the noun 'garden' is again used in 18.26 in relation to Peter (not to Judas) and without evocations of a struggle between Jesus and Judas. Fourth, the overall tone of Jn 18 is related to the portrayal of Jesus as king (see 18.33, 37). The reference to a 'fight' in 18.36 is explicitly related to the kingship of Jesus: 'My kingship is not of this world; if my kingship were of this world, my servants would fight, that I might not be handed over to the Jews; but my kingship is not from the world' (RSV).

Fifth, the suggested fresh meaning introduced by a link to Gen. 2–3 in Jn 18 does not fit well with the overall meaning of GJohn. Jesus is clearly portrayed as existing apart from creation (17.5, 24) and as taking an active role in creation (1.3, 10) elsewhere in GJohn. On the other hand, he is never explicitly (or even implicitly) portrayed as 'Adam' or 'new Adam'. If John were intended to portray a struggle in Jn 18 between the representative of the serpent (Judas) and Jesus as the new Adam, he may be expected to have made the connection clearer.

To sum up, although some elements in GJohn might be taken as oblique references to the OT that activate further and richer meaning, a careful consideration of the larger context of GJohn can help us bring some control over the free patterns of relationship evoked by perceived allusions.

The criteria discussed above provide an explicit set of questions for assessing creation imagery in GJohn. Such criteria will serve as the basis for the following investigation. In the next section I explain the approach and procedure taken in this study.

III. Approach and Procedure

Here I offer a full-scale inquiry of the place and significance of creation imagery in GJohn with a comprehensive treatment of the evidence. Specifically, this project distinguishes itself from previous attempts for the approach it takes. First, I will use an explicit set of methodological parameters that will be consistently applied in the study of creation imagery in GJohn. Second, I will perform a thorough assessment of significant scholarly suggestions about links between GJohn and Gen. 1–3. Third, I will try to elucidate the role that creation imagery plays in its particular literary contexts and in GJohn as a whole.

This investigation comprises three major parts preceded by this Introduction and followed by a corresponding Conclusion. Part I is devoted to the Johannine prologue (Chapter 1) and Jesus' prayer in Jn 17 (Chapter 2). I have treated both passages in the same Part of this study because of the close thematic and literary resemblances between the two texts, and because both passages contain direct assertions about the creation of the world (1.3, 10; 17.5, 24). In Part II, I consider a large body of material in which Jesus performs miracles and pronounces several teachings (1.19–17.4). Scholars have posited a number of instances of creation imagery at various points in this section of the Gospel. I assess some of those suggestions in three separate chapters (Chapters 3, 4, and 5). Chapter 3 is devoted to the idea that Jesus performing the works of his Father is an instance of creation imagery. I conclude that this is a valid instance and explain the role it plays in GJohn. In Chapter 4 I suggest that a case can be made to argue that Jn 6.19 and 9.6 reflect creation imagery. In Chapter 5 I contend against the idea that the seven days of creation in Gen. 1–2 have shaped the structure of GJohn.

Part III is devoted to the passion and resurrection narratives (Jn 18–21), and is composed of two separate chapters (Chapters 6 and 7). In Chapter 6 I explain that Jn 20.22 is an instance of creation imagery that plays an important role in the Gospel. A number of scholars have claimed that the mention of a garden (Jn 18.1, 26; 19.41) and Mary's identification of Jesus as gardener in Jn 20.15 are related to the garden of Eden. In Chapter 7 I evaluate this suggestion and judge that those passages cannot be taken as valid instances of creation imagery.

In this study I argue that John has intentionally included only a limited number of instances of creation imagery and that he has positioned them carefully to highlight their significance. I will show that creation imagery in GJohn is used in several (but similar) ways in varying contexts. First, John uses this imagery to portray Jesus in close association with his Father, existing apart from and prior to the created order in a relationship that legitimizes his participation in divine activities. Second, he uses this imagery to assert the primal and universal significance of Jesus and the message about him and to privilege him over other important figures in the story of Israel. Third, John uses creation imagery to link past reality with present and future reality, portraying Jesus as the agent of creation whom the reader should regard as the primal agent of revelation and salvation.

Part I

THE PROLOGUE AND JESUS' PRAYER

This part comprises two separate chapters. The first chapter is devoted to the Johannine prologue (1.1-18).[1] The second chapter focuses on Jesus' prayer in Jn 17. The main emphasis of each chapter is an explanation of the place and significance of creation imagery in its literary context. Consequently, I will not address all the exegetical and theological issues associated with these passages.

There are at least two reasons for studying Jn 1.1-8 and Jn 17 in the same part of this investigation. The first reason is that direct references to the creation of the world in GJohn occur only in 1.3, 10; 17.5, 24.[2] Those references are the clearest instances of creation imagery in GJohn and, therefore, they should provide us with explicit indications of the way that John has used this imagery. The second reason is that John uses similar vocabulary in the prologue and in Jesus' prayer, signalling the literary relationship between both texts.[3] Jesus is referred to as Ἰησοῦς χριστός

---

1. It has been recently posited that there is no such thing as 'the prologue' (1.1-18) in GJohn. Instead, a few scholars have suggested that Jn 1.1-5 alone forms the preface or preamble to the Gospel. Cf. J. R. Michaels, *The Gospel of John* (NICNT; Grand Rapids: Eerdmans, 2010), p. 45, and P. J. Williams, 'Not the Prologue of John', *JSNT* 33 (2011), pp. 375–86. The link between the close association of the Word and God (1.1) and of the Son and the Father (1.18) may indicate at least that Jn 1.1-18 forms a literary unit. Cf. N. W. Lund, 'The Influence of Chiasmus upon the Structure of the Gospels', *ATR* 13 (1931), pp. 41–6. When I refer to the 'prologue' in this investigation, I am thinking about this literary unit (1.1-18). A recent defence of the view that Jn 1.1-18 is a literary unit can be found in T. Thatcher, 'The Riddle of the Baptist and the Genesis of the Prologue: John 1.1-18 in Oral/Aural Media Culture', in Le Donne and Thatcher (eds.), *Media Culture*, pp. 29–48.

2. There is also a reference to the creation of the world in 12.28 according to a reading preserved in D. However, it is clear that this idiosyncratic reading was influenced by 17.5.

3. E. Käsemann, for example, deemed that Jesus' prayer is to be regarded as the 'counterpart' of the prologue; see his *The Testament of Jesus: A Study of the Gospel of John in the Light of Chapter 17* (trans. G. Krodel; NTL; London: SCM, 1968), p. 3.

only twice in GJohn, in 1.17 and in 17.3 (cf. 20.31; ιης χρς, D; IC O XC, W). Other significant words that occur in both texts are: ζωή (1.4; 17.2-3), ὄνομα (1.12; 17.6, 11-12, 26), δόξα (1.14; 17.5, 22, 24), and ἀλήθεια (1.14, 17; 17.17, 19).[4]

Also, both passages occupy strategic places in the structure of GJohn. It is widely recognized that the opening section of a Gospel is programmatic, since it shapes the way that readers should engage the rest of the narrative.[5] In Jn 1.1-18 the narrator shares information with the reader that is not readily available to the characters portrayed in the story that follows. Similarly, Jn 17 is a key unit of material for the understanding of GJohn because it provides the most extended instance of Jesus addressing his Father. As for content, it is evident that Jn 17 is one of the densest sections of GJohn: 'The prayer gathers up much of what has been said…and presupposes everywhere the total picture of Christ and His work'.[6] Its present location, 'at the close of Jesus' farewell lends climactic force to their witness and underscores their pivotal importance in the thematic structure of the Fourth Gospel'.[7]

4. R. E. Brown, *The Gospel according to John* (AB, 29–29a; 2 vols.; Garden City: Doubleday, 1966–1970), vol. 2, p. 745, considered that both the prologue and Jesus' prayer have a 'hymnic quality'.

5. E. S. Malbon, 'Ending at the Beginning: A Response', *Semeia* 52 (1990), pp. 175–84 (177); M. D. Hooker, 'The Johannine Prologue and the Messianic Secret', *NTS* 21 (1974), pp. 40–58 (40).

6. C. H. Dodd, *The Interpretation of the Fourth Gospel* (Cambridge: Cambridge University Press, 1953), p. 417. See also Käsemann, *Testament*, p. 3, 'Regardless of how the question of the original position of this chapter [Jn 17] is answered, it is unmistakable that this chapter is a summary of the Johannine discourses'.

7. M. L. Appold, *The Oneness Motif in the Fourth Gospel: Motif Analysis and Exegetical Probe into the Theology of John* (WUNT, 2/1; Tübingen: J. C. B. Mohr, 1976), p. 280.

Chapter 1

CREATION IMAGERY IN THE PROLOGUE

Having established in the introductory chapter the set of questions that I will use to interrogate the evidence related to creation imagery in GJohn, here I will attempt a detailed examination of the relationship between Jn 1.1-18 and Gen. 1–2. My goal is to arrive at a properly nuanced esti- mate of the place and significance of creation imagery in the opening section of the Gospel. I will argue that John evokes the Genesis account of creation in Jn 1.1-5.[1] John uses those instances of creation imagery (along with 1.10) to shape his portrayal of the Word/Jesus.

In this chapter, and in the rest of this study, I am assuming that the prologue (whatever its previous stages of composition)[2] forms an integral part of what we now know as GJohn. Scholars have suggested more than forty different reconstructions of the putative hymn behind the prologue. This shows the great difficulties associated with positing an independent hymn that circulated autonomously of GJohn.[3] Additionally, although there are a number of variant readings in 1.1-18, there is no manuscript evidence to support the claim that the prologue, or parts of it, circulated independently of the rest of the Gospel.[4] Finally, words,

---

1. Scholars agree that there are 'two' creation accounts in Gen. 1–2 that are distinguishable both in the MT and the LXX. Cf. S. Brayford, *Genesis* (SCS; Leiden: Brill, 2007), p. 226. However, for the sake of convenience, in this study I will use 'the Genesis account/story of creation' to refer to Gen. 1–2 without distinguishing two separate narratives.

2. Cf. S. de Ausejo, '¿Es un himno a Cristo el prólogo de San Juan? Los himnos cristológicos de la Iglesia primitiva y el prólogo del IV Evangelio', *EstBíb* 15 (1956), pp. 381–427.

3. M. Hengel, 'The Prologue of the Gospel of John as the Gateway to Christ- ological Truth', in *The Gospel of John and Christian Theology* (ed. R. Bauckham and C. Mosser; Grand Rapids: Eerdmans, 2008), pp. 265–94.

4. The unit of material of GJohn 'that is supported by the greatest number of [early] witnesses is John 1', according to J. Chapa, 'The Early Text of John', in *The Early Text of the New Testament* (ed. C. E. Hill and M. J. Kruger; Oxford: Oxford University Press, 2012), pp. 140–56 (143).

concepts, and images found in the prologue are used elsewhere in the Gospel, showing the literary relationship between Jn 1.1-18 and the rest of GJohn.[5]

I. Assessment

Scholars have posited a number of instances of creation imagery in the prologue. Here I will assess those suggestions that meet our minimum requirement of verbal parallels between GJohn and Genesis.[6] Specifically, I will evaluate four suggested links between the Johannine prologue and the Genesis account of creation: (1) the phrase ἐν ἀρχῇ, (2) the noun ὁ λόγος, (3) the words πάντα and ἐγένετο, and (4) the cluster ζωή, φῶς, σκοτία, φαίνω. In addition, I will assess the proposal that the structure of the Johannine prologue emulates the seven days of creation.[7]

a. *John 1.1-2 and Genesis 1.1*

John 1.1-2

[1] ᾿Εν ἀρχῇ ἦν ὁ λόγος, καὶ ὁ λόγος ἦν πρὸς τὸν θεόν, καὶ θεὸς ἦν ὁ λόγος. [2] οὗτος ἦν ἐν ἀρχῇ πρὸς τὸν θεόν.

Genesis 1.1 LXX

[1] ᾿Εν ἀρχῇ ἐποίησεν ὁ θεὸς τὸν οὐρανὸν καὶ τὴν γῆν

---

5. E. Harris, *Prologue and Gospel: The Theology of the Fourth Evangelist* (JSNTSup, 107; Sheffield: Sheffield Academic Press, 1994), p. 25.

6. For example, Minear, *Christians*, p. 84, suggests that 'grace and truth' in Jn 1.17 'opened the way to the return to the situation of Genesis 1', and A. García-Moreno, *Temas teológicos del Evangelio de Juan: La creación* (Madrid: Rialp, 2007), p. 168, sees in Jn 1.13 a reference to the newborn as new Adam.

7. Virtually all Johannine commentators assert that Jn 1.10 is a clear reference to creation. A few have also seen there an allusion to or echo of a specific OT text. Hoskyns, 'Genesis', p. 216, related ὁ κόσμος in Jn 1.10 to Gen. 1. See also Terian, 'Creation', p. 50, who thinks that Jn 1.10 corresponds to Gen. 1.1. However, this noun occurs only in Gen. 2.1 (MT צבא). In Ps. 33.6 צבא is used in the MT, but the LXX has ἡ δύναμις (32.6). The noun κόσμος is used in creation contexts in, e.g. Jn 17.24; Mt. 13.35; 24.21; Lk. 11.50; Rom. 1.20; Eph. 1.4; Heb. 4.3; 9.26; 1 Pet. 1.20; Rev. 13.8; 17.8. Other Jewish texts deem that the κόσμος is created by God (2 Macc. 7.23; 13.14; *4 Macc.* 5.25; Wis. 9.9; 11.17; *Pr. Man.* 2; cf. *Odes* 16.19; Philo, *Leg. All.* 1.1; *Dec.* 101). On the other hand, the noun κόσμος is commonplace. Therefore, it is better to take Jn 1.10 as an instance of creation imagery but it is hardly an oblique reference to a particular OT text.

There are similarities in terms of vocabulary, theme, tone, and syntactical pattern. The phrase ἐν ἀρχῇ occurs in the two texts, once in Genesis and twice in GJohn.[8] The noun θεός occurs also in both texts, once with definite article in Gen. 1.1 and three times in GJohn, twice as the object of a preposition and with the article, πρὸς τὸν θεόν, and once as the predicate of a sentence but without the article, θεός.[9] The definite nominative article ὁ occurs in both texts, but in GJohn it accompanies λόγος while in Gen. 1.1 it identifies θεός.[10] In Gen. 1.1 the noun θεός occurs after the main verb while in Jn 1.1 it precedes the verb (θεὸς ἦν ὁ λόγος). The sentences in which θεός is used are different. 'God' is the subject of the verb ποιέω in Gen. 1.1, while 'God' functions as the predicative in a sentence with the verb ἦν. There is also a common theme in these two texts, since both refer to a general idea of 'beginning', although Gen. 1.1 refers to the beginning of creation while Jn 1.1 indicates the existence of the Word before creation (cf. Jn 1.3). As for tone, a narrator speaks in both texts. In terms of syntactical patterns, ἐν ἀρχῇ is used in both texts at the beginning of a sentence.[11] Dale Allison has noted that,

---

8. Aquila (according to cursives 135 343-344, Jerome) has εν κεφαλαιω (or εν τω κεφαλαιω, according to cursives 78-413) instead of ἐν ἀρχῇ. Symmachus and Theodotion use *in principio* (according to Jerome) and another version (known as ὁ Ἑβραῖος) uses a transliteration of בראשית (βρασιθ, according to 135; βαρησηθ, 73; βαρησειθ, 57'-78 [57'=57+413]; βρησιθ, Origen's Hexaplorum).

9. Cf. P. Borgen, *Philo, John and Paul: New Perspectives on Judaism and Early Christianity* (BJS, 131; Atlanta: Scholars Press, 1987), p. 76, and idem, *Logos Was the True Light and Other Essays on the Gospel of John* (Trondheim: Tapir, 1983), p. 14.

10. The noun אלהים lacks the article in the MT. Genesis has האלהים (with the article) elsewhere (e.g. 5.22; 6.11; 20.6; 35.7; 48.15).

11. The Hebrew בראשית (Gen. 1.1) is used in Jer. 26.1; 27.1; 28.1; 49.34 (cf. Ezek. 36.11, מראשתיכם). Where בראשית is found, only in the case of Jer. 26.1 does the LXX have ἐν ἀρχῇ (Jer. 33.1 LXX; cf. Ezek. 36.11). The phrase ἐν ἀρχῇ is used a number of times in the LXX where the MT uses תחלה (Judg. 20.18; Ruth 1.22; 2 Kgdms 17.9 [2 Sam. 17.9 MT]; 21.9, 10; 4 Kgdms 17.25 [2 Kgs 17.25]; 2 Esd. 4.6 [Ezra 4.6]; Dan. 9.23), ראש (3 Kgdms 20.9 [1 Kgs 21.9]; 20.12 [1 Kgs 21.12]; 1 Chron. 16.7; 2 Chron. 13.12; Ps. 136.6 [137.6]; Sir. 36.14), or קצה (Judg. 7.17, 19; cf. 1 Esd. 8.67 [Ezra 9.2, ראשון]). In other cases ἐν ἀρχῇ seems to have no correspondence with any particular Hebrew term (Isa. 51.9; Jer. 33.1 [26.1 MT]; 28.58 [51.58]; Ezek. 21.24; 42.10). Only in Gen. 1.1 is ἐν ἀρχῇ used in the same phrase with ὁ θεός (cf. 2 Chron. 13.12, ἐν ἀρχῇ κύριος). Apart from Gen. 1.1 and Prov. 8.23, the phrase occurs in creation contexts only in Sir. 36.14, δὸς μαρτύριον τοῖς ἐν ἀρχῇ κτίσμασίν σου, 'Give testimony to your creations in the beginning' (36.20 NETS; cf. 24.9).

> It is not just the shared phrase, *en archē*, that sends one back to Gen. 1.1.
> There is additionally a deeper parallel of sound and order: *en archē*
> prefacing a sentence at the beginning of a book + verb (*epoiēsen* / *ēn:ē*
> and *n* are common) + *ho* + two-syllable subject with two vowels ending
> in *-os* (*the–os* in Genesis, *log–os* in John).[12]

Now we should ask whether the similarities noted above are common-place or not. Among the canonical gospels, GJohn is distinctive in the way that it opens its narrative. Mark begins his account with ἀρχὴ τοῦ εὐαγγελίου (1.1), Luke with ἐπειδήπερ πολλοὶ (1.1),[13] and Matthew with βίβλος γενέσεως (1.1). Although Mark uses the noun ἀρχή, the combination with the preposition ἐν is peculiar to John. The combination ἐν ἀρχῇ does not occur elsewhere in GJohn, although the noun ἀρχή alone is used in 2.11; 6.64; 8.25, 44; 15.27; 16.4. None of these instances, however, is used in creation contexts. The phrase ἐν ἀρχῇ is used in several OT books[14] but only twice elsewhere in the NT (Acts 11.15; Phil. 4.15). Other than in Jn 1.1, the phrase is used in creation contexts only in Gen. 1.1 and Prov. 8.23.[15] In the latter text 'wisdom' says: 'before eternity he established me, in the beginning (ἐν ἀρχῇ)'. Proverbs refers to the deity as κυριός (8.22, 26). However, only in Gen. 1.1 is the phrase the opening of the book, where it is said by the narrator, and the deity is referred to as θεός. These three phenomena occur in Jn 1.1-2 as well.

As for prominence, there is one quotation from Gen. 28.12 in Jn 1.51 but no quotations from Proverbs in GJohn. On the one hand, Günter Reim finds no allusions to Proverbs in GJohn, only linguistic and theological formal parallels (Jn 3.12-13 / Prov. 30.4; 7.34 / 1.28; 7.37 / 18.4; 9.31 / 15.29) that are not evidence of direct or indirect literary dependence.[16] On the other hand, Reim suggests at least six obvious

12. Allison, *Moses*, p. 20.
13. If we regard 1.1-4 as a conventional introduction, then the beginning of Jesus' story would be, ἐγένετο ἐν (1.5).
14. See n. 11 above.
15. Cf. Ps. 101.26 [102.26 MT]: κατ᾽ ἀρχάς (לפנים). Codex Alexandrinus (and perhaps one additional minuscule) omits the phrase ἐν ἀρχῇ in Prov. 8.23.
16. G. Reim, *Studien zum alttestamentlichen Hintergrund des Johannesevangeliums* (SNTSMS, 22; Cambridge: Cambridge University Press, 1974), p. 162. The editors of NA[28] deem Jn 1.1 / Prov. 8.22-26; 3.13 / 30.4; 7.34 / 1.28; 7.38 / 18.4; 9.31 / 15.8; 9.31 / 15.29; 14.23 / 8.17; 17.12 / 24.22 as allusions. One instance does not even have verbal parallels (Jn 9.31 / Prov. 15.8). John 17.12 and Prov. 24.22 share two words that are commonplace and that are used differently in each passage (φυλάσσω, ἀπώλεια). John 14.23 and Prov. 8.17 share a verb that is commonplace (ἀγαπάω). John 7.38 and Prov. 18.4 share words with similar meanings (κοιλία, καρδία) and words with a similar root (ζάω, ζωή), but they are used differently in each passage. John 7.34 and Prov. 1.28 have a similar phrase: ζητήσετέ με καὶ οὐχ

allusions, five probable allusions, and three possible allusions to Genesis in GJohn.[17] Prominence also involves asking whether a particular OT passage was well known in ancient texts and, consequently, more likely to be a source of allusion. Quotations from Gen. 1.1 can be found in Josephus (*Ant.* 1.27), Philo (*Rer. Div. Her.* 122; *Op. Mund.* 26–27), Justin Martyr (*1 Apol.* 59, 64), Melito (*Pasc.* 47), and Theophilus (*Autol.* 2.10). Almost all of these works have the phrase ἐν ἀρχῇ in combination with the noun ὁ θεός (with the definite article).[18] Allusions to Gen. 1.1 are also found in *2 Bar.* 21.4; *4 Ezra* 6.1, 38; Melito, *Pasc.* 104; and Philo, *Quaest. in Gen.* 4.215; *Op. Mund.* 29; *Vit. Mos.* 2.266; *Plant.* 86; *Praem. Poen.* 1; *Sacr.* 8 (cf. *1 En.* 69.17-21; *2 En.* 47.2). On the other hand, it is difficult to find quotations from or allusions to Prov. 8.22-23 in ancient sources (Tertullian, *Herm.* 20, saw in Jn 1.1 a reference to Prov. 8.23), and Prov. 8.23 itself can be regarded as an allusion to Gen. 1.1. Since Gen. 1 is a more prominent text than Prov. 8, and since there are important linguistic similarities between Gen. 1 and Jn 1.1-2, it is more likely that John was being primarily influenced by the Genesis account of creation.

Now we should consider whether ancient readers of John saw in 1.1-2 a link to Gen. 1.1. Origen, for example, related Jn 1.1-2 to Gen. 1.1, but explained that the expression 'was in the beginning' (Jn 1.1-2) is older than 'in the beginning God made heaven and earth' (Gen. 1.1), because the Word is to be regarded as older than creation (*Comm. Jo.* 2.36).[19]

εὑρήσετέ / ζητήσουσίν με κακοὶ καὶ οὐχ εὑρήσουσιν. John 3.13 and Prov. 30.4 share a recognizable similarity. Jesus tells Nicodemus that no one (οὐδείς) has ascended (ἀναβέβηκεν) into heaven (οὐρανόν) but he who descended (καταβάς) from heaven (οὐρανοῦ), and in Prov. 30.4 a certain man asks 'Who has ascended (ἀνέβη) to heaven (οὐρανόν) and come down (κατέβη)?' John 1.1 and Prov. 8.23 both have the phrase ἐν ἀρχῇ.

17. Reim, *Studien*, p. 98. *Offensichtliche Anspielungen*: Jn 4.34 / Gen. 2.2; 20.22 / 2.7; 8.44 / 3.4; 6.50-51 / 3.22; 8.56 / 17.17; 1.51 / 28.12. *Wahrscheinliche Anspielungen*: Jn 8.51 / Gen. 2.17; 8.39 / 4.1-2; 8.39 / 15.6; 3.16 / 22.2 and 22.12; 5.46 / 49.10. *Mögliche Anspielungen*: Jn 3.31 / Gen. 2.7; 14.6 / 3.24; 8.35 / 21.10. Menken, 'Genesis', pp. 85–8, 90–1, considers that Jn 1.51 is a quotation from Gen. 28.12 and that Jn 2.5 and 8.44 are minor allusions to Gen. 41.55 and Gen. 3–4, respectively.

18. All those texts have ἐν ἀρχῇ ἐποίησεν, except *Pasc.* 47, which has the verb first followed by the prepositional phrase. *Quis rerum divinarum heres sit* 122 and *Op. Mund.* 27 do not have the noun θεός and *Ant.* 1.27 has κτίζω instead of ποιέω. Likewise, Aquila, Symmachus, and Theodotion have κτίζω instead of ποιέω in Gen. 1.27.

19. Modern commentators who see a link between the two texts include: Bultmann, *John*, p. 20; R. H. Lightfoot, *St. John's Gospel: A Commentary* (Oxford:

The phrase ἐν ἀρχῇ in Jn 1.1-2 as tied to Gen. 1.1 fits into the line of argument that John develops in 1.1-10. According to Jn 1.3, everything came into being through the Word, and he played a decisive role in the becoming of all things. Likewise, Jn 1.10 states that the world came into being through the Word. In light of these verses, it is not difficult to see creation imagery in Jn 1.1-2. Therefore, it is highly likely that in these two verses John was drawing on and creatively deploying a phrase found in Gen. 1.1 (ἐν ἀρχῇ).

b. *John 1.1, 14 and Genesis 1*

John 1.1, 14

¹ Ἐν ἀρχῇ ἦν ὁ λόγος,
    καὶ ὁ λόγος ἦν πρὸς τὸν θεόν,
καὶ θεὸς ἦν ὁ λόγος.
    ¹⁴ καὶ ὁ λόγος σὰρξ ἐγένετο κτλ.

Genesis 1.3, 6, 9, 11, 14, 20, 24 LXX

καὶ εἶπεν ὁ θεός κτλ.

Some scholars have proposed that λόγος in Jn 1.1 (cf. 1.14) refers to the phrase 'and God said' in Gen. 1 (cf. Philo, *Somn.* 1.75).[20] Jeannine Brown, for instance, asserts that the noun λόγος 'evokes the recurring Genesis language of "God said"'.[21] However, this supposed direct reference to Genesis does not fulfil our criterion of similar vocabulary, since no words are shared between the two texts.[22] The word λόγος does

Clarendon, 1956), p. 78; C. K. Barrett, *The Gospel according to St John* (London: SPCK, 2nd edn, 1978), p. 151; G. R. Beasley-Murray, *John* (WBC, 36; Waco, Tex.: Word, 1987), p. 10; C. S. Keener, *The Gospel of John: A Commentary* (2 vols.; Peabody: Hendrickson, 2003), vol. 1, p. 366.

20. The phrase ויאמר אלהים is consistently used in Gen. 1 MT. The phrase 'God said / saying' is used in Gen. 1.22, 26, 28, 29 LXX, but without depicting a divine act of creation.

21. J. K. Brown, 'Creation', p. 277. Cf. Michaels, *John*, p. 50; Borgen, *Logos*, pp. 14, 100; E. Hühn, *Die alttestamentlichen Citate und Reminiscenzen im Neuen Testamente* (Tübingen: J. C. B. Mohr, 1900), p. 70.

22. E. Haenchen, 'Probleme des johanneischen "Prologs"', *ZTK* 60 (1963), pp. 305–34 (313). Furthermore, there are conceptual differences between Gen. 1 and Jn 1.1, 14. Dodd, *Interpretation*, p. 269, has observed, 'In the act of creation the word was to go forth from God, but before creation was begun it was "with God" [Jn 1.1]'.

figure prominently in the Johannine prologue,[23] and it is closely related to a verified instance of creation imagery in vv. 1-2, ἐν ἀρχῇ. Therefore, one wonders whether λόγος is used in other creation contexts in the OT. Psalms is a prominent OT book in GJohn, since John cites it at least seven times.[24] In Ps. 32.6 [33.6 MT] the word of the Lord is the agent of God in creation: τῷ λόγῳ τοῦ κυρίου οἱ οὐρανοὶ ἐστερεώθησαν κτλ. In the same way, John indicates that everything came into being through ὁ λόγος (1.3, δι' αὐτοῦ, 'through him'). But apart from that, there are no other similarities between the two texts.

Second-Temple Jewish texts confirm that λόγος was frequently used in creation contexts. In the LXX the λόγος takes an active role in creation (Wis. 9.1; *Pr. Man.* 3).[25] In Wis. 9.1 God is referred to as the One who made all things through his word (ὁ ποιήσας τὰ πάντα ἐν λόγῳ σου). In *Pr. Man.* 3 the One who made the sky and the earth is the same one who 'shackled the sea by the word of [his] ordinance (τῷ λόγῳ τοῦ προστάγματός σου)'. Other Second-Temple texts that relate the word of God to God's act of creation are *Odes* 16.19; *2 Bar.* 14.16-17; *Sib. Or.* 3.20; 2 Pet. 3.5; Theophilus, *Autol.* 1.7; Justin, *Dial.* 61 (cf. 4Q381 1, 3-7, דבריו; Heb. 11.3, ῥήματι θεοῦ).[26]

23. It occurs four times (three times in v. 1 and once in v. 14) and it is the referent of the pronouns οὗτος, αὐτοῦ, and αὐτῷ in 1.2-4. Some even regard 'Logos' as the implicit subject of the verb ἦν in 1.9, 10. Others regard 'light' as the subject of the verb ἦν in 1.9, 10. Cf. Michaels, *John*, pp. 61, 64.

24. Reim, *Studien*, p. 160, counts seven explicit citations of Psalms in GJohn (Jn 19.24 / Pss. 22.19; 13.18 / 41.10; 15.25 / 69.5; 2.17 / 69.10; 19.28 / 69.22; 10.34 / 82.6; 12.13 / 118.25-26). Daly-Denton, *David*, pp. 27–8, counts ten citations, seven readily identifiable and Jn 7.38 / Pss. 78.16, 20; 19.28 / 69.22; 19.36 / 34.21. She includes in her list of seven quotations six of Reim's quotations and Jn 6.31 / Ps. 78.24.

25. Others have attempted to trace links between John's λόγος and the 'logos' of the Stoics, the gnostic 'logos', or the מימרא of the Targumim. For a critical evaluation of these putative links, see J. F. McHugh, *A Critical and Exegetical Commentary on John 1–4* (ed. G. N. Stanton; London: T&T Clark International, 2009), pp. 91–6; C. A. Evans, *Word and Glory: On the Exegetical and Theological Background of John's Prologue* (JSNTSup, 89; Sheffield: Sheffield Academic Press, 1993), pp. 47–76, 100–45; P. M. Phillips, *The Prologue of the Fourth Gospel: A Sequential Reading* (LNTS, 294; London: T&T Clark International, 2006), pp. 90–106, 131–6.

26. M. Endo, *Creation and Christology: A Study on the Johannine Prologue in the Light of Early Jewish Creation Accounts* (WUNT, 2/149; Tübingen: Mohr Siebeck, 2002), p. 210, mentions other texts that refer to the word of God in the context of creation: e.g. *2 En.* 33.4; *Apoc. Abr.* 9.9; 22.2; *Jos. Asen.* 12.2; Sir. 39.17;

Now there remain two questions to ask. The first question is whether ancient readers of Jn 1.1-2 saw creation imagery in the use of the noun λόγος. The second question is whether λόγος as an instance of creation imagery fits the line of argument John is developing. A few ancient readers of GJohn regarded ὁ λόγος as an instance of creation imagery. Tertullian, for example, opposed those who saw in Gen. 1.1 the creation of the Son and deemed that ὁ λόγος was God's 'Reason' and 'Discourse' in the beginning (*Prax.* 5). Tertullian explains in *Prax.* 5 that the 'rational Artificer' created rational beings (Gen. 1.26). As for thematic coherence, it is evident that ὁ λόγος is used in a creation context in Jn 1.3, 10, where creation (including the 'world') is directly attributed to ὁ λόγος.

In light of the previous analysis, ὁ λόγος can be deemed to evoke creation-discourse, even if it does not directly allude to Gen. 1. John did not refer directly to Ps. 32.6, but his use of ὁ λόγος resembles the use of God's word in creation contexts in several texts of Second-Temple Judaism.

c. *John 1.3 and Genesis 1–2*

John 1.3

³ πάντα δι' αὐτοῦ ἐγένετο, καὶ χωρὶς αὐτοῦ ἐγένετο οὐδὲ ἕν ὃ γέγονεν

Genesis 1.1–2.7 LXX

³ ... γενηθήτω ... ἐγένετο κτλ. ⁶ ... γενηθήτω ... ἐγένετο οὕτως ⁹, ¹¹ ... ἐγένετο οὕτως κτλ. ¹⁴⁻¹⁵ ... γενηθήτωσαν ... ἐγένετο οὕτως ²⁰, ²⁴ ... ἐγένετο οὕτως ²¹ ... πᾶσαν ψυχὴν ... πᾶν πετεινὸν κτλ. ²⁵ ... πάντα τὰ ἑρπετὰ κτλ. ³¹ ... τὰ πάντα ὅσα ἐποίησεν κτλ. ²·¹ ... πᾶς ὁ κόσμος αὐτῶν ²·², ³ ... ἀπὸ πάντων τῶν ἔργων κτλ. ²·⁴ ... ὅτε ἐγένετο κτλ. ²·⁷ ... ἐγένετο ὁ ἄνθρωπος κτλ.

There are similarities between Jn 1.3 and Gen. 1–2 in terms of vocabulary. Both πάντα and ἐγένετο are used in Jn 1.3 and in the Genesis story of creation. The plural adjective-pronoun πάντα is used in Gen. 1.25, 31 in reference to God's creation.[27] Additionally, other forms of the

42.15. See also *4 Ezra* 6.38, where it is said that the word of the Lord accomplished the work of creation. For examples of the use of λόγος in creation contexts in the works of Philo, see McHugh, *John*, p. 94.

27. The Papyrus of the Bohairic translation that has both GJohn and Gen. 1–4 (Boᵏ) omits παντα in 1.25. Instead of καλὰ λίαν, Philo has in Gen. 1.31 another instance of πάντα (αγαθα παντα). In Gen. 1.31 Aquila has πᾶς instead of πάντα. Manuscript 664 in Gen. 1.24 uses πάντα with reference to the creation of 'all the beasts' (παντα τα ερπετα), according to N. Fernández-Marcos and A. Sáenz-Badillos,

adjective πᾶς are used in Gen. 1.21; 2.1, 2, 3 with reference to the creation of all living creatures and all birds (1.21), all reptiles (1.25), and all the 'cosmos' of heaven and earth (2.1), and to refer more generally to God's creation as a whole (1.31; 2.2, 3). John uses the aorist ἐγένετο twice in 1.3. This noun is used nine times in the Genesis account (1.3, 6, 9, 11, 15, 20, 24; 2.4, 7).[28] Furthermore, other forms of γίνομαι are used in both texts (γέγονεν, Jn 1.3; γενηθήτω, Gen. 1.3, 6; γενηθήτωσαν, Gen. 1.14). The verb γίνομαι is used to assert that something came into existence by God's command: light (1.3), the firmament (1.6), the gathering of the waters (1.9), vegetation (1.11), stars (1.14-15), animals (1.20, 24), heaven and earth (2.4), and man himself (2.7).[29] However, there is no verse in the Genesis account of creation where both πᾶς and γίνομαι occur together, as they do in Jn 1.3. Genesis 1.31 is an exception, but in this case, γίνομαι is not related to a divine act of creation.

It is also possible to claim that Jn 1.3 and Gen. 1–2 share common themes and emphases. Both texts refer to the creation of everything that exists,[30] and both emphasize the idea of creation. Similarly, the number of occurrences of πᾶς and γίνομαι (three times in Jn 1.3) shows the emphasis on the divine act of creation in the Genesis account.

The word combination πᾶς and γίνομαι is not a commonplace in GJohn. John uses both words separately in other passages, but he never uses them together in the same verse. In the rest of the NT there are at

Anotaciones críticas al texto griego del Génesis y estudio de sus grupos textuales (TSt, 12; Madrid: Consejo Superior de Investigaciones Científicas, 1972), p. 14. The adjective πᾶς is also used in Gen. 1.26 (πάσης, πάντων), 1.28 (πάντων, πάσης, πάντων), 1.29 (πᾶν, πάσης, πᾶν), and 1.30 (πᾶσιν, παντί, πάντα).

28. Cursive 82, Eusebius, and the Armenian translation omit the verb ἐγένετο in Gen. 2.4.

29. The LXX has γενηθήτω...ἐγένετο οὕτως in 1.6, but the MT lacks ויהי־כן (cf. 1.20). In Gen. 2.4 the MT has ברא instead of היה. The narrator also uses the verb γίνομαι in Gen. 1.5, 8, 13, 19, 23, 31.

30. Some scholars have argued that πάντα in Jn 1.3 does not refer to 'all things created' but to 'all things made by the Logos', i.e. revelation and salvation. Ed. L. Miller, '"In the Beginning": A Christological Transparency', *NTS* 45 (1999), pp. 587–92 (589 n. 10); idem, *Salvation-History in the Prologue of John: The Significance of John 1:3/4* (Leiden: Brill, 1989), pp. 45–89; T. E. Pollard, 'Cosmology and the Prologue of the Fourth Gospel', *VC* 12 (1958), pp. 147–53; I. de la Potterie, *La Vérité dans Saint Jean* (AnBib, 73–74; 2 vols.; Rome: Biblical Institute Press, 1977), vol. 1, pp. 162–3. Cf. P. Lamarche, 'Le Prologue de Jean', *RSR* 52 (1964), pp. 497–537 (527). Nevertheless, Jn 1.10 has a clear statement of creation that is parallel to Jn 1.3, πάντα δι' αὐτοῦ ἐγένετο (v. 3) / ὁ κόσμος δι' αὐτοῦ ἐγένετο (v. 10). McHugh, *John*, p. 13, comments that John might be intending both senses, that πάντα refers to both creation and salvation.

least three more instances where Jesus' role in creation is prominent: 1 Cor. 8.6; Col. 1.13-18; Heb. 1.2-3. 1 Corinthians 8.6 and Col. 1.16 say that Jesus participated in the creation of 'all things' (τὰ πάντα),[31] but do not use the verb γίνομαι. In other OT texts where creation is a conspicuous idea, the verb γίνομαι is used, but not πάντα (Pss. 32.9 [33.9 MT]; 89.2 [90.2]; 103.20 [104.20]; 148.5).

There is evidence from Qumran that היה and כל occur in the same sentence in creation contexts. According to 1QS XI, 11, 'By his knowledge everything shall come into being [נהיה כול], and all that does exist [וכ{ע}ול הויה] he establishes with his calculations and nothing is done outside of him'[32] (cf. Philo, *Op. Mund.* 13). Where Gen MT has היה, Gen LXX has γίνομαι (e.g. 1.3, 6; 2.7). Similarly, where Gen MT has כל, Gen LXX has πᾶς (Gen. 1.21, 25, 31; 2.1-3).[33]

Ancient and modern Johannine readers have seen language in Jn 1.3 that evokes the Genesis account of creation. For example, Chrysostom asserts that Jn 1.3 is a summary reference to Gen. 1 (*Hom. Jo.* 5.1; *NPNF*[1], vol. 14, p. 21).[34] More recently, Raymond Brown has argued that Jn 1.3 is linked to Gen. 1, since both texts use the verb γίνομαι.[35]

---

31. In all three passages (1 Cor. 8.6; Col. 1.16; Heb. 1.2) Jesus' role in creation is conveyed by the phrase δι' plus genitive, as in Jn 1.3. The verb used to describe the act of creation is implicit in 1 Cor. 8.6, but it is explicit in Col. 1.16 (κτίζω) and Heb. 1.2 (ποιέω). In Rev. 4.11 the adjective πᾶς is put together with the verb κτίζω. Cf. O. Hofius, 'Struktur und Gedankengang des Logos-Hymnus in Joh 1,1–18', in *Johannestudien: Untersuchungen zur Theologie des vierten Evangeliums* (ed. O. Hofius and H. C. Kammler; WUNT, 88; Tübingen: Mohr Siebeck, 1996), pp. 1–23 (6 n. 36).

32. F. García-Martínez and E. J. C. Tigchelaar (eds.), *The Dead Sea Scrolls Study Edition* (Leiden: Brill, 1999), pp. 98–9.

33. Cf. Bultmann, *John*, p. 37; R. Schnackenburg, *The Gospel according to St John* (trans. K. Smyth; HTKNT; 3 vols.; London: Burns & Oates, 1968–1982), vol. 1, p. 238. In Wis. 9.1 πάντα is used in a creation context, but without the verb γίνομαι. A creation context is also in view in *Odes* 16.18, where it is said that the Lord 'was before anything came to be' (*OTP*, vol. 2, p. 750). Endo, *Creation*, p. 210, has also observed that creation is portrayed using the idea of 'all' (e.g. πᾶς) in several Jewish texts: *Jub.* 12.4; *2 En.* 33.8; 66.4, 5; *Jos. Asen.* 12.1; *Sib. Or.* 1.7-8; 3.20.

34. Irenaeus, *Haer.* 3.8.3, related Jn 1.3 to Ps. 32.6 [33.6 MT].

35. Brown, *John*, vol. 1, p. 6. Cf. also Michaels, *John*, p. 51; von Wahlde, *John*, vol. 2, p. 28; McHugh, *John*, p. 12; P. Borgen, 'Creation, Logos and the Son: Observations on Joh 1:1-18 and 5:17-18', *ExAud* 3 (1987), pp. 88–97 (92). D. A. Carson, *The Gospel according to John* (Grand Rapids: Eerdmans, 1991), p. 118, relates Jn 1.3 to Gen. 1 and Prov. 3.19; 8.30, but neither γίνομαι nor πᾶς is used in Proverbs to indicate creation.

In light of the previous analysis, it is likely that John intended to evoke the Genesis account of creation when he used the word combination γίνομαι and πᾶς in Jn 1.3. It seems natural to see creation imagery in Jn 1.3, because John has already evoked Gen. 1.1 in Jn 1.1.[36]

d. *John 1.4-5 and Genesis 1–2*

John 1.4-5

⁴ ἐν αὐτῷ <u>ζωὴ</u> ἦν, καὶ <u>ἡ ζωὴ</u> ἦν <u>τὸ φῶς</u> τῶν ἀνθρώπων· ⁵ καὶ <u>τὸ φῶς</u> ἐν τῇ <u>σκοτίᾳ φαίνει</u>, καὶ ἡ <u>σκοτία</u> αὐτὸ οὐ κατέλαβεν.

Genesis 1–2 LXX (Life)

²⁰ ... ψυχῶν <u>ζωσῶν</u> κτλ. ²¹ ... πᾶσαν ψυχὴν <u>ζώων</u> κτλ. ²⁴ ... ἐξαγαγέτω ἡ γῆ ψυχὴν <u>ζῶσαν</u> κτλ. ³⁰ ... ψυχὴν <u>ζωῆς</u> κτλ. ²·⁷ ... πνοὴν <u>ζωῆς</u> ... εἰς ψυχὴν <u>ζῶσαν</u>. ²·⁹ ... καὶ τὸ ξύλον <u>τῆς ζωῆς</u> κτλ. ²·¹⁹ ... ὃ ἐὰν ἐκάλεσεν αὐτὸ ᾿Αδὰμ ψυχὴν <u>ζῶσαν</u> κτλ.

Genesis 1 LXX (Light and Darkness)

² ... καὶ <u>σκότος</u> ἐπάνω κτλ. ³ ... γενηθήτω <u>φῶς</u> καὶ ἐγένετο <u>φῶς</u>. ⁴ καὶ εἶδεν ὁ θεὸς <u>τὸ φῶς</u> ... <u>τοῦ φωτὸς</u> καὶ ... <u>τοῦ σκότους</u> ⁵ καὶ ἐκάλεσεν ὁ θεὸς <u>τὸ φῶς</u> ... καὶ <u>τὸ σκότος</u> κτλ. ¹⁴ ... γενηθήτωσαν <u>φωστῆρες</u> ... εἰς <u>φαῦσιν</u> κτλ. ¹⁵ καὶ ἔστωσαν εἰς <u>φαῦσιν</u> ... ὥστε <u>φαίνειν</u> κτλ. ¹⁶ καὶ ἐποίησεν ὁ θεὸς τοὺς δύο <u>φωστῆρας</u> ... τὸν <u>φωστῆρα</u> τὸν μέγαν ... καὶ τὸν <u>φωστῆρα</u> τὸν ἐλάσσω κτλ. ¹⁷ ... ὥστε <u>φαίνειν</u> ἐπὶ τῆς γῆς, ¹⁸ ... ἀνὰ μέσον <u>τοῦ φωτὸς</u> καὶ ἀνὰ μέσον <u>τοῦ σκότους</u> κτλ.

There are similarities between Jn 1.4-5 and Gen. 1–2 in terms of vocabulary. The noun ζωή is used twice in Jn 1.4, and appears as well in Gen. 1.30; 2.7, 9 (always in the genitive form).[37] The concept of life is expressed also in Gen. 1.20, 21, 24; 2.7, 19 through ζῶσαν (1.24; 2.7, 19,

---

36. A. T. Lincoln, *The Gospel according to Saint John* (BNTC; London: Continuum, 2005), pp. 98–9. Cf. E. Haenchen, *John 1* (trans. R. W. Funk; Hermeneia; Philadelphia: Fortress, 1984), p. 112; F. J. Moloney, *The Gospel of John* (SP, 4; Collegeville: Liturgical, 1998), p. 42.

37. The construction נפש plus חי is used to describe both animals (1.20, 21, 24; 30; 2.19) and humankind (2.7). The adjective חי is translated by the noun ζωή only in 1.30. In 1.30 a group of cursives (group *d* except cursive 106), the original reading of cursive 56, and the Armenian and Syrian Palestinian translations have ζωσαν (verb ζάω) instead of ζωῆς. In this same verse Aquila and Symmachus have the neuter noun ζῷον (ζώῳ and τοῖς ζῷοις, respectively) instead of τοῖς θηρίοις, 'the wild animals', and they also have ζῶσα (verb ζάω) instead of ζωῆς. Likewise, Philo and the Armenian translation have ζωσαν (verb ζάω) instead of ζωῆς in 2.7. In this same verse (2.7) Chrysostom omits ζωῆς.

verb ζάω; cf. 1.20, ζωσῶν) or ζῷων (noun ζῷον).[38] The noun ζωή is used in the Genesis account of creation with reference to the breath of human life (2.7), the tree of life (2.9), and animal life (1.30). Apart from the presence of ζωή, there are no other clear similarities between Jn 1.4, on the one hand, and Gen. 1.30; 2.7. The use of this noun in the two passages is different. In both sentences of Jn 1.4 it functions as the subject, first, without the article, to indicate that life was in the Word (cf. 5.26; 6.68), and secondly, with the article, to state that the life that was in the Word was the light of humankind (cf. 6.63; 11.25; 14.6). On the other hand, in the Genesis creation account the noun is always used in the genitive to modify the nouns ψυχή (1.30), πνοή (2.7), and ξύλον (2.9), and the other grammatical forms from the same root also modify ψυχή (1.20, 21, 24; 2.7, 19).

The words 'light', 'darkness', and 'to shine' are used both in Jn 1.4-5 and Gen. 1.[39] John uses the noun φῶς, with the article, in relation to life and men in 1.4, and to darkness in 1.5.[40] 'Light' is a predominant theme in Gen. 1, where it is mentioned in the narration of the first (1.3-5) and fourth (1.14-19) days of creation. The noun φῶς is used with the article in Gen. 1.4, 5, 18 and without it in 1.3.[41] The idea of light is also expressed through the nouns φωστήρ (Gen. 1.14, 16) and φαῦσις (1.14,

---

38.   Instead of ζωσῶν in Gen. 1.20, Aquila has ζώσης, Symmachus has ζῶσαν, and Theodotion has ζώσας. In 1.21 ζῷων is replaced by ζωσων (cursive 82, a number of other cursives, the Armenian translation, and, according to Fernández-Marcos and Sáenz-Badillos, *Anotaciones*, p. 14, manuscripts 246 and 664) or ζωσαν (cursives 72 25 54 730, and the Ethiopian and Bohairic translations). In 1.24 ζῶσαν does not occur in the original reading of cursive 75 and Eusebius. The plural 'the animals' (θηρίον) in 2.19, 20 is replaced by ζῷα (2.19) and ζῴοις (2.20) in Aquila and Symmachus.

39.   Cf. Borgen, *Logos*, pp. 15, 99–100; W. S. Kurz, 'Intertextual Permutations of the Genesis Word in the Johannine Prologues', in *Early Christian Interpretation of the Scriptures of Israel: Investigations and Proposals* (ed. C. A. Evans and J. A. Sanders; JSNTSup, 148; Sheffield: Sheffield Academic Press, 1997), pp. 179–90 (181, 188).

40.   The noun occurs also in Jn 1.7-9. The pronouns αὐτοῦ and αὐτόν (masculine) in Jn 1.10 refer to λόγος (1.1-3) not to φῶς (neuter, 1.9).

41.   The article precedes the noun (το φως, 1.3) in cursive 106. Cursives 125 and 664, and the mixed manuscripts 19 and B^s omit τό φῶς (1.4). This noun, however, occurs in the genitive form (φωτός) in Hippolytus (1.4). Instead of τῆς ἡμέρας in 1.14, B^s and cursive 75 have του φωτος. In 1.18 the Old Latin has *diem*, 'day', and manuscript 664 has θηρος, 'wild animal' (Fernández-Marcos and Sáenz-Badillos, *Anotaciones*, p. 14) instead of φωτός, and the cursive 646 adds το φως after θεός: 'and God saw that *the light* was good'.

15).[42] Like Jn 1.5, Gen. 1 contrasts light and darkness, since it says that God separated light from darkness (1.4-5) and created luminaries to separate day from night (1.14, 16) and light from darkness (1.18). Unlike Jn 1.4, the Genesis account does not relate directly light to life, nor to humanity.[43]

The noun 'darkness' is used in both texts, but while the feminine noun σκοτία, with the article, occurs twice in Jn 1.5, the Genesis account uses rather the neuter σκότος,[44] with the article (1.4, 5, 18) and without it (1.2).[45] John states that the light shines in the darkness and that the darkness has not overcome it, while Gen. 1 recounts that darkness was separated from light (1.4, 18), and that God called it night (1.5). As for the verb φαίνω, it occurs in Jn 1.5 and Gen. 1.15, 17.[46] The main difference between the two texts is that GJohn says that φῶς 'shines' (φαίνω), while in Gen. 1 the luminaries (φωστήρ) and the stars (ἀστήρ) 'shine' (φαίνω).[47]

The word combination 'life', 'light', 'darkness', and 'to shine' is rare in both the NT and the OT, although each separate word is commonplace. The nouns 'darkness' (σκότος) and 'light' (φῶς) and the verb 'to

42.   The LXX has φῶς where the MT has אור. The nouns φωστήρ (Gen. 1.14, 16) and φαῦσις (Gen. 1.14, 15) are used where the MT has מאור. As for variants in the LXX, (1) the Bohairic papyrus that has both the text of GJohn and Gen. 1–4 omits τόν φωστῆρα (1.16), and (2) Aquila has φωστῆρας instead of φαῦσιν in Gen. 1.15. This latter noun is used by Theodoret of Cyrrhus (Gen. 1.17) instead of ὥστε φαίνειν. According to J. W. Wevers, *Notes on the Greek Text of Genesis* (SBLSCS, 35; Atlanta: Scholars Press, 1993), p. 9 n. 27, it might be expected that Aquila changed φαῦσιν to φωστῆρας for the sake of consistency in light of Gen. 1.14.

43.   Köstenberger, *Theology*, p. 339, suggests that light is created first in Gen. 1.3-5, 14-18 in order to enable life to exist (1.20-31). With this, Köstenberger intends to show that there is a similarity between Genesis and GJohn in the way that both texts relate life and light. However, although God creates light first in Genesis, there is no clear indication there that light is related to the existence of life.

44.   The feminine σκοτία is used in Job 28.3; Isa. 16.3; Mic. 3.6, but none of these verses is located in creation contexts.

45.   The MT uses the masculine חשך, 'darkness', in these verses. As for variant readings in the LXX, (1) the noun 'darkness' occurs without the article in cursive 31 (Gen. 1.5), (2) του σκοτους is used instead of τῆς νυκτός in cursive 75 (Gen. 1.14), and (3) the Old Latin has *noctem* where Greek manuscripts have σκότους in 1.18.

46.   There are two additional occurrences of the verb φαίνω in other manuscripts. Instead of φαῦσιν in Gen. 1.14, cursives 75 and 509, Eusebius of Caesarea, Severianus Gabalitanus, and two translations (Old Latin and Ethiopian) have φαινειν; and although cursive 129 preserves φαῦσιν, it adds immediately after this noun the phrase της ημερας του φαινειν. According to Fernández-Marcos and Sáenz-Badillos, *Anotaciones*, p. 14, manuscript 664 has φαναι instead of φαίνειν in Gen. 1.15.

47.   Cf. Wevers, *Notes*, p. 9.

shine' (λάμπω) are used in 2 Cor. 4.6 without the noun 'life'.[48] In the OT 'light' (φῶς, λαμπρότης), 'darkness' (σκότος), and 'to shine' (φαίνω, φωτίζω) are used in Isa. 60.1-3 in an eschatological context, but without the noun 'life'.

Concepts of light and life are prominent in creation contexts in Second-Temple Jewish texts, although light is far more conspicuous. The idea of life occurs in relation to the Creator God in, for example, *Jub.* 12.4; *2 En.* 30.10; *4 Ezra* 6.47-48; *Jos. Asen.* 8.10-11; 12.1; *2 Bar.* 23.5; Philo, *Op. Mund.* 30. The idea of light figures in long narratives about God's creation (*Jub.* 2; *1 En.* 69.16-25; *2 En.* 24–33; *4 Ezra* 6.38-54; *Sib. Or.* 1.5-35; *LAE* 60; Josephus, *Ant.* 1; 1QM X; 1QHᵃ IX; 4Q381 1; Philo, *Op. Mund.* 22–35; cf. Ps. 103.2 [104.2 MT]; 4Q392; 11Q5 XXVI).[49]

God is portrayed as the Creator of light (*Jub.* 2.2; *2 En.* 25.1-3; *2 Bar.* 54.13; 4Q392 1, 4; cf. *Sib. Or.* 1.10) and of those elements that impart light in the earth, such as the sun, the moon, the stars (*Jub.* 2.8; *2 En.* 30.2, 5; *4 Ezra* 6.45; 1QM X, 11; 1QHᵃ IX, 10-11; 4Q381 1, 5), and the light of the lightning (1QHᵃ IX, 12; *1 En.* 69.23), that comes from God's own eye (*2 En.* 29.1-2). God is also portrayed as separating light from darkness in *Jub.* 2.8-10; *2 En.* 27.4; 11Q5 XXVI, 11; Philo, *Op. Mund.* 33.[50] In *2 En.* 25.4 God commands the light to go to the highest place and to become the foundation of the highest things, and the light becomes itself the highest thing that exists. In the same way, Philo deems that light was made to crown God's creation (*Op. Mund.* 29), and even indicates that the 'invisible light' is an image of the divine word (θείου λόγου, *Op. Mund.* 31). According to *2 En.* 27.1-3, light was even used to create the waters, since they were surrounded with light when they were created. Similarly, in *4 Ezra* 6.40, light comes from God's treasuries in order to enable his creation to appear (cf. 4Q392 1, 7; *2 Bar.* 54.13). It is

48. In 2 Pet. 1.19 it is said that the prophetic word (λόγος) shines (φαίνω) like a light (λύχνος) in a dark (αὐχμηρός) place.

49. Endo, *Creation*, pp. 216–19. The idea of darkness is also prominent in some of these texts. *Jubilees* 2.2 and 4Q392 1 portray God as the Creator of darkness. In other cases darkness is described as already existing (*2 En.* 25.1; *4 Ezra* 6.38; *LAB* 60.2) and as being the lowest thing that exists (*2 En.* 26.3). In *LAB* 60.2 darkness is closely related to the creation of light: 'silence spoke a word and the darkness became light' (*OTP*, vol. 2, p. 373). According to Philo, God himself gave to the air the name of 'Darkness' (*Op. Mund.* 29).

50. In *2 En.* 30.15 light and darkness have an ethical sense, since it is said that God pointed out to Adam light as the good things and darkness as the bad things (cf. *2 Bar.* 18.1-2; *Jos. Asen.* 8.10). By contrast, 4Q392 1, 5-6 says that God does not need to separate light from darkness. For Philo, darkness withdrew, moved out, and retired after the coming of the light (*Op. Mund.* 33, 35).

also said that light is a blessing for paradise: 'the light which is never darkened was perpetually in paradise' (*2 En.* 31.2; *OTP*, vol. 1, p. 154; cf. *2 En.* 65.10).

On the one hand, some church fathers saw in Jn 1.4-5 creation imagery, but they did not make a direct link to Gen. 1. Hilary (d. 367) indicates that the Word was the life that made creation possible (*On the Trinity* 2.20). Chrysostom sees in the word 'life' a reference not only to the act of creation but also to divine providence (*Hom. Jo.* 5.3). M.-É. Boismard used Irenaeus, *Epid.* 38, as evidence that a link to Gen. 1 was early made by readers of Jn 1.4-5.[51] However, a closer reading of *Epid.* 38 reveals that while Irenaeus indicates that God sent his creative 'Word' to deliver those who had lost life, and that God's light appeared and destroyed death (humanity's darkness), he did not make a direct link between the two texts. On the other hand, modern readers of GJohn have explicitly related both texts.[52] Craig Evans, for example, sees a parallel between Gen. 1.15 and Jn 1.5 in terms of the verb 'to shine',[53] and Antonio García-Moreno notices the use of same noun (φῶς) in both texts.[54]

If John has evoked the Genesis story of creation when he used the phrase 'in the beginning' (1.1) and when he indicated that 'all things were created by him' (1.3), it is reasonable to think that he was also using vocabulary from Gen. 1–2 in the following two verses (1.4-5).

51. M.-É. Boismard, *Le Prologue de Saint Jean* (LD, 11; Paris: Cerf, 1953), p. 17 n. 3.

52. Boismard, *Prologue*, pp. 24–38; McDonough, *Creator*, p. 20; Keener, *John*, vol. 1, p. 386; B. Lindars, *The Gospel of John* (NCB; London: Oliphants, 1972), p. 85; Phillips, *Prologue*, pp. 166–7; Carson, *John*, p. 119 (who entertains the possibility of a link to Gen. 1.27 in Jn 1.4). Brown, *John*, vol. 1, pp. 26–7, relates Jn 1.4 to the tree of life in the garden of Eden and Jn 1.5 to the fall of Adam and Eve. Similarly, Borgen, *Logos*, p. 108, relates Jn 1.5 to Adam's fall (cf. *Apoc. Adam* 1.12). Nevertheless, J. Painter, 'Rereading Genesis in the Prologue of John?', in *Neotestamentica et Philonica: Studies in Honor of Peder Borgen* (ed. D. E. Aune, T. Seland, and J. H. Ulrichsen; NovTSup, 106; Leiden: Brill, 2003), pp. 179–201 (182), rightly comments that Jn 1.5 states that 'the light was not overcome by the darkness' and 'nowhere suggests that the light was withdrawn'. Against Brown, see Michaels, *John*, p. 56 (cf. von Wahlde, *John*, vol. 2, p. 5).

53. Evans, *Word*, p. 78.

54. García-Moreno, *Temas*, p. 148. Two others who have seen a clear reference to Gen. 1 in John's use of the noun light in 1.4-5 are: Borgen, 'Creation', p. 92, and G. H. van Kooten, ' "The True Light which Enlightens Everyone" (*John* 1:9): John, *Genesis*, the Platonic Notion of the "True, Noetic Light", and the Allegory of the Cave in Plato's *Republic*', in van Kooten (ed.), *The Creation of Heaven and Earth*, pp. 149–94 (149).

However, the way in which 'life', 'light', 'darkness', and 'to shine' are used in the two texts is different. This observation, along with the assessment of the evidence pondered above, leads to the conclusion that in using these words John is not making a direct reference to the Genesis narrative, but rather he is only drawing on and creatively deploying terms and images stemming from Gen. 1–2.

e. *The Prologue's Structure and Genesis 1–2*
Mary Coloe has proposed that the structure of Jn 1.1-18 resembles the structure of Gen. 1.1–2.4a. She indicates that both narratives have an introduction (Jn 1.1-2; Gen. 1.1-2) and a conclusion (1.18; 2.4a) that bracket three strophes (strophe 1, Jn 1.3-5, 14 and Gen. 1.3-5, 14-19; strophe 2, Jn 1.6-8, 15 and Gen. 1.6-8, 20-23; strophe 3, Jn 1.9-13, 16-17 and Gen. 1.9-13, 24-31). Her main conclusion is that the Genesis narrative leads to a seventh-day climax which is absent from the Johannine prologue. Therefore, Coloe deems, John maintains that the fulfilment of creation was not possible within Israel because Jesus was sent to finish the work of his Father (Jn 4.34; 5.17; 19.30).[55]

It seems that Coloe is proposing a forced structure to understand both texts (Genesis and GJohn), since there is not enough word agreement between the suggested corresponding strophes. The verbal parallels are limited to the introductions ('in the beginning') and the imagery in the 'first strophe' ('life', 'light', 'darkness', and 'to shine'). It is almost impossible to find similar parallels between the suggested second strophe, third strophe, and conclusion of the two passages. Even the proposed structure for the Genesis narrative seems problematic in itself, although her observation that Gen. 1.1–2.3 forms a literary unit might be correct.[56] As for 'strophe 3', I am unable to see similarities between Gen. 1.9-13 and Gen. 1.26-31, although there are a number of verbal parallels between vv. 11-13 and 24-25. Furthermore, I have been unable to find in Second-Temple Jewish texts any evidence that ancient readers saw in the Genesis account of creation the structure Coloe is proposing. In some of those texts a sequence of seven days can be discerned (e.g. *Jub.* 2.1-33; Josephus, *Ant.* 1.27-36; *4 Ezra* 6.38-54), but there is no recognition of her three strophes.

55. Coloe, 'Structure', pp. 40–55; idem, *God Dwells with Us*, pp. 15–29; idem, 'Creation', p. 4.

56. W. P. Brown, *Structure, Role, and Ideology in the Hebrew and Greek Texts of Genesis 1:1–2:3* (SBLDS, 132; Atlanta: Scholars Press, 1993), p. 26.

There is no evidence that ancient readers of GJohn saw in the prologue a structure parallel to that of the Genesis creation account. Even modern commentators have proposed a great diversity of structures for understanding Jn 1.1-18, which leads to the conclusion that John perhaps did not intend a rigid structure when articulating the prologue.[57] For all these reasons, Coloe's proposal is not compelling.[58]

II. The Significance of Creation Imagery in the Prologue

In the previous section I established that there is creation imagery in the Johannine prologue. John asserts that the world was created through the Word (1.10), uses terms and images stemming from Gen. 1–2 (Jn 1.1-5), and evokes other creation-discourses by using ὁ λόγος. The question that needs to be answered now is how John uses these instances of creation imagery.

a. *John 1.1-2*
The evocation of the opening words of Gen. 1 in Jn 1.1-2 takes the reader back to the Genesis account of creation. From the first verse, the only character in this narrative is God, who is portrayed as making heaven and earth. The Johannine reader familiar with this verse will immediately notice that, in contrast, John includes another figure along with God, since what follows ἐν ἀρχῇ is not ὁ θεός, but rather ὁ λόγος.[59] This, however, does not mean that John is attempting to replace ὁ θεός with ὁ λόγος. Instead, it seems that he is emphasising the close association that ὁ λόγος had with God in the beginning. This emphasis is signalled by the three consecutive clauses in vv. 1-2 that assert the relationship between ὁ λόγος and God. The first clause (ὁ λόγος ἦν πρὸς τὸν θεόν) indicates that ὁ λόγος is distinguishable from 'God', but the immediately following one indicates that he is, at the same time, closely related to 'God', since θεὸς ἦν ὁ λόγος.[60] This does not mean that ὁ λόγος has replaced ὁ θεός, because

---

57. Endo, *Creation*, pp. 189–202, has found almost fifteen different modern proposals for the structure of the Johannine prologue. See also the diverse ways in which the major editions of the Greek NT divide the prologue (McHugh, *John*, p. 68).

58. Du Rand, 'Creation', p. 38, finds Coloe's structure to be helpful.

59. Haenchen, *John 1*, p. 109; Beasley-Murray, *John*, p. 10; Phillips, *Prologue*, p. 149.

60. It is better to take the noun θεός here as a reference to God instead of as a reference to the general idea of 'divinity' (cf. θεῖος, Acts 17.29; 2 Pet. 1.3-4; θειότης, Rom. 1.20). If John is evoking Gen. 1.1 in Jn 1.1-2, the most plausible identification of θεός is with the God of Genesis. Literarily, one can identify λόγος with Jesus Christ and θεός with the Father, in light of 1.18.

John immediately repeats that οὗτος ἦν ἐν ἀρχῇ πρὸς τὸν θεόν.[61] Thus, John is not intending a simple identification of the two figures, since he places ὁ λόγος at the side of God by bracketing θεὸς ἦν ὁ λόγος with two very similar statements that ὁ λόγος existed with God.[62] The two ideas expressed in these three clauses are to be read as complementary.

The phrase ἐν ἀρχῇ is also intended to portray ὁ λόγος as existing apart from and prior to creation.[63] Several commentators have observed that 'in the beginning' (Jn 1.1) precedes the creation of all that exists (Jn 1.3).[64] In consequence, John (by evoking Gen. 1.1) is indicating that ὁ λόγος is not part of 'all things' that were created (1.3), but that he existed with God before creation. There is a distance between the created world (1.3, 10) and God,[65] and John has put ὁ λόγος at the side of God.

Earlier in this chapter it was determined that the use here of ὁ λόγος could be deemed to evoke creation-discourse, even if it does not directly allude to Gen. 1. However, scholars have found it difficult to decide categorically on this noun's background. A case can be made for relating it in various ways to the Greek Hellenistic world, or with Gnostic systems, or with Hellenistic Judaism, or with the Hebrew Bible, or with

---

61. Bultmann, *John*, p. 34; Brown, *John*, vol. 1, pp. 5, 24; Michaels, *John*, p. 47; Keener, *John*, vol. 1, p. 373. But cf. Haenchen, *John 1*, p. 112; McHugh, *John*, p. 11.

62. The preposition πρός before an accusative noun can mean 'with God' or 'towards God' (Brown, *John*, vol. 1, pp. 4–5; Schnackenburg, *John*, vol. 1, p. 233; Carson, *John*, p. 116; Lincoln, *John*, p. 97; McHugh, *John*, pp. 9–10; Moloney, *John*, p. 35; Keener, *John*, vol. 1, p. 370). The sense would be, then, 'in the presence of God' (e.g. Haenchen, *John 1*, p. 109; Schnackenburg, *John*, vol. 1, p. 234) or 'turned towards and in close fellowship with God' (e.g. I. de la Potterie, 'L'emploi dynamique de εἰς dans Saint Jean et ses incidences théologiques', *Bib* 43 [1962], pp. 366–87 [379–81]; Beasley-Murray, *John*, p. 10; Phillips, *Prologue*, p. 152). In light of the phrase 'in the bosom of the Father' in Jn 1.18, we can privilege the second option, i.e. the Word existed in close association with God in the beginning.

63. M. J. J. Menken, 'What Authority Does the Fourth Evangelist Claim for His Book?', in *Paul, John, and Apocalyptic Eschatology* (ed. J. Krans et al.; NovTSup, 149; Leiden: Brill, 2013), pp. 186–202 (196), has claimed that ἐν ἀρχῇ is used to signal the authority of GJohn. By beginning his Gospel with a phrase that is the opening of the book of Genesis, John 'contends that his book is divine revelation to a higher degree than the Scriptures'. John probably intended to write an authoritative text for his audience, but it is difficult to take ἐν ἀρχῇ as signalling the superiority of GJohn over the Scriptures of the time (cf. 5.39).

64. Lightfoot, *John*, p. 78; Haenchen, *John 1*, p. 109; Schnackenburg, *John*, vol. 1, p. 232; Carson, *John*, p. 114; Lincoln, *John*, p. 94.

65. Schnackenburg, *John*, vol. 1, p. 234.

Rabbinic and Targumic literature.[66] In light of this, one should ask why John selected a noun that was widely used in a variety of settings in antiquity and has used it in an allusion to Gen. 1.1 (ἐν ἀρχῇ). A plausible answer has been provided by Peter Phillips: 'Λόγος represents a flux of ideas and meanings interacting with one another crossing a number of different cultural milieux'.[67] If Phillips is correct, it is possible to conclude that the noun λόγος in Jn 1.1-2 is an instance of creation imagery intended to signal the universal significance of the Word in creation. This idea is even clearer in Jn 1.3, 10.

b. *John 1.3, 10*

The word combination γίνομαι and πᾶς in Jn 1.3 is another instance of creation imagery. Instead of listing each thing created by God in Genesis, John uses γίνομαι in two statements (one positive and the other negative) with πᾶς in the first, to indicate that everything was created through ὁ λόγος. Both statements signify totality or universality. 'It is thus stated as strongly as possible that everything without exception has been made by the Logos.'[68] This idea is even stronger if we take as the conclusion of v. 3 the phrase 'not one thing was created that has been created'.[69] The

---

66. The noun 'word' is used in a number of texts; e.g. *Trim. Prot.* 35.1-6 (Gnostic); *Odes* 12.8, 10; 16.18-19 (Christian); Philo, *Fug.* 101; *Somn.* 1.230; *Cher.* 35, 127 (Hellenistic Jewish); *Tg. Neof.* Gen. 1.1; *Tg. Onq.* Gen. 20.3 (Targumic exegesis, cf. מימרא). 'Torah' and 'wisdom' are also used in creation contexts in, e.g. *Gen. Rab.* 1.1 (Rabbinic) and Sir. 24 (cf. Prov. 8), respectively. Fuller lists of the use of 'word' in creation contexts are found in Evans, *Word*, pp. 47–121; Phillips, *Prologue*, pp. 73–138; McHugh, *John*, pp. 91–6; Schnackenburg, *John*, vol. 1, pp. 481–93; Dodd, *Interpretation*, pp. 263–85. Cf. G. Schwarz, 'Gen 1 1 2 2a und John 1 1a.3a – ein Vergleich', *ZNW* 73 (1982), pp. 136–7, who compares Jn 1.1-3 with *Tg. Neof.*

67. Phillips, *Prologue*, p. 149. Similar ideas have been asserted by Moloney, *John*, pp. 42–3, and Carson, *John*, p. 116. Cf. A. Jeannière, '«En arkhê ên o logos». Note sur des problèmes de traduction', *RSR* 83 (1995), pp. 241–7 (244–7); T. Engberg-Pedersen, '*Logos* and *Pneuma* in the Fourth Gospel', in *Greco-Roman Culture and the New Testament* (ed. D. E. Aune and F. E. Brenk; NovTSup, 143; Leiden: Brill, 2012), pp. 27–48 (27–8).

68. Bultmann, *John*, p. 37.

69. Some manuscripts do not have punctuation in Jn 1.3-4 (e.g. Papyrus[66.75*] ℵ A B). Other manuscripts have a full stop after οὐδὲ ἕν, so that a new sentence can begin with ὃ γέγονεν ἐν αὐτῷ (e.g. C D L 050, in a correction to Papyrus[75], in the lectionary 2211, ancient versions such as the Old Latin, Vulgata, Syriac, and Sahidic). This punctuation enjoyed almost universal support in the second and early third centuries, according to K. Aland, 'Eine Untersuchung zu Joh 1:3. 4. Über die Bedeutung eines Punktes', *ZNW* 59 (1968), pp. 174–209. The other reading has a

absence of the article at the beginning of v. 3 indicates that 'everything' (distributive rather than collective) should be understood as 'every single thing',[70] in which case, John is indicating that ὁ λόγος has a claim on every individual thing that has been created.[71] In v. 3, then, John is highlighting the universal significance of ὁ λόγος in creation.[72]

A noticeable difference between Jn 1.3 and the Genesis account of creation is the use of ποιέω in, e.g. Gen. 1.1, 7, 31; 2.2 but the use of δι' αὐτοῦ ἐγένετο in Jn 1.3, 10.[73] Elsewhere in GJohn διά plus a genitive pronoun referring to Jesus is used to signal his role in bringing salvation into the world (e.g. 3.17; 10.9; 14.6). Additionally, πᾶς is used elsewhere in GJohn in relation to Jesus' ministry (e.g. 3.35; 5.20; 13.3; 16.15; 17.7, 10; 19.28). If read in light of the Gospel as a whole, Jn 1.3 might be an indication for the reader that there is a link between creation and salvation, between past reality and present and future reality, and that Jesus is to be regarded as the privileged agent of both creation and salvation.

---

full stop after ὃ γέγονεν, at the end of v. 3, so that a new sentence can begin as the opening of v. 4 (ἐν αὐτῷ). This reading is supported by, e.g. Ψ 33, corrections in א and 050, two families of manuscripts ($f^{1.13}$), the Majority text, and two ancient versions (Syriac, Bohairic). If one takes ὃ γέγονεν along with ἐν αὐτῷ, the next verb in v. 4 should be ἐστιν instead of ἦν (McHugh, *John*, p. 15; cf. א D Italae), but if one takes ὃ γέγονεν along with οὐδὲ ἕν, one would expect ὧν ἐγένετο or οὐδὲν, ὅ τι γέγονεν (Phillips, *Prologue*, pp. 163–4; cf. οὐδέν in Papyrus⁶⁶ א* D). The decision is difficult. Here I read ὃ γέγονεν joined with οὐδὲ ἕν, because (1) John elsewhere begins sentences with ἐν and a pronoun (B. M. Metzger, *A Textual Commentary on the Greek New Testament* [Stuttgart: United Bible Societies, 2nd edn, 1994], p. 168; cf. 13.35; 15.8) and (2) the idea that ὁ λόγος (i.e. Jesus) has life 'in him' (1.4) occurs elsewhere in GJohn (e.g. 5.26; cf. 5.40; 6.53). Many others prefer this punctuation, including Schnackenburg, *John*, vol. 1, p. 240; Haenchen, *John 1*, pp. 112–13; Michaels, *John*, p. 54; von Wahlde, *John*, vol. 2, pp. 3, 28; Carson, *John*, p. 118; Lincoln, *John*, p. 92; Barrett, *John*, p. 157. For a recent reading of ὃ γέγονεν joined with ἐν αὐτῷ, see J. Nolland, 'The Thought in John 1:3c-4', *TynBul* 62 (2011), pp. 295–312.

   70. McHugh, *John*, p. 11.
   71. Barrett, *John*, p. 157.
   72. Schnackenburg, *John*, vol. 1, p. 238.
   73. A. H. Franke, *Das alte Testament bei Johannes. Ein Beitrag zur Erklärung und Beurtheilung der johanneischen Schriften* (Göttingen: Vandenhoeck & Ruprecht, 1885), p. 117, has observed that in Jas 3.9 γίνομαι has replaced the verb ποιέω found in Gen. 1.26. The construction in Jn 1.3 can mean that ὁ λόγος is the (1) mediator or intermediary of creation (Beasley-Murray, *John*, p. 11; Haenchen, *John 1*, pp. 112–13), (2) instrument (von Wahlde, *John*, vol. 2, p. 3), (3) personal agent (Carson, *John*, p. 118), or (4) the creator himself, 'by ὁ λόγος' (Schnackenburg, *John*, vol. 1, p. 236).

There is a clear contrast between Jn 1.3 and 1.1-2. John uses only γίνομαι in 1.3 (three times), while he uses only the verb ἦν in the first two verses (four times).[74] With this, John draws a clear contrast between God and ὁ λόγος who 'existed' in the beginning, on the one hand, and all creation that came into being through ὁ λόγος. John portrays ὁ λόγος as existing at the side of the Creator and apart from the created order.[75] However, that 'everything' was created through ὁ λόγος would indicate that there is a relationship between ὁ λόγος and creation. Creation is not to be regarded as alien territory that ὁ λόγος enters in his incarnation (1.14), but as his possession where the work of revelation and redemption will be carried out.[76]

Without being linked to Gen. 1–2 specifically, Jn 1.10 is a direct reference to the creation of the world.[77] Its central clause repeats almost exactly 1.3a, πάντα δι' αὐτοῦ ἐγένετο / ὁ κόσμος δι' αὐτοῦ ἐγένετο (v. 10). John thus highlights the idea that the world was created through ὁ λόγος.[78] This instance of creation imagery (1.10) also helps to portray ὁ λόγος as existing apart from the created order. However, the separation is even wider due to the world's rejection of the one through whom it was created. They failed to recognize him, and even his own did not receive him (1.11).[79] Thus John uses creation imagery to highlight the irony that

74. McHugh, *John*, p. 12.
75. Lightfoot, *John*, p. 79; Lincoln, *John*, p. 99; Keener, *John*, vol. 1, p. 369.
76. Lincoln, *John*, p. 99; Barrett, *John*, p. 25.
77. McHugh, *John*, pp. 40–1, relates each phrase in 1.10 to Gen. 1–2 in this way: the world was created through ὁ λόγος, therefore, the world is good (Gen. 1); ὁ λόγος was in the world, therefore, ὁ λόγος beckoned humanity to enjoy perfect happiness (Gen. 2); but ὁ λόγος was rejected (Gen. 3). To warrant this reading, McHugh refers to *Tg. Neof.* 3.8, where the 'word' of the Lord is related to the garden of Eden. However, there are few clues in 1.10 itself to posit that John was intending such links.
78. In light of the masculine pronoun αὐτόν, the implicit subject in 1.10 should be ὁ λόγος (Brown, *John*, vol. 1, p. 10; von Wahlde, *John*, vol. 2, pp. 7, 29 n. 25; McHugh, *John*, p. 40). Others think that the implicit subject of the first clause in 1.10 is φῶς (Hoskyns, *Gospel*, vol. 1, p. 141; cf. Michaels, *John*, p. 64).
79. Some interpret τὰ ἴδια and οἱ ἴδιοι in 1.11 in a 'universal' sense: 'his creation' and 'his creatures' (e.g. Bultmann, *John*, p. 56; Borgen, *Logos*, p. 17; von Wahlde, *John*, vol. 2, p. 30). They indicate that both τὰ ἴδια in 1.11 and πάντα in 1.3 are neuter plural and both should refer to creation and that both οἱ ἴδιοι in 1.11 and ἄνθρωποι in 1.4 are masculine plural and should refer to people in a general sense. Additionally, they observe a parallelism between 1.9 and 1.10, 'the *world* was made through him' / 'He came to *his own*' and 'the *world* did not know him' / '*his own* did not receive him'. Others prefer to see in 1.11 a reference to Israel (e.g. Barrett, *John*, p. 163; Brown, *John*, vol. 1, p. 10; Carson, *John*, p. 124; Keener, *John*, vol. 1,

creation has rejected his creator. The rejection by the world seems 'universal' in 1.10, but the possibility of becoming children of God is open to all (ὅσοι) who want to receive him, those who believe in his name (1.12). With this, John links past reality (creation) with present reality (revelation and salvation), since the agent of creation is also the agent of redemption.[80] The universal rejection of ὁ λόγος (1.10) is then contrasted with his 'universal' openness to all who want to recognize and receive him (1.12).[81] Those who believe in the name of the one through whom the world was created can experience a new beginning, since they will be born of God (1.13). The one who was 'in the beginning' bringing into existence the world (1.1-3, 10) is the same one who is able to provide a new beginning for those who receive him (1.12-13).

c. *John 1.4-5*

The cluster ζωή, φῶς, σκοτία, φαίνω evokes the Genesis account of creation. John 1.4-5 makes no direct reference to Gen. 1–2. Rather John seems to draw on and creatively deploy terms and images stemming from that passage in ways different from their original use. In Gen. 1 φῶς came into being (ἐγένετο) and life was a quality of created animals and humans (Gen. 1.20-21, 24, 30). In Jn 1.4 there is a direct link between life and light that it is not readily apparent in Gen. 1. In Jn 1.4 the life was (ἦν) the 'light of men',[82] but in Gen. 1 light and luminaries were created before the creation of the man. Furthermore, in Jn 1.4-5 life is mentioned first, then light is referred to in relation to that life, and, lastly, darkness is mentioned, but in Gen. 1–2 darkness is mentioned first (1.2),

---

p. 398). They appeal to the coming of wisdom in Sir. 24 (cf. Prov. 8.22-31), the use of ἴδιος in 4.44, and the contrast between ὁ κόσμος in Jn 1.11 and τὰ ἴδια / οἱ ἴδιοι in 1.12. Given the use of ambiguity in Jn 1.4-5, it would not be rare to see the same here in 1.11: 'his own' might be a reference to both his own creation and his own people (e.g. Chrysostom, *Hom. Jo.* 9.1; Hoskyns, *Gospel*, vol. 1, p. 146; Phillips, *Prologue*, p. 190; T. L. Brodie, *The Gospel according to John: A Literary and Theological Commentary* [New York: Oxford University Press, 1993], p. 140; Michaels, *John*, p. 67).

80. In light of the 'historical' comment in Jn 1.6-8 and of the reference to 'children of God' in 1.12, I take 1.9-11 as anticipated references to the work of Jesus, ὁ λόγος made flesh. These verses anticipate the incarnation, which is fully asserted in 1.14. Others who share this opinion include Schnackenburg, *John*, vol. 1, p. 258, and Lincoln, *John*, p. 101 (cf. Brown, *John*, vol. 1, p. 10; Michaels, *John*, p. 64). For a different opinion (i.e. 1.9-11 refers to a period previous to the incarnation), see Haenchen, *John 1*, p. 117.

81. Hoskyns, *Gospel*, vol. 1, p. 141.

82. Michaels, *John*, pp. 55 n. 4, 63.

then light (1.3), and, lastly, life (1.20). In Genesis God separated light from darkness (1.4-5, 14-18; cf. Ps. 103.20 [104.20 MT]), but in Jn 1.5 darkness attempted to grasp or to overcome light.[83]

These differences between Jn 1.4-5 and Gen. 1–2 already indicate that John is referring to something beyond creation. This is confirmed by the fact that in 1.4-5 the reader encounters what will become a Johannine feature: ambiguity. The words 'life', 'light', 'to shine', 'darkness', and 'to overcome' are all open to several interpretations. Scholars debate whether 'life was in him' refers to life in Gen. 1.30; 2.7, 9 (cf. Gen. 1.20-21, 24; 2.19), the life that every human being has had from the beginning of time up until the present, or a special life that is found in the Word (i.e. eternal life).[84] Scholars also debate whether 'and the life was the light of men' means that through ὁ λόγος all humanity has received spiritual or intellectual perception. Some even propose that this clause is an anticipated reference to Jesus as the light who brings revelation and judgement.[85] The noun 'darkness' has been interpreted as referring to the darkness in creation (Gen. 1.2), the fall of Adam and Eve (Gen. 3), or unbelief and those who will reject Jesus.[86] Given that all the verbs in Jn 1.1-4 are in the imperfect (ἦν), aorist (ἐγένετο), or perfect (γέγονεν) tenses, scholars wonder whether φαίνει in the present tense (1.5) refers to a continual activity of ὁ λόγος since creation (a gnomic present) or only to a current manifestation of the light (i.e. incarnation).[87] Commentators also discuss whether κατέλαβεν in the aorist tense in 1.5 refers to a specific opposition of the darkness to the light or to a complexive opposition (i.e. a series of attempts).[88]

83. Painter, 'Rereading', p. 186.

84. Brown, *John*, vol. 1, pp. 7, 27; Michaels, *John*, p. 54; von Wahlde, *John*, vol. 2, p. 4.

85. Michaels, *John*, p. 55; McHugh, *John*, p. 16; Hoskyns, *Gospel*, vol. 1, p. 138; Brown, *John*, vol. 1, p. 7.

86. Brown, *John*, vol. 1, pp. 8, 26–7; Schnackenburg, *John*, vol. 1, p. 245; Lincoln, *John*, p. 99.

87. Beasley-Murray, *John*, p. 11; Barrett, *John*, p. 158; Schnackenburg, *John*, vol. 1, pp. 245, 247; von Wahlde, *John*, vol. 2, p. 5; Michaels, *John*, p. 56; Haenchen, *John 1*, pp. 114–15.

88. Additionally, there is discussion whether κατέλαβεν here means 'to understand' or 'to overcome'. Bultmann, *John*, pp. 46–8, related 1.5 to 1.10-11 (οὐκ ἔγνω, οὐ παρέλαβον) and concluded that κατέλαβεν should have an intellectual meaning (cf. Schnackenburg, *John*, vol. 1, pp. 246–7; Beasley-Murray, *John*, p. 11). Others relate Jn 1.5 to 12.35 (where καταλαμβάνω has an aggressive sense) and suggest the translation 'to overcome' (cf. Moloney, *John*, pp. 36–7, 43; Hoskyns, *Gospel*, vol. 1, p. 138).

With respect to these debates, Jn 1.4-5 itself offers little basis for choosing one particular interpretation over others. I suggest that John has intentionally selected these images of life, light, and darkness and the tenses of the verbs in order to link creation to the story that follows in the rest of the Gospel, in which Jesus will act as the privileged agent of revelation, judgement, and salvation.[89] The coming of ὁ λόγος in the flesh is an idea that the reader will encounter clearly in 1.14.[90] However, John will later comprehensibly apply to Jesus in the story that follows (e.g. 5.26; 8.12; 9.5; 11.25) terms and images stemming from Gen. 1–2. Therefore, John's use of these terms and images might be an indication of his attempt to relate the work of creation to the work of salvation, and the original darkness to the opposition that Jesus will suffer in his earthly ministry.[91] Since life and light are related to ὁ λόγος from the beginning, he is authorized to partake in other divine activities, as will be seen in Jesus' works elsewhere in GJohn.

If John distinguished between God and creation and put ὁ λόγος at the side of God in 1.1-3, here in 1.4-5 he begins to hint at the relationship between ὁ λόγος and his creation. In these two verses 'λόγος now approaches humanity, first by giving life and then by that life being the light of humanity'.[92] On the other hand, darkness remains alienated from the source of life and light (cf. 1.10-11).[93] The gifts of life and light that are found in ὁ λόγος are not restricted to a particular group, but are here portrayed as being available to humankind (τῶν ἀνθρώπων) as a whole (Jn 1.4). Therefore, humankind who remains in darkness can find life and light only by returning to their origin, i.e. ὁ λόγος, who is later revealed to be Jesus Christ (1.17).[94] Additionally, light and life are almost universal religious symbols, well represented in Jewish, early Christian, pagan, and Gnostic literature.[95] These observations lead to the conclusion that by using creation imagery John signals the universal significance of ὁ λόγος in creation.

89. The ambiguity of some or all of these words 'life', 'light', 'darkness', 'to shine', and 'to overcome' has been noted; see e.g. Hoskyns, *Gospel*, vol. 1, p. 139; Lightfoot, *John*, p. 89; Dodd, *Interpretation*, p. 284; Barrett, *John*, p. 158; Phillips, *Prologue*, p. 174; Carson, *John*, p. 119; Keener, *John*, vol. 1, p. 387.
90. Hengel, 'Prologue', pp. 268–71; Dodd, *Interpretation*, pp. 268–72.
91. Cf. O. Cullmann, 'The Theological Content of the Prologue of John in Its Present Form', in *The Conversation Continues: Studies in Paul & John in Honor of J. Louis Martyn* (ed. R. T. Fortna and B. R. Gaventa; Nashville: Abingdon, 1990), pp. 295–8 (296–7).
92. Phillips, *Prologue*, p. 169.
93. Lincoln, *John*, p. 99.
94. Bultmann, *John*, p. 47.
95. Moloney, *John*, p. 43; Carson, *John*, p. 118; Keener, *John*, vol. 1, pp. 382–7.

d. *The Rest of the Prologue*
I have noted that creation imagery in the prologue (1.1-5, 10) is used in a threefold way. First, John portrays ὁ λόγος in close association with God, existing apart from and prior to the created order in a relationship that legitimizes his participation in divine activities. Second, John uses creation imagery to assert the universal significance of ὁ λόγος. Third, John uses creation imagery to link past reality with present reality. John portrays ὁ λόγος as the agent of creation and also hints at his significance in the works of revelation, judgement, and salvation.[96] Other verses in the prologue support these ideas.

The close association between ὁ λόγος and God (1.1-2) is distinctive because none of the other characters in the prologue has the same relationship with God. To be sure, John (1.6) and those who have received the Word (1.12-13) have a special relationship with God. However, unlike ὁ λόγος, who exists in close association with God, John is sent from (ἀπεσταλμένος παρά) God,[97] and in distinction from ὁ λόγος, who existed (ἦν) in the beginning, those who receive the Word become (γενέσθαι, 1.12) children of God because they are born of God (ἐγεννήθησαν, 1.13).[98] The unique association between ὁ λόγος and God is emphasised in 1.14, in the declaration that the Word who became flesh is μονογενής, 'only, unique'.[99] Since this adjective occurs in 1.14 in relation to πατήρ and δόξα, the uniqueness of the Word who became flesh should be related to these two nouns. The unique association of ὁ λόγος and ὁ θεός begins here to take shape as a relationship between the Father and

96. This link between creation and redemption is found in other OT texts: e.g. Isa. 45.18-19, 22.

97. Unlike ὁ λόγος, who 'existed' (ἦν) in the beginning, has a close association with God, is identified as 'God', and has become flesh (σάρξ, 1.14), John is a man (ἄνθρωπος) who appeared (ἐγένετο) with a mission from God.

98. The metaphor can be translated 'born' or 'begotten', but the selection of one of these two options do not alter the basic meaning that God is the source of the believers' new life. Cf. M. J. J. Menken, '"Born of God" or "Begotten by God"? A Translation Problem in the Johannine Writings', *NovT* 51 (2009), pp. 352–68 (367).

99. MM, pp. 416–17. The translation 'only begotten' (e.g. Lightfoot, *John*, p. 86; J. V. Dahms, 'The Johannine Use of Monogenēs Reconsidered', *NTS* 29 [1983], pp. 222–32) has been abandoned by most modern commentators, who now prefer 'only, unique' or 'only son/Son' (e.g. Brown, *John*, vol. 1, p. 13; Michaels, *John*, p. 80; Lincoln, *John*, p. 105; Phillips, *Prologue*, p. 205; Keener, *John*, vol. 1, p. 416; cf. D. Moody, 'God's Only Son: The Translation of John 3:16 in the Revised Standard Version', *JBL* 72 [1953], pp. 213–19; P. Winter, 'ΜΟΝΟΓΕΝΗΣ ΠΑΡΑ ΠΑΤΡΟΣ', *ZRGG* 5 [1953], pp. 335–63; G. Pendrick, 'ΜΟΝΟΓΕΝΗΣ', *NTS* 41 [1995], pp. 587–600).

the Son.[100] This paternal imagery will become clearer in the rest of the Gospel, where John portrays God as the Father of Jesus.[101] The use of the term μονογενής in relation to πατήρ and following Jn 1.13 indicates that the Word who became flesh possesses a unique relationship with the Father that is distinguishable from that of those who believe in ὁ λόγος.[102] This relationship is also distinctive in that the Son has a unique glory.[103] Again, this association between Jesus and his glory will become clearer as the Gospel unfolds (e.g. 7.18; 8.54; 17.5).

The uniqueness of Jesus in relation to the Father is explicitly indicated in 1.18.[104] I suggested above that John was not intending a simple identification between ὁ λόγος and 'God' in 1.1 because the phrase θεὸς ἦν ὁ λόγος is bracketed by ἦν πρὸς τὸν θεόν (1.1-2). Something similar can be perceived in 1.14, 18. The Word who became flesh is unique in his relationship with the Father (παρὰ πατρός), but he is also μονογενὴς θεός. Since this phrase can lead the reader to think that John has collapsed God into Jesus Christ, the following phrase clarifies that this μονογενὴς θεός exists in the bosom of the Father (1.18).[105] The two statements should be read as complementary.

---

100.   Bultmann, *John*, p. 71. The absence of the noun υἱός and of the articles in μονογενής and πατήρ has led some commentators to see in 1.14 a 'general' description of a 'son' in relation to a 'father' (McHugh, *John*, pp. 47, 58; Lincoln, *John*, p. 105) instead of a 'Father–Son' relationship. However, in light of GJohn as a whole (cf. 3.16), one should see here early indications of the 'Father–Son' relationship.

101.   John uses πατήρ more than one hundred times. The 'Father–Son' imagery in reference to the relationship between God and Jesus is prominent in GJohn.

102.   Michaels, *John*, p. 80; Lincoln, *John*, p. 105.

103.   Schnackenburg, *John*, vol. 1, p. 270; Lincoln, *John*, p. 105.

104.   The phrase μονογενὴς θεός (or ὁ μονογενὴς θεός) has better manuscript support (e.g. Papyrus[66] Papyrus[75] ℵ B C 33) and is a more difficult reading than ο μονογενης υιος (e.g. A Θ), because the latter idea is repeated elsewhere in GJohn (3.16, 18). However, Bultmann, *John*, p. 82 n. 2 (cf. Moloney, *John*, p. 46), considered that θεός here is so difficult that it 'is most likely the result of an error in dictation'. Notwithstanding this observation, μονογενὴς θεός is not impossible within Johannine thought (1.1; 20.28). Cf. Beasley-Murray, *John*, pp. 2–3; Michaels, *John*, p. 92 n. 78; Lincoln, *John*, p. 108; Phillips, *Prologue*, pp. 216–17. Among those who prefer μονογενης υιος are von Wahlde, *John*, vol. 2, p. 12; Haenchen, *John 1*, p. 121; Schnackenburg, *John*, vol. 1, p. 280. Recently, B. J. Burkholder, 'Considering the Possibility of a Theological Corruption in Joh 1,18 in Light of Its Early Reception', *ZNW* 103 (2012), pp. 64–83 (83), has argued (*c.* B. Ehrman, *The Orthodox Corruption of Scripture* [New York: Oxford University Press, 1993], pp. 78–82) that 'extant evidence from early Alexandria does not provide any conclusive evidence that the variant in Joh 1,18 [μονογενὴς θεός] would have arisen from theological motives'.

105.   Barrett, *John*, p. 169.

The unique status of ὁ λόγος in relation to God prior to creation highlights his privilege over other important figures mentioned in the prologue. There are distinctions between John (1.6, 15) and ὁ λόγος.[106] John himself recognizes that ὁ λόγος made flesh existed before him (πρῶτός μου ἦν, v. 15; cf. 1.30; 3.28).[107] A second distinction between ὁ λόγος and John is that the former exists in the bosom of the Father (1.18).[108] The Word was active before coming to the world, since he partook in the divine activity of creation (v. 3), while John begins his activity on earth by testifying about ὁ λόγος (v. 7). A third distinction is that ὁ λόγος is identified as θεός (1.1; cf. 1.18) and as having become flesh (σάρξ, v. 14), but John is identified as ἄνθρωπος (v. 6). A fourth difference between ὁ λόγος and John is that the former is portrayed as the 'light of men' (1.4) and as the 'true light' (1.9), while the latter is portrayed positively as testifying about the light (1.7; cf. v. 15) and negatively as not being the light (1.8).[109] A fifth difference is that although both ὁ λόγος and John have a name (ὄνομα, vv. 6, 12), people can become children of God only by believing in the name of ὁ λόγος (v. 12), while John was sent so that people may believe through him (v. 7).

The other human character that can be seen in relation to ὁ λόγος made flesh is Moses (Jn 1.17). It is suggestive that the prologue begins with creation (1.3) and finishes with a reference to Moses and the law given through him (1.17). By beginning with the existence of ὁ λόγος before creation, John is probably implying the primal significance of Jesus over Moses. Through ὁ λόγος people can receive the right to become God's children (1.12) and grace (1.16; cf. 1.14). There is a striking parallel between 'everything came into being through the Word (δι᾽ αὐτοῦ ἐγένετο)' in 1.3 and 'grace and truth came through Jesus Christ (διὰ ᾽Ιησοῦ Χριστοῦ ἐγένετο)' in 1.17. On the other hand, Moses is not portrayed as bringing something into existence, since it is said that the law was given (ἐδόθη, passive voice) through him (διὰ Μωϋσέως) (v. 17).

The universal significance of ὁ λόγος is highlighted elsewhere in the prologue. In 1.9 John states that the true Light gives light to every man (πάντα ἄνθρωπον), thus indicating that the light of ὁ λόγος is not restricted

---

106. Hoskyns, *Gospel*, vol. 1, p. 141.

107. Carson, *John*, p. 114, has noted that John repeatedly uses εἰμί and γίνομαι side by side to establish a contrast, and gives as an example 8.58, where Jesus is portrayed as saying that 'before Abraham came into existence (γενέσθαι), I am (εἰμί)'.

108. Elsewhere John characterizes Jesus as being 'sent' by God (e.g. 3.17; 5.36; 17.3).

109. Barrett, *John*, p. 160; Borgen, *Logos*, p. 102.

to a particular group in history, but rather gives light to every human being.[110] Elsewhere in the Gospel, the light that Jesus brings can mean revelation for those who receive it or judgement for those who reject it (3.19-21; cf. 1.11-12; 9.35-41).[111] Scholars debate whether Jn 1.9 refers to the light that Jesus brings with his incarnation (1.14) or to a time prior to the incarnation. The use of the verb ἦν in 1.4, 9 might refer the reader back to 1.1-2 (cf. 1.4), where this verb is used to talk about a time previous to the incarnation. The present tense of the verb φωτίζει (cf. also φαίνει in 1.5), however, might indicate that John is referring to the reality that he and his readers are experiencing. The phrase ἐρχόμενον εἰς τὸν κόσμον in 1.9 might be a reference to the incarnation, the coming of the Word to the world (1.14), or to a time previous to the incarnation. Whichever option one takes, it is clear that the light associated with ὁ λόγος has a universal significance, since the true Light gives light to every human being for revelation, leading to either salvation or judgement.[112]

John also uses creation imagery to assert the primal significance of Jesus and the message about him and to link past reality with present reality. Since ὁ λόγος was involved in the first divine activity, creation of 'everything' (1.3), Jesus' mission now concerns all humanity, 'since all

110.   Bultmann, *John*, p. 53; Hoskyns, *Gospel*, vol. 1, p. 141; Lightfoot, *John*, p. 89; Schnackenburg, *John*, vol. 1, p. 253; Lincoln, *John*, p. 101; McHugh, *John*, p. 32 (but cf. Keener, *John*, vol. 1, p. 394). If we take ἐρχόμενον εἰς τὸν κόσμον as modifying ἄνθρωπον, the universal significance of the true Light is even more emphatic because the translation would be, 'every human being who comes into the world'. This option is preferred by Hoskyns, *Gospel*, vol. 1, p. 141; Lightfoot, *John*, p. 89; Bultmann, *John*, p. 52 n. 1; Michaels, *John*, p. 61. The other popular option (a periphrastic construction ἦν...ἐρχόμενον, 'was coming') is preferred by Brown, *John*, vol. 1, p. 10; Moloney, *John*, p. 43; Beasley-Murray, *John*, p. 12; Lincoln, *John*, p. 101; von Wahlde, *John*, vol. 2, p. 6; Keener, *John*, vol. 1, p. 395. The decision is not an easy one. Although a relative clause appears between ἦν and ἐρχό-μενον (this never happens elsewhere in GJohn), although the phrase 'all who come into the world' is found in rabbinic literature (*Lev. Rab.* 31.6), and although the verb ἦν appears alone (not in periphrasis) in Jn 1.1-2, 4, I am inclined to understand ἐρχόμενον in relation to ἦν. There are three main reasons for taking this view. First, the coming of Jesus as the light of the world is a prominent feature in Johannine thought (e.g. 3.19; 12.46). Second, periphrastic constructions are used elsewhere in GJohn (e.g. 1.28; 3.23; 10.40). Third, the Word who is the true Light appears also in relation to the world in the next verse (1.10).

111.   Beasley-Murray, *John*, p. 12; Barrett, *John*, p. 161.

112.   The adjective 'all' (πᾶς) is also used in Jn 1.7, 16 in reference to the testimony of John and in reference to the 'fullness' believers have received.

men are the creation of God by the Word'.[113] Since everything owes its existence to him, he can be the privileged agent of revelation, leading to either salvation or judgement.[114] The involvement of ὁ λόγος in the divine activity of creation authorizes his participation in other divine activities described in the prologue: (1) granting the authority to become God's children (1.12),[115] (2) manifesting God's glory (1.14), (3) manifesting grace and truth (1.17), and (4) revealing God (1.18). These divine activities can only be performed by someone who is identified with life (salvation) and light (revelation).[116] The precise sense in which Jesus performs those divine activities is to be disclosed gradually, as the story that follows unfolds.[117]

III. Conclusion

Although it is not possible to assert that the Genesis account of creation influenced the whole composition of the Johannine prologue, I have found evidence that allows us to conclude that John drew on and creatively deployed terms and images stemming from Gen. 1–2 (Jn 1.1-5) or other creation-discourse (ὁ λόγος, 1.1, 14). John uses all these instances, along with the direct assertion of the creation of the world in 1.10, in a three-fold way. First, John intended to portray the Word/Jesus in close association with God existing apart from and prior to the created order in a relationship that legitimizes his participation in divine activities. Second, John asserts the primal and universal significance of the Word/Jesus and privileges him over John and Moses. Third, John uses creation imagery to link past reality with present and future reality, portraying the Word/Jesus as the agent of creation who is to be regarded as the privileged agent of revelation and redemption as well.

---

113.   Hoskyns, *Gospel*, vol. 1, p. 137.
114.   Schnackenburg, *John*, vol. 1, p. 238.
115.   Dodd, *Interpretation*, p. 282; Weidemann, 'Protology', p. 306.
116.   Schnackenburg, *John*, vol. 1, p. 244; Beasley-Murray, *John*, p. 11; Barrett, *John*, pp. 157–8; Carson, *John*, p. 120.
117.   McHugh, *John*, p. 16.

Chapter 2

CREATION IMAGERY IN THE PRAYER OF JESUS

In the previous chapter I concluded that John uses creation imagery in the prologue to shape his portrayal of the Word/Jesus. In this chapter I will argue that although instances of creation imagery in Jn 17.5 and 17.24 are used in a different context (a prayer of Jesus), they function in ways similar to the ones in the prologue. After assessing the problems associated with the background, text, and syntax of the references to creation in Jn 17.5 and 17.24, I will explain how John employs this imagery in the broader context of Jesus' prayer.

I. Assessment

The two instances of creation imagery in the prayer of Jesus are straightforward: 'before the world was' (v. 5) and 'before the foundation of the world' (v. 24). A few scholars have tried to tie those phrases to specific passages in the OT. Wisdom's speech in Prov. 8.23-25 (along with Wis. 7.25) has been seen as either the source of allusion or at least the background to the creation statements in Jn 17.[1] In Prov. 8 'wisdom' says that she was founded (θεμελιόω) before the present age, and that she was begotten (γεννάω) before God made the earth, depths, springs of water, mountains, and hills (vv. 23, 25). Unlike Jn 17.5 and 17.24, where Jesus partakes of God's glory and is the recipient of God's love, Prov. 8 does not refer to a shared glory between God and 'wisdom', nor does it explicitly indicate God's love for 'wisdom'. In Wis. 7.25 there is the mention of both 'glory' and 'wisdom'. However, Wis. 7.25 indicates that 'wisdom' was an emanation (ἀπόρροια) of the pure glory of the Almighty. This language of an 'emanation of the glory' is not used in Jn 17.5 or 17.24; the glory described in those verses is one shared between the Father and Jesus.[2]

1. Brown, *John*, vol. 2, p. 754; Lindars, *John*, p. 521.
2. Keener, *John*, vol. 2, p. 1063 n. 118.

The construction πρὸ τοῦ is used before a phrase five times in Prov. 8.23-24 in order to indicate that 'wisdom' existed before the created things.[3] But unlike Jn 17.24, where it is said that God loved Jesus, Prov. 8.23-24 lacks explicit indications that God loved 'wisdom' (cf. 8.17, 21). The only clear similarity between Jn 17.5, 24 and these wisdom passages is the construction πρὸ τοῦ before a phrase, but this is hardly enough evidence to posit that John intended a link to Prov. 8.23-25. The differences between the portrayal of Jesus' relationship with his Father in Jn 17 and the relationship of 'wisdom' with God in Prov. 8 and Wis. 7 are stronger than the similarities. Additionally, the construction πρὸ τοῦ is used before a phrase elsewhere in the LXX in reference to the existence of God himself (Ps. 89.2 [90.2 MT]).

The noun καταβολή is not found in the LXX in creation contexts.[4] In Second-Temple Jewish and Christian texts καταβολή is used several times. The construction καταβολῆς κόσμου occurs after a preposition elsewhere in the NT to refer to the creation of the world (Eph. 1.4; 1 Pet. 1.20; Mt. 13.35; 25.34; Lk. 11.50; Heb. 4.3; 9.26; Rev. 13.8; 17.8).[5] In some cases this phrase is used to assert that a divine action is as old as the creation of the world (Mt. 13.35; 25.34; Heb. 4.3; Rev. 17.8). In 1 Pet. 1.20 the phrase is used to indicate that Jesus was foreknown or chosen before the foundation of the world. In Eph. 1.4 it is said that God chose the saints before creation. The preposition attached to καταβολῆς κόσμου signals whether the divine action in question is as old as creation or even older than creation.

3. πρὸ τοῦ αἰῶνος ἐθεμελίωσέν (v. 23); πρὸ τοῦ τὴν γῆν ποιῆσαι, πρὸ τοῦ τὰς ἀβύσσους ποιῆσαι, πρὸ τοῦ προελθεῖν τὰς πηγὰς (v. 24); πρὸ τοῦ ὄρη ἑδρασθῆναι (v. 25). Additionally, the construction προ plus πάντων βουνῶν occurs in v. 25.

4. Schnackenburg, *John*, vol. 3, p. 439 n. 89. Schnackenburg claims that the phrase has its background in the divine predestination language of the rabbis. However, it is always difficult to date rabbinic traditions as early as the first century C.E. Cf. C. H. Williams, 'John and the Rabbis Revisited', in *Engaging with C. H. Dodd on the Gospel of John: Sixty Years of Tradition and Interpretation* (ed. T. Thatcher and C. H. Williams; Cambridge: Cambridge University Press, 2013), pp. 107–25 (114–16, 122–3).

5. This phrase does not occur in the LXX. The phrase πρὸ τοῦ αἰῶνος (Prov. 8.23; cf. Sir. 24.9; 42.21; Tob. 6.18) is perhaps the closest equivalent in the LXX to the use of a preposition before καταβολῆς κόσμου. The phrase ἀπὸ καταβολῆς κόσμου occurs in Mt. 13.35 in the context of an OT quotation from Ps. 78.2, where we find the phrase מני־קדם, 'from of old', in the MT and the phrase ἀπ' ἀρχῆς (77.2) in the LXX (cf. Neh. 12.46; Isa. 23.7; 45.21; Mic. 5.1; Hab. 1.12).

The noun καταβολή is used several times in Philo and Josephus and it also occurs in *Ep. Arist.* 89, 129; and *T. Mos.* 1.14.[6] However, it refers to creation only in *Ep. Arist.* 129, where it is said that 'one creation exists' (μιᾶς καταβολῆς οὔσης), and in *T. Mos.* 1.14, in a context where pre-existence is ascribed to Moses.[7] In this text Moses himself says that God designed, devised, and prepared him before the foundation of the world in order to be the mediator of God's covenant. In this case the noun καταβολή is used to indicate that a divine action is even older than creation.[8]

In light of the evidence considered above, we can conclude that while John does use creation imagery in 17.5 and 17.24, he is not attempting to link it to a specific precursor text. Before explaining the use and significance of those instances in the larger context of Jesus' prayer, it is now necessary to address the textual and syntactical problems of the statement in 17.5.

The phrase πρὸ τοῦ τὸν κόσμον εἶναι παρὰ σοί has three textual variants.[9] The original reading of Papyrus⁶⁶ and two Old Latin manuscripts (a f) is παρὰ σοί πρὸ τοῦ κτλ. A correction made to Papyrus⁶⁶ that cannot be established with absolute certainty has παρὰ σοί twice, before πρὸ τοῦ κτλ. and after εἶναι. The original reading of Codex Bezae is παρα σοι προ του γενεσθαι τον κοσμον. (This reading is also found, with minor

---

6. The phrases 'before time' and 'before the foundation of the world' are also used in *Odes* 41.14-15, where they are applied to the 'Word' and the 'Messiah'. Christian influences are evident there. The noun καταβολή is used without referring to creation in 2 Macc. 2.29; Josephus, *Ant.* 12.64; 18.163-164, 274; *War* 2.260, 409, 417; Philo, *Op. Mund.* 132; *Sobr.* 45; *Rer. Div. Her.* 115; *Vit. Mos.* 1.279; *Spec. Leg.* 3.36; *Leg. Gai.* 54, 125. This noun is also found in several papyri in the sense of 'payment', according to MM, p. 324.

7. A. M. Denis, *Fragmenta pseudepigraphorum quae supersunt Graeca* (PVTG, 3; Leiden: Brill, 1970), p. 63. The phrase *ab initio orbis terrarum* occurs in the Latin manuscript of *T. Mos.* 1.14, 17. See J. Tromp, *The Assumption of Moses: A Critical Edition with Commentary* (SVTP, 10; Leiden: Brill, 1993), p. 8; Ashton, *Understanding*, p. 455.

8. T. F. Glasson, *Moses in the Fourth Gospel* (SBT; London: SCM, 1963), p. 77, judged that there was no real significance behind the similarity between *T. Mos.* 1.14 and Jn 17.24 because this was only a 'coincidence'.

9. The construction πρὸ τοῦ is used before a present tense verb only here in Jn 17.5, according to BDF, §403. John uses πρὸ τοῦ before an aorist verb elsewhere (1.48; 13.19). See also the list of phrases found in G. Lindeskog, *Studien zum neutestamentlichen Schöpfungsgedanken* (UUÅ, 11; Uppsala: Lundequist, 1952), pp. 204–7, e.g. ἀπὸ κτίσεως κόσμου (Rom. 1.20); ἀπ' ἀρχῆς κτίσεως (2 Pet. 3.4); πρὸ τῶν αἰώνων (1 Cor. 2.7).

variations, in a correction to D² and in Irenaeus and Epiphanius.[10]) If πρὸ τοῦ τὸν κόσμον εἶναι παρὰ σοί was original, the reading found in Papyrus⁶⁶ can be explained as an attempt to disambiguate the text. By placing παρὰ σοί before πρὸ τοῦ κτλ., the reading 'the world [instead of Jesus] was with yourself' is avoided. The reading found in Codex Bezae (D) can be explained as influenced either by the creation statement in Jn 1.10 (ὁ κόσμος δι' αὐτοῦ ἐγένετο) or by Jn 8.58 (γενέσθαι).[11] Since παρά plus a dative noun occurs before a verb elsewhere in GJohn (1.39; 14.17, 23, 25), the reading εἶναι παρὰ σοί is more difficult. For these reasons, here I will deem πρὸ τοῦ τὸν κόσμον εἶναι παρὰ σοί as the original reading.

This reading, however, has a syntactical problem. The prepositional phrase παρὰ σοί can be seen as adverbial along with πρὸ τοῦ τὸν κόσμον εἶναι, both phrases modifying εἶχον. The idea would be that Jesus had glory with the Father or in the presence of the Father before the creation of the world. The use of παρὰ σοί would be similar to the use of παρὰ σεαυτῷ in the same verse.[12] On the other hand, παρὰ σοί can be regarded as modifying its nearest word, the infinitive εἶναι. The translation would be: 'before the world was in existence beside you'.[13] J. M. Ballard claimed that this translation 'adds to the doctrine of Creation' because it would imply that God allowed a κόσμος to exist alongside of him, thus emphasizing 'the oneness of this creation, "before" which there was no other, but God alone'.[14] Ballard's translation would also imply that in the beginning the world was with God, but that at some point the world separated from him.[15]

John uses παρά plus a dative noun after an aorist infinitive in 4.40, and so it is not impossible that he intended the phrase παρὰ σοί to be understood as modifying εἶναι in 17.5. However, there is no other place

---

10. Other variants found mainly in the church fathers can be seen in M.-É. Boismard, 'Critique textuelle et citations patristiques', *RB* 57 (1950), pp. 388–408 (394). Bultmann, *John*, p. 495, conjectured that John added πρὸ τοῦ τὸν κόσμον εἶναι to his source.

11. Brown, *John*, vol. 2, p. 743. See also 12.28 (D).

12. Dodd, *Interpretation*, p. 260; Lindars, *John*, p. 520; Michaels, *John*, p. 861.

13. J. M. Ballard, 'The Translation of John xvii. 5', *ExpTim* 47 (1935–1936), p. 284.

14. Ballard, 'Translation', p. 284.

15. Ballard also contended that his translation avoids redundancy, because παρὰ σοί in direct relation to εἶχον adds nothing to the idea already conveyed by the use of δόξασον before παρὰ σεαυτῷ. If John intended to link παρὰ σοί to εἶχον, he would have put the prepositional phrase next to the verb, not separated by πρὸ τοῦ τὸν κόσμον εἶναι ('Translation', 284). However, repetition is thoroughly in accordance with Johannine style (e.g. Jn 1.1-18).

in GJohn where it is said that the world existed in the presence of or near the Father. Furthermore, it is said in Jn 1.1 (although a different preposition is used) that the Word (not the world) was with God. Therefore, it is better to understand παρὰ σοί as referring to Jesus in the presence of his Father.

In sum, no specific link between Jn 17.5, 24 and a particular precursor text can be detected; the original reading of the creation statement in Jn 17.5 is πρὸ τοῦ τὸν κόσμον εἶναι παρὰ σοί; and the phrase παρὰ σοί should be taken as modifying εἶχον: Jesus (not the world) existed in the presence of the Father.

II. The Significance of John 17.5, 24

Creation imagery is strategically placed within Jn 17, as it occurs at the beginning (v. 5) and at the end (v. 24) of Jesus' prayer.[16] John 17.5 occurs in the context of Jesus' twofold petition to his Father to glorify him: 'Father...glorify your Son' (v. 1) and 'Father, you glorify me' (v. 5). Jesus will be glorified so that he can glorify the Father (v. 1), and he will also be glorified with the glory he already had (v. 5). In the same way, Jn 17.24 occurs in the context of Jesus asking his Father to allow his followers to be with him so that they can see his glory. The Father gave glory to Jesus because he loved him before the foundation of the world (v. 24).

John 17.5 and 17.24 highlight Jesus' existence with the Father in a glorified status, apart from and prior to the created order.[17] According to v. 5, Jesus possessed glory before the world was created. Similarly, v. 24 emphasizes the existence of Jesus before the existence of the world. Jesus was loved by the Father and shared his glory 'before the foundation of the world'.[18] The glory Jesus had before creation (v. 5) was given

---

16. There are several links between the opening section and the closing section of the prayer: both begin with πάτερ (vv. 1, 24), both highlight the theme of 'knowledge' (vv. 3, 25), both refer to creation (vv. 5, 24; see Carson, *John*, p. 569), both are related to Jesus' glory (vv. 1, 4-5, 24; see Moloney, *John*, pp. 460, 472; Lightfoot, *John*, pp. 300–301), the phrase ὃ δέδωκας occurs in both sections (vv. 2, 24; Beasley-Murray, *John*, p. 304), and the divine name figures prominently in vv. 6, 26 (Lincoln, *John*, p. 440).

17. This could imply that Jesus' coming to the world entailed a forfeiture of his glory. Cf. E. Haenchen, *John 2* (trans. R. W. Funk; Hermeneia; Philadelphia: Fortress, 1984), p. 152; Carson, *John*, p. 557. For a different opinion, see Käsemann, *Testament*.

18. Both verses share the same structure: relative pronoun (ἣ / ἣν) plus past tense verb (imperfect εἶχον; perfect δέδωκας).

by his Father (v. 24). If any ambiguity remains concerning Jesus' existence with God before creation in Jn 1.1-2, it vanishes in Jn 17.5. In light of these verses, one should not make a distinction between the pre-existence of the Word and the pre-existence of Jesus,[19] for here it is the human Jesus who refers to his own glory that he shared with God before the creation of the world.[20]

Since Jesus exists apart from and prior to creation, there is a sharp distinction between Jesus and the created order. The noun κόσμος in Jn 17.5 and 17.24 refers to the created world, but this same noun refers in 17.14 and 17.16 (cf. v. 25) to those who oppose Jesus and his followers.[21] There is not only a distinction between Jesus and those who oppose him, but also between Jesus and the world as creation. He is over all humanity (πάσης σαρκός, v. 2) because he existed before them. Similarly, Jesus' glory existed prior to creation, since it has its origins in the Father's love for his Son prior to the foundation of the world.[22]

Since Jesus exists apart from creation, he is at the side of God the Father. The prepositional phrase παρὰ σοί in v. 5 highlights this idea. Similarly, the phrase 'you loved me before the foundation of the world' in v. 24 helps to signal the close association between Jesus and his Father. The surrounding context (especially vv. 11, 21-22) repeats this theme of Jesus' close association or oneness with his Father. In vv. 11, 21-22 Jesus refers three times to the unity of believers in light of the unity he has with his Father. The structure of the sentences in those verses is strikingly similar, but there is a significant difference. The lack of explicit verbs in phrases referring to the unity of Jesus and the Father is in contrast to the explicit use of ὦσιν to refer to the unity Jesus asks for the believers.

v. 11	ἵνα ὦσιν ἓν	καθὼς ἡμεῖς
v. 21	ἵνα πάντες ἓν ὦσιν,	καθὼς σύ, πάτερ, ἐν ἐμοὶ κἀγὼ ἐν σοί
v. 22	ἵνα ὦσιν ἓν	καθὼς ἡμεῖς ἓν

Since there are no explicit verbs in the phrases that convey the unity between Jesus and the Father, it is not clear whether Jesus refers to the

19. J. D. G. Dunn, *Christology in the Making: A New Testament Inquiry into the Origins of the Doctrine of the Incarnation* (London: SCM, 1980), pp. 239–45.

20. See M. J. J. Menken, 'Observations on the Significance of the Old Testament in the Fourth Gospel', in Van Belle, van der Watt, and Maritz (eds.), *Theology and Christology*, pp. 155–75 (169).

21. P. S. Minear, 'John 17:1-11', *Int* 32 (1978), pp. 175–9 (178), has rightly observed that John uses κόσμος 'more often than any other New Testament book, and more often in this chapter than in any other'.

22. Bultmann, *John*, p. 496 n. 5.

unity that he (1) had with the Father before the world was, (2) has had during his earthly ministry, (3) will have in his final exaltation, or (4) a combination of all or several of these options.[23] In contrast to his prayer for the unity of believers, Jesus never prays for his oneness with God, 'since that oneness is presupposed, eternally secured, pre-existently present and never relinquished'.[24]

Along with vv. 5, 25 and vv. 11, 21-22, other verses in this prayer highlight the idea of a close association between Jesus and his Father. The Father gave his name to Jesus (vv. 11-12), and he in turn revealed it to men (vv. 6, 26). In the prologue it has been anticipated that people can become children of God through believing in τὸ ὄνομα αὐτοῦ (v. 12). Again, it is not possible to know when exactly Jesus received the name from the Father (δέδωκας, vv. 11-12).[25] Jesus' authority to give eternal life can also be deemed to imply a close association between Jesus and the Father (v. 2). Here Jesus has received a prerogative traditionally belonging to God: authority over all flesh.[26] People can acquire this eternal life when they believe both in the Father as the only true God and in Jesus Christ as the one sent by the Father (v. 3). The one in whom was life in the beginning (1.4) is now able to give eternal life (17.2). Since salvation is associated with both the Father and the Son (cf. 17.20, τῶν πιστευόντων...εἰς ἐμέ), it is possible to conclude that this statement in 17.3 also highlights unity between Jesus and his Father. This special relationship between them is also asserted in v. 10, which describes the Father and the Son sharing everything they have.

23.   Several manuscripts (e.g. ℵ² A C³ Θ Ψ *f*¹³ Majority text) have the present tense εσμεν in v. 22, but the reading without the verb is to be preferred, since it is supported by better manuscripts (Papyrus⁶⁰.⁶⁶ [ℵ*] B C* D). The phrase ἵνα ὦσιν ἓν καθὼς ἡμεῖς in v. 11 is omitted in Papyrus⁶⁶* it ly (the Lycopolitan tradition). Since this reading is not attested in other manuscripts, I follow here the reading that includes the phrase.

24.   Appold, *Oneness*, p. 282.

25.   The clause ᾧ δέδωκας implies that the Father gave his name to Jesus, the reading of Papyrus⁶⁰ A B *f*¹³ Majority text in v. 11, and Papyrus⁶⁶ᶜ ᵛⁱᵈ (uncertain) B L W 33 and the Coptic tradition in v. 12. With slight modifications, other witnesses imply that the Father gave his name to the Son: ο δεδωκας D* (v. 11), ℵ² (v. 12); ω εδωκας Papyrus⁶⁶ᵛⁱᵈ.¹⁰⁷ ℵ L W (v. 11), C* (v. 12). The phrase is absent from Papyrus⁶⁶* ℵ* in v. 12. Several witnesses imply that in vv. 11-12 what the Father gave to the Son was the group of disciples, not his name, since these witnesses have the phrase ους δεδωκας: e.g. D¹ N (v. 11); e.g. A C³ D Majority text (v. 12). However, this reading (ους δεδωκας) can be explained as one influenced by 17.6, τοῖς ἀνθρώποις οὓς ἔδωκάς μοι. Since the reading ᾧ δέδωκας is well attested, I will use it here as the preferred reading.

26.   Moloney, *John*, p. 461; Keener, *John*, vol. 2, p. 1053.

The two instances of creation imagery in Jn 17 are used to signal that Jesus existed apart from and prior to creation, partaking of divine glory stemming from the Father's love for the Son. Some of these ideas occur also in the prologue. Here in the prayer, Jesus asks the Father to glorify him with the glory that he had before the creation of the world (17.5), so that his disciples can see his glory (17.24). Similarly in the prologue, the narrator confesses that 'they' have seen the glory of him (1.14) through whom the world was created (1.10).[27] The narrator explains there that the Word's glory is like the glory of the μονογενοῦς παρὰ πατρός (1.14) and that the Word existed in the beginning πρὸς τὸν θεόν (1.1-2). Likewise, Jesus prays that he may be glorified παρὰ σεαυτῷ with the glory he had παρὰ σοί (17.5). In Jn 17.1-5 Jesus' glory is related to his authority to give eternal life, and in Jn 1.12 those who believe receive authority to become God's children. In his prayer Jesus indicates that he has revealed the Father's name to the world (17.6, 26) and in the prologue those who believe in the Word's name receive authority to become children of God (1.12).

Therefore, John uses creation imagery in the prayer of Jesus to support the claim found in the prologue that Jesus existed apart from and prior to creation at the side of the Father, partaking of his glory. However, there is an evident difference between the prologue and Jesus' prayer. In distinction from Jn 1.3 and 1.10, where the Word's active involvement in the act of creation is explicit, Jn 17 offers no explicit indication of Jesus' participation in creation. Only implicitly can one read in Jn 17.24 that the world has its origins in God.[28]

27. Du Rand, 'Creation', pp. 42–3, argues that δόξα in GJohn reveals the nature of God in creation. This idea is endorsed by McDonough, *Creator*, p. 222. However, in Jn 17 Jesus' glory goes beyond the act of creation because it is a glory that he shared with the Father prior to the foundation of the world. There is no explicit indication in GJohn that Jesus' participation in the creation of the world was a manifestation of God's glory. Thus it is difficult to see 'glory' itself as directly tied to the divine act of creation. Elsewhere John has developed the idea of Jesus' glory and glorification in light of passages from Isaiah, not from Gen. 1–3 or other creation narratives (see Jn 12.41). Cf. J. Frey, '"…dass sie meine Herrlichkeit schauen" (Joh 17.24) Zu Hintergrund, Sinn und Funktion der johanneischen Rede von der δόξα Jesu', *NTS* 54 (2008), pp. 375–97 (384–6); C. H. Williams, 'Isaiah in John's Gospel', in *Isaiah in the New Testament* (ed. S. Moyise and M. J. J. Menken; London: T&T Clark International, 2005), pp. 101–16 (111), 'Jewish precedents for making God's glory the object of Isaiah's vision would undoubtedly have paved the way for the interpretation of Jesus as the embodiment of that glory'.

28. Bultmann, *John*, p. 521.

John 1.10

ὁ κόσμος δι' αὐτοῦ [ὁ λόγος] ἐγένετο
καὶ ὁ κόσμος αὐτὸν οὐκ ἔγνω

John 17.24-25

ἠγάπησάς με πρὸ καταβολῆς κόσμου
πάτερ δίκαιε, καὶ ὁ κόσμος σε οὐκ ἔγνω

The conjunction καί in Jn 17.25 can be taken as relating ἠγάπησάς με πρὸ
καταβολῆς κόσμου to ὁ κόσμος σε οὐκ ἔγνω.[29] The Father loved the Son
before the divine act of creation (17.24), and although the world was
created by God, this world did not know him (v. 25). This idea is clearer
in 1.10. Although the world was created through the Word, the world did
not know him. The most significant difference between the two texts is
that in 1.10 the world came into existence through the Word, while in
17.25 it is only by implication that one could understand that the Father
created the world. It is striking that in the first case (1.10) the world fails
to recognize the Word, but in the second case (17.25) the world fails to
recognize the Father himself. This observation goes some way toward
our argument that in GJohn creation imagery is intended to highlight
Jesus' close association with the Father.

John 17.5 and 17.24 also occur in a context in which past reality is
linked to present and future reality. Throughout Jn 17 there are 60 verbal
forms (including participles and infinitives) that occur in the aorist (42×),
perfect (19×), or imperfect tenses (4×).[30] By contrast, there are only 34
verbal forms that occur in the present tense.[31] Only one verb (γνωρίσω,
v. 26) is used in the future tense. The emphasis in this prayer is on divine

29. Bultmann, *John*, p. 521. The conjunction καί in the phrase καὶ ὁ κόσμος σε
οὐκ ἔγνω (17.25) can also be read as related to καὶ οὗτοι ἔγνωσαν ὅτι σύ με ἀπέστειλας
in v. 25 instead to the preceding phrase in v. 24, ἠγάπησάς με πρὸ καταβολῆς κόσμου.
E. A. Abbott, *Johannine Grammar* (London: Adam & Charles Black, 1906), p. 148,
suggested this connection. However, Michaels, *John*, p. 881 n. 85, has observed that
Abbott's reading is difficult to sustain because the phrase καὶ ὁ κόσμος κτλ. forms a
symmetrical contrast with ἐγὼ δέ σε ἔγνων. Michaels rightly proposes that the
conjunction καί in the phrase καὶ ὁ κόσμος κτλ. (v. 25) has an adversative force.
However, he posits that the contrast is between the phrase 'the world did not know
him' (v. 25) and the world's potential belief and knowledge (vv. 21, 23) and the
disciples' future vision of Jesus' glory (v. 24). It is puzzling that Michaels does not
explain how the phrase 'since the foundation of the world' fits into his suggestion.

30. Aorist tense: vv. 1-6, 8, 11-12, 14-15, 17-18, 21, 23-26. Perfect tense: vv. 1-2,
4, 6-14, 19, 22-24. Imperfect tense: vv. 5-6, 12.

31. Present tense: vv. 3, 5, 7, 9, 11, 13-17, 19-24.

past actions and realities that warrant present petitions. However, this does not mean that the future is not prominent in Jn 17. Future ideas are conveyed through the present imperative (e.g. v. 17) or through clauses introduced by ἵνα (v. 15).

Twice Jesus asks the Father to glorify him (vv. 1, 5, δόξασον), implying that there is an aspect of his glorification that is still awaiting consummation. As for his disciples, Jesus asks his Father to keep them safe (v. 11, τήρησον) and to sanctify them (v. 17, ἁγίασον). Both imperatives imply future divine actions.[32] The conjunction ἵνα is used before a subjunctive verb to indicate a future action of Jesus in favour of the Father (v. 1), future divine actions in favour of the disciples (vv. 11, 13, 15, 19, 21-24, 26),[33] and future consequences for the world (vv. 21, 23).[34]

In this broad context creation imagery in Jn 17 is intended to highlight the link between past reality and present and future reality. In the first case (17.5) the glory that Jesus had prior to the creation of the world is the same glory that he will receive in his glorification by the Father. In the second case (17.24) Jesus asks his Father to allow his disciples to see the glory that he received from him when he was loved before the foundation of the world. The ultimate glory of Jesus in the Father is tied to his pre-existent glory.[35] Therefore, there is a link between primal reality (signalled by creation imagery in vv. 5, 24) and present and future reality.[36]

Jesus' glorious existence in the past, prior to creation, enables him to be authorized to provide his disciples and the world with the possibility of a new reality. The disciples will see the glory that Jesus shared with his Father prior to the foundation of the world (v. 24), and they will have

32. The verb θέλω in 17.24 refers to Jesus' will in favour of his disciples. The construction πρὸς σὲ ἔρχομαι in 17.11, 13 conveys the idea that Jesus *will* go to the Father.

33. In Jn 17.13, 23 the participles πεπληρωμένην and τετελειωμένοι bear the idea of something that is not finished yet.

34. The phrases in vv. 21 and 23 are almost identical: ἵνα ὁ κόσμος πιστεύῃ ὅτι σύ με ἀπέστειλας and ἵνα γινώσκῃ ὁ κόσμος ὅτι σύ με ἀπέστειλας. Another Johannine way to assert future actions could be the present participle in 17.20, τῶν πιστευόντων, 'those who *will* believe'.

35. Brown, *John*, vol. 2, p. 754.

36. Even the 'present reality' signalled by καὶ νῦν (17.5) can be seen as 'eschatological reality', as has been argued by A. Laurentin, '*We'attah – Kai nun.* Formule caractéristique des textes juridiques et liturgiques (à propos de Jean 17,5)', *Bib* 45 (1964), pp. 413–32 (418–32). Cf. Barrett, *John*, p. 514, 'the beginning and end of time are here [17.24] brought together to find their meaning in the historical mission of Jesus and its results'.

access to the knowledge of the Father that enables eternal life (vv. 2-3). They will also receive the love of the Father, which is the same love that the Father gave to the Son prior to creation (vv. 24, 26). This new reality (eternal life) for the disciples will enable them to gain a privileged association with God (vv. 21, 24, 26), which ultimately will result in the world believing that Jesus was sent from the Father (vv. 21, 23). Since knowing the Father through the Son is what provides eternal life (vv. 2-3), the world that has been the result of a divine act of creation in the beginning will also have the opportunity to obtain eternal life. More specifically, through the testimony of the unity of the disciples, the world can believe that Jesus was sent by the Father. This begins the process of the world being brought into its proper relationship with its Creator.[37] Creation imagery in Jn 17 is thus used to assert the universal significance of Jesus and the message about him.

III. Conclusion

In the prayer of Jesus John further supports some of the claims intro-duced earlier in the prologue. John uses creation imagery in two strategic places (17.5 and 17.24) in order to portray Jesus existing apart from and prior to creation, having a close association with his Father that stems from the glory and love they share. This authorizes his participation in divine activities. Specifically, Jesus is authorized to reveal God's name to his disciples and to bring eternal life to those who believe in the Father through the Son. Those instances are also used to assert the universal significance of Jesus and the message about him. Although the primary emphasis in Jesus' prayer is on the disciples receiving divine blessings (e.g. glory, unity, eternal life), there are also indications that through those disciples the 'world' will also have access to the knowledge of God that imparts eternal life (vv. 21, 23). By linking past reality with present and future realities, John portrays Jesus as the privileged agent of revelation and redemption who also existed with the Father before the foundation of the world.

The reader has encountered the first instances of creation imagery in the prologue (1.1-5, 10). Now, at the end of Jesus' ministry and right before his passion and resurrection (Jn 18–20), the reader again encounters creation imagery. In both cases (the prologue and Jesus' prayer) those instances function in similar ways, although they are located in different contexts. Throughout GJohn the reader learns to trust both the narrator

37. Bultmann, *John*, p. 522.

and Jesus himself. Therefore, it is significant that creation imagery is put on the lips of the narrator (1.1-5, 10) and on the lips of Jesus (17.5, 24). The location of creation imagery in Jn 17 may have made a deep impression on John's readers, to help them to fix key ideas introduced earlier in the prologue.

Part II

The Earthly Ministry of Jesus

In the previous part I addressed those passages in GJohn in which creation imagery is explicit: the prologue (1.1-18) and Jesus' prayer (17.5, 24). In the next three chapters I turn my attention to the large body of text found between these two units of material, where John describes Jesus' ministry (Jn 1.19–17.4).[1] I argue that John has used a few and less explicit instances of creation imagery in this section of the Gospel, but he has put them in strategic places to highlight some of the ideas introduced in the prologue.

The following chapters support my main argument that John uses limited (albeit significant) instances of creation imagery by performing two tasks. The first task is showing that John seems to draw on and creatively deploy terms and images stemming from OT narratives where creation imagery plays a prominent role as he portrays Jesus performing the works of his Father (Chapter 3) and performing two distinctive actions: walking on the sea and healing a man born blind (Chapter 4). The second task is a thorough assessment of the claim that John has used the seven days of creation in the composition of his Gospel (Chapter 5). There are reasons to judge that John did not intend to mimic the structure of Gen. 1–2 to arrange his narrative.

Scholars have suggested a number of instances of creation imagery in Jn 1.19–17.4. A couple of these suggestions appear impressive at first glance, but they fall apart when considered in light of GJohn as a whole.[2]

---

1. I include 17.1-4 here because the reference to Jesus accomplishing the works of his Father links Jesus' ministry (1.19–16.33) to Jesus' prayer. Scholars traditionally divide GJohn into four sections: (1) prologue (1.1-18), (2) Jesus' public ministry (1.19–12.50), (3) Jesus' farewell discourses, death, and resurrection (13.1–20.31), and (4) epilogue (21.1-25). Cf. C. H. Williams, 'The Gospel of John', in *The Oxford Handbook of the Reception History of the Bible* (ed. M. Lieb, E. Mason, J. Roberts, and C. Rowland; Oxford: Oxford University Press, 2011), pp. 104–17.

2. For instance, the contrast between 'eating' and 'death' in Gen. 3 is related to 'eating' and 'life' in Jn 6.50-51. See A. Guilding, *The Fourth Gospel and Jewish Worship: A Study of the Relation of St. John's Gospel to the Ancient Jewish*

There are other proposed instances where similar vocabulary shared between GJohn and Gen. 1–3 can be detected, but the vocabulary is commonplace.[3] There are yet some other proposals based only on putative conceptual parallels between GJohn and Gen. 1–3.[4] All those suggestions fail to meet our criteria set out in the Introduction. In all those cases it seems that the scholarly claims have exceeded the data available. Therefore, none of them is deemed here as a valid instance of creation imagery.

Lectionary System (Oxford: Clarendon, 1960), pp. 61–3; J. Luzárraga, 'Presentación de Jesús a la luz del A.T. en el Evangelio de Juan', *EstEcl* 51 (1976), pp. 497–520 (508); M.-É. Boismard, *Moïse ou Jésus: Essai de Christologie Johannique* (BETL, 84; Leuven: Leuven University Press, 1988), pp. 82–3.

3. See, for example, πνεῦμα in Jn 1.32-33 and Gen. 1.2. E. Schweizer, *The Holy Spirit* (trans. R. H. Fuller and I. Fuller; Philadelphia: Fortress, 1980), p. 68; Engberg-Pedersen, '*Logos* and *Pneuma*', p. 27.

4. Cf. 'divine image' in Jn 14.23 and Gen. 1.26. See Brodie, *John*, p. 467.

Chapter 3

JESUS PERFORMING GOD'S WORKS
AND CREATION IMAGERY

This chapter has three sections. The first section is devoted to an assessment of the evidence offered to support the claim that John evokes Gen.
2.1-3 in his portrayal of Jesus performing God's works. In the second
section I will attempt to show that this motif occupies a prominent and
strategic place in GJohn. In the final section I will explain the significance of the Johannine instances of creation imagery related to the idea
of Jesus performing the works of his Father. In this chapter I will show
that John is drawing on and creatively deploying terms and images stemming from Gen. 2.1-3. John also reflects Jewish discussions about God's
rest after creation as he portrays Jesus performing works in 5.20, 36; 9.3-
4; and 17.4 (cf. 5.17). I will also show that John deploys this language at
strategic places in his Gospel in order to shape his presentation of Jesus
and his message and in order to support some of the assertions found
earlier in the prologue.

I. Assessment

By contrast with the chapter devoted to the Johannine prologue (Chapter
1), in which I compared a sequence of verses in GJohn (1.1-5) with the
Genesis account of creation, here I will take into account several verses
scattered through the Gospel in which Jesus is portrayed as performing 'works' (4.34; 5.20, 36; 7.3, 21; 9.3-4; 10.25, 32-33, 37-38; 14.10-
12; 15.24; 17.4).[1] I will now look in detail at the similarities that three

---

1.   John uses the noun ἔργον in several contexts in relation to Jesus' ministry or to
human actions (3.19, 21; 7.7; 8.39, 41). Cf. J. van der Watt, '"Working the Works of
God": Identity and Behaviour in the Gospel of John', in Krans et al. (eds.), *Paul,
John*, pp. 135–50 (137). In the following analysis I will take into account only those
occurrences in which the noun 'work' is related to Jesus' ministry.

representative verses in particular (Jn 4.34; 5.36; 10.32) share with Gen. 2.1-3, but in the overall discussion I will take into account all of the other relevant passages.

a. *Similarities and Prominence*

Genesis 2.1-3 LXX

¹ καὶ <u>συνετελέσθησαν</u> ὁ οὐρανὸς καὶ ἡ γῆ καὶ πᾶς ὁ κόσμος αὐτῶν. ² καὶ <u>συνετέλεσεν</u> ὁ θεὸς ἐν τῇ ἡμέρᾳ τῇ ἕκτῃ <u>τὰ ἔργα αὐτοῦ ἃ ἐποίησεν</u>, καὶ κατέπαυσεν <u>ἐν τῇ ἡμέρᾳ τῇ ἑβδόμῃ</u> ἀπὸ πάντων <u>τῶν ἔργων αὐτοῦ, ὧν ἐποίησεν</u> ³ καὶ εὐλόγησεν ὁ θεὸς <u>τὴν ἡμέραν τὴν ἑβδόμην</u> καὶ ἡγίασεν αὐτήν, ὅτι ἐν αὐτῇ κατέπαυσεν ἀπὸ πάντων <u>τῶν ἔργων αὐτοῦ</u>, ὧν ἤρξατο ὁ θεὸς <u>ποιῆσαι</u>.

John 4.34

... ἐμὸν βρῶμά ἐστιν ἵνα <u>ποιήσω</u> τὸ θέλημα τοῦ πέμψαντός με καὶ <u>τελειώσω</u> <u>αὐτοῦ τὸ ἔργον</u>.

At the end of the narrative of Jesus' encounter with the Samaritan woman, when the disciples have returned from buying food in a town, Jesus tells them that his food is to do the will of the One who sent him and 'to finish his work' (4.34). There are a number of similarities between this verse and Gen. 2.1-3. The phrase αὐτοῦ τὸ ἔργον (Jn 4.34) is similar to τὰ ἔργα αὐτοῦ (Gen. 2.2)[2] and τῶν ἔργων αὐτοῦ (Gen. 2.2, 3).[3] In both cases (Gen. 2 and Jn 4) the pronoun αὐτοῦ refers to God.[4] The 'One who sent' Jesus is identified as God the Father elsewhere in GJohn (14.24). However, the word order and the number of the nouns are different. The plural noun with the definite article is followed by the pronoun in Gen. 2.2, 3,[5] while in Jn 4.34 the pronoun precedes the

2. Some ancient translations (e.g. Arabic, Armenian, Bohairic) and a couple of Latin writers (Augustine and Irenaeus) have the adjective 'all, every' before τὰ ἔργα αὐτοῦ in Gen. 2.2. The phrase πάντων τῶν ἔργων αὐτοῦ (Gen. 2.2, 3) might have influenced this reading. The adjective πάντων (2.2) does not occur in several Christian witnesses (e.g. Ambrose and Augustine). Likewise, Augustine omits πάντων in Gen. 2.3.

3. The phrase מלאכתו, 'his work', is used three times in those verses in the MT (Gen. 2.2-3).

4. The variant τα εργα αυτα (cursive 106, Gen. 2.2) refers not to God but to his works of creation. The pronoun αὐτοῦ is omitted in cursives 72 53' (53+664) 127. If the original reading was τὰ ἔργα αὐτοῦ ἃ ἐποίησεν, it is possible to postulate that the scribe's eye went from the α of ἔργα to the relative pronoun ἃ, thus omitting the pronoun.

5. There is no article in cursives 53 and 59 (Fernández-Marcos and Sáenz-Badillos, *Anotaciones*, p. 15) in Gen. 2.2 (ἔργων αὐτοῦ) and the pronoun αὐτοῦ does not occur in the group *d* (44 107 125 370 610), cursive 75, a couple of church

singular noun.⁶ A further difference between the two texts is that in Gen. 2 the narrator is speaking, while in Jn 4 a character (Jesus) is speaking.

There is also a similarity between the verb τελειόω in Jn 4.34 and the verb συντελέω in Gen. 2.1, 2, since both verbs share the same verbal root τελεω,⁷ and both carry the general meaning 'to complete, to finish, to bring to an end'.⁸ Some scholars have observed that there is a strong tendency in the Johannine writings to avoid compound verbs, and this could be a reason why, if John is using Gen. 2.1-2 in some way, he prefers τελειόω instead of συντελέω.⁹ Since both verbs are commonplace,¹⁰ it is necessary to determine how prominent the construction τελειόω/τελέω/συντελέω + ἔργον is. The word combination τελειόω and ἔργον (Jn 4.34) occurs in 2 Esd. 16.3, 16 [Neh. 6.3, 16 MT] to describe the rebuilding of Jerusalem's wall. In spite of this similarity, there is no explicit indication in Neh. 6.3, 16 that τὸ ἔργον is God's work, and John never quotes or alludes to the book of Nehemiah (cf. Jn 5.2). Therefore, while not impossible, it seems quite unlikely that Jn 4.34 is a reference to this OT book.¹¹

The construction τελέω + ἔργον is used three times in the LXX to indicate the fulfilment of a task that is not related to creation (1 Macc. 4.51; Sir. 7.25; 38.27). This same idea is conveyed through the construction

fathers (Augustine and Irenaeus), and the Vulgata (cf. cursive 31, where the phrase αὐτοῦ, ὧν ἐποίησεν is altogether omitted). Cursive 509 lacks the noun ἔργων in Gen. 2.3.

6.   In the MT the noun is singular (מלאכתו), but the LXX apparently understood the singular in a collective sense and translated it using the plural form. Cf. Wevers, *Notes*, p. 20.

7.   Instead of συνετελέσθησαν (Gen. 2.1), other witnesses have συνετελεσθη (e.g. 413 Ethiopic), συνετελεσεν (392; see Gen. 2.2), συνετελεστη (527), or ετελεσθησαν (Philo).

8.   See BDAG, pp. 975, 996; LSJ, pp. 1726, 1770; MM, pp. 613, 629. According to L&N, p. 658, the verbs τελέω, ἐκτελέω, ἀποτελέω, ἐπιτελέω, συντελέω, and τελειόω are all part of the same semantic field: 'to bring an activity to a successful finish, to complete, to finish, to end, to accomplish'. In Isa. 44.24 ὁ συντελῶν is used to portray God as Creator.

9.   Weidemann, 'Protology', p. 314. Weidemann refers to R. Morgenthaler, *Statistik des neutestamentlichen Wortschatzes* (Zurich: Gotthelf Verlag, 3rd edn, 1992), pp. 15–17, who points out that constructions with σύν are typically Markan–Lukan–Pauline.

10.   The verb συντελέω is absent from GJohn but it occurs elsewhere in the NT (Mk 13.4; Lk. 4.2, 13; Acts 21.27; Rom. 9.28; Heb. 8.8).

11.   τὸ ἔργον appears along with ἐπλήρωσαν in Acts 14.26, and τὰ ἔργα is used along with πεπληρωμένα in Rev. 3.2.

συντελέω + ἔργον in the LXX in reference to a sacred task such as constructing a house for the Lord (Exod. 36.2; 40.33; 3 Kgdms 7.26 [1 Kgs 7.40 MT]; cf. 1 Esd. 6.9) or making a burnt offering (2 Chron. 29.34), as well as to tasks that are not necessarily sacred (Exod. 5.13; Hos. 13.2; Prov. 22.8; cf. Sir. 38.8). However, none of those instances has the phrase 'God's work'.

Scholars have proposed several OT texts as the background to Jn 4.34. Masanobu Endo asserts that the word combination 'to do (ποιέω)' and 'to accomplish (τελειόω)' occurs only six times in the OT (Ps. 37.7; Dan. 8.12, 24; 11.36; Isa. 55.11; 2 Chron. 31.21) and concludes that 'the ministry of the Son of God in Jn 4.34 may allude to the figure of the word of God in Isa. 55.11'.[12] However, Endo's word search is not accurate; the noun ἔργον and the verb ποιέω do not occur in Isa. 55.11 LXX. It seems that Endo has searched for עשה and צלח instead of ποιέω and τελειόω, and has restricted his search to צלח instead of including כלה, 'to accomplish, to fulfil'. Other scholars have suggested that in Jn 4.34, 'Almost certainly Jesus is echoing Deuteronomy 8:3'.[13] However, there are no significant words shared between the two texts. A similar critique can be made of McHugh and Boismard and Lamouille, who suggested that Jesus' declining to eat in Jn 4.34 is meant to recall Abraham's servant's refusal to drink and eat when seeking a wife for Isaac (Gen. 24).[14]

John 5.36

... τὰ γὰρ ἔργα ἃ δέδωκέν μοι ὁ πατὴρ ἵνα τελειώσω αὐτά, αὐτὰ τὰ ἔργα ἃ ποιῶ κτλ.

The idea that Jesus performs the works of his Father occurs again in Jn 5. In his discourse Jesus asserts that both his Father and he himself are 'working' (5.17).[15] His miraculous healing at the pool provoked discussions between him and the Jews (5.16-23) and the crowd (7.20-24), because he performed this 'work' on a Sabbath (5.9-10, 16).

12. Endo, *Creation*, pp. 240–1 (248).
13. Carson, *John*, p. 228. Cf. Barrett, *John*, p. 240; Lindars, *John*, p. 194; Brown, *John*, vol. 1, p. 173. Cf. Michaels, *John*, p. 261.
14. McHugh, *John*, p. 292, referring to M.-É. Boismard and A. Lamouille, *Un évangile pré-johannique* (EBib, 17–18, 24–25, 28–29; Paris: Gabalda, 1996).
15. A. T. Hanson, *The Prophetic Gospel: A Study of John and the Old Testament* (Edinburgh: T. & T. Clark, 1991), pp. 70–1, proposes that Jn 5.17 is influenced by Hab. 1.5. Cf. Mihalios, *Hour*, pp. 96–7. The verbal parallel is striking but there is nothing in the context of Hab. 1 that may indicate that the 'work' will be done during the Sabbath. Besides, Habakkuk is not a prominent text in GJohn. Thus Hanson's suggestion is not compelling.

There are similarities between Jn 5.36 and Gen. 2.2-3.[16] The plural noun with the article (τὰ ἔργα) and a relative clause (ἃ ἐποίησεν, ὧν ἐποίησεν, Gen. 2.2; ἃ ποιῶ, Jn 5.36)[17] following the noun ἔργον occur in both texts.[18] There is also a similarity in terms of chronological context. According to Gen. 2.3 LXX, God left off from all his work of creation on the seventh day (τὴν ἡμέραν τὴν ἑβδόμην).[19] Similarly, the events narrated in Jn 5 took place on a Sabbath (σάββατον, 5.9, 10, 16, 18; cf. 7.22, 23).[20] In both cases (Gen. 2 and Jn 5) the 'seventh day' is emphasized, since it is repeated twice in Gen. 2.2-3[21] and several times in Jn 5.[22] As for differences, the pronoun αὐτοῦ is not used in Jn 5.36, the noun follows

16. Keener, *John*, vol. 1, p. 649, links the miracle of Jesus in Jn 5 to Gen. 1.26, but the similarities between the two texts are not prominent.

17. The relative pronoun ὧν (Gen. 2.2) does not occur in cursive 72 probably by homoioteleuton, and the phrase ὧν ἐποίησεν does not appear in two versions (Ethiopian and Arabic). In Gen. 2.3 ὧν ἤρξατο ὁ θεὸς ποιῆσαι follows τῶν ἔργων αὐτοῦ. In this verse, instead of the aorist infinitive ποιῆσαι, several witnesses have the present infinitive ποιειν (cursive 508, group *b* [19-108-118-314-537], Chrysostom, and Hippolytus).

18. The phrase τὰ ἔργα σου...ἃ ποιήσεις is used as a reference to future divine acts of mercy in Isa. 64.3 LXX, where the Sabbath context is absent.

19. Unlike Gen. 2.2 MT, where it is said that God finished his work of creation on the 'seventh day', Gen. 2.2 LXX (except cursive 527, which omits the phrase) states that God finished his work on the 'sixth day'. The LXX's reading is also found in the Samaritan Pentateuch and the Syriac Peshiṭta (Wevers, *Notes*, p. 20) and in Philo, *Leg. All.* 1.2. Aquila, Symmachus, and Theodotion (according to majuscule M, cursives 17–135, and possibly cursives 127–344) still preserve 'seventh day'.

20. Although the reading found in the MT might give room to posit that God still worked during the seventh day, it is too much to claim that John found a basis in this for deeming that creation was incomplete, as has been argued by A. J. Droge, 'Sabbath Work/Sabbath Rest: Genesis, Thomas, John', *HR* 47 (2007–2008), pp. 112–41 (129–30). Droge considers that for John, 'the deity finished his work only on the seventh day... The demiurge rested on the seventh day only after he had finished some tantalizingly unspecified "sabbath work" of creating the heavens and the earth.' Droge speculates that 'one can well imagine that its author [John] would not easily have accepted the pronouncement at Genesis 1:31 that "*Elohim* saw every-thing that he had made, and *it was very good, indeed*"' (Droge's emphasis).

21. Cursive 527 omits 'seventh day' in Gen. 2.2, but this might be explained as an scribal error, since it is possible that the hand behind 527 went from κατέπαυσεν ἐν (2.2) to ὁ θεός in 2.3, because 'God' is the obvious subject of the verb (cf. the reading preserved in, e.g. the Origenic recension [except cursive 426], 53-56*-664*, the Ethiopic translation, and Augustine).

22. The similarity is closest in Gen. 2.2-3 MT, where שבת is used to depict God's rest. The LXX describes God's rest using κατέπαυσεν, while Aquila uses the aorist διέλιπεν (according to 135 344' [344+127]), and the imperfect διέλειπεν is attested in the majuscule M.

the verb in Gen. 2.2 (συνετέλεσεν + τὰ ἔργα αὐτοῦ) but precedes the verb in Jn 5.36 (τὰ ἔργα + τελειώσω), and the narrator is speaking in Gen. 2.2 but a character (Jesus) is speaking in Jn 5.36.[23]

The idea that Jesus performs 'works' occurs also in Jn 9.3-4, in the context of another healing that took place on a Sabbath (9.14, 16). Jesus refers to the miracle as τὰ ἔργα τοῦ θεοῦ (9.3) and τὰ ἔργα τοῦ πέμψαντός με (9.4).[24] The first phrase is similar to τὰ ἔργα αὐτοῦ (Gen. 2.2), but instead of a verb of completion (τελέω or συντελέω), this phrase is accompanied by φανερόω in Jn 9.3. This could be due to the context, where it is appropriate to find this verb in relation to the noun 'light' (9.5; cf. 3.21).[25] God's works, both in Gen. 2.2 and Jn 9.3-4, are related to the day of God's rest.

John 10.32

... πολλὰ ἔργα καλὰ ἔδειξα ὑμῖν ἐκ τοῦ πατρός· διὰ ποῖον αὐτῶν ἔργον ἐμὲ λιθάζετε;

In a dialogue with Jesus the Jews request, 'If you are the Christ tell us plainly' (10.24). In response, Jesus asserts that the works (τὰ ἔργα) that

---

23. This difference is not prominent, since in GJohn there is an overlap between Jesus' voice and the narrator's voice. Cf. R. A. Culpepper, *Anatomy of the Fourth Gospel: A Study in Literary Design* (Philadelphia: Fortress, 1983), pp. 16–18.

24. There is an important textual problem in 9.4. There are three possible readings: (1) ἡμᾶς δεῖ ἐργάζεσθαι τὰ ἔργα τοῦ πέμψαντός ἡμᾶς ('we...us'), (2) ἐμέ... με, and (3) ἡμᾶς...με. The decision is difficult. The earliest reading is the first one (Papyrus[66.75]; cf. א* L W), but the reading supported by the majority of manuscripts is the second one (e.g. א[1] A C Θ Ψ *f*[1.13] Majority text). The third reading occurs only in a few manuscripts from the fourth century onwards (B D [δει ημας]). The most difficult reading is the first one. The reader expects the subject to be Jesus ('I') not the disciples ('we'; cf. 3.21; 6.27-29; 14.12) because of 4.34; 5.17, 36 and because Jesus alone is the one who heals the man in Jn 9. Similarly, the reader expects 'the One who sent me [Jesus]' instead of 'sent us [the disciples]' (4.34; 5.23, 24, 30, 37; 6.38, 39, 44; 7.16, 18, 28, 33; 8.16, 18, 26, 29) because the Father sends Jesus, John (1.33), and the Spirit/Counsellor in Jesus' name (14.26; cf. 15.26; 16.7), but the disciples are sent by Jesus (13.20; 20.21), not directly from the Father. If 'I...me' (shortest reading) was original, R. Bultmann speculated that the Christian community behind GJohn changed it to 'we...us' in 'order to give the statement the character of a universally valid principle' (*John*, p. 332 n. 7). On the other hand, Metzger, *Commentary*, p. 194, deemed that if 'we...us' was original, it is 'slightly more probable that copyists would have altered ἡμᾶς to ἐμέ than vice versa'. Considering the difficulties in deciding between these two readings, commentators usually embrace reading number three ('we...me').

25. The phrase τὰ...ἔργα τοῦ θεοῦ ἀνακαλύπτειν occurs in Tob. 12.11 in a context where creation is not in view.

he performs (ἃ ἐγὼ ποιῶ) in his Father's name testify about him (10.25). These works are called 'the works of my Father' in 10.37 and simply 'the works' in 10.38. Here in 10.32 we find for the first and only time in GJohn that Jesus refers to the works that he performs as 'good works' (cf. 10.33).[26] The adjective καλός is used several times in Gen. 1 in order to indicate that God's creation was 'good'.[27] Yet apart from this similarity, it is difficult to find other correspondences between Gen. 1 and Jn 10.

The adjective καλός occurs elsewhere in GJohn, always in relation to Jesus ('good shepherd', 10.11, 14) or to a miracle performed by him ('good wine', 2.10).[28] This adjective is commonplace in the LXX. It is peculiar that John uses the adjective in relation to Jesus,[29] because 'good works' is always used in relation to people in other canonical texts (Mt. 5.16; 26.10 / Mk 14.6; 1 Tim. 3.1; 5.10, 25; 6.18; Tit. 2.7, 14; 3.8, 14; Heb. 10.24; 1 Pet. 2.12). In context, the use of καλός in Jn 10.32-33 would take the reader back primarily to 10.11, 14, where it is said that Jesus is the 'good (καλός) shepherd'.[30] Furthermore, the discourse about the shepherd and the sheep in Jn 10 seems to have been developed in light of Ezek. 34, not in light of Gen. 1–2.[31]

26. The uncial W and a manuscript of the Old Latin (b) do not have καλός in 10.32. Several witnesses have ἔργα καλά (e.g. ℵ A K and possibly Papyrus[45] Papyrus[75]), but others have καλὰ ἔργα (e.g. Papyrus[66] D L Majority text).

27. See vv. 4, 8, 10, 12, 18, 21, 25. The adjective refers to light (1.4), the sky (1.8), earth and seas (1.10), the products of the earth (1.12), luminaries and stars (1.18), and animals (1.21, 25). The whole of God's creation is seen as 'very good' (καλὰ λίαν) in Gen. 1.31. The adjective used in the MT is טוב (except 1.8). Philo and Aquila have the adjective ἀγαθός instead of καλός in Gen. 1.31.

28. For this reason J. Heath, ' "Some Were Saying, 'He is Good' " (John 7.12b): "Good" Christology in John's Gospel?', *NTS* 56 (2010), pp. 513–35 (521), deems that the application of the adjective 'good' to Jesus is a theme of 'relative prominence' in GJohn. For some commentators, however, the use of the adjective καλός in GJohn is not significant (cf. Beasley-Murray, *John*, p. 175; Carson, *John*, p. 396).

29. John uses the noun ἀγαθός in 1.46; 5.29; and 7.12 but never to refer to the works performed by Jesus. In Jn 7.12 people say that Jesus is ἀγαθός, 'good' (not his works; cf. Mk 10.17 / Lk. 18.18; Lk. 9.33). The adverb καλῶς is used several times in GJohn (4.17; 8.48; 13.13; 18.23), but only in 18.23 is it used in relation to Jesus.

30. As for the literary relationship between 10.22-39 and 10.1-21, see Dodd, *Interpretation*, pp. 355–6.

31. Cf. Manning, *Echoes*, pp. 111–19; Dodd, *Interpretation*, p. 358. The noun καλός is used in Ezek. 34.18 to refer to 'good pasture'. There is no reference to 'good works' in Ezek. 34, and it is doubtful that John took this adjective from Ezek. 34.18. The designation 'good shepherd' (Jn 10.11, 14) is unparalleled in the OT (Heath, 'Christology', p. 529).

There are some similarities between the Johannine claim that Jesus performs God's works and Gen. 1–2, but there are also noticeable differences. Therefore, the overall result of this enquiry so far is inconclusive. A link to Gen. 1–2 has still not been convincingly demonstrated. It is necessary to see whether the words ἔργον, τελειόω, and καλός were used in creation contexts in Second-Temple literature and to consider ancient Jewish exegetical traditions about God's rest after the creation of the world in order to establish the plausibility of a link to Gen. 1–2 in GJohn.

b. *Interpretative Traditions*
Both ἔργον and συντελέω are used in Second-Temple Jewish texts in creation contexts. The noun ἔργον is frequently used to depict God's creation (Wis. 13.1; *Jub.* 2.3, 4; *4 Ezra* 6.38, 43; *LAE* 51.2; *Odes* 16.12; Philo, *Spec. Leg.* 2.59; *Dec.* 97; Josephus, *Ant.* 1.33; cf. Sir. 42.16; *Pss. Sol.* 18.1; Heb. 1.10; 4.4).[32] In fact, phrases that are used both in GJohn and Gen. 2.2-3 occur in creation contexts in Second-Temple texts: πάντα ἔργα θεοῦ (*1 En.* 2.2), πάντων τῶν ἔργων αὐτοῦ (*1 En.* 5.1; cf. Philo, *Leg. All.* 1.16, 18; *Poster. C.* 64), τά ἔργα αὐτοῦ πάντα ὅσα ἐποίησεν (*1 En.* 5.2), *opera tua* (*4 Ezra* 6.40; cf. *mirabilia tua*, 6.48), *omnibus factis quae fecisti* (*4 Ezra* 6.54), 'all the works of God' (בל מעשי אל, 4Q392 1, 7), 'his works' (*Jub.* 2.1, 3, 16, 25; *Odes* 16.12).[33] The verb συντελέω was used in quotations from Gen. 2.1-2 in Second-Temple Jewish texts (*Jub.* 2.16; Philo, *Rer. Div. Her.* 122; *Leg. All.* 1.1-3), but other related words were used when Gen. 2.1-2 was alluded to in *Sib. Or.* 1.21 (τελέω) and Philo (*Spec. Leg.* 2.58; *Dec.* 99, τελείωσις; *Spec. Leg.* 2.59, τέλειος; *Spec. Leg.* 2.260, τελεσφορέω).[34]

---

32. The phrase 'God's works' is used in the LXX in reference to God's creation (Pss. 8.4; 101.26; Isa. 64.7). This phrase is also used in the OT and other ancient Jewish literature to depict a number of divine or human activities: the law given to Moses (Exod. 32.16), commandments given by God (Jer. 31.10), a divine favour (Ps. 77.7; Tob. 12.6, 7, 11; 2 Macc. 3.36), divine judgement (Ps. 63.9; Jer. 28.10), historical acts of redemption (Ps. 65.5), God's will (4Q266 II, 14-16; 1QS IV, 4), acts of legal piety (*T. Benj.* 10.3), or cultic service (Num. 3.7, 8; 4.3, 4, 16, 23, 27, 30; 1 Esd. 7.2, 3, 9, 15). I have taken these examples from S. Pancaro, *The Law in the Fourth Gospel* (NovTSup, 42; Leiden: Brill, 1975), pp. 380–4, and U. C. von Wahlde, 'Faith and Works in Jn VI 28-29. Exegesis or Eisegesis?', *NovT* 22 (1980), pp. 304–15 (308).

33. R. L. Bensly, *The Fourth Book of Ezra* (TS, 3/2; Cambridge: Cambridge University Press, 1895), pp. 23–4; M. Black, *Apocalypsis Henochii Graece* (PVTG, 3; Leiden: Brill, 1970), pp. 19–20; García-Martínez and Tigchelaar (eds.), *Scrolls*, p. 788.

34. Philo uses συντελέω elsewhere in contexts where creation is not in view (*Ebr.* 52, 53; *Mut. Nom.* 270; *Somn.* 2.23, 29; *Abr.* 240; *Spec. Leg.* 1.67; cf. *Somn.* 2.116).

The goodness of God's creation is an idea found in Second-Temple Jewish literature but it is conspicuously absent in some texts in which Gen. 1–2 has been clearly used.[35] The hand behind *2 Enoch* portrays God as asserting how good his creation was (*2 En.* 25.3; 26.2; 27.3).[36] The narrator in Sir. 39.16 (cf. v. 25) proclaims that all the works of the Lord are 'very good' (τὰ ἔργα κυρίου πάντα ὅτι καλὰ σφόδρα). Philo portrays God as contemplating 'what had been so well created (τὰ γεγονότα καλῶς)' (*Dec.* 97) and asserts elsewhere that God's 'goodness and kindness' (ἡ ἀγαθότης καὶ ἡ χρηστότης) were the impetus for his creation (*Quaest. in Gen.* 2.13). The creation of light (*Apoc. Abr.* 22.1-2) and of each part of the human body (*T. Naph.* 2.8) is also portrayed as 'good' (*OTP*, vol. 1, pp. 700, 811).[37] On the other hand, there is no mention of the goodness of God's creation in several narratives where Gen. 1–2 has been clearly used (*Jub.* 2.2-16; *4 Ezra* 6.38-54; *Odes* 16.10-13, 16; cf. Philo, *Op. Mund.* 40, 42-43, 46-47, 62).[38] Josephus, for example, indicates that he will narrate the story of creation as it is found in the 'sacred books', but he omits statements such as 'and God saw that it was good' in his narrative (*Ant.* 1.27-37).

The statement that God rested on the seventh day (Gen. 2.3) is asserted in several texts (e.g. Exod. 20.11; 31.17; *Jub.* 2.1, 25; *2 En.* 32.2; *LAE* 51.2; *Hell. Syn. Pr.* 5.2; Philo, *Cher.* 87; cf. *Odes* 16.12),[39] but it also gives rise to some speculation (cf. Ps. 120.4 [121.4 MT]; *Ep. Arist.* 210).[40] Josephus' assertion that God 'took a rest from his works' (λαβεῖν

35. Cf. H. Spieckermann, 'Is God's Creation Good? From Hesiodos to Plato and from the Creation Narratives (Genesis 1–3) to Ben Sira', in *Beyond Eden: The Biblical Story of Paradise (Genesis 2–3) and Its Reception History* (ed. K. Schmid and C. Riedweg; FAT, 2/34; Tübingen: Mohr Siebeck, 2008), pp. 79–94.

36. In other texts from the Second-Temple period ἔργον καλός (or ἔργα καλά) is used to describe human actions (e.g. *T. Ash.* 4.2; *Ep. Arist.* 18, 272; *Sib. Or.* 3.220).

37. In 4Q440 3 I, 22 the phrase '(in) your goodness' (ובטובה{ב}ו) appears possibly in a creation context: '[…] your [gl]ory to everything which exists […] you, my God, are the pure one (?) in all […] us all to make us do it, because […]…and {in} your goodness you established […the aby]ss of your awesome mysteries […] your glorious Sabbath' (lines 19-24) (García-Martínez and Tigchelaar, *Scrolls*, p. 921).

38. God's creation is called 'great works' (μέγιστα ἔργα) in *Jub.* 2.3. Cf. 'wonderful works' in a creation context in 4Q392 1, 7 (פלא[י]ם מעשי).

39. A quotation from Gen. 2.2 LXX occurs in Heb. 4.4. This text is combined with Ps. 94.11 LXX (95.11 MT) in Heb. 4.3 in order to explain that God's works were accomplished (γενηθέντων) since the foundation of the world and, therefore, he rested on the seventh day (Heb. 4.10). God had a Sabbath but, in the author's view, a Sabbath rest remains for the people of God (Heb. 4.9).

40. Dodd, *Interpretation*, p. 320; Moloney, *John*, p. 174.

ἀπὸ τῶν ἔργων ἐκεχειρίαν, *Ant.* 1.33 [Thackeray, LCL]) has been interpreted as if he 'implies that [God] had merely taken a respite from His activities and that He intended to resume them'.[41] More explicit are some lines attributed to Aristobulus. Although he possibly wrote as early as the second century B.C.E., his reflections on the Sabbath are known to us only through a fragment preserved in the work of Eusebius (*Praep. ev.* 13.12.9-16):

> And it is plainly said by our legislation that God rested on the seventh day. This does not mean, as some interpret, that God no longer does anything. It means that, after he had finished ordering all things, he so orders them for all time. For the legislation signifies that in six days he made heaven and earth and all things which are in them in order that he might make manifest the times and foreordain what precedes what with respect to order. For, having set all things in order, he maintains and alters them so... And the legislation has shown plainly that the seventh day is legally binding for us as a sign of the sevenfold principle which is established around us. (*Aristob.* 5.11-12; *OTP*, vol. 2, pp. 841–2)[42]

Aristobulus indicates that there are 'some' who interpret the biblical text to mean that God no longer does anything. Unlike them, Aristobulus deems that God's creation was a work of 'ordering' and that he is still active in maintaining and altering the times. Aristobulus does not state whether there are others who endorse his interpretation, but at least his comments might indicate that Gen. 2.2-3 elicited curiosity at that time.[43]

   The clearest evidence of speculation about God's rest after creation is found in Philo.[44] In his account of the creation of the world Philo asserts

41. L. H. Feldman, *Judean Antiquities 1–4: Translation and Commentary* (Leiden: Brill, 2000), p. 12 n. 55.

42. Denis, *Fragmenta*, pp. 221–8; C. R. Holladay, *Fragments from Hellenistic Jewish Authors* (SBLTT, 39; 4 vols.; Atlanta: Scholars Press, 1995), vol. 3, pp. 183–5.

43. Furthermore, Aristobulus did not assert explicitly that God is active during the Sabbath (M. H. Burer, *Divine Sabbath Work* [BBRSup, 5; Winona Lake: Eisenbrauns, 2012], pp. 69–71). Cf. G. Swart, 'Aristobulus' Interpretation of LXX Sabbath Texts as an Interpretative Key to John 5:1-18', *JSem* 18 (2009), pp. 569–82 (572); L. Doering, *Schabbat: Sabbathalacha und –praxis im antiken Judentum und Urchristentum* (TSAJ, 78; Tübingen: J. C. B. Mohr [Paul Siebeck], 1999), pp. 306–15. Swart deems that Aristobulus alluded not only to Gen. 2.2-3 but also to Exod. 20.10, 11; Deut. 5.14 (p. 572).

44. Putting together several fragments of 4Q176 (frgs. 16, 17, 18, 22, 23, 33, 51, 53), García-Martínez and Tigchelaar, *Scrolls*, p. 361, propose the following translation: 'Because he created every [spirit] of the eternal [generation]s, and [according to] his judgement [he established] the paths of them all. The ear[th] he cre[ated with] his [rig]ht (hand) before they existed, and he con[tinually superv]ises everything

that God finished his creation in six days (*Leg. All.* 1.1-4), but he immediately adds (1.5) that 'on the seventh day' (ἑβδόμῃ ἡμέρᾳ) God begins (ἄρχεται) the configuration (διατυπώσεως) of divine things (θειοτέρων). For Philo, God never leaves off making (παύεται…ποιῶν) because his intrinsic nature is to make (τὸ ποιεῖν) (1.5). Philo interprets God's rest in Gen. 2.2-3 in light of the verb found in the LXX, 'Moses says "caused to rest" [κατέπαυσεν] not "rested" [ἐπαύσατο]; for He causes to rest that which, though actually not in operation, is apparently making, but He Himself never ceases making [οὐ παύεται δὲ ποιῶν αὐτός]' (*Leg. All.* 1.5-6 [Thackeray, LCL]). Similarly, Philo asserts: 'God, when…causing to cease, does not cease making, but begins the creating of other things' (*Leg. All.* 1.18 [Thackeray, LCL]).[45] Elsewhere Philo explains that God's rest is not 'mere inactivity' (*Cher.* 87). Since God is by nature active, he never ceases to do what is good (καλῶν) and beautiful (τὰ κάλλιστα). God's working, Philo says, is a working with absolute ease, without toil and without suffering (*Cher.* 87), because God is by nature untiring (*Cher.* 87, 90).[46]

Jesus' assertion that his 'Father is working' (5.17) in a context where he has healed a person on a Sabbath, and his reference to the healing on a Sabbath of a man born blind as 'the works of God' (9.3-4), might indicate that Jewish speculations about God's rest after creation are part of the background to those Johannine passages.[47] Since there is evidence that readings of Gen. 2.2-3 elicited those speculations, it is also highly possible that Gen. 2.2-3 is relevant for understanding Jn 5 and Jn 9. Our survey of Second-Temple Jewish texts has provided additional evidence of the possibility of a link between the Genesis story of creation and

th[ere is in it. And in] his mystery he causes the lot to fall on man in order to give […]' (lines 2 and 3). This text might indicate that God 'continually [even during the Sabbath] supervises' his creation, but the fragmentary state of the text does not allow any firm conclusion.

45. Cf. P. Borgen, *Early Christianity and Hellenistic Judaism* (Edinburgh: T. & T. Clark, 1996), p. 113, also related Jn 5 to Philo, *Migr. Abr.* 89–93.

46. Rabbinic material pertinent to the discussion about God's rest and God's work is found in Str-B, vol. 2, pp. 461–2; Dodd, *Interpretation*, pp. 320–8; H. Odeberg, *The Fourth Gospel: Interpreted in Its Relation to Contemporaneous Religious Currents in Palestine and the Hellenistic-Oriental World* (Uppsala: Almqvist & Wiksell, 1929), pp. 201–4; Burer, *Work*, pp. 78–100. However, it is always difficult to date the origin of the traditions contained in Rabbinic material. Cf. P. W. Ensor, *Jesus and His 'Works': The Johannine Sayings in Historical Perspective* (WUNT, 2/85; Tübingen: J. C. B. Mohr, 1996), p. 186.

47. Borgen, *Early Christianity*, p. 105; Bultmann, *John*, p. 246.

those Johannine passages in which Jesus is portrayed as performing God's works. Now it is time to see if early readers of GJohn made this link and to assess the thematic coherence of those Johannine passages when considered in light of Gen. 2.

c. *History of Interpretation and Thematic Coherence*

Some ancient Christian writers linked several passages in which John portrays Jesus as performing God's works with the idea of creation. Irenaeus quotes Jn 9.3 in order to prove that the One who created humanity in the beginning is the Father, commenting: 'the work of God is the fashioning of man (*Opera autem Dei plasmatio est hominis*)' (*Haer.* 5.15.2).[48] Irenaeus explains that Jn 9.3 means that Jesus' disciples will be able to see the hand of God that formed humanity in the beginning at work in the restoration of the blind man (*Haer.* 5.15.2; cf. 5.15.4). Tertullian uses Jn 10.25 to indicate that 'the Creator's works testify at once to His goodness, since they are good' (*Marc.* 2.5; *ANF*, vol. 3, p. 301). Athanasius relates Jn 5.17 to the first three verses of the Johannine prologue and concludes that the Father is in the Son and the Son is in the Father because the Word of God performs the works of the Creator God (*C. Ar.* 2.15-16 [*NPNF*[2], vol. 4, pp. 354–60]; cf. *Inc.* 18.1-3).[49] Chrysostom deems that the 'works' mentioned in Jn 9.3-4 were a proof that Jesus was taking part in God's work of creation (*Hom. Jo.* 56.2). There is evidence, then, that some Johannine passages (5.17; 9.3-4; 10.25, 38) were read in relation to creation by ancient interpreters of GJohn.[50]

In terms of thematic coherence, there is little evidence in the surrounding context of Jn 4.34 to suggest that John is using Gen. 2.2-3.[51] The context of Jn 5.20, 36 is more promising, since the language of 'works' is used in discussions about God working on the Sabbath. Jesus' assertion

---

48. A. Rousseau, L. Doutreleau, and C. Mercier, *Irénée de Lyon: Contre les Hérésies* (SC, 153; 2 vols.; Paris: Cerf, 1969), vol. 2, p. 204.

49. In *Barn.* 5.5 Jesus is portrayed as being involved in creation.

50. See also Ephrem the Syrian, *Commentary on Tatian's Diatessaron* 13.4, who portrays Jesus as the creator in Jn 5.17. C. McCarthy, *Saint Ephrem's Commentary on Tatian's Diatessaron: An English Translation of Chester Beatty Syriac MS 709* (JSSSup, 2; Oxford: Oxford University Press, 1993), pp. 206–7.

51. Although Gen. 48.22 might be in view in Jn 4.5, it is evident that Genesis was not an important text in the composition of Jn 4. Reim, *Studien*, p. 98, deems that Jn 4.34 is an 'obvious allusion' (*Offensichtliche Anspielungen*) to Genesis. Cf. J. K. Brown, 'Creation', p. 285; Coloe, *God Dwells with Us*, p. 197; von Wahlde, *John*, vol. 2, pp. 187, 194.

that his Father is 'working until now' (5.17) resonates with Jewish
discussions about God's rest after creation in Gen. 2.2-3 (e.g. Philo, *Leg.
All.* 1.1-6; *Cher.* 87, 90; *Aristob.* 5.11-12).[52]

Several clues in the context of Jn 9.3-4 would indicate that this is an
instance of creation imagery. It is possible that discussions about God's
rest that stemmed from Gen. 2.2-3 are part of the background to the
healing of a man born blind on a Sabbath. Jesus' assertion that he is the
light of the world (9.5; cf. 8.12) and his act of giving sight to a man born
blind invites a link to the prologue, where the Word is associated with
the light (1.4-5, 9) in a context where creation is a prominent idea (1.3,
10).[53] The mention of the devil being a murderer and a liar 'from the
beginning' (8.44, ἀπ' ἀρχῆς) takes John's readers back to Gen. 3, where
the serpent is portrayed as liar.[54] Thus 8.44 might prepare Johannine
readers to see creation imagery in Jn 9.3-4.

As for Jn 10.25, 33, 37-38; 14.10-12; and 15.24, there are few clues in
their literary contexts to suggest that John is evoking Gen. 1–2.[55] Apart
from a few verbal parallels between those texts and Gen. 1–2, it is
difficult to see how Gen. 1–2 would fit into the line of argument that
John is developing. John 17.4 is a more promising text because there the

52. The healing of the man narrated in Jn 5 resurfaces in 7.20-24, but the
discussion there is related to Moses and circumcision, not to God's rest. John seems
to use two arguments to defend Jesus' right to heal on a Sabbath, one based on
God's work (Jn 5) and one based on the practice of circumcision. Cf. Terian,
'Creation', p. 55.

53. Ensor, *Works*, p. 126. Cf. F. Grob, *Faire l'oeuvre de Dieu: Christologie et
éthique dans L'Evangile de Jean* (Paris: Presses Universitaires de France, 1986),
p. 43; Minear, *Christians*, p. 92; C. Koch, 'Geschaffen, um Gott zu sehen. Die
Heilung des Blindgeborenen als „Schöpfungsereignis" in Joh 9,1-38', in *Horizonte
biblischer Texte* (ed. A. Vonach and G. Fischer; OBO, 196; Göttingen: Vandenhoeck
& Ruprecht, 2003), pp. 195–222 (204); M. Rae, 'The Testimony of Works in the
Christology of John's Gospel', in Bauckham and Mosser (eds.), *Gospel of John*,
pp. 295–310 (305–6); Hoskyns, *Gospel*, vol. 2, p. 407; Lightfoot, *John*, p. 199;
Lincoln, *John*, p. 281; von Wahlde, *John*, vol. 2, p. 425. For a reading of Jn 9 in light
of the prologue, see Koch, 'Geschaffen', pp. 201–2.

54. Ensor, *Works*, p. 284 n. 17. The devil was frequently associated with the
serpent of Gen. 3 in Jewish tradition; e.g. Wis. 2.23-24 (see Rev. 12.9; 20.2; *LAE*
16.1–18.3; *2 En.* 31.3-6; cf. *Apoc. Sedr.* 5.1-6; *Apoc. Abr.* 23.1, 11). Cf. E. C.
Bissell, 'The "Protevangelium" and the Eighth Psalm', *JBL* 6 (1886), pp. 64–8 (66);
J. H. Charlesworth, *The Good and Evil Serpent: How a Universal Symbol Became
Christianized* (ABRL; New Haven: Yale University Press, 2010), p. 315; Keener,
John, vol. 1, p. 760; Menken, 'Genesis', p. 91.

55. Painter, 'Earth', p. 78, and idem, 'Inclined', p. 349, thinks that John 'picked
up' the Hebrew '*tob*' (the goodness of God's creation) in Jn 10.32.

phrase 'by completing the works' is used close to a clear reference to the creation of the world (17.5).[56]

In light of all the evidence assessed above, it can be concluded that, on the one hand, John is not making a direct use of Gen. 1–2 when portraying Jesus as performing the works of his Father (Jn 5.20, 36; 9.3-4; 17.4),[57] but he is drawing on and creatively deploying terms, images, and concepts stemming from Gen. 1–2. On the other hand, there is no evidence to take Jn 4.34; 7.3, 21; 10.25, 33, 37-38; 14.10-12; 15.24 as instances of creation imagery.

II. The Place of the Works Performed by Jesus

Now it is time to elucidate the place that the idea of Jesus performing 'works' occupies in John's argument. Five features of this motif will show its prominent and strategic place in GJohn. The first feature is the sheer number of times it figures in several sections of the Gospel. Although references to Jesus performing works are lacking in the first sections of the Gospel (1.1–4.33) and in the passion and resurrection narratives, they appear in 4.34; 5.20, 36; 7.3, 21; 9.3-4; 10.25, 32-33, 37-38; 14.10-12; 15.24; 17.4. If repetition is an indication of importance, it can be concluded that John regarded the idea of Jesus performing works as quite significant.[58]

The second feature is the almost exclusive appearance of those instances on Jesus' lips. Jesus uses the language of 'works' when addressing his disciples (4.34; 9.3, 4; 14.10, 11, 12; 15.24), the Jews (5.20, 36; 10.25, 32, 37, 38), the crowds (7.21), and his Father (17.4). Since the main character in the Johannine narrative is Jesus himself, the reader attributes great importance to his words.[59] The third feature is the use of

---

56. M. Hengel, 'The Old Testament in the Fourth Gospel', *HBT* 12 (1990), pp. 19–41 (33).

57. Droge, 'Sabbath', p. 133; Weidemann, 'Protology', p. 314; Reim, *Studien*, p. 98; Minear, *Christians*, pp. 87–8.

58. The noun ἔργον in relation to Jesus is always accompanied by an article (4.34; 5.36; 7.3; 9.3-4; 10.25, 37-38; 14.10, 11; 17.4) or an adjective (μείζωνα, 5.20; ἕν, 7.21; πολλὰ ἔργα καλὰ, ποῖον, 10.32; καλοῦ, 10.33).

59. John puts the noun ἔργον on the lips of Jesus fifteen times, but he only puts this noun on the lips of other characters twice in his Gospel: once on the Jews' lips (10.33) and once on the lips of Jesus' brothers (7.3). The references to the works performed by Jesus are made when he is in Judea (5.20, 36; 7.21; 9.3-4; 10.25, 32, 37-38; 14.10-12; 15.24; 17.4), although there are also a few instances when he is in Samaria (4.34) and Galilee (7.3).

τὸ ἔργον in conjunction with the verb τελειόω.[60] Jesus uses this combination the first time and the last time he refers to the Father's work (4.34; 17.4). The first time appears along with Jesus' reference to the 'One who sent' him. Jesus speaks of 'the One who sent' him eighteen times in GJohn, and 4.34 is Jesus' first use of this phrase.[61] In between these two instances, there are two miracle stories that are referred to as 'works' (5.20, 36; 9.3, 4).[62]

The fourth feature is that Jesus attributes to God the works that he performs by using the pronoun αὐτοῦ (4.34; 14.10), direct references to God, or peculiar expressions. Jesus indicates that the works that he performs are the works of God (τοῦ θεοῦ, 9.3),[63] the works of his Father (τοῦ πατρός μου, 10.37), or the works of the One who sent him (τοῦ πέμψαντός με, 9.4). Jesus also asserts that he performs works in the name

---

60. A. Vanhoye, 'L'œuvre du Christ, don du Père (Jn 5,36 et 17,4)', *RSR* 48 (1960), pp. 377–419 (415–19); Moloney, *John*, pp. 143, 191; Schnackenburg, *John*, vol. 1, p. 447, and others have argued that there is a distinction between ἔργον (singular) and ἔργα (plural). Moloney, for example, thinks that the singular refers to the whole mission of Jesus, while the plural refers to the deeds Jesus performs. This distinction seems artificial (see Bultmann, *John*, p. 265 n. 6). Jesus uses both the singular (4.34; 17.4) and the plural (5.36) forms along with the verb τελειόω without making any conceptual distinction. The plural form is used more times (5.20, 36; 7.21; 9.3, 4; 10.25, 32, 33, 37, 38; 14.10, 11) than the singular form. Furthermore, in 10.32 the construction has to be understood as plural: διὰ ποῖον αὐτῶν ἔργον, 'for which of those works' (KJV).

61. Michaels, *John*, p. 261.

62. The story in Jn 5 has numerous points of resemblance with the story in Jn 9: the use of the verb ἐργάζομαι (5.17; 9.4), the mention of the Sabbath (5.9, 10, 16, 18; 9.14, 16), the initial inability of the two healed people to identify who the healer was (5.11; 9.12), the Jews' concern for the day of the healing (5.10; 9.16), Jesus' subsequent encounter with the healed person (5.14; 9.35), and the Jews' inquiry about the identity of the healer (5.12-13; 9.12). Cf. Lightfoot, *John*, pp. 16, 138; Bultmann, *John*, p. 239; Culpepper, *Anatomy*, pp. 139–40; J. L. Staley, 'Stumbling in the Dark, Reaching for the Light: Reading Characters in John 5 and 9', *Semeia* 53 (1991), pp. 55–80 (58). Some scholars have also related Jn 9.3-4 to Jn 6.28 (von Wahlde, *John*, vol. 2, p. 425) or Jn 3.21 (Michaels, *John*, pp. 541–2). However, the links between Jn 5 and 9 are stronger (*c.* von Wahlde see Haenchen, *John 2*, p. 37).

63. In Jn 6.28-29 the 'works of God' is used in a context where Jesus' mission is not being described. According to J. D. M. Derrett, 'Τί ἐργάζῃ; (Jn 6,30): An Unrecognized Allusion to Is 45,9', *ZNW* 84 (1993), pp. 142–4, Jn 6.30 is an instance of irony in which the creation (the crowd) asks the Creator: 'What work do you do?' Derrett finds this same irony in Isa. 45.9, 'Shall the clay say to the potter, "What are you doing, since you are not working, nor do you have hands?"'

of his Father (10.25), that his works are 'from the Father' (10.32), and that the Father gave him 'works' to complete (5.36; 17.4). He even claims, 'the Father who dwells in me does the works' (14.10; cf. 5.20).

The fifth feature surfaces when comparing GJohn with the other canonical gospels. There are a few instances where ἔργον is related to Jesus in the Synoptic Gospels (Mt. 11.2; Lk. 24.19),[64] but only in Mt. 11.19 is this noun put on the lips of Jesus: 'wisdom (ἡ σοφία) is vindicated by her deeds (ἔργων)'. Here it is implied that although both Jesus and John were rejected by 'this generation' (11.16), their final vindication will be based on their 'deeds'.[65] Unlike GJohn, the Synoptic Gospels do not indicate that Jesus' works were directly related to God's works. The Synoptic Gospels use the nouns δύναμις (Mt. 11.20, 21, 23; 13.58; Mk 6.2, 5; Lk. 10.13; 19.37), σημεῖον (Mt. 12.38; Mk 8.11; Lk. 11.16, 29; 23.8; cf. Jn 2.11, 18, 23; 3.2; 4.48, 54; 6.2, 14, 26, 30; 7.31; 9.16; 10.41; 11.47; 12.18, 37; 20.30-31), and τέρας (Mt. 24.24; Mk 13.22; cf. Jn 4.48; Acts 2.22) to refer to miracles, but John distinctively puts ἔργον on the lips of Jesus in contexts where miracles are in view (5.20, 36; 9.3; 10.25).[66] Furthermore, John uniquely links the noun ἔργον and Jesus' miracles to Sabbath controversies.[67]

In sum, when referring to Jesus, ἔργον seems to occupy an important place in Johannine thought.[68] Phrases such as 'the works of my Father', 'the works of God', and 'the works of the One who sent me' are distinctively Johannine. The noun ἔργον is used in several strategic places in GJohn (e.g. Sabbath controversies), bracketing most of Jesus' earthly ministry (4.34; 17.4).

---

64. In Mt. 11.2 the narrator says that John the Baptist heard about 'the deeds of Christ' (τὰ ἔργα τοῦ Χριστοῦ), and in Lk. 24.19 Cleopas tells the one who was walking with him that Jesus the Nazarene was a prophet powerful in 'deed and word' (ἐν ἔργῳ καὶ λόγῳ). The noun ἔργον is also used to refer to 'good' (Mt. 5.16; 26.10; Mk 14.6) or 'bad' (Mt. 23.3, 5; Lk. 11.48; cf. ἐργάται in Lk. 13.27) human deeds or to the physical work of a servant (Mk 13.34; cf. ἐργάζωμαι and ἐργάτης in Mt. 9.37, 38; 20.1, 2, 8; 21.28; Lk. 10.2).

65. J. Nolland, *The Gospel of Matthew: A Commentary on the Greek Text* (NIGTC; Grand Rapids: Eerdmans, 2005), p. 464.

66. H. Van den Bussche, 'La structure de Jean I-XII', in *L'Évangile de Jean: Études et Problèmes* (RechBib, 3; Bruges: Desclée De Brouwer, 1958), pp. 61–109 (79), asserted that there is not a 'material' distinction between 'signs' and 'works' in GJohn, but their *valeur de signification* is different.

67. Dodd, *Interpretation*, p. 320.

68. M. de Jonge, 'Signs and Works in the Fourth Gospel', in *Miscellanea Neotestamentica* (ed. T. Baarda, A. F. I. Klijn, and W. C. van Unnik; NovTSup, 48; Leiden: Brill, 1978), pp. 107–26 (122).

III. The Significance of the Works Performed by Jesus

John seems to draw on and creatively deploy terms and images stemming from Gen. 1–2 in Jn 5.20, 36; 9.3-4; 17.4. Furthermore, Jewish discussions about God's rest after creation seem to be part of the background to 5.17, 20, 36; 9.3-4. The question that needs to be answered now is how John uses those instances of creation imagery.

a. *The Works Performed by Jesus and Creation Imagery*

In Jn 5 the narrator identifies a particular day in his narrative for the first time: ἦν δὲ σάββατον ἐν ἐκείνῃ τῇ ἡμέρᾳ (5.9).[69] In this temporal setting Jesus claims that he is 'working' (5.17; cf. v. 36) and asserts that he will perform 'greater works' (5.20). Since the previous miracle is referred to as σημεῖα καὶ τέρατα (4.48), it is striking that this miracle is called 'work' (5.20, 36).

The idea of Jesus performing works is used in order to portray him in close association with his Father. Jesus claims that his Father is working until now and he too is working (5.17). The Jews do not dispute that God is able to work 'until now', perhaps because they would agree that the Creator is still active after creation (e.g. Philo, *Leg. All.* 1.1-6; *Cher.* 87, 90; *Aristob.* 5.11-12). However, they persecute Jesus because he is healing a man on the Sabbath (5.16, 18). By claiming that not only 'his Father' but also he himself are authorized to work on the Sabbath, Jesus is declaring his unique relationship with him.[70]

The narrator reports that the Jews realize that Jesus is calling God his own Father and that they see in Jesus' words a claim of equality with God (5.18). In the following verses Jesus will refer several times to the Son and the Father (5.19, 20, 21, 22, 23, 26),[71] but he never mentions that he is making himself 'equal with God'. On the one hand, it seems that 'making himself equal with God' would imply independence from God and a challenge to the distinction between Creator and creation.[72] On the

69. John often indicates the temporal settings of his narrative: e.g. 'on the next day' (1.29, 35, 43), 'on the third day' (2.1; cf. 2.19), 'a few days' (2.12), 'two days' (4.40), 'after two days' (4.43), 'it was about the tenth hour' (1.39), 'at night' (3.2), 'about the sixth hour' (4.6), 'yesterday at the seventh hour' (4.52; cf. 4.53).

70. Lightfoot, *John*, pp. 139, 141, 150; Bultmann, *John*, p. 246; Lindars, *John*, p. 229; R. Hakola, *Identity Matters: John, the Jews and Jewishness* (NovTSup, 118; Leiden: Brill, 2005), pp. 120, 126, 134. Some scholars suggest Jesus is making here a claim to divinity (Michaels, *John*, p. 304; von Wahlde, *John*, vol. 2, pp. 221, 259; cf. Hoskyns, *Gospel*, vol. 1, p. 296; Carson, *John*, p. 251).

71. Haenchen, *John 1*, p. 248; Lightfoot, *John*, p. 139; Carson, *John*, p. 249.

72. Hakola, *Identity*, p. 126 n. 48; Barrett, *John*, p. 256 (e.g. 1 Kgs 8.23; Isa. 40.25; Jer. 10.6). The phrase 'equal with God' is echoed in other texts, and seems to

other hand, neither Jesus nor the narrator rejects the assertion that he is 'equal with God'.[73] Instead, the following verses can be deemed to explain the close and unique relationship between the Son and the Father.[74] Similarly to the prologue, where the phrase θεὸς ἦν ὁ λόγος (1.1) is bracketed by πρὸς τὸν θεόν (1.1-2), and μονογενής is accompanied by παρὰ πατρός and ὁ ὢν εἰς τὸν κόλπον τοῦ πατρὸς (1.14, 18), here too the unique relationship between Jesus and his Father, described as 'equality with God' (5.18), is clarified by the following verses.

    This clarification includes two elements. The first element is Jesus' indirect negation that he is 'making' (ποιῶν, 5.18) himself something. Instead, he asserts that the Son can do (ποιεῖν) nothing by himself (ἀφ᾽ ἑαυτοῦ, v. 19; ἀπ᾽ ἐμαυτοῦ, v. 30); rather, whatever the Father 'does' (ποιῇ; cf. ποιοῦντα), the Son does (ποιεῖ) likewise (v. 19).[75] The second element is Jesus' description of his relationship with the Father in terms of dependence, not independence.[76] Jesus' right to work on the Sabbath is grounded in his dependence on the Father. Jesus does what he sees his Father doing (5.19; cf. 3.32; 8.38), he judges according to what he hears from the Father (3.32; 5.30), and he seeks the will of the One who sent him (5.30; cf. 4.34). The relationship between the Father and the Son is also asserted in terms of love (5.20): as the Father gave glory to Jesus because he loved (ἠγάπησας) him before the foundation of the wold (17.24), so the Father shows the Son everything he does because he loves (φιλεῖ) him (5.20). This relationship of dependence between the Son and

be a common expression for human arrogance and pride (e.g. Gen. 3.5; Isa. 14.14; Ezek. 28.2; 2 Macc. 9.12; Philo, *Leg. All.* 1.49). See W. A. Meeks, 'Equal to God', in Fortna and Gaventa (eds.), *The Conversation Continues*, pp. 309–21 (312); Dodd, *Interpretation*, pp. 326–7; Carson, *John*, p. 249. Some scholars have suggested a close link between Jn 5.18 and Gen. 3.5-6 (cf. Brown, *John*, vol. 1, p. 213; von Wahlde, *John*, vol. 2, p. 222; Hakola, *Identity*, p. 126), but the lack of signifi-cant similar vocabulary deters us from exploring this possibility further. See also E. W. Grinfield, *The Christian Cosmos: The Son of God the Revealed Creator* (London: Seeley, Jackson & Halliday, 1857), p. 50, who said the Jews 'probably suspected him [Jesus] of claiming to be the Creator'.

    73.   Some scholars believe that the Jews are asserting something that is truth within the narrative world of GJohn, i.e. that Jesus is equal with God (e.g. Bultmann, *John*, p. 244; Lightfoot, *John*, p. 139; Moloney, *John*, p. 170; Michaels, *John*, p. 307), while other scholars deem that 'equal with God' is a misleading interpreta-tion of the declaration of Jesus (e.g. Beasley-Murray, *John*, p. 75; Haenchen, *John 1*, p. 249; Dodd, *Interpretation*, p. 328; Keener, *John*, vol. 1, pp. 646–7).

    74.   Barrett, *John*, p. 256; Lightfoot, *John*, p. 141.

    75.   Michaels, *John*, p. 307; Keener, *John*, vol. 1, p. 648; von Wahlde, *John*, vol. 2, p. 222; Lincoln, *John*, p. 202.

    76.   Bultmann, *John*, p. 245; Moloney, *John*, p. 170; Lightfoot, *John*, p. 139.

his Father allows Jesus to claim that he will receive the same honour his Father receives from people (5.23).

Therefore, Jesus is to be seen at the side of the Creator God, who has been at work since the creation of the world 'until now' (5.17), and not on the side of creation.[77] Jesus has demonstrated that he has authority over God's creation (a sick man, 5.8), and has implied that the Sabbath regulation that binds creation does not apply to him.[78] Unlike humankind, which received life from God (Gen. 2.7) through the Word (Jn 1.4), Jesus has been granted life in himself (ἐν ἑαυτῷ, 5.26; cf. 1.4).[79]

Jesus' position in relation to his Father legitimizes his participation in divine activities.[80] Jesus claims that the Father will show him 'greater works' (μείζονα ἔργα, 5.20) that are related to his right to give life and to execute judgement (5.21-30).[81] In Jewish thought working on the Sabbath, the bestowal of life, and the execution of judgement were regarded as God's prerogatives (5.21, 26, 27).[82] Those divine rights and authority are granted to Jesus, who is executing them in the present and will execute them in the future. Since the Father raises (ἐγείρει) the dead and makes them live (v. 21), those who listen to Jesus' voice and believe the Father can now possess eternal life, avoid condemnation, and cross over from death to life (v. 24). Jesus has even already 'raised' (ἔγειρε) a man with the authority of his voice (5.8).[83] Likewise, in the future the

---

77. Borgen, *Early Christianity*, p. 116, concludes, 'the Sabbath issue contributed to the formulation of a "high Christology"' in the community behind GJohn.

78. Moloney, *John*, p. 170; Beasley-Murray, *John*, p. 75; Lindars, *John*, p. 218; Bultmann, *John*, pp. 245–6; Carson, *John*, pp. 247, 249.

79. See Keener, *John*, vol. 2, p. 645.

80. Barrett, *John*, p. 266.

81. Moloney, *John*, p. 182; Lincoln, *John*, p. 203; von Wahlde, *John*, vol. 2, pp. 231, 244, 252; Dodd, *Interpretation*, p. 326. Other scholars suggest that the 'greater works' are further miracles (e.g. Beasley-Murray, *John*, p. 76) or Jesus' death and resurrection (e.g. Keener, *John*, vol. 1, p. 648; cf. Hoskyns, *Gospel*, vol. 1, p. 303). However, neither Jesus' other miracles (e.g. the healing of a man born blind or Lazarus' resurrection) nor his resurrection is labelled 'greater works' in GJohn.

82. Gen. 1–3; Deut. 32.39; 1 Sam. 2.6; 2 Kgs 5.7; Ezek. 37.3-12; Hos. 6.2; Wis. 16.13 (Hoskyns, *Gospel*, vol. 1, p. 299; Lightfoot, *John*, p. 142; Barrett, *John*, p. 260; von Wahlde, *John*, vol. 2, pp. 221, 244; Carson, *John*, pp. 250–2; Keener, *John*, vol. 1, p. 645).

83. Borgen, 'Creation', p. 90. E. Straub, 'Alles ist durch ihn geworden. Die Erschaffung des Lebens in der Sabbatheilung Joh 5,1-18', in *Studien zu Matthäus und Johannes / Études sur Matthieu et Jean* (ed. A. Dettwiler and U. Poplutz; ATANT, 97; Zurich: Theologischer Verlag Zürich, 2009), pp. 157–67 (160), has observed that 5.3 ('a great number of sick, blind, lame, and paralyzed people') and

dead will hear the voice of the Son of God and will come out of their tombs to receive either life or condemnation (vv. 25, 28-29).[84]

The works that Jesus performs are also intended to link past and present reality with future reality. In the prologue the Word who was in the beginning with God partook in the divine activity of creation (1.3, 10), bringing life and light unto humankind (1.4-5). Now Jesus is working along with his Father (5.17) and will continue doing greater works: the dead will hear (ἀκούσουσιν, 5.25, 28) the voice of the Son of God, they will come out of their tombs (ἐκπορεύσονται, 5.29), and they will live (ζήσουσιν, 5.25). Through his works Jesus makes known that the Father is still active and will continue being active, bringing life and judgement into his creation. Therefore, Jesus is to be regarded both as the agent of creation (1.3, 10) and as the agent of revelation, judgement, and redemption.

The Sabbath does not limit the works the Father has given to Jesus. In addition, the Father's works are not restricted to a particular group. The divine work of judgement will result in 'all people' (πάντες) honouring both the Father and Jesus (5.23). Likewise, the divine work of giving life will be available to 'all (πάντες) who are in the tombs' (5.28). Jesus can perform these works of universal significance because of his claim over 'everything' that the Father has. The Father shows the Son 'everything' (πάντα) he does (5.20) and has given to him 'all' (πᾶσαν) judgement (5.22). For the reader who knows that 'everything' (πάντα) was created through the Word (1.3),[85] it is no surprise that he will continue performing divine works that will have a universal significance.

Jesus' decision to 'raise' just one person (5.6) foreshadows 5.21, 'the Son gives life to whomever he wishes' (cf. Minear, *Christians*, p. 87). Straub also suggests that Jesus' question in 5.6 ('Do you want [θέλεις] to become well?') is related to Jesus' words in 5.40, 'you are not willing (θέλετε) to come to me'. Those parallels would indicate that the miracle in Jn 5 refers to Jesus giving life to a man (Borgen, 'Creation', p. 92; Straub, 'Erschaffung', p. 160; cf. Lincoln, *John*, pp. 199–200). For a different opinion, see Bultmann, *John*, p. 246.

84.   Unlike those who hear the voice (τῆς φωνῆς, vv. 25, 28) of Jesus and his message (τὸν λόγον μου, v. 24), the Jews are portrayed as never having heard God's voice (φωνὴν αὐτοῦ, 5.37) and as not having God's word (τὸν λόγον αὐτοῦ) in them (5.38). Cf. Straub, 'Erschaffung', pp. 161, 166; Swart, 'Sabbath', pp. 580–1; Koester, *Symbolism*, p. 93. X. Léon-Dufour, *Lecture de l'Évangile selon Jean* (4 vols.; Paris: Seuil, 1990), vol. 2, p. 80, and Rae, 'Works', p. 297 n. 4, see here a link to Gen. 1, where God's word is related to creation (cf. Sir. 42.15). However, there is a lack of verbal parallels between 'God's word' in Gen. 1 and Jn 5.

85.   Painter, 'Light', p. 40.

The noun 'work' in relation to Jesus also occurs in 5.36. There it asserts the primal significance of Jesus and the message about him and it privileges him over other important figures.[86] One of those figures is John, whom people regard highly in GJohn, since the Jews[87] 'wanted to rejoice greatly for a while in his light' (5.35). Although John shed light upon those who heard him (5.35; cf. 1.7), he was merely a lamp (5.35), not the light (1.8-9). He was a witness to the truth (5.33), but the reader knows he was not the 'true light' (1.9). John's testimony was important, but the works the Father gave Jesus to complete are a 'greater testimony' (5.36).[88] Those works associate Jesus with the Father in a unique way, because both are working on the Sabbath (5.17-20). Since Jesus is able to perform those divine works, he and his message are to be regarded as privileged over John's.

The other figure mentioned in Jn 5.36-47 is Moses. He is also well regarded by the Jews, since they have placed their hopes in him (5.45). However, Moses is not a competitor with Jesus, because John portrays him as being a witness to Jesus. John describes Moses as having written about Jesus himself (5.46). Since the law was given through Moses (1.17), the reference to 'Scripture' in 5.39 can also be an indication that Moses was a witness to Jesus through the Scripture he wrote. By implication, Jesus is to be regarded as existing 'before' Moses (cf. 1.15; 8.58).[89] Jesus, who is at the side of the Creator God (1.3, 10) and who is authorized to work on the Sabbath (5.17, 36), is privileged over Moses.[90]

---

86. The noun certainly refers to what he has done on the Sabbath (5.17). See Brown, *John*, vol. 1, p. 224; Lindars, *John*, p. 22; Lincoln, *John*, p. 206. Others deem that 'works' in 5.36 includes also the whole activity of Jesus in his earthly ministry (Bultmann, *John*, p. 265; Lightfoot, *John*, p. 146; Carson, *John*, p. 261).

87. In light of 5.33, Jesus seems to be talking to the Jews here (cf. 1.19-28; 5.16).

88. Some manuscripts (e.g. Papyrus[66] A B) have the nominative case and masculine gender μείζων, 'I who am greater than John'. This reading makes clearer our point that the works that Jesus performs privilege him over John. However, it is better to follow the shorter reading μείζω (e.g. א L Θ Majority text), because this reading explains the origin of the former. Since the two previous words before μείζω end with ν, it is possible to think that a copyist unintentionally added a ν to μείζω. Cf. Hoskyns, *Gospel*, vol. 1, p. 303; Barrett, *John*, p. 266; Carson, *John*, p. 261 n. 3.

89. Some scholars have attempted to find indications of the pre-existence of Jesus in Jn 5. They argue that Jesus received the works from the Father (5.36) in his pre-existence (Bultmann, *John*, p. 254) and that the 'seeing' of Jesus in 5.19 is 'intrinsically related' to the notion of his pre-existence in heaven (von Wahlde, *John*, vol. 2, p. 241). However, it is difficult to nail down the idea of pre-existence in Jn 5, since there are no explicit indications of it there (cf. Michaels, *John*, pp. 302, 308).

90. Moses and the practice of circumcision are referred to in 7.20-24, where Jesus discusses his right to perform works on the Sabbath.

John uses the works that Jesus performs to assert the primal significance of Jesus and to privilege him over John and Moses.[91]

At several points in this discussion, I have noticed how the prologue relates to Jn 5. Here I would like to underscore further links between the two texts. In the prologue the Word is portrayed as the one through whom everything was created (1.3). But although he was behind the divine work of creation, the world did not recognise him (1.10). Notwithstanding this rejection, those who believe in his name receive the right to become God's children (1.12), because while no one has ever seen God, the Word made flesh has made him known (1.18). This Word made flesh took up residence among 'us' (1.14). Similarly, Jesus claims that the Father is behind the works that he performs on the Sabbath (5.19-20, 36). But although he does what the Father has given him to do, the Jews persecute him (5.16), try to kill him (5.18), and are not willing to come to him (5.40). They have failed to receive the one who has come in the Father's name (5.43), because they have never seen God (5.37). Therefore, the word of God has not taken up residence in them (5.38). These literary connections between the two texts help the reader to relate the Word's work of creation in the beginning with Jesus' earthly ministry.

The other mention of Jesus performing the works of the Father on a Sabbath occurs in Jn 9.3-4. Unlike in Jn 5, in Jn 9.3-4 the reference to the works that Jesus performs comes in a dialogue with his disciples, not with the Jews.[92] In the preceding context (Jn 8) Jesus has made at least two claims. The first claim is that one's identity is directly related to one's paternity; one's paternity is reflected in the 'works' one performs. If the Jews try to kill Jesus, they should be linked to a killer, and since the devil has been a killer from the beginning, the devil should be their father (8.38-44; cf. 10.10). Conversely, if Jesus can demonstrate that he[93]

91. Von Wahlde, *John*, vol. 2, p. 246.

92. The mention of the disciples here is perhaps striking, since the last time John mentioned them was in 6.71 (cf. 7.3; 8.31). See Bultmann, *John*, p. 330; Brown, *John*, vol. 1, p. 371; Lightfoot, *John*, p. 202; von Wahlde, *John*, vol. 2, p. 424. If these disciples are the twelve, 'this is the first indication that they came up to Jerusalem with Jesus' (Brown, *John*, vol. 1, p. 371; cf. Michaels, *John*, p. 542).

93. Traditionally it has been suggested that 'we' refers to 'Jesus and his disciples' (Brown, *John*, vol. 1, p. 372; Barrett, *John*, p. 357; Schnackenburg, *John*, vol. 2, p. 241; Hoskyns, *Gospel*, vol. 2, p. 406; Lightfoot, *John*, p. 202; Moloney, *John*, p. 291; Beasley-Murray, *John*, p. 155; Carson, *John*, p. 362; Keener, *John*, vol. 1, p. 779). J. L. Martyn, *History and Theology in the Fourth Gospel* (Louisville: John Knox, 3rd edn, 2003), p. 28, saw here the voice of the 'Johannine Church'. C. H. Dodd, *Historical Tradition in the Fourth Gospel* (Cambridge: Cambridge University Press, 1963), p. 186, proposed this to be part of 'proverbial wisdom', where 'we' refers to humankind generally. A. von Harnack, *Das 'Wir' in den Johanneischen*

performs the works of the One who in the beginning brought light to his creation (Gen. 1.3), he will be able to claim he is the Son of God (8.28, 38, 42; cf. 8.23). The second claim is that Jesus existed 'before Abraham' (8.58). To support both claims, Jesus performs a 'work' (9.4) by bringing light into God's creation, represented by a man born blind (9.1-7).[94] By performing this miracle, Jesus manifests nothing but the 'works of God' in this man (9.3).[95] Just as in Jn 5 Jesus said that he performs divine activities such as bringing life and judgement, here too in Jn 9 Jesus performs divine activities such as bringing light (9.1-7) and judgement (9.39-41; cf. 8.16, 26).[96]

In light of this, the reader cannot conclude with some of the characters in the narrative that Jesus is associated with demons (8.48, 52; cf. 10.21).[97] Rather, the reader realizes that Jesus exists in close association with his Father and apart from the created order. This legitimizes his participation in divine activities. Jesus is regarded here as the privileged agent of revelation,[98] whose activities cannot be limited by the Sabbath

Schriften (SPAW; Berlin: Akademie der Wissenschaften, 1923), p. 107, took 'we' as an emphasized 'I' (cf. 3.11). More recently, Michaels, *John*, p. 543; J. C. Poirier, '"Day and Night" and the Sabbath Controversy of John 9', *FN* 19 (2006), pp. 113–19 (117); J. D. M. Derrett, 'Miracles, Pools, and Sight: John 9,1-41; Genesis 2,6-7; Isaiah 6,10; 30,20, 35,5-7', *BeO* 36 (1994), pp. 71–85 (73), have argued that 'we' includes Jesus and the man born blind. In light of Jn 4.34-38 and 14.12 (cf. 20.21), it is possible to think that Jesus is including his disciples here, although none of them helps him to heal the blind man. Whatever option one takes, it should be acknowledged that 'we' is a difficult textual variant.

94. Lindars, *John*, pp. 341–2.

95. A few scholars have proposed that Jesus' answer ends with 'his parents sinned[.]' and that a new mini-discourse is found in 9.3b-4, '[B]ut in order that the works of God...no one can work'. W. H. Spencer, 'John ix.3', *ExpTim* 55 (1944), p. 110; J. C. Poirier, '"Day and Night" and the Punctuation of John 9.3', *NTS* 42 (1996), pp. 288–94; Poirier, 'John 9', pp. 113–19. This punctuation 'relieves the text of a bizarre theodicy' (Poirier, 'John 9.3', p. 294), but does not affect our point here, that this miracle is a manifestation of the works of God in favour of God's creation. Poirier's suggestion has been challenged by T. Nicklas, *Ablösung und Verstrickung: 'Juden' und Jüngergestalten als Charaktere der erzählten Welt des Johannesevangeliums und ihre Wirkung auf den impliziten Leser* (RST, 60; Frankfurt: Peter Lang, 2002), pp. 313–14 (cf. Keener, *John*, vol. 1, p. 779).

96. Lightfoot, *John*, p. 199, has rightly observed that both life and light are important ideas in the prologue in relation to the Word, and that life figures prominently in Jn 5, while light is used in Jn 9. Cf. Terian, 'Creation', pp. 54, 60. Elsewhere in GJohn, references to God's works are located close to references to 'life' (10.25-38; 14.6-19; 17.2-4).

97. Painter, 'Earth', p. 78.

98. Cf. φανερωθῇ in 9.3.

(9.14, 16).[99] At the same time, the work of God performed by Jesus in Jn 9 can be seen as an illustration of his earlier claim that he existed before Abraham (8.58), because he demonstrates that he is able to bring light into God's creation. This singular miracle (cf. 9.32; 15.24) indicates that Jesus and the message about him are privileged over this patriarchal figure.

The third instance where John seems to draw on and creatively deploy terms and images stemming from Gen. 1–2 in his portrayal of Jesus performing works is in Jn 17.4. Here Jesus asserts that he has glorified the Father on earth by performing his work (v. 4).[100] Jesus' authority to give people eternal life (17.2) is related to the work he has performed. Since eternal life is achieved by knowing the only true God (17.3), and since Jesus has made God known (cf. 1.18),[101] the way to obtain eternal life is by knowing the only true God as revealed by Jesus Christ (17.3). Jesus has the authority to reveal God (and therefore to give life) because the Father has granted him authority over all humanity (17.2). This is part of the glory Jesus has received from the Father, a universal authority to reveal God and to bestow life. Those who receive eternal life through Jesus can relate properly to God. Therefore, the Father is glorified when people know him through Jesus Christ. This is part of the glory Jesus gives to the Father, a proper relationship between him and those who believe (cf. 5.20-23).

The work that Jesus has completed (17.4) appears here in relation to the authority he has received over all humanity (17.2)[102] and is used

99. Although some scholars have attempted to see the 'Sabbath' elsewhere in GJohn, this day is explicitly referred to only in relation to Jesus' two healings (Jn 5.9, 10, 16, 18; 7.22, 23; 9.14, 16) and in 19.31 (cf. 20.1, 19). See also the reading of Jn 6.59 preserved in D (Mk 1.21; Lk. 4.16, 31). I have found unpersuasive Droge's suggestions ('Sabbath', pp. 131–3) that the Sabbath is referred to in Jn 1.19–2.1, in the story of Jesus and the Samaritan, and in the resurrection of Lazarus. Consider, for example, the way that Droge 'discovers' the number 'seven' in Jn 4, 'the Samaritan woman has had five husbands, a lover, and now Jesus' (p. 133 n. 51).

100. The reading ετελειωσα (aorist indicative) can be related to the rest of v. 4 only if the conjunction και is added (D). Otherwise, v. 4 has to be seen as having two sentences. Although this is possible, it is better to follow the earliest reading, τελειώσας (e.g. Papyrus[66] ℵ A B C), and to relate it to the verb ἐδόξασα.

101. Moloney, *John*, p. 460.

102. Commentators typically observe that 'all flesh' refers to humanity in the broadest possible sense. Lightfoot, *John*, p. 300, regarded 'all flesh' as referring to humankind as contrasted with God (cf. Gen. 9.17; Num. 16.22; Ps. 78.39; Isa. 40.5; 49.26; Ezek. 21.4; Sir. 17.4; 39.19; 4Q511 35 1 [בכול בשר]; *Jub.* 25.22; Rom. 3.20). See Keener, *John*, vol. 2, p. 1053 n. 37; Lindars, *John*, p. 518.

to link past reality with present and future reality.[103] Jesus has the power to execute judgement over all humanity (5.20-23) and to confer life to those the Father has given him (17.2).[104] Therefore, the significance of Jesus is universal in scope.[105] The divine activities Jesus has completed (bringing life and executing judgement) warrant his petition for a future glorification (17.5).[106] But the works that he performs are possible because the Father has granted him authority in the past.[107] These ideas (17.1-4) support some of the claims found in the prologue: as the Word who was with God in the beginning (1.1-2) and had life in himself (1.4) came in the flesh from the Father, displaying glory (1.14) in order to make God known (1.18), so Jesus Christ makes known the only true God (17.3) because he shares the glory of his Father (17.1-4) and has received authority over all flesh to give eternal life (17.2).[108]

b. *The Works Performed by Jesus Elsewhere in GJohn*
The language of 'works' is deployed in other places in GJohn where there is no clear evidence of creation imagery.[109] I will now briefly consider those instances (4.34; 10.25, 32-33, 37-38; 14.10-11; 15.24),[110]

---

103.   Bultmann, *John*, p. 496. Bultmann also deemed that the knowledge of God through Jesus allows man to find 'his way back to his Creator' and, therefore, the world can recover its character of creation (pp. 495–6).

104.   Brown, *John*, vol. 2, p. 740; Schnackenburg, *John*, vol. 3, p. 171; Bultmann, *John*, pp. 494, 496; Moloney, *John*, p. 461.

105.   Beasley-Murray, *John*, p. 296; Hoskyns, *Gospel*, vol. 2, p. 590; Schnackenburg, *John*, vol. 3, p. 171; Lightfoot, *John*, p. 297. Haenchen, *John 2*, p. 150, thinks that the universal authority Jesus received is a 'hyperbole' because 'it exaggerates the reality'. However, in the literary world of John, Jesus' universal authority is real (cf. 3.16, 35; 12.31-32; 13.3). Some commentators argue that the power Jesus has to give life is limited to those the Father has given him (17.2; e.g. Brown, *John*, vol. 2, p. 740). However, through his disciples, Jesus will be able to give 'the world' the opportunity to believe in him (17.20-21; 20.21-22) and, therefore, to achieve eternal life.

106.   Barrett, *John*, p. 504; Haenchen, *John 2*, p. 151.

107.   Moloney, *John*, p. 463, saw in the aorist ἔδωκας (17.2) a reference to the incarnation (1.14). According to Barrett, *John*, p. 502, it is also possible to see in this verse a reference to a time previous to the incarnation (thus Carson, *John*, p. 555).

108.   Schnackenburg, *John*, vol. 3, p. 172; Bultmann, *John*, p. 494 n. 6; Moloney, *John*, pp. 461, 464; Lightfoot, *John*, p. 300; Barrett, *John*, p. 502; von Wahlde, *John*, vol. 2, p. 717; Haenchen, *John 2*, p. 151; Michaels, *John*, p. 859; Keener, *John*, vol. 2, p. 1054.

109.   For a different opinion, see Rae, 'Works', pp. 302–8 (cf. Weidemann, 'Protology', p. 315; Painter, 'Earth', p. 77).

110.   In Jn 7.3 Jesus' brothers advise him to go to Judea so his disciples may see his 'works'. Since it has been stated clearly that the work that Jesus performs is the

highlighting how they support some of the ideas found in Jn 5.17, 20, 36; 9.3-4; 17.4.

There is in Jn 4.34 a close association between Jesus and the One who sent him.[111] Jesus takes part in the work of the Father in order to complete it. It is implied that both the Father and the Son are at work. This idea is illustrated in 4.38, where Jesus indicates to his disciples that there are 'others' who 'have laboured' (ἄλλοι κεκοπιάκασιν). In context, the only one who has been 'working' is Jesus, since he has been fulfilling his mission while talking to the Samaritan woman. However, the reader learns in 4.34 that what Jesus does is nothing but the work of the Father. Therefore, one can conclude that 'others' in 4.38 is a reference to both the Father and the Son (cf. 5.17).[112] This association between Jesus and his Father is unique, since he was not sent as a witness to the Father (cf. John as a witness of Jesus; 1.7; 3.28), nor was he sent to reap the fruits of the work of God (as the disciples are sent, 4.38). Jesus was sent to complete God's work.[113]

Jesus performing the work of the Father is related, in the context of Jn 4, to his partaking in the divine activity of offering eternal life to people beyond Israel. Scholars have disputed the meaning of 'work' in

---

work of the Father (αὐτοῦ τὸ ἔργον, 4.34; cf. 5.36), it is perhaps surprising that Jesus' brothers say 'your works' (σοῦ τὰ ἔργα, 7.3). Since Jesus has said that he does not receive honour from men (5.41), it is confusing that his brothers see Jesus' works as a source of reputation for himself (7.4). These observations, along with John's comment that Jesus' brothers do not believe in him (7.5), may indicate that they did not understand the meaning of Jesus performing the works of the Father as a witness to his close association with God. Several manuscripts indicate that Jesus' brothers say 'your works' or the 'works that you perform' in 7.3: σοῦ τὰ ἔργα (e.g. Papyrus[66]), τὰ ἔργα σοῦ (e.g. L W Ψ), τὰ ἔργα ἅ σὺ (e.g. Θ). Other manuscripts do not have the possessive pronoun (e.g. ℵ* D). Here I follow the earliest reading, σοῦ τὰ ἔργα.

111.   Lindars, *John*, p. 194, even sees in Jn 4.34 a 'complete identity of will' between Jesus and the Father (cf. Schnackenburg, *John*, vol. 1, p. 448).

112.   Schnackenburg, *John*, vol. 1, p. 447. Bultmann, *John*, p. 199, opined that 'others' in 4.38 cannot refer to the Father and Jesus, since the Father works through the Son. However, in Jn 5.17 it is clear that both Jesus and his Father are working. Bultmann suggested that 'others' might refer to the Baptist and the disciples, but both have been absent from the narrative in 4.7-30. Other suggestions (John and John's disciples, John and Jesus, Moses and the prophets; Michaels, *John*, p. 266) are not convincing because none of those characters (apart from Jesus) plays an important role in 4.4-30. Cf. J. A. T. Robinson, 'The "Others" of John 4,38: A Test of Exegetical Method', *SE* 1 (1959), pp. 510–15.

113.   In Jn 4.34 and 5.36 Jesus is portrayed as being sent (πέμψαντος, ἀπέσταλ-κεν) by the Father. Additionally, Vanhoye has observed several verbal parallels between 5.36 and 17.4 ('L'œuvre', p. 378).

4.34,[114] but its meaning should first be related to what Jesus has been doing in Jn 4.7-33. According to those verses, Jesus has been offering the Samaritan woman 'eternal life' (4.10, 14; cf. v. 36), since he himself is the one who gives life. In light of this, the work of Jesus seems to be not only offering life but also actually bestowing it. In the prologue the reader has learned that the one who was involved in the creation of the world gives light to 'everyone' (πάντα ἄνθρωπον, 1.9) and gives people the possibility of becoming children of God (1.12). Here in Jn 4.34 the reader finds confirmation of that, since the one who does the works of the Father is offering life to a Samaritan woman. The gift that Jesus offers has significance beyond Israel.[115]

Jesus has referred to the works of his Father in dialogues with his disciples (4.34; 9.3-4) and in discussions with the Jews (5.20, 36). Jesus will again refer to them in a discussion with the Jews (10.25, 32-33, 37-38)[116] and in a dialogue with his disciples (14.10-12; cf. 15.24). In his last direct encounter with the Jews (Jn 10)[117] Jesus uses the works that he performs to support his claim that he has a close and a unique relationship with his Father.[118] In Jn 8.39-59 Jesus asserted that one's works reveal one's father. Jesus illustrated this point by performing a work of the One who sent him (9.3-6). Here in Jn 10 Jesus will again claim that he is the Son of God (10.36), because he performs the works of his Father (10.37-38). Jesus' discourse in Jn 10.25-38 supports the claim about his unique association with his Father found in 5.17-47.[119]

Jesus asserts in 10.25 that the works that he performs in his Father's name (ἐν τῷ ὀνόματι τοῦ πατρός μου) testify about him (μαρτυρεῖ περὶ ἐμοῦ). In context, these works testify that he is the Christ (10.24), the Son

114. Lightfoot, *John*, p. 125; Bultmann, *John*, p. 194 n. 3; Michaels, *John*, p. 267; Moloney, *John*, p. 143, and others.

115. Cf. Hoskyns, *Gospel*, vol. 1, p. 270.

116. M. Asiedu-Peprah, *Johannine Sabbath Conflicts as Juridical Controversy* (WUNT, 2/132; Tübingen: J. C. B. Mohr, 2001), pp. 24–5, considers that the controversy between the Jews and Jesus begins in Jn 5.1-47, is developed in 9.1–10.18, and concludes in 10.19-21.

117. Lightfoot, *John*, p. 211.

118. Bultmann, *John*, p. 362 n. 5, rightly observed that Jesus' discourse in Jn 10 is 'framed by the ἔργα motif'.

119. Beasley-Murray, *John*, p. 174. The reference to the man born blind in Jn 10.21 might indicate that the 'works' in Jn 10.25, 32-33, 37-38 refer to this miracle performed by Jesus. Other scholars think that the 'works' in Jn 10 refer more broadly to Jesus' miracles and words (e.g. Bultmann, *John*, p. 390; Lincoln, *John*, p. 305).

of God (10.36),[120] and one with his Father (10.30). Previously, Jesus has said that the works testify (μαρτυρεῖ περὶ ἐμοῦ) that the Father has sent him (5.36)[121] and that he has come in his Father's name (ἐν τῷ ὀνόματι τοῦ πατρός μου, 5.43).[122] Since Jesus performs God's works, he is authorized to give people eternal life (10.28; cf. 10.10), which is a divine prerogative (5.24; cf. 1.4; 5.21, 25-26, 29).[123] Instead of accepting these claims, the Jews try to kill Jesus (5.18; 10.31).[124] They are unable to receive the one who has been working with the Father since the creation of the world (1.3, 10-11; 5.17-20). Instead of receiving the one who came in the Father's name (1.12; 5.43; 10.25),[125] they accuse him of blasphemy (10.33), because they believe he is making himself 'a god' (10.33, ποιεῖς σεαυτὸν θεόν; cf. 5.18, ἴσον ἑαυτὸν ποιῶν τῷ θεῷ).[126] However, the only thing Jesus is 'making' (i.e. 'performing') is the works of his Father (10.37-38; cf. 5.19).

There are at least three indications about the unique relationship between Jesus and his Father in Jn 10.28-38. For Jesus, these indications are natural implications in light of the works that he performs (10.25, 32-33, 37-38). The first indication is that both Jesus and the Father share the power to preserve the sheep in their hand (10.28-29).[127] The sentences are remarkably similar: οὐχ ἁρπάσει τις αὐτὰ ἐκ τῆς χειρός μου (10.28); οὐδεὶς δύναται ἁρπάζειν ἐκ τῆς χειρὸς τοῦ πατρός (10.29). Jesus and the Father

---

120.   The verbatim quotation from Ps. 81.6 (82.6 MT) in 10.34 is usually read as an argument from the lesser to the greater (Beasley-Murray, *John*, p. 175; Lightfoot, *John*, p. 208): if others (judges, angels, or Israel) were called 'gods' in the Scriptures, how much more should Jesus, who is one with the Father, be called the Son of God. Commentators refer to this argument as *a fortiori* (Barrett, *John*, p. 385; Lindars, *John*, p. 373), *a minori ad maius* (Bultmann, *John*, p. 389), or *qal wahomer* (Lincoln, *John*, p. 308; von Wahlde, *John*, vol. 2, p. 475). This kind of argument might be found in Jn 7.23 (Michaels, *John*, p. 604 n. 50; Borgen, *Early Christianity*, p. 110; H. Weiss, 'The Sabbath in the Fourth Gospel', *JBL* 110 [1991], pp. 311–21 [313]).
121.   Bultmann, *John*, p. 305; Lindars, *John*, p. 368.
122.   Von Wahlde, *John*, vol. 2, p. 472.
123.   Barrett, *John*, pp. 381, 386; Lincoln, *John*, p. 305.
124.   Bultmann, *John*, p. 387; Barrett, *John*, p. 384 (cf. Hoskyns, *Gospel*, vol. 2, p. 443).
125.   Elsewhere in GJohn, Jesus is portrayed as revealing the Father's name: 17.6, 26; cf. 12.13, 28; 17.11, 12.
126.   Lindars, *John*, p. 372; Beasley-Murray, *John*, p. 175; von Wahlde, *John*, vol. 2, p. 480.
127.   There is a very difficult textual problem in 10.29. Metzger, *Commentary*, p. 198, judged that the reading preserved in B* is perhaps original: 'that which the Father has given me is greater than all' (Hoskyns, *Gospel*, vol. 2, p. 451; Michaels, *John*, p. 599).

are one in securing the sheep.[128] The second indication is that Jesus and the Father are 'one' (10.30). Since the adjective is neuter (ἕν), it is natural to think that Jesus is not attempting here to equate himself with the Father, but rather to assert the unique and close association he has with him (1.1-3; 5.19-20; 8.16; 12.44-45).[129] Jesus is neither the Father nor a 'second' Father, but one with the Father.[130] The third indication (10.38) is that the Father is in Jesus (ἐν ἐμοὶ ὁ πατὴρ) and Jesus is in the Father (κἀγὼ ἐν τῷ πατρί).[131] The absence of an explicit verb (i.e. 'is', 'was', or 'will be') might indicate that the mutual indwelling of the Father and Jesus is not limited by temporal categories.

Jesus again refers to the works that he performs in a dialogue with his disciples in Jn 14. The argumentation in this unit of material is similar to that found in Jn 10: the works that Jesus performs are expressive of his unity with the Father.[132] In Jn 10 Jesus uses three explicit statements about his unity with the Father (10.28-29, 30, 38) and refers to the works that he performs three times (10.25, 32-33, 37-38). Here in Jn 14 Jesus offers six statements about his special association with the Father and two references to the works that he performs (14.10-11; cf. 15.24). Jesus claims that knowing him means knowing the Father (14.7), that those who have seen him have seen the Father (14.9), and that he is in the Father and the Father is in him (14.10-11).[133] Jesus also states that people should believe in both God and himself (14.1), that no one comes to the Father except through him (14.6), and that his disciples have already known and seen the Father (14.7). Additionally, Jesus claims in Jn 15.23 that the one who hates him hates his Father too. All these unique claims are based on the works that he performs: 'believe because of the works

128.   Lincoln, *John*, p. 306; Beasley-Murray, *John*, p. 174; Lightfoot, *John*, p. 214; Keener, *John*, vol. 1, p. 825. Some commentators have related Jn 10.28-29 to Deut. 32.39 and Isa. 43.13 (e.g. von Wahlde, *John*, vol. 2, p. 472) or to Isa. 48.11-13 (Hoskyns, *Gospel*, vol. 2, p. 450). However, the idea of protection (Jn 10.28-29) is absent from those OT texts. It is more promising to relate Jn 10.28-29 to Ps. 94.7 (95.7 MT) (Keener, *John*, vol. 1, p. 825). Michaels, *John*, p. 601, observes that 'one Shepherd' in Jn 10.16 could easily refer to the Father or to the Son.

129.   Bultmann, *John*, p. 387; Lightfoot, *John*, p. 208; Lindars, *John*, p. 371.

130.   Michaels, *John*, p. 601; Beasley-Murray, *John*, p. 175.

131.   Lindars, *John*, p. 376.

132.   Barrett, *John*, pp. 460, 481; Schnackenburg, *John*, vol. 3, pp. 69, 116.

133.   This statement is similar to that found in Jn 10.38 and 17.21, but there is a variation. In Jn 14.10-11 Jesus mentions himself first, but in Jn 10.38 and 17.21, the Father is mentioned first (cf. Schnackenburg, *John*, vol. 3, p. 69; Lincoln, *John*, p. 391; Bultmann, *John*, p. 609; Barrett, *John*, p. 460).

themselves' (14.11).[134] Jesus offers the same claims and the same evidence to both Jews (Jn 10) and disciples (Jn 14). Jesus does not disclose a mystery to his disciples about his works that has been hidden from the Jews during his earthly ministry.[135] However, the reaction of the Jews and the disciples is different. The Jews accuse Jesus of blasphemy (10.33), while the disciples seem to remain silent (14.10-11; 15.24; cf. 4.33-34; 9.2-4).

In the prologue the close association between ὁ λόγος and God (1.1-2) appears along with statements about ὁ λόγος partaking in the divine work of creation (1.3, 10). This close association authorizes Jesus Christ (the Word made flesh) to make God known (1.18). Similarly, Philip's demand in 14.8 ('show us the Father') is followed by Jesus' statement about his unique relationship with the Father (14.9-10), supported by the divine works that he performs (14.10-11).

Some scholars have argued that Jesus' cry on the cross (τετέλεσται, 19.30; cf. 19.28) was intended as an allusion to the completion of creation in Gen. 2.2 (συνετέλεσεν).[136] Martin Hengel, for example, observed that Jesus' death takes place on the sixth day and that the narrator refers to the next day as a 'great Sabbath' (ἦν μεγάλη ἡ ἡμέρα ἐκείνου τοῦ σαββάτου, 19.31). Hengel suggested that Jesus finishes the work of creation and salvation on the cross and then he 'rests' in the grave.[137] Therefore, Jesus completes his work of 'new creation'.[138] The evidence to support this link is found in (1) the words τελέω and σάββατον in Jn 19.28-31, and the verb συντελέω and the phrase τῇ ἡμέρᾳ τῇ ἕκτῃ in Gen. 2.1-2, and (2) the Genesis background to Jn 5.17-36 and 17.4. Hengel also referred to rabbinic material where Adam is portrayed as being created on the sixth day and disobeying God's commandment the same day at the tenth hour.[139] According to Hengel, this rabbinic

134.   For John, the works that Jesus performs are works that 'no one else did' (15.24). Not only his claims, but also the evidence Jesus offers is unique (cf. 9.32). See Haenchen, *John 2*, p. 138; Michaels, *John*, p. 823; Lindars, *John*, p. 495.

135.   Lincoln, *John*, p. 391; Bultmann, *John*, p. 609.

136.   Coloe, 'Creation', p. 6; Weidemann, 'Protology', pp. 321–2; J. K. Brown, 'Creation', pp. 285–6; Droge, 'Sabbath', pp. 131, 134; H. Saxby, 'The Time-Scheme in the Gospel of John', *ExpTim* 104 (1992), pp. 9–13 (11); M. Girard, 'La structure heptapartite du quatrième évangile', *SR* 5 (1975–1976), pp. 350–9 (354); Reim, *Studien*, p. 99; E. Stauffer, *Jesus and His Story* (trans. D. M. Barton; London: SCM, 1960), p. 117.

137.   Hengel, 'Old Testament', pp. 33–4.

138.   Hengel, 'Prologue', p. 70.

139.   Hengel, 'Old Testament', p. 34, referred to Str-B, vol. 4, pp. 1126–7. See *Pesiq. Rab.* 46.2; *Pesiq. Rab Kah.* 23.1; *Midr. Ps.* 92 §3; *Lev. Rab.* 29.1.

background allows one to understand that 'the Son "finishes" the work of God's Creation, which had been upset, indeed destroyed, by human sin'.[140]

However, this suggested link between GJohn and Gen. 2 seems implausible for several reasons. The first reason is that there is no extant evidence that the Genesis text was used or alluded to in Second-Temple Jewish texts in ways that resemble what scholars propose is going on in Jn 19.28-31. Rabbinic texts are not contemporary to the final redaction of GJohn, and it is always difficult to be certain whether traditions contained there can be dated back to the first century C.E. The second reason is that although the words used in Jn 19.28-31 and Gen. 2.1-2 share conceptual similarities, they are indeed different, making it difficult for a reader to establish a direct connection.

The third reason is that the language of fulfilment in Jn 19.28-30 is used in a context where a reference to the Scripture is made. Scholars have noted that in Jn 12.38–19.37 the Scripture is always referred to by using a fulfilment formula in relation to Jesus' death (πληρωθῇ, 12.38; 13.18; 15.25; 19.24, 36, 37; cf. 17.12).[141] John 19.28 is not an exception.[142] The uses of τελέω and τελειόω in Jn 19.28-30 point to John's idea that through the cross the Scriptures are fulfilled.[143] Jesus' cry on the cross recalls not only the completion of God's works (5.36; 17.4) but also his love for his own (εἰς τέλος, 13.1)[144] and the fulfilment of the Scripture. The fourth reason is that the phrase 'great Sabbath' in Jn 19.31 is intended to highlight the Sabbath in Passover-week, rather

ET W. G. Braude, *Pesikta Rabbati: Discourses for Feasts, Fasts, and Special Sabbaths* (YJS, 18; 2 vols.; New Haven: Yale University Press, 1968), vol. 2, p. 791; J. Neusner, *Pesiqta deRab Kahana: An Analytical Translation* (BJS, 123; 2 vols.; Atlanta: Scholars Press, 1987), vol. 2, p. 83; W. G. Braude, *The Midrash on Psalms* (YJS, 13; 2 vols.; New Haven: Yale University Press, 1959), vol. 2, pp. 111–12; H. Freedman and M. Simon, *Midrash Rabbah: Leviticus* (London: Soncino, 1939), p. 369.

140. Hengel, 'Old Testament', p. 34.

141. F. J. Moloney, 'The Gospel of John: The "End" of Scripture', *Int* 63 (2009), pp. 356–66 (357).

142. The phrase ἵνα τελειωθῇ ἡ γραφή (19.28) is omitted by Papyrus[66*] and two Coptic versions. Although some manuscripts have πληρωθη instead of τελειωθῇ (e.g. ℵ Dˢ), it is better to prefer here the most difficult reading, τελειωθῇ.

143. Moloney, 'Scripture', p. 359; Michaels, *John*, p. 961.

144. Daly-Denton, *David*, p. 221; U. Schnelle, *Theology of the New Testament* (trans. M. E. Boring; Grand Rapids: Baker Academic, 2009), p. 698; Schnackenburg, *John*, vol. 3, p. 288; Brown, *John*, vol. 2, p. 908.

than divine rest after creation. This is supported by the fact that the same adjective (μέγας) is also used in Jn 7.37 in reference to a Jewish festival (cf. 18.28; 19.14).[145]

IV. Conclusion

John uses creation imagery in contexts where Jewish discussions about God's rest after creation are in view (5.20, 36; 9.3-4; cf. 5.17) and in Jn 17.4. John attributes to Jesus the performance of the works of God at various strategic places in his narrative in order to show that Jesus has a close association with his Father, apart from and prior to the created order. The Sabbath law that binds all creation does not apply to Jesus and his Father. He shares uniquely in this divine exemption. Jesus is able to perform divine activities that are God's prerogatives even on the Sabbath. Therefore, the reader can see that Jesus and the message associated with him have a universal significance and that he is privileged over other important figures in John's narrative, i.e. John the Baptist, Moses, and Abraham.

145.   Lindars, *John*, p. 584; Bultmann, *John*, p. 676 n. 6; Schnackenburg, *John*, vol. 3, p. 288; Michaels, *John*, p. 966; Beasley-Murray, *John*, p. 353; Barrett, *John*, p. 55; Carson, *John*, p. 622; Lightfoot, *John*, p. 326; Hoskyns, *Gospel*, vol. 2, p. 634; von Wahlde, *John*, vol. 2, p. 816; Brown, *John*, vol. 2, p. 934.

Chapter 4

Two Possible Instances of Creation Imagery

In the previous chapter I suggested that the Johannine claim that Jesus performs the works of his Father can be taken as an instance of creation imagery (5.20, 36; 9.3-4; 17.4; cf. 5.17). In the present chapter I will examine two stories where John portrays Jesus as performing two distinctive actions: walking on the sea (6.19) and healing a man born blind (9.6). The evidence will show that it is possible to deem both acts as creation imagery. Both instances are positioned in strategic places in GJohn and they are used in similar ways, although they occur in varying contexts. The story of Jesus walking on the sea is used to convey the idea that he comes in the name of the Father in order to reveal God. The healing story is used to convey the idea that Jesus is from God and that he has the authority to perform divine activities. In both cases (6.19; 9.6) John might be using creation imagery to assert the primal significance of Jesus and the message about him and to privilege him over other important figures in John's narrative—Moses and Abraham.

I. Jesus Walking on the Sea

a. *Assessment*

Scholars have proposed a number of OT texts as the background to Jn 6.16-21.[1] In particular, some scholars have suggested that Jesus' distinctive action in Jn 6.19 is somehow linked to Job 9.8.[2] It is our task here to attempt a thorough assessment of the evidence in order to arrive at a properly nuanced estimate of this proposed relationship.

---

1. Pss. 28.3; 76.20; 106.29-30 LXX; Isa. 41–54; Exod. 14–15. See Dodd, *Interpretation*, p. 345 n. 1; C. H. Williams, *I am He: The Interpretation of 'Anî Hû' in Jewish and Early Christian Literature* (WUNT, 2/113; Tübingen: Mohr Siebeck, 2000), pp. 219, 227–8; Lincoln, *John*, p. 219.

2. D. F. Strauss, *The Life of Jesus Critically Examined* (trans. G. Eliot; London: Swan Sonnenschein, 1898), p. 504; Hoskyns, *Gospel*, vol. 1, p. 327; Haenchen, *John 1*, p. 280; Beasley-Murray, *John*, p. 89; Moloney, *John*, p. 203; von Wahlde, *John*, vol. 2, p. 273.

John 6.19

... θεωροῦσιν τὸν Ἰησοῦν <u>περιπατοῦντα</u> <u>ἐπὶ</u> τῆς <u>θαλάσσης</u> κτλ.

Job 9.8 LXX

ὁ τανύσας τὸν οὐρανὸν μόνος καὶ <u>περιπατῶν</u> ὡς ἐπ' ἐδάφους <u>ἐπὶ</u> <u>θαλάσσης·</u>

There are similarities as well as differences between these two texts. The clearest similarity is the noun θαλάσσης (Genitive) preceded by the preposition ἐπί.[3] The article (τῆς), however, is absent from Job 9.8.[4] The noun θάλασσα occurs always with the article in Jn 6.16, 17, 22; cf. 6.25. The 'sea' in Jn 6 is early identified as 'the Sea of Galilee', 'the Sea of Tiberias' (6.1), but in the episode of Jesus walking on the sea, the noun lacks any identification, making the similarity with Job 9.8 even closer.[5] The participle form of περιπατέω is used in both texts with different functions: modifying θεωροῦσιν in Jn 6.19 and as a subject in Job 9.8.[6]

The verb περιπατέω and the noun θάλασσα are commonplace, but the verb περιπατέω before the construction ἐπὶ (τῆς) θαλάσσης is rather unusual. It is used only once in the LXX, in Job 9.8. In the NT it is used four times outside GJohn,[7] always in the narratives of Jesus walking on the sea (Mt. 14.25, περιπατῶν ἐπὶ τὴν θάλασσαν; Mk 6.48, περιπατῶν ἐπὶ τῆς θαλάσσης; Mt. 14.26[8] and Mk 6.49, ἐπὶ τῆς θαλάσσης περιπατοῦντα).[9]

---

3. Papyrus[45] (Jn 6.19) has the accusative form την θαλασσαν (cf. ℵ B P W Δ in Mt. 14.25 and L W in Mt. 14.26) and cursive 406 (Job 9.8) has θαλασσην. The preposition ἐπί is omitted in Codex Sinaiticus (S*) and three cursives (55 255* 728) (Job 9.8).

4. Didymus uses the article.

5. The MT has ורך על־במתי ים, 'trampled the waves of (the) sea'. The LXX adds ὡς ἐπ' ἐδάφους, but some witnesses have περιπατῶν ἐπὶ θαλάσσης ὡς ἐπ' ἐδάφους (three manuscripts of Jerome's Latin translation [La^A], Lucianic witnesses [L'-406], some ancient translations [e.g. Coptic, Ethiopic, Armenian], and a number of church fathers [e.g. Eusebius, Didymus]).

6. The participle occurs with the definite article (ο) in cursive 754, the Sahidic version, and some church fathers (e.g. Chrysostom, Theodoret of Cyrrhus). Other witnesses have the aorist ο περιπατησας (cursive 55 and Anastasius), *et ambulat* (Jerome's Latin translation, Chromatius Aquileiensis, and Pseudo-Vigilius), *qui ambulat* (Eusebius Varcellensis), or *qui ambulavit* (Ambrose).

7. Similar ideas (using different words) occur in Rev. 10.2, 5, 8; 15.2, where an angel is portrayed as standing on the sea and victorious people are depicted as standing on a sea of glass.

8. See περιπατοῦντα ἐπὶ τῆς θαλάσσης (e.g. Θ *f*[13]).

9. There are several differences between the narrative of Jesus walking on the sea in GJohn and the corresponding narratives in GMatthew and GMark. The disciples think that the one walking on the sea is a 'ghost' and cry out, according to Mt. 14.26

Since the account of Jesus walking on the sea is found in GMark, GMatthew, and GJohn, it is reasonable to think that John knew the tradition that shaped the Markan (and Matthaean) episode. Therefore, it could be argued either that John was only reproducing an earlier tradition and was not intending a link to Job 9.8, or that John reproduced the tradition precisely because a link to Job 9.8 served his purposes.

In order to enhance or diminish the plausibility of a link to Job 9.8 in Jn 6.19, we need to ask whether the book of Job is a prominent text in GJohn,[10] and we need to explore extant Jewish traditions. It seems that Job is not a noticeable text in GJohn. John never quotes from this OT book. Some scholars have attempted to discern allusions to Job in GJohn, but the proposed links seem too slight to carry much conviction. The editors of NA[28] suggest the following allusions: Jn 3.20 / Job 24.13-17; 4.37 / 31.8; and 19.30 / 19.26-27.[11] Apart from the reference to light in Jn 3.20 and Job 24.13-17, it is difficult to see how the two texts are related in terms of vocabulary. As for Jn 4.37, it seems that John is reproducing a well-known saying rather than a specific text.[12] The only link between Jn 19.30 and Job 19.26-27 LXX is the verb 'to finish'.

Several texts from the Second-Temple period have been used to illuminate the interpretation of Jn 6.19. Here I will give attention to two of them.[13] The narrator in 2 Macc. 5 explains how Antiochus hurried away to Antioch after having defiled the temple, 'thinking in his arrogance

and Mk 6.49, but these details do not appear in GJohn. There is also a noticeable similarity: all three accounts have the phrase ἐγώ εἰμι· μὴ φοβεῖσθε (Mt. 14.27; Mk 6.50; Jn 6.20). For a detailed comparison of these accounts, see Brown, *John*, vol. 1, pp. 253–4; B. Grigsby, 'The Reworking of the Lake-Walking Account in the Johannine Tradition', *ExpTim* 100 (1989), pp. 295–7 (295–6). Cf. R. Nicholls, *Walking on the Water: Reading MT. 14:22-23 in the Light of Its Wirkungsgeschichte* (Leiden: Brill, 2008), pp. 42–7.

10. A link to Job 9 is clearer in GMark, since the verb παρέρχομαι is used in Mk 6.48 and Job 9.11. This detail is absent from the Johannine account. Cf. R. B. Hays, 'Can the Gospels Teach Us How to Read the Old Testament?', *ProEccl* 11 (2002), pp. 402–18 (410).

11. Reim, *Studien*, p. 159, counts Job 35.13 and Jn 9.31 among his suggested *formale Parallelen*.

12. Michaels, *John*, p. 265; Bultmann, *John*, p. 198 n. 2.

13. Cf. J. P. Heil, *Jesus Walking on the Sea: Meaning and Gospel Functions of Mt. 14:22-23, Mark 6:45-52 and John 6:15b-21* (AnBib, 87; Rome: Biblical Institute, 1981), pp. 19–21, 30. Heil mentions *T. Naph.* 6.1-10 (λαῖλαψ μεγάλη ἀνέμου), 1QH[a] XV, 2-6; 1QH[a] XI, 6, 13. Heil concludes: 'These Qumran *hodayot* contain the same combinations of motifs as these NT sea-rescue stories [Mt. 14.22-33; Mk 6.45-52; Jn 6.15-21]: the ship…the storm-tossed sea…and the divine rescue, which is indicated by a divine activity upon the chaotic waters' (p. 30). This is perhaps more

(ἀπὸ τῆς ὑπερηφανίας) that he could make the land navigable and the sea (τὸ πέλαγος) passable (πορευτόν) on foot, because his heart was elated' (5.21; cf. 9.8). Having experienced God's judgement, Antiochus later confesses, 'no mortal should think that he is equal to God (ἰσόθεα)' (9.12; cf. Jn 5.18, ἴσον...τῷ θεῷ). The wording in 2 Macc. 5.21; 9.8 is different from that of Jn 6.19 and Job 9.8, but the text is relevant because it indicates that crossing the sea on foot is a divine activity that is not within the capacity of human beings.[14]

The other text that needs to be taken into account is *Pr. Man.* 2–3, where God is portrayed as the Creator of the sky and the earth (*Pr. Man.* 2). In this context it is said that God 'shackled the sea by the word (τῷ λόγῳ) of [his] ordinance', 'shut up the deep', and 'sealed it with [his] awesome and notable name (ὀνόματι)' (NETS). Jarl Fossum suggests that as the 'Name of God' was 'instrumental in suppressing the sea', so 'Jesus the Word = Name is able to subdue the sea'.[15] Fossum contends that the 'I am' statement in Jn 6.20 may hint to the divine Name and therefore, 'When Jesus utters "I am" while walking on the sea, he appears as the personified divine Name'.[16] However, in *Pr. Man.* 2–3 the

clearly seen in Mk 6.51 and Mt. 14.32, where it is indicated explicitly that the wind ceased. In Jn 6, however, it is only said that 'the boat came to the land' (6.21), without explicitly saying that the wind ceased.

14. H. van der Loos, *The Miracles of Jesus* (NovTSup, 9; Leiden: Brill, 1965), p. 658, argues, 'It is nowhere said in the Old Testament that people walked on water'. Based on Sir. 24.5-6, Lincoln, *John*, p. 218, says, 'walking on the sea can also be attributed to Wisdom'. But as has been observed by Schnackenburg, *John*, p. 446 n. 67, 'The frequently cited text Sir 24:5–6, which refers to wisdom, is not relevant to this context'.

15. J. E. Fossum, *The Image of the Invisible God: Essays on the Influence of Jewish Mysticism on Early Christology* (NTOA, 30; Göttingen: Vandenhoeck & Ruprecht, 1995), p. 128. Fossum also refers to a note in the Talmud (*b. B. Bat.* 73a) where 'Seafarers used to smite the stormy sea with clubs on which was engraved the phrase "I am who I am, Yah, the Lord of Hosts"'. Additionally, we could add *Odes* 39, where it is said that the Lord has bridged the rivers 'by his word, and he walked and crossed them on foot' (39.9; *OTP*, vol. 2, p. 768). This text also relates the name of God to the ability to walk on the water: 'put on the name of the Most High and know him, and you shall cross without danger' (39.8; *OTP*, vol. 2, p. 768). Cf. W. Berg, *Die Rezeption alttestamentlicher Motive im Neuen Testament – dargestellt an den Seewandelerzählungen* (HSTE, 1; Freiburg: HochschulVerlag, 1979), pp. 92–4.

16. Fossum, *Image*, pp. 128–9. In the OT God is portrayed as ruling over the sea (Pss. 73.12-17; 76.17, 20 LXX; Wis. 14.3-4) and as being the Creator of the seas (Pss. 95.5; 104.24-25; 146.6 MT). Cf. P. J. Madden, *Jesus' Walking on the Sea: An Investigation of the Origin of the Narrative Account* (BZAW, 81; Berlin: W. de Gruyter, 1997), pp. 24–5.

'Name' is used in suppressing the sea, while in Jn 6.20 Jesus pronounces ἐγώ εἰμι to his fearful disciples but not in order to subdue the sea.[17]

Apart from Job 9.8 and 2 Macc. 5.21, the motif of 'walking on water' is absent from the LXX.[18] Therefore, if the OT influenced John when he was writing (or as he preserved a former tradition) about Jesus walking on the sea, the most likely candidate should be Job 9.8, where creation imagery is explicit. This could be further supported by looking at an early Christian interpretation of Jesus walking on the sea that is preserved in *Sibylline Oracles*.

The narrator behind the 'hymn to Christ' found in *Sib. Or.* 6 portrays Jesus walking on the waves in a context where his dominion over creation is highlighted. The narrator describes how the 'Son of the Immortal' 'will show heavenly paths', 'teach all with wise words', and 'raise the dead' (6.9-14; *OTP*, vol. 1, p. 407). In this context the speaker says that the Son of the Immortal 'will walk the waves' (6.13), and that in his hand 'are the whole world and earth and heaven and sea' (6.16-17). Similarly, the narrator behind *Sib. Or.* 8.273-274 portrays Jesus

---

17. It seems more natural to relate *Pr. Man.* 2–3 to the Markan storm-stilling story (4.35-41). This story, however, is absent from the Johannine account.

18. The idea of 'someone' walking on water is widespread in Greek and Roman traditions, as has been shown by A. Yarbro-Collins, 'Rulers, Divine Men, and Walking on the Water (Mark 6:45-52)', in *Religious Propaganda and Missionary Competition in the New Testament World* (ed. L. Bormann, K. del Tredici, and A. Standhartinger; NovTSup, 74; Leiden: Brill, 1994), pp. 207–27. The sources Collins lists tell us that gods such as Poseidon (Homer, *Il.* 13.16-30) and Neptune (Virgil, *Aen.* 5.1081-1085) were able to cross the sea in their chariots; that walking on water was proverbial for the humanly impossible and for the arrogance of the ruler aspiring to empire (Herodotus, *Hist.* 7.35 and Dio Chrysostom 3.30-31 on Xerxes; and Menander frg. 924K on Alexander the Great); that walking on water was the unrealistic type of thing that one sometimes dreams (Dio Chrysostom, 11.129); that heroes and legendary characters associated with the gods such as Euphemus (Asclepiades of Tragilus or Asclepiades of Myrleia), Euphemus of Taenarum (Apollonius Rhodius, *Argon.* 1.179-184), Orion (Apollodorus, *The Library* 1.4.3), and Heracles (Seneca, *Herc. fur.* 322–324; Julian, *Oration* 7.219D) were able or received from the gods the ability to walk on water. On the other hand, in a magical papyrus (*PGM* XXXIV.1-24), it is said that walking on water is something that the properly trained or instructed person can accomplish (cf. *Sword of Moses*). None of these sources, however, has the wording found in Jn 6.19, περιπατοῦντα ἐπὶ τῆς θαλάσσης. The phrases found in the sources listed by Collins are: τὴν θάλασσαν... διαπορεύεσθαι (Euphemus), διαβαίνειν τὴν θάλασσαν (Orion), βαδίσαι...τῆς θαλάττης (Heracles), διά τῆς θαλάττης τὸν πεζὸν (Xerxes), βαδίζειν ἐπὶ τῆς θαλάττης (see Dio Chrysostom, 11.129). Barrett's judgement (*John*, p. 279) in this regard is pertinent: 'non-biblical parallels are relatively unimportant'.

walking on the sea in a context where creation is prominent. The narrator says that Christ 'will come to creation not in glory, but as a man' (8.256; *OTP*, vol. 1, p. 424; cf. 8.269). In his coming, says the narrator, Christ 'will fashion the original man' (8.259) and will display his power over creation: 'doing all with a word, healing every disease…[calming] the raging sea by walking on it with feet of peace and with faith' (8.272-74; *OTP*, vol. 1, p. 424).[19]

In other early Christian interpretations of the event (besides the *Sibylline Oracles*) a link to Job 9.8 cannot be supported. Tertullian sets the event in a creation context but links it to a psalm that he did not identify, 'a psalm is, in fact, accomplished by this crossing over the lake. "The Lord", says the psalmist, "is upon many waters"' (*Marc.* 4.20; *ANF*, vol. 3, p. 379). The *Acts of Paul* refers to walking on the sea without a creation context, 'the Lord came to [Paul], walking upon the sea (ἦλθεν πρὸς αὐτὸν ὁ κύριος πε[ρ]ιπατ[ῶν ἐπ]ὶ [τῆς θα]λάσσης)' (*Acts Paul* 10).[20] Paul's reaction ('you are my Lord Jesus Christ, the king') is followed by the indication that 'walking on the sea (περιπατῶν ἐπὶ τῆς θαλάσσης), [the Lord] went before [Paul and Artemon]' on their way to Rome.[21]

It can be concluded that a link to Job 9.8 in Jn 6.19 is possible. It is significant that the participle 'walking' is used before ἐπὶ (τῆς) θαλάσσης only in Jn 6.19 and in the LXX (Job 9.8) and four more times in the NT, always in the narrative of Jesus walking on the sea. Therefore, it might be that John was using and creatively deploying language stemming from Job 9.8 where creation imagery is prominent. However, we can only regard this as a possibility because Job is not a noticeable text in GJohn.

---

19. In *T. Adam* 3.1 Adam tells Seth that God will come into the world and will perform miraculous things such as opening the eyes of the blind and 'walk[ing] on the waves of the sea' (*OTP*, vol. 1, p. 994). On the other hand, in *Apoc. Elij.* 3.8 it is said that the 'son of lawlessness' (the antichrist) will 'walk upon the sea and the rivers as upon dry land' (*OTP*, vol. 1, p. 745).

20. C. Schmidt and W. Schubart, *ΠΡΑΞΕΙΣ ΠΑΥΛΟΥ: Acta Pauli nach dem Papyrus der Hamburger Staats und Universität-Bibliothek* (Glückstadt: J. J. Augustin, 1936), p. 52 lines 27-28. ET J. K. Elliott, *The Apocryphal New Testament: A Collection of Apocryphal Christian Literature in an English Translation* (Oxford: Clarendon, 1993), pp. 383–4.

21. In *Ep. Apos.* 5 there is a summary of several miracles performed by Jesus. Among them, we find: 'Then he walked on the sea, and the winds blew, and he rebuked them, and the waves of the sea became calm' (Elliott, *Apocryphal*, p. 560).

b. *The Significance of Jesus' Act*

Since there is at least a reasonable possibility that John may be using an instance of creation imagery in his portrayal of Jesus walking on the sea, we need to ask now what role such an act plays in Jn 6. By demonstrating the literary relationship between Jn 6.19 and the surrounding context (6.1-13, 25-71) and other relevant sections of GJohn (1.11-12; 5.43), I will argue that John uses the episode of Jesus walking on the water to convey the idea that Jesus comes in order to reveal God and that he has to be regarded as privileged over Moses.

The story of Jesus walking on the sea is located in a strategic place. This story is embedded between Jesus' miraculous provision of food for a large crowd (6.1-15) and Jesus' discourse about the bread of life (6.26-40). Since Jn 6.16-21 seems to interrupt a natural flow between the miracle and the discourse, the story of Jesus walking on the sea might have made a deep impression on Johannine readers. By placing this story in this particular location, John may be doing more than just following the tradition.[22] He also might be calling his reader's attention to 6.16-21.

The central point of Jn 6.16-24 seems to be both that Jesus walked on the sea and that he said of himself ἐγώ εἰμι.[23] This is supported by the fact that the narrator anticipates in 6.17 that 'Jesus had not yet come to them', making the coming of Jesus the central point of the story, and by the fact that the transition from the scene of distress (6.16-19) to the scene of gladness (6.21) is the pronouncement of ἐγώ εἰμι (6.20). Jesus walking on the sea marks a major change in the narrative.

On the other hand, in Job 9 God is portrayed as having power over creation, since he 'ages' and 'overturns' mountains (9.5), shakes what is under heaven (9.6), speaks to the sun (9.7), seals up the stars (9.7), and causes the sea-monsters to bow down (9.13). God is able to do that because he is the Creator: he 'alone stretched out the sky' (9.8) and 'made Pleiades...and made the chambers of the south' (9.9).[24] The power of God as Creator is seen in the fact that he 'walks on the sea as on dry

22. John probably knew that the tradition of Jesus walking on water was attached to the discourse of the living bread (Mk 6.30-44; Mt. 14.13-21). See Loos, *Miracles*, p. 650; Brown, *John*, vol. 1, p. 252; Barrett, *John*, p. 279; L. Th. Witkamp, 'Some Specific Johannine Features in John 6.1-21', *JSNT* 40 (1990), pp. 43–60 (51); Hoskyns, *Gospel*, vol. 1, p. 326; Beasley-Murray, *John*, p. 87; von Wahlde, *John*, vol. 2, pp. 280, 282; Carson, *John*, p. 273; M. Labahn, *Offenbarung in Zeichen und Wort: Untersuchungen zur Vorgeschichte von Joh 6,1–25a und seiner Rezeption in der Brotrede* (WUNT, 2/117; Tübingen: Mohr Siebeck, 2000), pp. 247–71.
23. Schnackenburg, *John*, vol. 2, pp. 11, 27; Grigsby, 'Reworking', p. 296.
24. See also Job 8.3, where God is called ὁ τὰ πάντα ποιήσας, and Job 10.3, 8-9, where God is portrayed as the Creator of man.

ground' (9.8).[25] If John is drawing on and creatively deploying language
from Job 9.8, Jesus would be performing in Jn 6.19 an act that resembles
that of the Creator God. In the middle of darkness, great wind, and rough
water, Jesus is able to walk on the sea.[26]

Jesus has previously shown his authority over the created order by
providing food in abundance for five thousand men (6.10-11) in a setting
where the natural context is prominent. The miracle takes place on a
mountain (6.3, 15) and 'there was a lot of grass in that place' (6.10).[27]
The mention of Philip being unable to provide food for the people seems
to indicate that Jesus' miracle is humanly impossible (6.5-7). Only one
who took an active role in creation (1.3, 10) can be able to provide food
for so many people. Similarly, only one who took an active role in
creation can be able to display his power over creation by walking on the
sea (6.19).[28] Thus the event narrated in Jn 6.16-21 provides further
disclosure about the one who has just multiplied food.[29]

The story of Jesus walking on the sea is also related to Jesus' previous
discussion with the Jews in 5.43.[30] This discussion occurs in the broader
context of Jesus' insistence that he performs the works of God even on
a Sabbath (5.17, 20, 36). Jesus claims, 'I have come (ἐλήλυθα) in my
Father's name (ἐν τῷ ὀνόματι τοῦ πατρός μου), and you do not receive
(λαμβάνετε) me' (5.43). This statement is similar to the one in Jn 1.11-12,

---

25. See also Job 38.16, 'Did you walk in the tracks of the deep?' (ἐν ἴχνεσιν
ἀβύσσου περιεπάτησας).

26. Madden, *Sea*, p. 109, says that darkness in Jn 6.17 connected with the strong
wind and the rough sea are 'reminiscent of the chaotic scene in Gen 1:2'. However,
the scenes are quite different. The only point of contact is the concept of darkness
(σκοτία, Jn 6.17; σκότος, Gen. 1.2; cf. the longer reading preserved in Jn 6.17 ℵ D).
In Jn 6.17 a strong wind causes the sea to become rough, while in Gen. 1.2 the spirit
of God is being carried along over the water.

27. This detail also occurs in Mk 6.39 and Mt. 14.19. Cf. Little, *Echoes*, p. 142.
W. A. Meeks, *The Prophet-King: Moses Traditions and the Johannine Christology*
(NovTSup, 14; Leiden: Brill, 1967), p. 97 n. 4, takes the reference to the grass in
Jn 6.10 as a 'subtle allusion to the Good Shepherd's care for the sheep'.

28. Culpepper, *Anatomy*, pp. 106–7.

29. Lincoln, *John*, p. 217; G. R. O'Day, 'John 6:15-21: Jesus Walking on Water
as Narrative Embodiment of Johannine Christology', in *Critical Readings of John 6*
(ed. R. Alan Culpepper; Leiden: Brill, 1997), pp. 149–59 (152). Bultmann, *John*,
p. 218, rightly observed that Jesus walking on the sea shows 'Jesus' freedom from
the laws of nature that bind man', and that this miracle 'is meant to teach the
superiority and otherness of the revelation, as opposed to all forms of earthly natural
life'.

30. O'Day, 'John 6:15-21', p. 157, suggests that Jn 6.15-21 is an illustration of
Jesus' claim in 5.19, 'whatever the Father does, the Son does likewise'.

where it is said that 'his own did not receive (παρέλαβον) him', but others 'received (ἔλαβον) him' because they believed 'in his name' (τὸ ὄνομα αὐτοῦ). In 5.37 John portrays Jesus saying that the Jews 'have never seen (ἑωράκατε) his [the Father's] form (εἶδος)'. In the prologue the narrator says that 'no one has ever seen (ἑώρακεν) God', but 'the one who is in the bosom of the Father, has made him known' (1.18). In both cases creation imagery is important (1.3, 10; 5.17, 20, 36).

The evidence that some will reject the Son but some will receive him (1.11-12) is found in the story that follows the prologue. There are some who do not want to receive the one who came in the Father's name (5.43) and who have never seen the Father (5.37). However, there are some who receive the one who came in the Father's name because they see the manifestation of someone who acts as the Creator God, walking on the sea (6.19). This conclusion is supported by three details in Jn 6.16-21. The first detail is the narrator's clarification that the disciples see (θεωροῦσιν) Jesus walking on the sea. Unlike Mk 6.49 and Mt. 14.26, where the disciples are portrayed as seeing (ὁράω) a 'ghost', Jn 6.19 highlights that the disciples see Jesus.[31] In the discourse that follows Jesus will say that 'everyone who looks (ὁ θεωρῶν) on the Son and believes in him' has eternal life (6.40). Later Jesus will also shout out: 'he who sees (ὁ θεωρῶν) me sees (θεωρεῖ) the One who sent me' (12.45). And in his prayer he will assert his desire that his disciples see (θεωρῶσιν) his glory, which is associated with the Father's love for the Son before the foundation of the world (17.24).

The second detail is Jesus' use of ἐγώ εἰμι in 6.20. This phrase is used as a form of self-identification but in the hands of John, it serves to explain the significance of Jesus' act in 6.19.[32] In other words, Jesus uses ἐγώ εἰμι here in 6.20 as divine self-proclamation.[33] Jesus is able to use

31. The emphasis in the story in GJohn is not on what Jesus does (Mk 6.48-49; Mt. 14.25-26) but on what the disciples see.

32. C. H. Williams, 'Interpretations of the Identity and Role of Jesus', in *The Biblical World* (ed. J. Barton; 2 vols.; London: Routledge, 2002), vol. 2, pp. 332–54 (354).

33. C. H. Williams, '"I Am" or "I Am He"? Self-Declaratory Pronouncements in the Fourth Gospel and Rabbinic Tradition', in *Jesus in Johannine Tradition* (ed. R. T. Fortna and T. Thatcher; Louisville: Westminster John Knox, 2001), pp. 343–52 (345–7, 350); idem, *I am He*, pp. 227–8. 'I am' is hardly only a formula of self-identification here in Jn 6.20, where the narrator has already indicated that the disciples 'caught sight of Jesus' (6.19). Furthermore, ἐγώ εἰμι· μὴ φοβεῖσθε 'is the traditional formula of greeting used by the deity in his epiphany' (Gen. 26.24; 46.3; Isa. 41.13-14). See Bultmann, *John*, pp. 215–16; A. Feuillet, 'Les *Ego eimi* christo-logiques du quatrième Évangile (à suivre)', *RSR* 54 (1966), pp. 5–22 (19–21); cf.

ἐγώ εἰμι because he has come in his Father's name (1.12; 5.43). Through the pronouncement of ἐγώ εἰμι while performing an act that resembles that of the Creator God (6.19), Jesus is presumably making God known (1.18).[34] In his prayer Jesus will say twice retrospectively that he has manifested the Father's name (σου τὸ ὄνομα; τὸ ὄνομά σου) to the disciples (17.6, 26).

The third detail is that the name of the Father and the name of Jesus have been previously related either to the reception or the rejection of the one sent by God (1.11-12; 5.43). Jesus comes (ἐληλύθει) to his disciples (6.17) and they want to receive (λαβεῖν) him (6.21). Unlike those who do not receive (λαμβάνετε, 5.43; παρέλαβον, 1.11) the one who comes (ἐλήλυθα, 5.43; ἦλθεν, 1.11; cf. 1.9, 15) from God, the disciples are willing to receive him who walks on the sea using a divine self-proclamation.[35] This reading finds support when considered in light of other passages in GJohn. Elsewhere ἔρχομαι in the perfect tense (3.2, 19; 7.28; 8.42; 12.46; 16.28; 18.37) is used of the coming of Jesus to bring revelation,[36] and the verb λαμβάνω is used in 13.20 to assert that whoever accepts Jesus accepts the One who sent him. Furthermore, the coming of Jesus is related to the name of the Lord in 12.13 (quotation from Ps. 118.25-26).

So, there are many literary connections between Jn 6.19 and the preceding context. Now it is time to see how this passage relates to the context that follows. Jesus' dialogues in 6.25-71 are shaped by references to an important figure in the story of Israel: Moses. Moses and the miracle associated with him—providing manna for people—are mentioned three times (6.31-32, 49, 58). On the other hand, Jesus is presented as offering people a superior 'true bread from heaven' that is capable of giving life (6.27, 32-33, 35, 48, 50-51, 58). Jesus' interlocutors cannot accept that Jesus is able to provide this kind of food because he is 'the son of Joseph, whose father and mother [people] know' (6.42). The reader, however, has just read an episode in which Jesus walks on water and uses a divine self-proclamation (6.19-20). If the reader detected in

---

Lincoln, *John*, pp. 219–20. According to Madden, *Sea*, p. 111 n. 107, there are six instances in the LXX that contain the command μὴ φοβοῦ or μὴ φοβεῖτε plus the phrase ἐγώ εἰμι (Gen. 26.24; 46.3; Jer. 1.8, 17; 26.28; 49.11).

   34. Lincoln, *John*, p. 221.

   35. O'Day, 'John 6:15-21', pp. 157–8, judges that the negative portrayal of the disciples in 6.60-71 should deter us from seeing in Jn 6.21 the disciples' joyous reception of Jesus. However, Jn 6.60, 66 states that 'many' (not all) of his disciples were offended at Jesus' words, and that 'many' (not all) of his disciples quit following him, but the twelve decided to remain with him (6.67-70).

   36. Potterie, *Vérité*, p. 102 n. 60; Heil, *Jesus*, p. 146.

Jn 6.19-20 a link to Job 9.8, where the Creator God is portrayed as walking on the sea, it would be relatively easy for such a reader to come to the conclusion that Jesus has a close association with God that legitimizes his participation in the divine activity of giving bread from heaven.[37] Therefore, the reader could see the primal significance of Jesus and the message about him and privilege over Moses.[38]

II. The Healing of a Man Born Blind

a. *Assessment*
Despite the fact that there are no significant verbal parallels between Jn 9.6 and Gen. 2.7,[39] a number of scholars have suggested that the use of mud in the healing of a man born blind alludes to the creation of Adam.[40]

---

37. Others have attempted to explain the literary relationship between Jn 6.16-21 and its following context differently. Lindars, *John*, p. 245, suggests that walking on the sea was attached to the feeding discourse because 'The abiding presence of Jesus is a feature of the Church's Eucharistic teaching'. However, a Eucharistic reading of Jn 6 is problematic, since there are virtually no explicit references to the Lord's Supper in GJohn. Others have attempted to see an Exodus motif in Jn 6: as the manna story is related to Israel crossing the Red Sea, so the discourse about bread from heaven is linked to Jesus walking on the water (Beasley-Murray, *John*, p. 89; von Wahlde, *John*, vol. 2, p. 280; Carson, *John*, p. 273; cf. C. H. Giblin, 'The Miraculous Crossing of the Sea [Jn 6,16-21]', *NTS* 28 [1983], pp. 96-103 [98]). However, the images are different. On the one hand, Israel walks on dry land when crossing the sea. On the other hand, Jesus walks on the sea. Cf. Lindars, *John*, p. 246.

38. Cf. Dodd, *Interpretation*, p. 344. O'Day, 'John 6:15-21', p. 158, also notes that the identification of Jesus as 'the prophet who is to come into the world' in Jn 6.14 is intended to put into the mouth of people the claim that he is 'the prophet-king like Moses' (cf. Meeks, *Moses*).

39. Minear, *Christians*, p. 93, points out that both texts share the same verb (ποιέω). Koch, 'Geschaffen', pp. 206-7, suggests a few parallels between the two texts: (1) both the creation of man and the healing of the man have two parts, the preparation of the material and the use of it; (2) the use of ἐπιχρίω in Jn 9.6 implies that Jesus not only put clay in the man's eyes but also communicated spirit to him, as God gives to the man the breath of life in Gen. 2.7.

40. Lightfoot, *John*, p. 202; W. F. Hambly, 'Creation and Gospel: A Brief Comparison of Genesis 1,1–2,4 and John 1,1–2,12', in *Studia Evangelica* (ed. F. L. Cross; TUGAL, 103; Berlin: Akademie Verlag, 1968), pp. 69–74 (69 n. 4); Culpepper, *Anatomy*, p. 34; Lindars, *John*, p. 343; Brodie, *John*, p. 347; Keener, *John*, vol. 1, p. 780; Painter, 'Light', p. 42; McDonough, *Creator*, p. 35; J. W. Holleran, 'Seeing the Light: A Narrative Reading of John 9. II', *ETL* 69 (1993), pp. 354–82 (359 n. 112); Derrett, 'Miracles', p. 76. Barrett, *John*, p. 358, rightly concluded that an allusion here to Gen. 2.7 is improbable.

Here I ask instead whether this distinctive action[41] can be related to a broader background in which the noun πηλός is used in creation contexts.

John 9.6

Ταῦτα εἰπὼν ἔπτυσεν χαμαὶ καὶ ἐποίησεν <u>πηλὸν</u> ἐκ τοῦ πτύσματος καὶ ἐπέχρισεν αὐτοῦ τὸν <u>πηλὸν</u> ἐπὶ τοὺς ὀφθαλμοὺς

Isaiah 64.7 LXX

καὶ νῦν, κύριε, πατὴρ ἡμῶν σύ, ἡμεῖς δὲ <u>πηλὸς</u> ἔργον τῶν χειρῶν σου πάντες·

Job 10.9 LXX

μνήσθητι ὅτι <u>πηλόν</u> με ἔπλασας, εἰς δὲ γῆν με πάλιν ἀποστρέφεις

Jesus manifested (φανερωθῇ) the works of God (τὰ ἔργα τοῦ θεοῦ) in the man born blind by anointing his eyes with clay (πηλός, 9.3-6). Similarly, Isaiah says that God's people are the clay (πηλός), the work (ἔργον)[42] of God's hands (Isa. 64.7).[43] In the context of Isa. 64.7 people are portrayed as not having seen with their eyes (οἱ ὀφθαλμοὶ ἡμῶν εἶδον), but it is nevertheless said that they will see God's works (τὰ ἔργα σου) that he will do (ἃ ποιήσεις) (64.3). Despite these similarities, there are also important differences. For example, there is no mention of light in Isa. 64.7.

Some similarities can also be observed between Jn 9.6 and Job 10.[44] Job refers to God as the One who fashioned and made him (10.8) of clay

41. Scholars often recognize the difficulties associated with the interpretation of this act (e.g. Carson, *John*, p. 363). Some have proposed that the use of mud indicates that Jesus is a 'folk healer' (e.g. B. J. Malina and R. L. Rohrbaugh, *Social-Science Commentary on the Gospel of John* [Minneapolis: Fortress, 1998], pp. 170, 175), one who breaks the law by mixing clay on the Sabbath (e.g. Bultmann, *John*, p. 332 n. 3; Schnackenburg, *John*, vol. 2, p. 242; von Wahlde, *John*, vol. 2, p. 425), or a prophet like Elisha (e.g. M. Edwards, *John* [Oxford: Blackwell, 2004], p. 152).

42. The plural εργα is used in Codex Sinaiticus (S), the Hexaplaric recension (*O''*), the Lucianic recension (*L'''*-233), the Catena (*C''*), a number of cursives (e.g. 403' [403+613] 407 544), and three church fathers (Theodoret of Cyrrhus, Chrysostom, and Jerome).

43. J. D. M. Derrett, 'John 9:6 Read with Isaiah 6:10; 20:9', *EvQ* 66 (1994), pp. 251–4, has related the anointing in Jn 9.6 to the verb שׁעע found in Isa 6.10; 29.9. His suggestion is unlikely, because none of the verbs used in the LXX (καμμύω, Isa. 6.10; κραιπαλάω, Isa. 29.9) occurs in Jn 9.6. Derrett also suggests that Jn 9.6 is to be read in light of Gen. 2.5-7 (p. 255).

44. A few commentators point to Job 10.9 when explaining Jn 9.6. Cf. Hoskyns, *Gospel*, vol. 2, p. 408; Brown, *John*, vol. 1, p. 372; Michaels, *John*, p. 546 n. 38; McDonough, *Creator*, p. 35. In Job 10.9 cursive 106 has the dative form (πηλω)

(πηλός, 10.9),[45] and to people as the works of God's hands (ἔργα χειρῶν σου) (10.3; cf. v. 8). Job's situation bears some resemblance to that of the man born blind. In both cases people deem that their unfortunate condition is related to sin (Jn 9.2-3; Job 10.7, 14-15; cf. 9.20-21). Despite these similarities, there are once again important differences. For example, Job's sickness is not related to blindness.[46]

The strongest similarity between Jn 9.6, Isa. 64.7, and Job 10.9 is the noun πηλός, which is commonplace in the LXX but unusual in the NT. Outside GJohn, it is used only in Rom. 9.21, where a creation context is in view. In the LXX the noun can be used either in a literal sense or in a figurative sense.[47] In this latter category the noun is used in creation contexts in Job 33.4-6; 38.14; Sir. 33.10-13; Isa. 29.16 (cf. Rom. 9.20-21; *LAB* 53.13); 45.9.[48]

John uses the word πηλός several times (9.6, 11, 14, 15),[49] and this highlights how the healing he narrates is distinctive: this is the only time in the four canonical gospels when Jesus uses clay to restore someone's sight.[50] If John knew any or all of the Synoptic Gospels (or the traditions that shaped them), it is difficult to explain why he included the noun πηλός,[51] which the tradition preserved in the Synoptic Gospels lacks.

---

instead of the accusative form (πηλόν). Cursive 644 has a longer reading, using the adjective πηλινον. Cyril of Alexandria uses the same noun found in Gen. 2.7, χοῦν. Here I follow the reading attested in the majority of manuscripts, πηλόν.

45. The noun חמר occurs both in Isa 64.7 and Job 10.9.

46. Unlike Job, the man in Jn 9 is anonymous, as is expected of blind people of low social status in antiquity. Cf. D. Opatrný, 'The Figure of a Blind Man in the Light of the Papyrological Evidence', *Bib* 91 (2010), pp. 583–94 (585–7).

47. Literal sense: clay for buildings (Gen. 11.3; Exod. 1.14; Nah. 3.14), for moulding objects (Wis. 15.7, 8; Sir. 38.30; Bel 1.7), or simply the clay found in the streets (Zech. 10.5). Figurative sense: to express human fragility (2 Kgdms 22.43 / Ps. 17.43), disgrace (Pss. 39.3; 68.15), abundance (Zech. 9.3), or something of low value (Job 27.16; 30.19; Wis. 7.9; 15.10; Mic. 7.10; Isa. 14.23; 41.25).

48. There are two cases where the creation context is not clear, but one might argue that 'clay' is used in reference to creation (Job 4.19; Jer. 18.6).

49. K. H. Rengstorf, 'πηλός', *TDNT*, vol. 6, p. 118, says, 'such emphasis… suggests that there is more behind it [πηλός] than a mere stress on the fact that Jesus was showing His freedom in respect of the law of the Sabbath'.

50. Jesus spits on the eyes (Mk 8.23-25), touches the eyes (Mt. 9.27-29; 20.30-34; cf. Mt. 12.22; 15.30-31; 21.14), or uses only his voice (Mk 10.51-52; Lk. 18.42-43; cf. Lk. 4.18; 7.21-22) to restore blind men in the Synoptic Gospels. B. Witherington, *John's Wisdom: A Commentary on the Fourth Gospel* (Cambridge: Lutterworth, 1995), p. 180, has observed that the healing of blind people is the most common miracle in Jesus' ministry.

51. Jesus is portrayed as using 'clay' in order to mould 'twelve sparrows' in *Inf. Gos. Thom.* 2 (Elliott, *Apocryphal*, pp. 75–6).

One wonders whether John had in mind a larger OT background when he used this noun. As has been observed above, this noun is used in Isa. 64.7 and Job 10.9 in creation contexts.[52] It has also been already noted that Job is not a noticeable text in GJohn, but the book of Isaiah is one of John's favourites. As Catrin Williams has observed: 'Isaiah occupies a prominent, if not the highest, position among the scriptural texts that have contributed to the shaping'[53] of GJohn.

As for Second-Temple Jewish texts, the *Testament of Naphtali* and Qumran literature are particularly relevant.[54] God is portrayed as Creator in *T. Naph.* 2.2, since the narrator compares him with a potter who uses clay (πηλός) to form people.[55] The narrator behind this text indicates that the Most High created everything (2.3), including every human being according to his image (2.5).

The noun πηλός is used in the LXX in creation contexts where חמר appears in the MT (Job 10.9; 33.6; 38.14; Isa. 29.16; 45.9; 64.7). Similarly, a number of Qumran texts use חמר in creation contexts.[56] The narrator behind 1QS XI, 20-22 says that people (בן־אדם) born of woman are shaped from dust (מעפר) and saliva (מצירוק), and are moulded clay (חמר). In the *Hodayotª* (1QHª XX, 32-34) God is described as the One who is able to open people's mouths, and man is portrayed as clay (חמר) and saliva. Elsewhere in *Hodayotª* man is also referred to as created from clay (החמר) and water (IX, 21; cf. XI, 20-24; XIX, 3) in a context where God is represented as the One who fashioned every spirit, who stretched

---

52. The creation context is even clearer in some manuscripts of Isa. 64.7 that follow the MT (ואתה יצרנו) by adding και συ ο πλαστης ημων (uncial V, the Lucianic recension, some cursives, Theodoret; and Aquila and Theodotion, according to uncial Q and the Syro-Lucian tradition). This reading is explicitly marked as an addition to Origen's text in conformity with the MT.

53. Williams, 'Isaiah', p. 101. There are four explicit quotations from Isaiah in GJohn (Isa. 6.10 / Jn 12.40; 40.3 / 1.23; 53.1 / 12.38; 54.13 / 6.45) and numerous Isaianic motifs (Reim, *Studien*, p. 163).

54. See also *LAE* 27.2, where Adam recognizes that he was formed from 'clay' (*de limo terre plasmati*; J. H. Mozley, 'The Vitae Adae', *JTS* 30 [1929], pp. 121–49 [136]). The noun πηλός occurs also in *Jos. Asen.* 10.16; 13.7; 15.3; Philo, *Op. Mund.* 38; *Conf. Ling.* 1, 89, 103, 104; *Vit. Mos.* 1.38; *Leg. Gai.* 201; Josephus, *Ant.* 1.244; 4.275; *Apion* 2.252, in contexts where creation is not in view.

55. M. de Jonge, *The Testaments of the Twelve Patriarchs: A Critical Edition of the Greek Text* (PVTG, 1/2; Leiden: Brill, 1978), p. 114. In *2 En.* 65.2 God is portrayed as the One who created man and gave him eyes (cf. Ps. 93.9 LXX). However, *2 En.* 65.2 does not use the noun 'clay'.

56. D. Frayer-Griggs, 'Spittle, Clay, and Creation in John 9:6 and Some Dead Sea Scrolls', *JBL* 132 (2013), pp. 659–70.

out the heavens, and created the earth and the spirit of man (IX, 7-15; cf. XII, 29-38; XXII, 7; XXIII, 12).[57]

Since the same noun used in Jn 9.6 is used in creation contexts in Jewish literature, one wonders whether ancient readers related this Johannine verse to creation. There are at least three ancient Christian authors who posited this kind of connection. Irenaeus writes that the healing of the man born blind in GJohn was intended to show 'the Hand of God (*manum Dei*), the Hand which originally formed man (*ab initio plasmavit hominem*)' (*Haer.* 5.15.2). He adds that 'the works of God' (Jn 9.3) is 'the formation of man' (5.15.2), because in the beginning God formed man from clay. Irenaeus related Jn 9.6 to Gen. 2.7 and concluded that the one who formed the man in the beginning is the same one who is now healing the man born blind (5.15.3), since Jesus is creating eyes for this man (5.15.2, 4; 5.16.1).[58] Ephrem the Syrian understands that Jesus made eyes with the clay in order to give light to the man (*Commentary on Tatian's Diatessaron* 16.28).[59] Ephrem then related this miracle to the creation of light in Gen. 1 and concluded that Jesus is the Son of 'him whose hand had formed the First Adam from the earth' (16.28, 31).[60] Severus saw in this miracle a creation act and related it to the book of Job (ἢ ὡς ἡ βίβλος Ἰὼβ).[61]

It is significant that the noun πηλός is used five times in the story of the healing of the man born blind (Jn 9.6, 11, 14, 15) because this noun is used only once elsewhere in the NT (Rom. 9.21, where creation imagery is in view). Furthermore, πηλός occurs in a context where the reader is

57. García-Martínez and Tigchelaar (eds.), *Scrolls*, pp. 98–9, 192–7, 158–9, 164–7, 188–9. Cf. M. A. Daise, 'Biblical Creation Motifs in the Qumran Hodayot', in *The Dead Sea Scrolls Fifty Years after their Discovery* (ed. L. H. Schiffman, E. Tov, and J. C. VanderKam; Jerusalem: Israel Exploration Society, 2000), pp. 293–305 (296).

58. Rousseau, Doutreleau, and Mercier, *Irénée*, pp. 202–14; J. Keble, *Five Books of s. Irenaeus: Against Heresies* (Oxford: James Parker, 1872), pp. 485–8. Cf. A. C. Jacobsen, 'The Importance of Genesis 1–3 in the Theology of Irenaeus', *ZAC* 8 (2004), pp. 299–316. Similarly, Ammonius thinks that Jesus created eyes for the man and used mud because he 'wanted to show…that he himself is the one who made Adam from earth' (*Fragments on John* 317; Elowsky [ed.], *Scripture*, vol. 4a, p. 324).

59. Beasley-Murray, *John*, p. 151.

60. McCarthy, *Saint Ephrem*, pp. 258–9. Other Christian authors who saw creation imagery in Jn 9.6 include Chrysostom, *Hom. Jo.* 56.2, and Cyril of Alexandria, *Commentary on John* 6. Cf. J. A. Cramer (ed.), *Catenae Graecorum Patrum in Novum Testamentum* (8 vols.; Oxford: E Typographeo Academico, 1838–1844), vol. 2, pp. 286–9.

61. Corderio, *Catena*, pp. 250–1. For a list of church fathers who have related Jn 9.6 to Gen. 2.7, see Schnackenburg, *John*, vol. 2, p. 496 n. 13.

directed to the prologue and to Jewish discussions about God's rest after creation.[62] Jesus claims to be the 'light of the world' (9.5; cf. 1.9; 8.12) and to perform the works of the One who sent him (9.3-4; cf. 5.17, 20, 36).[63] The evidence allows us to claim that John is possibly using creation imagery as he portrays Jesus employing clay to heal a man born blind in Jn 9.6. The reader who knows that the Word was behind the divine act of creation (1.3, 10) can see in Jesus' action an instance of creation imagery.

b. *The Significance of Jesus' Miracle*
If John may be using creation imagery when portraying Jesus healing a man born blind, the question that needs to be answered now is what role this act plays in the larger literary context of Jn 9.6.

The location of Jesus' miracle in GJohn and the repeated mention of the use of 'mud' seem to indicate that John wanted to highlight this story. Since the reader has been reading long discourses and dialogues in Jn 7–8, the miracle in Jn 9 provides a much-needed change in the tone of the narrative.[64] This miracle is Jesus' third healing narrated so far. But unlike the two previous healings, where people were healed only by Jesus' word (4.50; 5.8), here the reader encounters a more elaborate procedure. Jesus spits on the ground, makes mud with the saliva, anoints the man's eyes with the mud, and commands him to go and wash in the pool of Siloam (9.6-7).[65] The detail that Jesus used mud in healing this man is repeated three more times in Jn 9.11, 14, 15.

Jesus has made a number of claims in the preceding sections of this Gospel when talking to the Pharisees (8.13), the Jews (7.15, 35), the crowd (7.20, 40), and the Jews who have believed in him (8.31).[66] His

62. Lightfoot, *John*, p. 202. Lindars, *John*, p. 343, and Hoskyns, 'Genesis', p. 216, deem that the indication that the man was blind 'from birth' in 9.1 highlights that Jesus' miracle is a 'creative act' (cf. Koch, 'Geschaffen', pp. 205–6). However, this is unlikely.

63. S. van Tilborg, 'Cosmological Implications of Johannine Christology', in Van Belle, van der Watt, and Maritz (eds.), *Theology and Christology*, pp. 483–502 (490). H. Hübner, *Vetus Testamentum in Novo* (vol. 1/2; Göttingen: Vandenhoeck & Ruprecht, 2003), pp. 372–3, thinks that there is a parallel between 'ground' (χαμαί) in Jn 9.6 and 'dust' (χοῦν) in Gen. 2.7. However, since the words are different, it is difficult to justify a literary link here.

64. Brown, *John*, vol. 1, p. 376.

65. Haenchen, *John 2*, p. 38; von Wahlde, *John*, vol. 2, pp. 425–6.

66. A full list of correspondences between Jn 7–8 and Jn 9 can be seen in J. W. Holleran, 'Seeing the Light: A Narrative Reading of John 9. I', *ETL* 69 (1993), pp. 5–26 (10).

last claim in Jn 7–8 has been, 'before Abraham was, I am' (8.58).[67] Some have rejected Jesus because they think they know his origins (πόθεν εστίν, 7.27; cf. 7.41, 52). People have also questioned Jesus about his identity: 'Who are you?' (8.25); 'Who makes you yourself?' (8.53; cf. 5.18).[68] Others have even made judgements about his identity: Jesus is a Samaritan and is possessed by a demon (7.20; 8.48)[69] because he claims that he preceded Abraham (8.52-53). On the other hand, Jesus has claimed that he knows where he comes from (πόθεν ἔρχομαι, 8.14). Jesus comes from God (7.29; 8.42), since he is from above (ἐκ τῶν ἄνω), not from this world (ἐκ τούτου τοῦ κόσμου, 8.23).[70]

Jesus has taken the discussion that precedes the miracle in Jn 9 back to the beginning (8.33-58). Since the Jews are trying to kill Jesus, he asso-ciates them with the one who was a murderer and a liar in the beginning (ἀπ᾽ ἀρχῆς, 8.44; cf. 1 Jn 3.8-10; Gen. 3.1-5).[71] On the other hand, the Jews cannot accept that Jesus is claiming to have existed before Abraham (8.57).[72] For the Jews, Jesus is less than fifty years old (8.57) and cannot be 'greater' than Abraham (8.53).[73] In this context the use of mud in the healing of a man born blind would be a dramatic representation of Jesus' claims as found in Jn 8. By healing a man in Jn 9, Jesus is performing an act that resembles that of the Creator God. Jesus is performing here a divine activity in order to show that he is not possessed by a demon, but

67. This claim would mean that Jesus 'does not belong to the ranks of historical personages' (Bultmann, *John*, p. 327).

68. Bultmann, *John*, p. 325; Hoskyns, *Gospel*, vol. 2, p. 398; Barrett, *John*, p. 351; Lincoln, *John*, p. 275; Michaels, *John*, p. 528.

69. The Jews' accusation that Jesus is demon-possessed is countered by Jesus' assertion that the devil is the Jews' father (8.44) (Lindars, *John*, p. 332; cf. Lincoln, *John*, p. 274).

70. According to Lindars, *John*, p. 320, this (8.23) would sound to a Hellenistic reader like a 'radical dualism, the complete incompatibility between the eternal and the created orders'. Jesus' assertion that he is from 'above' would mean that he is from God, because for John 'origin is synonymous with membership' (Bultmann, *John*, p. 348 n. 2).

71. F. M. Braun, 'L'arrière-fond du quatrième Évangile', in *L'Évangile de Jean*, pp. 179–96 (181), even saw in the opposition between Jesus and 'the prince of the world' elsewhere in GJohn (e.g. 12.31; 14.30; 16.11) reminders of Gen. 3.15.

72. Lindars, *John*, p. 336; Hoskyns, *Gospel*, vol. 2, p. 401, and Brown, *John*, vol. 1, p. 360, have observed that γίνομαι is used both in 8.58 and 1.3 (cf. Bultmann, *John*, p. 327; Michaels, *John*, p. 533). Jesus is then claiming pre-existence here (Beasley-Murray, *John*, p. 139; cf. Moloney, *John*, p. 287).

73. This (8.53) would indicate that the Jews grasped Jesus' claims aright: Jesus is greater than Abraham and the prophets (Bultmann, *John*, p. 325; Hoskyns, *Gospel*, vol. 2, p. 398). Cf. Mt. 3.9; Lk. 3.8 (Terian, 'Creation', p. 58).

is rather to be regarded as existing before Abraham. Jesus' origins should be located in God himself. Just as in the prologue the sentence θεὸς ἦν ὁ λόγος (1.1) requires further clarification (πρὸς τὸν θεόν, 1.1-2), here in Jn 8–9 Jesus' claim that he exists before Abraham (8.58) is clarified by a miracle where he shows that God is with him (Jn 9.3, 33). The reader has encountered different opinions about Jesus' identity and origins in Jn 7–8, but the miracle that he performs in Jn 9 confirms his claim that he comes from God the Father as the light of the world.

In John's narrative world Jesus' miracle produces several reactions. On the one hand, the former blind man seems to acknowledge that Jesus is from God (παρὰ θεοῦ, 9.33). On the other hand, the Jewish leaders deny that Jesus comes from God (παρὰ θεοῦ, 9.16; cf. 9.29).[74] In between these two reactions, some Jews ask: 'A demon cannot open the eyes of the blind, can it?' (10.21; cf. 9.16). The question of Jesus' origins causes discussions both in Jn 8 and in Jn 9.[75] The reader who has the advantage of the prologue can see the miracle in Jn 9 in light of Jn 1.1-18. There the Word was in the beginning with God (1.1-2), taking an active role in creation (1.3, 10). The Word was the source of life and the 'light of humankind' (1.4), the 'true light' for humanity (1.9). Similarly, Jesus is the light of the world who gives sight to a man born in darkness (9.5-6).[76] The prologue has anticipated that the Word was from the Father (παρὰ πατρός, 1.14), and in Jn 9.33 the reader finds that the one who performed the miracle is from God (παρὰ θεοῦ). Therefore, creation imagery in Jn 9.6 is used to support the idea found in the prologue that Jesus existed with God in the beginning as the light of the world, and functions as a dramatic representation of Jesus' claims in Jn 7–8.

The location of Jesus' origins before Abraham, with the Creator God himself, authorizes his participation in divine activities.[77] Jesus brings light into the world (cf. Jn 1.9) by giving sight to a man born blind and by bringing judgement to those who do not believe.[78] Jesus asserts that he

---

74. They deny Jesus' claim in 8.40, 42 (Lindars, *John*, p. 345).

75. Hooker, 'Johannine Prologue', p. 47.

76. Lightfoot, *John*, p. 199; Moloney, *John*, p. 292; J. Painter, 'John 9 and the Interpretation of the Fourth Gospel', *JSNT* 28 (1986), pp. 31–61 (32–3). Since darkness is not explicitly mentioned in Jn 9, Lightfoot's opinion (*John*, p. 199) that Jesus' miracle represents the 'transition of…fallen man…out of darkness into full enlightenment' (cf. Brown, *John*, vol. 1, p. 376) is perhaps beyond John's intention.

77. Dodd, *Interpretation*, p. 257.

78. Barrett, *John*, p. 358. Lightfoot, *John*, p. 199, also linked this miracle to the feast of Tabernacles (7.2). However, since there is no explicit mention of this feast in Jn 8, Jn 9 cannot be tightly tied to the feast of Tabernacles (Holleran, 'John 9. I', p. 7).

has come into the world for judgement, 'that those who do not see may see, and those who see may become blind' (9.39).[79] These divine activities not only support Jesus' claim that he existed before Abraham, (8.58),[80] they also create conflict with those who regard themselves as disciples of Moses (9.28; cf. Mt. 23.2).[81] The Jews draw a contrast between Jesus and Moses (9.29; cf. 1.17; 5.46).[82] They assert that God spoke to Moses (Exod. 33.11), but they claim that they do not know where Jesus comes from (9.29). On the other hand, the former blind man seems to relate Jesus' miracle to Jesus' origins because he replies to the Jews: 'You do not know where he comes from, and yet he opened my eyes' (9.30). Since the Jews have introduced Moses into the discussion, the former blind man's assertion that 'never since the world began has it been heard that anyone opened the eyes of a man born blind' (9.32; cf. 15.24; Isa. 64.3)[83] might be read as implying that not even Moses was capable of such divine activity.[84] This unprecedented miracle shows that the relationship between God and Jesus is also unprecedented.[85] Therefore, the conclusion John wants his readers to draw from this miracle is that Jesus is uniquely related to God since he comes from him (παρὰ θεοῦ, 9.33).

In the prologue the narrator describes two groups: those who rejected (1.11) the one through whom everything was created (1.3, 10) and those

79. On the basis of Jn 5, Holleran, 'John 9. I', p. 16, and idem, 'John 9. II', p. 37, identifies the 'works of God' (9.3) with Jesus' authority to judge (9.39-41) (cf. Witherington, *John's Wisdom*, p. 181).

80. Carson, *John*, p. 358, understands Jesus' claim in Jn 8.58 as 'superiority' over Abraham.

81. Although there is a contrast here between Moses and Jesus (Barrett, *John*, p. 362; Beasley-Murray, *John*, p. 158), Jesus is not discrediting Moses (cf. Lindars, *John*, p. 348), since Moses is elsewhere a witness to Jesus (5.46) and the giver of the law (7.19) (Michaels, *John*, pp. 559–60).

82. Lincoln, *John*, p. 284; Brown, *John*, vol. 1, p. 374; Michaels, *John*, p. 559; Carson, *John*, p. 374. Cf. W. M. Wright IV, *Rhetoric and Theology: Figural Reading of John 9* (BZAW, 165; Berlin: W. de Gruyter, 2009), p. 181 n. 148. Another point of comparison between Jesus and Moses is that both have disciples (9.28) (G. Marconi, 'La vista del cieco. Struttura di Gv 9,1-41', *Greg* 79 [1998], pp. 625-43 [639]).

83. Lindars, *John*, p. 349, sees in Jn 9.32 'a hint of the creation of light' (Gen. 1.3). Since there are no verbal parallels between the two texts, Lindars' proposal is dubious. For ancient Hellenistic stories of the blind being cured, see F. Martin (ed.), *Narrative Parallels to the New Testament* (SBLRBS, 22; Atlanta: Scholars Press, 1988), p. 224.

84. Lindars, *John*, p. 348, 'the healing of the blind man provides part of Jesus' credentials to be one who is greater than Moses'.

85. Beasley-Murray, *John*, p. 158.

who received the Word (the true Light) who was in the beginning (1.12). In the same way, here in Jn 9, the narrator portrays the blind man as receiving the one who identifies himself with the 'light of the world' (9.5), while the Jews reject him because he was 'working' on the Sabbath by making mud (9.15-16).[86]

III. Conclusion

There are reasons to suggest that John might be using creation imagery in Jn 6.19 and 9.6. It is possible that John is drawing on and creatively deploying terms and images stemming from OT narratives where creation imagery plays a prominent role. In the first case (Jn 6.19) Jesus walking on the sea might be tied to a particular text, Job 9.8. In the second case (Jn 9.6) the use of mud in the healing of a man born blind might be related to a broader OT and Second-Temple Jewish background where 'mud' is used in creation contexts. In both cases Jesus' distinctive actions enhance the suggestion that John might have intended creation imagery when portraying Jesus in those texts. The reader who knows that Jesus, the Word made flesh, took an active role in creation (1.3, 10) can see creation imagery in Jn 6.19 and 9.6.

Each of those two instances is placed in a strategic location in GJohn. Since Jn 6.16-21 seems to interrupt the natural flow of Jn 6.1-15 and 6.25-71, the Johannine reader is forced to pay attention to the story of Jesus walking on the sea. Since there is a long section devoted to dialogues and discourses in Jn 7–8, the miracle story in Jn 9 is a much-needed change in the tone of the narrative for Johannine readers.

Both texts function in similar ways and are used to support some of the ideas found elsewhere in GJohn, particularly in the prologue. The portrayal of Jesus walking on the sea is used to illustrate the idea that Jesus comes in the name of the Father in order to reveal God (Jn 1.1-18; 5.17-47). Since he is able to perform an act that resembles that of the Creator God in Job 9.8, he and his message are to be regarded as privileged over Moses, through whom manna was given to Israel (6.26-58). The portrayal of Jesus giving sight to a man born blind is used to illustrate his claims that he comes from the Father (e.g. 8.42) and exists before Abraham (8.58). John asserts the primal significance of Jesus and privileges him over Abraham (8.58) and Moses (9.29), since Jesus has been able to partake in the divine activities of bringing light (9.5) and judgement (9.39-41).

---

86. Witherington, *John's Wisdom*, p. 181.

Chapter 5

THE STRUCTURE OF GJOHN AND GENESIS 1–2

In the two preceding chapters (Chapters 3 and 4) I have argued that John uses limited (albeit significant) instances of creation imagery in his portrayal of Jesus' earthly ministry. In the present chapter I will support this contention by arguing against the suggestion that John used the seven days of creation in the composition of his Gospel. I set out to perform a thorough assessment of the evidence that bolsters the idea that John used Gen. 1–2 in various ways to arrange his narrative. The overall result of this inquiry is that there are reasons to judge that John was not intending to use the seven days of creation in his Gospel. This chapter serves the important purpose of clearing away undisciplined claims about the impact of Gen. 1–2 upon GJohn.

I. The Seven Days of Creation and John 1–2

Some scholars have argued that there is a sequence of days in Jn 1.19–2.12 that represents a week.[1] Rudolf Bultmann, for example, proposed that if one 'counts 1.19ff. as the first day, and includes, apart from the times mentioned (1.29, 35, 43) an extra day for vv. 40-42, then one arrives at the conclusion that 2.1-12 occurred on the seventh day'.[2] Some other scholars have claimed that John's putative week was structured in

---

1. Abbott, *Johannine Vocabulary*, p. 213; see also the list of scholars in M. J. J. Menken, *Numerical Literary Techniques in John: The Fourth Evangelist's Use of Numbers of Words and Syllables* (NovTSup, 55; Leiden: Brill, 1985), p. 94.
2. Bultmann, *John*, p. 114 n. 3. Bultmann also referred to O. Baumgarten et al., *Die Schriften des Neuen Testaments* (ed. J. Weiss; 4 vols.; Göttingen: Vandenhoeck & Ruprecht, 3rd edn, 1918), vol. 4; A. Omodeo, *La Mistica giovannea: saggio critico con nuova traduzione dei testi* (CS; Bari, Italy: Gius, Laterza & Figli, 1930); E. Hirsch, *Das vierte Evangelium: in seiner ursprünglichen Gestalt* (Tübingen: J. C. B. Mohr, 1936).

light of the seven days of creation in Gen. 1–2.[3] In spite of its critics,[4] this interpretation is still used favourably in recent Johannine works.[5] The major conclusion drawn by those who see the seven days of creation in Jn 1–2 is that the evangelist wanted to portray the beginning of Jesus' ministry as a new creation.[6]

Many proponents of a close link between the structure of Jn 1–2 and the seven days of creation would agree with Thomas Brodie's opinion: 'The overall impression—without pursuing the complex details—is that John has indeed used the seven-day structure of Genesis, but in doing so has made important adaptations'.[7] However, if one is to arrive at a properly nuanced estimate of the use of creation imagery in GJohn, one needs to pursue the 'complex details'. This involves looking closely at the sequence of days in Jn 1–2, assessing whether the suggested similarities between the Johannine account and the Genesis story of creation are truly convincing, and spotting the main differences between Gen. 1–2 and Jn 1–2.

There are six chronological signs in Jn 1–2: 'the next day' (1.29, 35, 43), 'that day' (1.39), 'on the third day' (2.1), and 'a few days' (2.12). This unique collocation of notes of time is, however, far from a clear indication for the reader that there are six or seven days in the narrative. There is no explicit indication of where to find the 'first day', and the phrase 'a few days' in 2.12 does not specify the exact number of days meant. Some scholars have proposed several sequences of six or seven days in Jn 1–2,[8] but none of them is convincing.

3. E. B. Allo, *L'évangile spirituel de Jean* (Paris: Cerf, 1944), pp. 75–6; F. Quiévreux, 'La structure symbolique de l'Évangile de Saint Jean', *RHPR* 33 (1953), pp. 123–65; M.-É. Boismard, *Du baptême à Cana (Jean 1,19–2,11)* (Paris: Cerf, 1956), p. 15 n. 3.

4. Ashton, *Understanding*, p. 190; J. A. T. Robinson, *The Priority of John* (London: SCM, 1985), pp. 162–8; and the list of scholars in Menken, *Techniques*, pp. 81, 94 n. 89.

5. C. Claussen, 'Turning Water to Wine: Re-reading the Miracle at the Wedding in Cana', in *Jesus Research: An International Perspective* (ed. J. H. Charlesworth and P. Pokorný; Grand Rapids: Eerdmans, 2009), pp. 73–97 (93); Köstenberger, *Theology*, p. 349; R. Zimmermann, 'Symbolic Communication between John and His Reader: The Garden Symbolism in John 19–20', in Thatcher and Moore (eds.), *Anatomies of Narrative Criticism*, pp. 221–35 (232); Carson, *John*, p. 168.

6. Boismard, *Cana*, p. 15.

7. Brodie, *John*, pp. 130–1.

8. Saxby, 'Time-Scheme', p. 13.

It has been posited that the 'first day' begins in Jn 1.19 and ends in 1.28.[9] It is not impossible that the events narrated in 1.19-28 lasted one day, but it is far from clear that John wanted his readers to detect a day there. Other scholars have taken the prologue (1.1-18) as the 'first day' instead.[10] There is no doubt that the Genesis account of creation has influenced Jn 1.1-5, but it is difficult to see how Jn 1.1-18 can represent a 'first day'. It seems that John was intending to compress the whole story of creation with the words 'all things were created by him' (1.3) and was not interested in portraying a specific day in the prologue.

Some have also found an additional day in Jn 1.35-42. The sequence from 1.29-34 to 1.35-42 is straightforward.[11] Both sections begin with 'the next day' (τῇ ἐπαύριον; 1.29, 35).[12] However, some scholars have argued that it is not possible that the events narrated in 1.35-42 took place in one single day. Therefore, they propose that a new day has to be seen in 1.40-42.[13] In order to justify a separate day in 1.40-42, M.-É. Boismard and W. F. Hambly adopted the variant reading 'in the morning' (*mane*; πρωΐ) in 1.41, which is found in a series of Old Latin manuscripts from the fifth century onwards and in one manuscript of the Syriac version.[14] This reading, however, is too weakly attested to be taken as original.[15] Furthermore, since John has used explicit indications

9. Boismard, *Cana*, pp. 14–15; T. Barrosse, 'The Seven Days of the New Creation in St. John's Gospel', *CBQ* 21 (1959), pp. 507–16 (507); Brown, *John*, vol. 1, p. 106; P. Trudinger, 'The Seven Days of the New Creation in St. John's Gospel: Some Further Reflections', *EvQ* 44 (1972), pp. 154–9; K. Löning and E. Zenger, *Als Anfang schuf Gott: Biblische Schöpfungstheologien* (Düsseldorf: Patmos, 1997), p. 110.

10. Saxby, 'Time-Scheme', p. 10.

11. Boismard, *Cana*, pp. 14–15, also attempted to find two separate days in Jn 1.43-46 and 1.47-51. However, he later changed his mind, and took 1.43-51 as a single day: M.-É. Boismard and A. Lamouille, *L'évangile de Jean. Commentaire* (SQEF, 3; Paris: Cerf, 1977), p. 99.

12. John uses the adverb ἐπαύριον elsewhere in his Gospel. In Jn 6.22 and 12.12 this adverb is used to indicate that an event took place in the same location as a previous event. There is nothing in the context of Jn 6.22 or 12.12 that may indicate that this adverb evokes Gen. 1–2.

13. Boismard, *Cana*, pp. 14–15; Barrosse, 'Days', pp. 507–16; Brown, *John*, vol. 1, p. 106; Trudinger, 'Days', pp. 154–9. Cf. P. W. Skehan, 'The Date of the Last Supper', *CBQ* 20 (1958), pp. 192–9 (197–8), who proposed a separate day out of Jn 1.39, where the disciple stay with Jesus.

14. Boismard, *Cana*, pp. 82–4; Hambly, 'Creation', p. 70. Cf. Saxby, 'Time-Scheme', p. 10, who deems Jn 1.40-42 to be the 'fifth day'.

15. Metzger, *Commentary*, p. 172; Hoskyns, *Gospel*, vol. 1, p. 181; Menken, *Techniques*, p. 94 n. 87; Robinson, *John*, p. 163.

of time in 1.29, 35, 43, the reader expects a similar explicit indication in 1.40-42 if John were intending a separate day here.[16]

John states clearly that the events narrated in 2.1-11 took place 'on the third day' (τῇ ἡμέρᾳ τῇ τρίτῃ, v. 1).[17] Some scholars have posited that this phrase represents either the 'sixth day'[18] or the 'seventh day'.[19] But the 'third day' is hardly a direct way of designating a sixth or seventh day.[20] Trudinger argues that the 'sixth day' is referred to as the 'third day' in Jn 2.1 because Jesus' miracle at Cana points to the resurrection.[21] However, according to Jn 20.1, Jesus' resurrection took place 'on the first day of the week'.

In their search for a putative 'seventh day' in Jn 1–2 that can be matched to the day of rest of God in Gen. 2, some scholars have given attention to Jn 2.12.[22] Hambly, for example, contended that Jn 2.12 represents the seventh day when Jesus rested after the miracle at Cana.[23] This conclusion is implausible for at least four reasons. The first reason is that Jesus stayed in Capernaum 'a few days' (οὐ πολλὰς ἡμέρας, 2.12), while God's rest after creation in Gen. 2.2-3 comprised only a single day. The second reason is that the phrase 'after this' (2.12) is not as clear as

16. Cf. F. Neirynck, *Jean et les Synoptiques: Examen critique de l'exégèse de M.-É Boismard* (BETL, 49; Leuven: Leuven University Press, 1979), p. 195.

17. The phrase 'third day' is commonplace in the LXX (e.g. Gen. 22.4; 31.2, 5, 22; 34.25; 40.20; 42.18; Exod. 19.11; Num. 7.24; Judg. 20.30; Hos. 6.2).

18. B. W. Bacon, 'After Six Days: A New Clue for Gospel Critics', *HTR* 8 (1915), pp. 94–120; J. Frey, *Die johanneische Eschatologie* (WUNT, 110; 3 vols.; Tübingen: Mohr Siebeck, 1998), vol. 2, pp. 193–5; Trudinger, 'Days', p. 155; Brown, *John*, vol. 1, p. 106; M. W. G. Stibbe, *John* (Sheffield: JSOT Press, 1993), p. 46. Cf. Origen, *Comm. Jo.* 6.259. Frey also refers to H. Lausberg, *Der Vers J 1,27 des Johannes-Evangeliums: Rhetorische Befunde zu Form und Sinn des Texts* (NAWG, 6; Göttingen: Vandenhoeck & Ruprecht, 1984), p. 284; idem, *Der Vers J 1,19 des Johannes-Evangeliums (im Rahmen des ,redaktionellen Kapitels' J 1,19– 2,11). Rhetorische Befunde zu Form und Sinn des Textes* (NAWG, 2; Göttingen: Vandenhoeck & Ruprecht, 1987), p. 11; idem, *Die Verse J 2,10-11 des Johannes-Evangeliums. Rhetorische Befunde zu Form und Sinn des Textes* (NAWG, 3; Göttingen: Vandenhoeck & Ruprecht, 1986), pp. 122–5.

19. Cf. the list of scholars in T. E. Phillips, ' "The Third Fifth Day?" John 2:1 in Context', *ExpTim* 115 (2004), pp. 328–31 (328 nn. 1–2); Frey, *Eschatologie*, vol. 2, p. 194.

20. Robinson, *John*, p. 165; cf. Brown, *John*, vol. 1, p. 106.

21. Trudinger, 'Days', p. 156. Cf. idem, ' "On the Third Day There Was a Wedding at Cana": Reflexions on St John 2, 1-12', *DRev* 104 (1986), pp. 41–3 (42–3); Dodd, *Interpretation*, p. 300.

22. Lausberg, 'J 2,10-11', pp. 122–5; Frey, *Eschatologie*, vol. 2, p. 195; Trudinger, 'Days', p. 155.

23. Hambly, 'Creation', p. 71.

'the next day' (e.g. 1.43). Therefore, John does not indicate explicitly that Jesus' arrival to Capernaum took place 'the next day' after the miracle at Cana. The third reason is that other people stayed in Capernaum with Jesus: his mother and brothers, and his disciples (2.12). Since they did not take an active role in the previous miracle at Cana, it is difficult to think that they stayed with Jesus in order to rest. If John were intending to portray the seventh day in 2.12 as a day of rest for Jesus, the mention of his family and disciples would be unnecessary. The fourth reason is that John never indicates that Jesus stayed in Capernaum in order to rest. The reference to a royal official of Capernaum who has heard about Jesus before (4.46-47) might indicate that Jesus was already known in Capernaum as one who performs healings (cf. 20.30). Therefore, there is room to posit that Jesus' stay in Capernaum in 2.12 involved some kind of activity (cf. 4.40-41; 10.40-41).[24]

There are some time indicators in Jn 1.29, 35, 39, 43; 2.1, 12, but they are far from signalling a clear sequence of six or seven days that resembles the days of creation in Genesis. Only if there were conspicuous similarities between Jn 1–2 and Gen. 1–2 might one be inclined to believe that John intended to shape the inaugural days of Jesus' ministry in light of the days of creation of the Genesis account. But a close assessment of suggested similarities between the two texts will show that this is not the case.

It has been suggested that Jn 2.11 is an allusion to Gen. 2.3, because the verb ποιέω and the broad idea of 'beginning' are used in both texts.[25] However, the meanings of the texts are very different. John refers to the first (ἀρχήν) sign performed by Jesus while Gen. 2.3 refers to the works of creation that God 'began' (ἤρξατο) to make (cf. Jn 13.5).[26] Similarities

---

24. Brodie, *John*, pp. 131, 161, suggests that the 'day of rest' is to be found in Jn 1.39. But this is dubious, because the time when Jesus stayed with the baptist's former disciples was four o'clock in the afternoon ('the tenth hour'), if we assume John is following the Jewish time reckoning (Michaels, *John*, p. 120). Saxby, 'Time-Scheme', p. 12, proposed that after Jn 1.51 and before 2.1 one can find a 'Sabbath Day of Rest'. However, this is speculative, because there is nothing in the text to support his opinion.

25. Lausberg, 'J 2,10-11', pp. 123–4; Frey, *Eschatologie*, vol. 2, p. 195 n. 199. The phrase ὧν ἤρξατο ὁ θεὸς ποιῆσαι (Gen. 2.3) is omitted in cursive 121. Moore, 'Creation', p. 189, relates Jn 2.11 to Gen. 1.1.

26. Barrosse, 'Days', p. 508, suggested that in both cases (Jn 1–2 and Gen. 1–2) the narrator introduces a particular individual or pair on each of the 'six days', and concluded that John imitated the structure of Genesis. However, several days in Gen. 1 do not have a particular individual or pair. In day three (Gen. 1.9-13) there is the description of at least four things (waters, dry land, pasture, and fruit-bearing

have also been proposed between the first and second days of creation and the putative Johannine days of new creation. Paul Trudinger and Hambly claimed that just as in Gen. 1.1-5 the light is separated from darkness, so too in Jn 1.19-28 the light (Jesus) is separated from the darkness (priests and Levites) by the witness of the Baptist.[27] This link seems speculative because John never identifies the priests and Levites with darkness. People can walk in, love, or abide in darkness (3.19; 8.12; 12.46; cf. 12.35) but people are never identified as darkness in GJohn. Trudinger also attempted to relate the second day of creation (Gen. 1.6-8) to Jn 1.32-33, based on the use of the nouns οὐρανός and ὕδωρ in both texts.[28] However, this seems to be a forced link. Both nouns are commonplace, and even in Gen. 1–2 they are used in other days of creation (οὐρανός, Gen. 1.1, 9, 14, 15, 17, 20, 26, 28, 30; 2.1, 4; ὕδωρ, 1.2, 9, 10, 20, 21, 22). Likewise, these nouns are used elsewhere in Jn 1.19–2.12 (1.51; 2.7, 9).

For the putative third, fourth, and fifth Johannine days, a few scholars have only been able to propose conceptual parallels without identifying verbal similarities with Gen. 1–2. Hambly suggested that the separation between 'dry land' and the 'seas' in Gen. 1.9 has to be related to the two disciples mentioned in Jn 1.35-39. Hambly proposed that Andrew represents the Hellenised world and the other disciple, whose name is not mentioned in the narrative (1.40), represents the Jews. Both are united in Jesus, claimed Hambly.[29] Trudinger attempted to relate the 'dry land' in Gen. 1.9 to the place where Jesus stayed with the two disciples (1.39).[30] Since the identity of the 'other disciple' (Jn 1.40) is not revealed in the

---

trees). On the one hand, only in day four (Gen. 1.14-19) does the narrator say explicitly that God created *two* things. On the other hand, the only place in Jn 1–2 where two people are explicitly mentioned as a pair is 1.37 (cf. 1.40), which Barrosse identified as the 'third day'.

27. Trudinger, 'Days', p. 157; Hambly, 'Creation', p. 71. Quiévreux, 'Jean', p. 132, related the first day of creation (Gen. 1.3-5) to Jn 1.1-28 and argued that both texts have in common the topic of light. However, light is used explicitly only in Jn 1.4-5, 7-9.

28. Trudinger, 'Days', p. 157. Hambly, 'Creation', p. 71, suggested that Jesus standing in the waters below (Jn 1.32-33) is related to the second day of creation in Genesis. However, there is no explicit indication that Jesus was standing in the waters, since John seems to avoid any direct indication that Jesus was baptized by John. See P. Fredriksen, *From Jesus to Christ: The Origins of the New Testament Images of Jesus* (New Haven: Yale University Press, 1988), p. 24.

29. Hambly, 'Creation', p. 72.

30. Trudinger, 'Days', p. 157.

text, and since there is no explicit indication of 'dry land' in Jn 1.39, Hambly and Trudinger's opinions seem speculative.[31] Trudinger has also attempted to relate the putative fourth Johannine day (1.40-42) to the 'two great lights' in Gen. 1.14-19. Trudinger deemed that Jesus is the greater light and Peter is 'the greatest of the lesser lights'.[32] But since Peter is never identified as light in GJohn (cf. 12.36), Trudinger's suggested conceptual parallel is weak. For the putative fifth Johannine day (1.43-51), Trudinger proposed that the mention of the town 'Bethsaida' and of Andrew, Peter, and Nathanael were intended to evoke the sea and his creatures. He observed that Andrew and Peter were fishermen and Nathanael is mentioned again in Jn 21.1-3 in a context where the sea and fishing are mentioned. Therefore, Trudinger concluded, there is a link to the description of the sea and its creatures in Gen. 1.20-23.[33] Yet, without significant verbal parallels, Trudinger's suggestions are not compelling.

The suggested linkages between Jn 2.1-11 (supposed sixth or seventh day) and the Genesis account of creation require implausible readings of GJohn. Thomas Barrosse argued that Jn 2.1-11 represents the consummation of the new creation because this text refers to Jesus' passion and resurrection (19.30; 20.1, 19). For him, 'all the elements of the new creation have been assembled' in Jn 1.19-51. Therefore, Barrosse concluded, Jn 2.1-11 is tied to the completion of creation in Gen. 2.1-3.[34] Since there are others who will also be attracted to Jesus' group in GJohn (e.g. Samaritans, 4.39-42; a royal official, 4.46, 53; Jewish people, 12.11), it is an exaggeration to claim that all the elements of the new creation are assembled in Jn 1–2. Hambly argued that the marriage in Jn 2.1-11 points to the new humanity created by Jesus' union with his

31. Hambly, 'Creation', p. 157, and Trudinger, 'Days', p. 72, also claimed that just as in Gen. 1.9-13 trees produced fruit according to their kind, so too in Jn 1.40-41 Andrew produces 'fruit' when bringing Simon to Jesus. But without verbal links, this suggested conceptual parallel is unconvincing.

32. Trudinger, 'Days', p. 157. Hambly, 'Creation', pp. 72–3, proposed that as the 'sun, moon, and stars' were created to mark 'signs' and seasons in Gen. 1, so too Peter is a 'sign' for the union of gentiles and Jews because he brings together these two groups.

33. Trudinger, 'Days', pp. 157–8. He also argued that the reference to angels in Jn 1.51 alludes to Jacob (Gen. 28.12), who received the promise of numerous offspring (Gen. 22.14) found in Gen. 1.22. Hambly, 'Creation', p. 73, on the other hand, saw in the fish and birds of day five in Gen. 1 the calling of the gentiles in Jn 1.43-51.

34. Barrosse, 'Days', pp. 508, 513.

disciples. This new humanity is related to the creation of man and woman in Gen. 1.27, according to Hambly.[35] But the texts are different. Genesis 1.27 narrates the creation of man and woman in the image of God, while Jn 2.1-11 portrays Jesus manifesting his glory by turning water into wine.[36]

There are no significant similarities between Jn 1–2 and Gen. 1–2. Instead, it is easier to spot differences between the two texts. The phrase καὶ ἐγένετο ἑσπέρα καὶ ἐγένετο πρωί ἡμέρα is consistently used before 'day *x*' six times in Gen. 1–2 at the conclusion of each of God's works of creation to mark each day of creation (1.5, 8, 13, 19, 23, 31) while John uses τῇ ἐπαύριον at the beginning of three separate narratives (1.29, 35, 43). Although John uses ἡμέρα in 1.39; 2.1, 12, this noun is commonplace even in GJohn (e.g. 2.19; 4.40; 6.39; 8.56; 12.1; 19.31). Time markers are commonplace in the other canonical gospels. Mark uses phrases such as 'in those days' (1.9), 'after some days' (2.1), and 'on that day' (4.35). Even the adverb ἐπαύριον (Jn 1.29, 35, 43) is found in Mk 11.12 and Mt. 27.62 without any symbolic meaning.

To sum up, the claim that Jn 1–2 has been shaped by the seven days of creation in Gen. 1–2 is not adequately supported by the evidence. There are no significant similarities between the texts, and the sequence of days in Jn 1–2 is far from a clear indication for the reader that John was attempting to emulate Gen. 1–2.

II. Jesus' Miracles and the Genesis Creation Account

Other scholars have attempted to relate the seven days of creation to the structure of some other sections of GJohn[37] or even to the structure of

---

35. Hambly, 'Creation', p. 73. Brown, *John*, vol. 1, p. 109, claimed that the mother of Jesus in Jn 2 is the 'new Eve, the symbol of the Church' (cf. Barrosse, 'Days', p. 516). However, the only verbal link between Jn 2.4 and Gen. 2.22 is the noun 'woman', which is commonplace. John uses this noun to refer to his mother (2.4), the Samaritan woman (4.7), and Mary Magdalene (19.26).

36. Trudinger, 'Days', pp. 155–6, and Hambly, 'Creation', p. 74, saw in Jn 2.12 the 'rest' of Jesus that can be tied to the 'rest' of God in Gen. 2.2-3. But since the verbs used in each case are different (καταπαύω or διέλ[ε]ιπεν, שבת in Gen. 2.3-4; and μένω in Jn 2.12), one should conclude that John did not intend such a link. J. L. Staley, *The Print's First Kiss: A Rhetorical Investigation of the Implied Reader in the Fourth Gospel* (SBLDS, 82; Atlanta: Scholars Press, 1988), p. 83, deems that Jn 2.1-12 represents the 'seventh' Johannine day.

37. C. M. Carmichael, *The Story of Creation: Its Origins and Its Interpretation in Philo and the Fourth Gospel* (Ithaca: Cornell University Press, 1996), argued that Jn 1–5 is a replication of the seven days of creation in Gen. 1–2.

GJohn as a whole.[38] These proposals have not met with approval. Scholars have rejected or simply ignored them.[39] There is, however, one suggestion that has been influential in recent Johannine works. I refer here to the idea that Jesus' miracles resemble the seven days of creation. As early as 1928, Ernst Lohmeyer posited that John placed seven signs in his Gospel (2.1-12; 4.43-54; 5.1-9; 6.1-15; 6.16-21; 9.1-7; 11.1-45).[40] Based upon this suggestion, other scholars have proposed in passing that the seven Johannine signs are related to creation imagery or directly allude to the seven days of creation in Gen. 1–2.[41] Recently some scholars have attempted to provide a defence of this suggestion.

There are three recent proposals about the use of the seven days of creation in the sequence of the Johannine signs.[42] Here I aim to engage the arguments found in these proposals in order to show that it is implausible that John attempted to portray Jesus' signs as a sequence of seven miracles that allude to Gen. 1–2. First, I will describe briefly the differences among these three proposals. Second, I will consider whether John has attempted a pattern of seven in the narratives of Jesus' signs.

38. Girard, 'structure', p. 350, 'la structure de Gn 1,1–2,4a sous-tend la composition de l'évangile tout entier'. Girard suggested the following arrangement of seven days: day 1, Gen. 1.2-5 / Jn 1.19–2.12; day 2, Gen. 1.6-8 / Jn 2.13–4.54; day 3, Gen. 1.9-13 / Jn 5–6; day 4, Gen. 1.14-19 / Jn 7–9; day 5, Gen. 1.20-25 / Jn 10.1–11.53; day 6, Gen. 1.26-31 / Jn 11.54–19.42; day 7, Gen. 2.1-3 / Jn 20. Cf. J. Goettmann, *Saint Jean: Évangile de la Nouvelle Genèse* (Paris: Cerf, 1982); Boismard, *Prologue*, p. 137, 'Jean a voulu répartir la vie du Christ en 7 périodes de 7 jours, en 7 semaines…les 7 fois 7 jours de ministère messianique correspondent aux 7 jours de la création'.

39. See the reviews of Carmichael's work in C. H. Williams, *JTS* 49 (1998), pp. 531–2, and D. T. Runia, *RevBL* 1 (1999), pp. 299–301. I have been unable to find works that have engaged critically Girard's and Goettmann's proposals.

40. E. Lohmeyer, 'Über Aufbau und Gliederung des vierten Evangeliums', *ZNW* 27 (1928), pp. 11–36 (12 n. 1). See also Quiévreux, 'Jean', p. 130; Koester, *Symbolism*, p. 79. Lohmeyer also suggested a seven-fold division of the whole Gospel: 1.1-18; 1.19-51; 2.1–6.71; 7.1–12.50; 13.1–19.42; 20.1-31; 21.1-25. He argued that most of these sections are divided into seven scenes (pp. 13, 30–32). See also Brown, *John*, vol. 1, p. 525, and M. Girard, 'La composition structurelle des sept « signes » dans le quatrième évangile', *SR* 9 (1980), pp. 315–24. F. Zeilinger, *Die sieben Zeichenhandlungen Jesu im Johannesevangelium* (Stuttgart: Kohlhammer, 2011), finds seven *Zeichenhandlungen* in Jn 2–12.

41. E. Käsemann, *New Testament Questions of Today* (trans. W. J. Montague; London: SCM, 1969), pp. 161–2; R. A. Culpepper, 'Cognition in John: The Johannine Signs as Recognition Scenes', *PRSt* 35 (2008), pp. 251–60 (259); Painter, 'Earth', p. 77; Saxby, 'Time-Scheme', p. 13.

42. Rae, 'Works', pp. 302–8; J. K. Brown, 'Creation', pp. 287–8; Moore, 'Creation', pp. 184–271.

Third, I will judge whether the suggested similarities between Gen. 1–2 and the Johannine signs are persuasive.

All three scholars (Murray Rae, Jeannine Brown, and Anthony Moore) agree that the first four Johannine signs that correspond to the first four days of creation are: the wedding at Cana (2.1-11), the healing of the royal official's son (4.46-54), the healing of a man in Jerusalem (5.1-19), and the feeding of a multitude (6.1-15). Moore and Jeannine Brown consider that the fifth, sixth, and seventh signs that correspond to the fifth, sixth, and seventh days of creation are the story of Jesus walking on the sea (6.16-21), the healing of a man born blind (9.1-41), and the resurrection of Lazarus (11.1-53). On the other hand, Rae does not include the story of Jesus walking on the sea as a sign and considers that the fifth sign is the healing of a man born blind (9.1-41), that the sixth sign is the resurrection of Lazarus (11.1-53), and that the seventh sign comprises Jesus' death and resurrection. Moore and Jeannine Brown even include an 'eighth' sign that supposedly corresponds to an 'eighth day' that signals the beginning of a new creation. For Moore, this 'eighth sign' is the miraculous catch of fish (21.1-14),[43] while for Jeannine Brown the eighth sign is Jesus' resurrection.[44]

Although there are minor differences among the proposals, all three conclude that John intended the sequence of Jesus' miracles to follow the seven days of creation in order to portray Jesus as bringing a new creation or the renewal of creation. The few clear clues in the text of GJohn as to the number and sequence of miracles performed by Jesus help explain the differences among the scholars' proposals.

John numbered only two of the signs included in his Gospel. John concludes the story of the transformation of water into wine by indicating that this was the 'first' (ἀρχή) of Jesus' signs (2.11) performed in Cana of Galilee.[45] John also mentions the 'second' (δεύτερον) sign

43. Moore, 'Creation', pp. 184–271.

44. J. K. Brown, 'Creation', pp. 287–8; Rae, 'Works', pp. 302–8. As for Jesus' resurrection as a Johannine sign, see D. A. Smith, *Revisiting the Empty Tomb: The Early History of Easter* (Minneapolis: Fortress, 2010), p. 150. Rae arranges his suggested seven signs in a chiastic structure in which Jesus' death and resurrection correspond to the wedding at Cana (cf. J. A. Grassi, 'The Role of Jesus' Mother in John's Gospel: A Reappraisal', *CBQ* 48 [1986], pp. 67–80; Girard, 'signes', pp. 315–24).

45. The usual word for 'first' is πρῶτος (Papyrus[66*] f q; cf. Jn 2.10), but John might have used ἀρχή in order to recall the opening words of the prologue (Lindars, *John*, p. 132) or to stress that this is the 'beginning' of Jesus' public ministry (Schnackenburg, *John*, p. 335; von Wahlde, *John*, vol. 2, p. 85. Barrett, *John*, p. 192, deemed that John used ἀρχή because the miracle at Cana was a 'primary sign' representative of Jesus' work as a whole.

performed by Jesus when he returned from Judea to Galilee (4.54; cf. 6.1-2).[46] The other miraculous manifestations of Jesus in GJohn take place in Jerusalem (5.1, 14; 9.7, 11), Bethany (11.1, 18), on the other side of the Sea of Galilee (6.1), and on the Sea of Galilee (6.17). Since the two numbered signs (2.11; 4.54) take place in Galilee, one should not read 4.54 'as promising a whole series of signs up to seven... The numbering stops at two'.[47]

None of the other miracles in GJohn is numbered, and the reader can identify them as signs only because the word σημεῖον occurs in discussions surrounding them. The crowd in 7.31 refers to the healing of a man in Jerusalem (Jn 5) using the noun 'sign'. People refer to the miraculous provision of food in Jn 6.5-12 using that same noun in 6.14 (cf. 6.26). Some Pharisees are made to say that the healing of a man born blind was a sign (9.16). Similarly, Jewish authorities (11.47) and the crowd (12.18) say that the resurrection of Lazarus was a sign. Jesus' passion and resurrection might also be seen as signs if Jn 20.30 refers to Jn 19–20, and if Jn 2.18-22 is taken as an anticipated indication of Jesus' resurrection.[48] There is no explicit indication that Jesus' walking on the sea (6.16-21) was a sign. Since throughout the Gospel the narrator gives clear temporal indications (e.g. 5.9; 9.14), he might be expected to have been less ambiguous when numbering the signs, if he were intending to attach a special significance to the number of Jesus' miracles. Instead, the narrator only indicates that, although Jesus 'had performed many signs', people still refused to believe in him (12.37; cf. 2.23-25; 3.2; 20.30-31).

It is difficult to see in the signs performed by Jesus a sequence of seven days that allude to specific days in the Genesis creation account. The turning of water into wine took place 'on the third day' (2.1). The

46. Moloney, *John*, p. 163, has argued that the numbering of the two signs (2.11; 4.54) 'point forward (2:1–12) and backward (4:43–54) as a frame around episodes that...deal with responses to the word of Jesus'. The literary relationship between the two signs is made explicit in Jn 4.46, 'Jesus came again to Cana in Galilee where he had made the water wine'.

47. Michaels, *John*, p. 284. Cf. S. Temple, 'The Two Signs in the Fourth Gospel', *JBL* 81 (1962), pp. 169–74 (169), 'if an author were intending to draw attention to any given number of signs he would number all, either plainly or in a code, or number none, leaving the secret to be understood by the enlightened reader'.

48. J. K. Brown, 'Creation', pp. 287–8; Saxby, 'Time-Scheme', p. 12. A number of other 'signs' have been suggested by scholars: e.g. Jesus' cleansing of the temple (2.14-17), Jesus' teaching about the serpent in the wilderness (3.14-15), the anointing of Jesus (12.1-8), the triumphal entry (12.12-16). Cf. A. J. Köstenberger, 'The Seventh Johannine Sign: A Study in John's Christology', *BBR* 5 (1995), pp. 87-103 (96).

healing of two people in Jerusalem took place on the Sabbath (5.9; 9.14). Jesus performed the healing of the official's son at the seventh hour (4.52). The resurrection of Lazarus took place after four days of his burial (11.39). None of these explicit time indicators provides clear clues to relate Jesus' miracles to a sequence of seven days.[49]

Jeannine Brown has claimed that the resurrection of Jesus on the 'first day of the week' (Jn 20.1, 19; cf. v. 26) signals the beginning of a new week or a new creation.[50] She asserts that 'the first day of the new week (of re-creation) for John may be a way of referring to an eighth day of creation',[51] and that 'John alludes in these references [Jn 20.1, 19] to the week of creation in Genesis 1–2'.[52] However, there is nothing peculiar in the indication that Jesus' resurrection took place on the first day of the week. All three Synoptic Gospels have this detail (Mt. 28.1; Mk 16.2; Lk. 24.1).[53] Certainly, John repeats this detail twice (Jn 20.1, 19), because he has included the appearance of Jesus to his disciples behind closed doors on the same day (cf. 20.26; Lk. 24.13).[54] John's indication

49. It seems that John's primary concern was to relate Jesus' life to some Jewish festivals. The incident in the temple took place when the Passover was near (2.13). The provision of food for a multitude took place when 'the Jewish feast of the Passover was near' (6.4). The feast of the Tabernacles was near when Jesus' brothers encouraged him to reveal his signs in Judea (7.2-3). Jesus' discussion with the Jews in 10.22-39 took place when the Feast of Dedication arrived (10.22). Cf. Ashton, *Understanding*, p. 79. M.-É. Boismard claimed that the feasts in GJohn serve a septenary structure that portrays Christ as new creator ('L'évangile à quatre dimensions', *LumVie* 1 [1951], pp. 93–114; cf. Boismard, *Prologue*, pp. 136–8). Boismard's thesis has been adequately refuted by M. A. Daise, *Feasts in John: Jewish Festivals and Jesus' "Hour" in the Fourth Gospel* (WUNT, 2/229; Tübingen: Mohr Siebeck, 2007), pp. 40–7.

50. J. K. Brown, 'Creation', p. 283. She also lists other scholars who share her opinion: e.g. Carson, *John*, p. 635; F. J. Moloney, *Glory Not Dishonor: Reading John 13–21* (Eugene, Ore.: Wipf & Stock, 2004), p. 159. More recently, Coloe, 'Creation', pp. 6–7, has also supported this idea. The earliest scholarly indication of a connection between Jesus' resurrection and creation that I have been able to identify is found in Grinfield, *Cosmos*, p. 45.

51. J. K. Brown, 'Creation', p. 283.

52. J. K. Brown, 'Creation', p. 284. On the other hand, Brown, *John*, vol. 2, p. 1019, has suggested that the phrase 'that day' (20.19) might be an evocation of the OT concept of the day of the Lord (e.g. Isa. 52.6).

53. John's phrase (τῇ δὲ μιᾷ τῶν σαββάτων...πρωΐ) is closest to that of Mark (λίαν πρωΐ τῇ μιᾷ τῶν σαββάτων). The phrase 'first day of the week' (μία plus σαββάτων) occurs in all four gospels. Cf. Lindars, *John*, p. 599; Carson, *John*, p. 635.

54. See also v. 9 in the longer reading of GMark: 'early on the first day of the week (πρωΐ πρώτῃ σαββάτου)'. John offers more narratives of Jesus' appearance after his resurrection than the Synoptic Gospels.

in 20.19 is not out of narrative place because it 'establishes continuity with the opening lines of the preceding section [20.1]'.[55] Therefore, by placing Jesus' resurrection on the 'first day of the week' (Jn 20.1, 19) John may be following the tradition without intending to create an eighth day of new creation as a climax to Jesus' seven signs.[56]

Notwithstanding the problems associated with trying to relate Jesus' miracles to specific days in the Genesis creation account, Anthony Moore has claimed that John has placed in his Gospel words that are 'suggestive of intentional allusion or thematic cross-referencing' to the seven days of creation.[57] In what follows I will assess his suggested allusions, showing that they are not persuasive.

Moore observes that Jn 2.11 shares two words (ἐποίησεν ἀρχὴν) with Gen. 1.1 (ἀρχῇ ἐποίησεν).[58] Although the verb is used in exactly the same form in both texts, the noun is used in different cases. This combination of words is infrequent in the LXX, but it is used most of the time in creation contexts (Eccl. 3.11; Sir. 15.14; 16.26; Isa. 22.11; cf. Mt. 19.4).[59] Moore concludes that in 'repeating [these two words] John is drawing a parallel to tie the first miracle of Jesus to the first day of the Genesis creation narrative'.[60] This conclusion is problematic, since Gen. 1.1 is not technically the first day of creation but the summary of the divine work of creation that will be described in detail in Gen. 1.3-31.[61] The link seems forced because the first day of creation in Gen. 1.3-5 has to do with light and darkness yet these nouns are not used in Jn 2.1-11.[62] If we

---

55. Michaels, *John*, p. 1007. See also Brown, *John*, vol. 2, p. 1019.

56. Brown, *John*, vol. 2, p. 1025, reported that some scholars saw in the reference to 'eight days later' in Jn 20.26 a 'week' that matches the 'week' at the beginning of GJohn: 'the two weeks would share the theme of creation'. However, Brown rightly concludes, 'such imaginative interpretations are difficult to substantiate' (p. 1025).

57. Moore, 'Creation', p. 189.

58. Moore, 'Creation', pp. 189–90. Cf. S. Palmer, 'Repetition and the Art of Reading: καὶ τῇ ἡμέρᾳ τῇ τρίτῃ, "On the Third Day" in John's Gospel', in *Repetitions and Variations in the Fourth Gospel: Style, Text, Interpretation* (ed. G. Van Belle, M. Labahn, and P. Maritz; BETL, 223; Leuven: Peeters, 2009), pp. 403–17 (408).

59. Cf. Sir. 24.9, ἀπ' ἀρχῆς ἔκτισέν; 39.25, ἔκτισται ἀπ' ἀρχῆς.

60. Moore, 'Creation', p. 190.

61. Brayford, *Genesis*, p. 205.

62. Moore, 'Creation', p. 192, also suggests that there are similar ideas in Jn 2.1-11 and the first day of creation: 'Jesus' glory that is made manifest in the changing of water into wine is the glory of God who, "in the beginning" and "on the first day", separated the light from the darkness'.

are to find a parallel to the first day of creation in GJohn, the most natural place to find it would be Jn 1.4-5, where light and darkness are mentioned in a creation context (Jn 1.1-3).[63] Furthermore, there are other OT texts that are more prominent in Jn 2.1-11 than Gen. 1.1 because they are related to wine as an eschatological blessing (e.g. Isa. 24.4-5, 7, 11; Amos 9.11-13).

Moore also proposes two links between the second day of creation (Gen. 1.6-8) and Jn 4.46-54. According to him, the phrase δεύτερον σημεῖον (Jn 4.54) corresponds 'with the work of God in "a second day" (ἡμέρα δευτέρα) (Gen. 1.8)'[64] and the noun water (Jn 4.46) is related to the same noun in Gen. 1.6. Nevertheless, several objections can be made to Moore's suggestions. First, John uses the adjective 'second' in order to identify a sign not a day. Since the healing of the official's son is in fact the second sign performed by Jesus in GJohn, there is nothing in 4.54 that is in itself out of narrative place that requires the reader to look for allusions to explain it. Second, the noun 'water' in 4.46 refers to Jesus' first miracle in Jn 2.1-11 ('[Jesus] came again to Cana in Galilee where he had made the water wine') not to his second miracle (4.46-54). Therefore, it is difficult to claim that water in 4.46 was intended to relate Jesus' second miracle to the second day of creation in Genesis. Third, the adjective 'second' (Jn 3.4; 9.24; cf. 21.16) and the noun water (e.g. Jn 1.26; 2.7; 5.7) are commonplace.[65]

For the third day of creation (Gen. 1.9-13), Moore suggests only one link to the miracle narrated in Jn 5, the 'reference to the pool in the third sign can be seen then as a direct allusion to the gathered waters (seas) of the third day of creation'.[66] However, the nouns are quite different. John uses κολυμβήθρα (5.2), while the narrator in Genesis uses ὕδωρ. Consider also that John explicitly and repeatedly states that the day of the healing was a Sabbath (5.9, 10, 16, 18; 7.22-23).[67] It is difficult to see how a

---

63. S. D. Giere, *A New Glimpse of Day One: Intertextuality, History of Interpretation, and Genesis 1.1–5* (Berlin: W. de Gruyter, 2009), pp. 262–5.

64. Moore, 'Creation', p. 194.

65. The adjective 'second' is used eighteen times in Genesis: 1.8; 2.13; 4.19; 7.11; 8.14; 11.10; 22.15; 27.36; 29.33; 30.7, 12; 32.9, 20; 41.5, 43, 52; 45.6; 47.18. The noun water is used fifty-nine times in Genesis, and twelve times in four different 'days' and in the introduction to the narrative of creation: Gen. 1.2; day two, 1.6, 1.7; day three, 1.9, 10; day five, 1.20, 21, 22.

66. Moore, 'Creation', p. 219.

67. Rae, 'Works', p. 305, rightly observes that Jn 5 is related to discussions about God's rest after creation in Gen. 2.2, but he fails to explain how this close tie between Jn 5 and the Sabbath coheres with his suggestion that Jn 5 is related to the third day of creation.

reader would link a miracle that took place on the seventh day to the third day of creation.

Equally unconvincing is Moore's proposed connection between the fourth day of creation (Gen. 1.14-19) and what he calls the fourth Johannine sign (Jn 6.1-16, 22-71). Moore argues that the temporal setting of John's miracle in Jn 6.16 ('when evening came') is related to the establishment of the lights of the sky in Gen. 1.14-18.[68] Yet the Greek word for 'evening' in Jn 6 is not used in Gen. 1.14-19 or elsewhere in the Genesis account of creation.[69] Furthermore, the most natural text behind Jn 6 seems to be Exod. 16, because John relates the multiplication of bread to the story of Moses and the miraculous provision of manna in the desert (6.31-32).[70] If there is an OT background to Jn 6.1-16, the most natural place to look at is the book of Exodus and those traditions in which the manna story are preserved (Ps. 78.24; Jn 6.31).[71]

Moore's fifth day of new creation in GJohn is the story of Jesus walking on the water (6.16-21). He relates this story to the fifth day of creation in Genesis, when God created the great sea monsters, every creature among creeping animals, every winged bird, and quadrupeds and wild animals (Gen. 1.20-25). Moore finds that the noun θάλασσα is used both in Jn 6.16, 17, 18, 19 and Gen. 1.22.[72] But this is a very faint connection. The noun θάλασσα is also used in the third (Gen. 1.10) and the sixth days of creation (Gen. 1.26, 28).[73] It is difficult to see how a Johannine reader can relate Jn 6.16-21 only to the fifth day of creation when the same noun that supposedly links both passages occurs also on the third day and on the sixth day in the Genesis sequence. Furthermore, θάλασσα is used in Jn 21, a unit of material that Moore claims is the

---

68. Moore, 'Creation', p. 224. See also Little, *Echoes*, p. 150, who tries to relate the gathering of the waters in Gen. 1.9 to the 'gathering of bread' in Jn 6.12-13.

69. John uses 'evening' in 20.19. Matthew and Mark use this noun several times (Mk 1.32; 4.35; 6.47; 11.11; 14.17; 15.42; Mt. 8.16; 14.15, 23; 16.2; 20.8; 26.20; 27.57).

70. Borgen, *Early Christianity*, pp. 205–9; Moloney, *John*, p. 194; Lincoln, *John*, pp. 223–4.

71. Brown, *John*, vol. 1, p. 233, has also observed a number of parallels between Jn 6.1-15 and Num. 11.

72. Moore, 'Creation', p. 234. The noun 'sea' is also used in the same narrative in Mt. 14.22-27 and Mk 6.45-52.

73. John uses the noun 'sea' (singular) in accusative (6.16), nominative (6.18), and genitive (6.17, 19) forms. On the other hand, the dative form of sea (plural) is used in Gen. 1.22. The accusative singular form is used in the third day of creation (Gen. 1.10), and the genitive singular form is used in the sixth day of creation (Gen. 1.26, 28).

eighth Johannine day of new creation (21.1, 7). There are no other links between Jn 6.16-21 and Gen. 1.20-25 to suggest that John was intending his readers to relate both texts. On the contrary, the texts show strong dissimilarities. It is almost impossible to relate the birds, the creeping and wild animals, and the quadrupeds of Gen. 1.20-22 to the story of Jesus walking on the sea.[74]

Moore has tied the miracle described in Jn 9 to the sixth day of creation. He proposes that the healing of a man born blind in Jn 9 has four links to Gen. 1.26-31. The first and strongest link in Moore's view is the use of the noun ἄνθρωπος in Jn 9.1, 24, 30, 'the anonymous man (ἄνθρωπος) centre stage [in Jn 9], clearly corresponds to the sixth day, at the climax of which man (ἄνθρωπος) is created'.[75] The other three suggested links lack any verbal similarities. Moore considers that the parents of the man born blind (9.2, 3, 18, 20, 22, 23) 'may also contain an echo of Gen. 1.27: ἄρσεν καὶ θῆλυ ἐποίησεν αὐτούς'.[76] Moore also asserts that the former blind man uses the 'divine name' (ἐγώ εἰμι, 9.9) to identify himself because he has been made in God's image.[77] The fourth linkage suggested by Moore is found in Jn 9.7; for him, 'Siloam' is 'reminiscent of the quasi-apostolic commission of man by God in Gen. 1:28'.[78]

Several observations can be made in response to these suggested connections between Jn 9 and the sixth day of creation. First, the noun ἄνθρωπος is applied to several characters in GJohn without links to the creation of humans in Genesis: John the Baptist (1.6), the anonymous bridegroom (2.10), Nicodemus (3.1), Jesus himself (4.29; 9.11, 16; 10.33; 11.47; 18.14, 17; 19.5), a sick man (5.5; 7.23), and any Jewish person

74. Moore, 'Creation', pp. 234–5, also suggests that the wind in Jn 6.18 (πνέοντος) and the wind from God (πνεῦμα θεοῦ) in Gen. 1.2, and that the darkness (σκοτία) in Jn 6.17 and the darkness (σκότος) in Gen. 1.2 are all related. If that were the case, the story of Jesus walking on the sea would not be tied to the fifth day of creation, but to the introduction to the Genesis account of creation. Such suggested links would cause confusion to the Johannine reader, if John were intending to show that his narrative follows the sequence of the seven days of creation.
75. Moore, 'Creation', pp. 248–9.
76. Moore, 'Creation', p. 249.
77. Moore, 'Creation', pp. 250–1. The idea that the former blind man is using the divine name here has been supported by a minority of scholars (e.g. J. Marsh, *The Gospel of St John* [Harmondsworth: Penguin, 1968], p. 380; cf. Lightfoot, *John*, p. 203). Most commentators take the former blind man's use of ἐγώ εἰμι as self-identification without divine connotations. See Brown, *John*, vol. 1, p. 373; Lindars, *John*, p. 344; Barrett, *John*, p. 359; Lincoln, *John*, p. 282; Haenchen, *John 2*, pp. 38–9; von Wahlde, *John*, vol. 2, p. 426; Carson, *John*, p. 366. See also Michaels, *John*, p. 548; Moloney, *John*, p. 297.
78. Moore, 'Creation', p. 252.

(7.22). Second, the reference to the parents (οἱ γονεῖς) of the man in Jn 9 is very different to 'male' and 'female' (ἄρσεν καὶ θῆλυ) in Gen. 1.27. Third, the 'divine name' is not used in Gen. 1.26-27, and it is difficult to conclude that John is using it in 9.9. No character, apart from Jesus, is so closely identified with the name of the Father in GJohn. Elsewhere in GJohn, Jesus reveals his Father's name to his disciples (e.g. 17.6) but there is no indication that those who receive such a revelation will be able to appropriate it for themselves. Furthermore, those who receive the revelation brought by Jesus can be granted authority to become 'God's children' (1.13) and can then refer to God as 'God' and 'Father' (20.17). But there is no indication in GJohn that Jesus' disciples will use the Father's name for themselves. Fourth, although 'Siloam' means 'sent' in Jn 9.7, there is no indication in Gen. 1.28 that the man was sent in order to fulfil a commission. Fifth, John clearly indicates that the miracle described in Jn 9 took place on the Sabbath (9.14, 16) not on the sixth day. For all these reasons, a connection between Jn 9 and Gen. 1.26-31 seems unpersuasive.

In order to create a Johannine seventh day, Moore puts together Jn 11 and Jn 17, and posits that both units of material are tied to Gen. 2.1-3. The literary connections he proposes are: (1) the language of blessing and sanctification, (2) the use of the noun 'day', (3) the 'world' terminology, (4) the number of references to Jesus as 'Lord' in Jn 11, (5) the concept of 'rest', (6) the verb 'to do', and (7) vocabulary related to 'earth'.[79] Moore's suggestion, however, requires a sophisticated reading of GJohn, because the reader needs to relate a unit of material that describes a miracle performed by Jesus (Jn 11) to a unit of material that describes a prayer by Jesus (Jn 17), leaving aside a long section (Jn 12–16) and connecting both Jn 11 and Jn 17 to Gen. 2.1-3. This sophisticated reading was hardly intended by John. Furthermore, there are other objections that can be made to Moore's suggestion.

First, the verb ἁγιάζω is commonplace. It is used in different forms both in Gen. 2.3 and Jn 17.17, 19 (cf. 10.36) but not in Jn 11.[80] The same verb form (ἡγίασεν) is used both in Gen. 2.3 and Jn 10.36 but not in Jn 17.17, 19. The verb is used differently in each case. God sanctifies a day in Gen. 2.3, while Jesus asks his Father to sanctify his disciples (17.17, 19) and asserts that he sanctifies himself (17.19). The blessing of

---

79. Moore, 'Creation', pp. 253–65. Moore claims: 'Together, these two "separate" extracts from the Fourth Gospel [Jn 11 and Jn 17] are loaded with the language of the seventh day of creation (LXX Gen. 2:1-3)' (p. 253).

80. ἡγίασεν (Gen. 2.3; Jn 10.36), ἁγίασον (Jn 17.17), ἁγιάζω, and ἡγιασμένοι (Jn 17.19).

people in Genesis occurs in 1.28, on the sixth day of creation, not in Gen. 2.3, on the seventh day. Second, the verb for blessing (εὐλογέω) used in Gen. 2.3 does not occur in Jn 11 or Jn 17.[81] Moore claims that Jn 17 has to do with 'the blessing of the work that Jesus has done in the seven signs',[82] but there is nothing in Jn 17 that can give us a firm basis to support this claim. Jesus prays that he has glorified his Father by completing the work that he has given Jesus to do (17.4), but there is no explicit indication in Jn 17 that Jesus or his Father blesses the miracles performed by him.

Third, Moore's proposal that the reference to the last day (τῇ ἐσχάτη ἡμέρᾳ) in Jn 11.24 is an indication that the resurrection of Lazarus has to do with the seventh day of creation is unconvincing.[83] If John wanted to highlight the day when Lazarus was raised he could have used a clearer indication as he did in Jn 5.9 or Jn 9.14. Instead, John only indicates that Lazarus had been in the tomb for four days (11.17, 39). Furthermore, the reference to the last day seems to be an eschatological reference to a distant future without any reference to a specific day.[84] Jesus himself has used the 'last day' in Jn 6.39, 40, 44, 54[85] (Moore's fourth Johannine day).

Fourth, the noun 'world' (Gen. 2.1, Jn 11, and Jn 17) is commonplace.[86] It is used in every section of GJohn except in Jn 2, 5, 19, and 20. It is used eighteen times in Jn 17 but only two times in Jn 11.[87] John uses this noun in Jn 17.5 and 17.24 when referring to Jesus' glory before the foundation of the world, and in Jn 1.10 in order to indicate that the Word was behind the divine work of creation. The two references to the creation of the world in Jn 17 are not tied to Gen. 2, because the language used in 17.5, 24 is different from that of the Genesis account of creation. Furthermore, there is no clear indication in Jn 11.9, 27 that John used the noun 'world' as an allusion to the seventh day of creation.

Fifth, it is hardly possible that John's use of the noun 'Lord' seven times in John is intended to signal that the resurrection of Lazarus took place during the seventh day. One can easily spot seven instances of

81. The participle εὐλογημένος is used in Jn 12.13.
82. Moore, 'Creation', p. 254.
83. Moore, 'Creation', pp. 257–9.
84. Bultmann, *John*, p. 402; Hoskyns, *Gospel*, vol. 2, p. 469; Barrett, *John*, p. 395; Haenchen, *John 2*, p. 62; von Wahlde, *John*, vol. 2, pp. 499–500; Moloney, *John*, p. 338; Michaels, *John*, p. 631; Carson, *John*, p. 412.
85. A reference to the 'last day' also occurs in Jn 12.48 (cf. 7.37).
86. Moore, 'Creation', pp. 259-62.
87. John 11.9, 27; 17.5, 6, 9, 11 (×2), 13, 14 (×3), 15, 16 (×2), 18 (×2), 21, 23, 24, 25.

other words elsewhere in GJohn. Take for example the seven occurrences of the verb 'to carry, bear' in Jn 15.[88] If John wanted to signal the seventh day in Jn 11 by using seven times the word 'Lord' he could have used this device exclusively in the story of the resurrection of Lazarus.[89] Even more damaging to Moore's claim is the fact that 'Lord' is used eight times, not seven times, in Jn 11. Moore mentions Jn 11.3, 12, 21, 27, 32, 34, 39, but he omits the narrator's indication in 11.2 that 'Mary was the one who anointed the Lord'.

Sixth, Moore's claim that the concept of rest in Gen. 2.2-3 has been used in Jn 11 is unpersuasive because the verb καταπαύω, which is used in the Genesis account of creation, does not occur in the story of the resurrection of Lazarus. God is portrayed as resting in Gen. 2.2-3 after his work of creation, while Lazarus is described as sleeping (κοιμάω) in the tomb (11.11, 13).[90] Seventh, both the verb 'to do' and the noun 'earth' are commonplace. Even the phrase ἃ ἐποίησεν that is used both in Jn 11.45-46 and Gen. 2.2 is commonplace in the LXX,[91] and occurs also in Jn 21.25 (cf. Mt. 21.15). Similarly, the noun γῆ is used elsewhere in the narrative of creation (Gen. 1.1-2, 10-12, 14-15, 17, 20, 22, 25-26, 28-30) and elsewhere in GJohn (3.22, 31; 6.21; 8.6, 8; 12.24, 32; cf. 21.8, 9, 11).[92]

The previous assessment leads us to conclude that John was not intending to arrange the miracles of Jesus in a pattern of seven days that emulates Gen. 1–2. The proposal put forth by Rae, Jeannine Brown, and Moore, that John was imitating Gen. 1–2 when describing Jesus' miracles, must be regarded with much scepticism, if not rejected

88. See also the seven occurrences of 'world' in Jn 12.19, 25, 31 (×2), 46, 47 (×2). Quiévreux, 'Jean', p. 131, provides a number of examples where a reader can find seven times the same word or phrase in GJohn. Cf. Boismard, 'dimensions', pp. 94–114; Brown, *John*, vol. 1, p. cxlii, 106; Robinson, *John*, p. 163; Girard, 'structure', p. 359 nn. 42, 44; D. Muñoz-León, 'El Pentateuco en San Juan', in *Entrar en lo Antiguo: Acerca de la relación entre Antiguo y Nuevo Testamento* (ed. I. Carbajosa and L. Sánchez-Narravo; PD, 16; Madrid: Facultad de Teología San Dámaso, 2007), pp. 107–66 (136).
89. Jesus is called 'Lord' seven times in Jn 20.2, 13, 15, 18, 20, 25, 28. Following Moore's proposal one could argue that the multiplication of bread in Jn 6 corresponds to the third day of creation (instead of corresponding to the fourth day as Moore suggests) because the noun 'Lord' is used three times there (6.23, 34, 68).
90. Aquila (according to cursives 135 and 344' [344 + 127]) and Symmachus (according to cursive 135) have διέλιπεν instead of κατέπαυσεν in Gen. 2.2. The verb διαλείπω can mean 'cease from, cease to exist, abandon, to desist from an action or activity' (BDAG, p. 232; *PGL*, p. 355).
91. For example, Exod. 14.31; Deut. 34.12; Job 11.7; Joel 2.26.
92. See also the reading preserved in Papyrus[66] Jn 4.6.

altogether. Since John 'is quite ready to indicate numbers' elsewhere in his Gospel 'it is not easy to understand why he did not suggest this symbolism [seven signs] more strongly to his readers'.[93] Moore seems to exercise little exegetical controls over the allusions that occur to him, since he allows as evidence of links between GJohn and Gen. 1–2 words that are commonplace and even concepts that lack any verbal links. Upon closer examination, his suggested allusions prove to be dubious.

In order to complete this assessment of scholarly claims about the putative use of the seven days of creation in the composition of GJohn, I will consider, in the next section, evidence from extant early Jewish texts and information from the early Christian history of interpretation.

III. Further Assessment

a. *Interpretative Traditions*
Some extant texts from the Second-Temple period have used the seven days of creation.[94] Here I will judge whether *Jubilees*, *2 Enoch*, *4 Ezra*, *Antiquities* (Josephus), and *De opificio mundi* (Philo) have used or referred to Gen. 1–2 in ways that resemble what scholars propose is going on in the composition of GJohn. First, I will describe some features of the use of the seven days of creation in each of those Jewish texts. Second, I will contrast the use of the seven days of creation in those texts with some features of GJohn.

The hand behind the book of *Jubilees* is 'seriously concerned with chronological matters'[95] and shows a great deal of interest in the number

93. Schnackenburg, *John*, vol. 1, p. 65. John uses explicit numbers and time indicators elsewhere without attaching to them allusions to Gen. 1–2. For example, Jesus' dialogue with the Samaritan woman took place on the 'sixth hour' (4.6), the woman has had five husbands (4.18), Jesus stayed in Samaria two days (4.40), there were five stoas in Jn 5.2, the miracle in Jn 6 started with five loaves and two fish (6.9, 13), the events narrated in Jn 7.37-44 took place 'on the last day of the feast' (7.37), the events that are narrated in Jn 12 took place 'six days before the Passover' (12.1). None of these explicit indications of time and numbers coheres with a putative sequence of seven subtle days in the Johannine narrative.

94. There are a number of texts where creation narratives have been used but without reference to the seven-day structure found in Gen. 1–2, e.g. 1QM X, 8-18; 1QH[a] IX, 7-20; 4Q381 1 1-12; *Apoc. Abr.* 17.18; 21.1-6; *Sib. Or.* 1.5-35; 3.8-35. In *LAB* 60.2-3 there is the description of what was before creation and the first two days of creation. Only the second day is explicitly named, 'second (day)' (*secunda*). See D. J. Harrington (ed.), *Pseudo-Philon: Les Antiquités bibliques* (SC, 229; 2 vols.; Paris: Cerf, 1976), vol. 2, p. 368.

95. O. S. Wintermute, 'Jubilees', in *OTP*, vol. 2, p. 38.

seven: 'the author [of Jubilees] has used a system based on multiples of seven, the number of days in the week. Seven years are treated as a week of years, and seven weeks of years equal a jubilee'.[96] Four observations can be made about how the author of *Jubilees* uses the seven days of creation.

The first observation is that the sequence of seven days is explicit in *Jub.* 2. The reader finds clear clues to move from one day to another: τῇ πρώτῃ ἡμέρᾳ (2.2), ἐν τῇ δευτέρᾳ (2.4), τρίτῃ ἡμέρᾳ (2.5), τῇ τετάρτῃ (2.8), τῇ πέμπτῃ (2.11), and τῇ ἕκτῃ ἡμέρᾳ (2.13).[97] The second observation is that time indicators occur both at the beginning and at the conclusion of each day of creation, while in Gen. 1–2 time indicators occur only at the end of each day. For instance, *Jub.* 2.2-3 opens with 'for on the first day' and ends with 'he made seven great works on the first day' (*OTP*, vol. 2, p. 55). The third observation is the explicit indication of the number of things created each day: seven works on the first day (2.3), one work on the second day (2.4), four works on the third day (2.7), three works on the fourth day (2.10), three works on the fifth day (2.12), and four works on the sixth day (2.14). The fourth observation is the explicit and emphatic way that the hand behind *Jub.* 2 asserts that God created everything in six days (2.1, 16, 25; cf. 2.23).

The seven days of creation are also used in *2 Enoch*. The formula 'evening came, and morning came' is used to mark, at the same time, the close of daily work and the commencement of a new day. For instance, it is said that 'on the third day I [the Lord] commanded the earth to make trees grow' (30.1), but immediately the text goes: 'And thus I created the renewal of the earth. And then evening came and morning came—the fourth day' (*2 En.* 30.2; *OTP*, vol. 2, p. 148).[98] The number seven is used

96. Wintermute, 'Jubilees', p. 52 n. b. See, for example, *Jub.* 3.15, 17, 'during the first week of the first jubilee Adam and his wife had been in the garden of Eden for seven years tilling and warding it... At the end of seven years which he [Adam] completed there, seven years exactly...the serpent came and drew near to the woman' (*OTP*, vol. 2, pp. 59-60).

97. Denis, *Fragmenta*, pp. 71–3.

98. The other time markers are: 'and evening came, and morning came, the first day' (27.4); 'this first-created day I named for myself. Then evening came and morning, and it was the second day' (28.5); 'and the third day came' (29.6); 'and on the third day I commanded the earth' (30.1); 'and then evening came and morning came—the fourth day' (30.2); 'And on the fourth day I commanded' (30.2); 'then evening came and morning came—the fifth day' (30.7); 'and on the fifth day I commanded' (30.7); 'and evening came and morning came—the sixth day' (30.8); 'and on the sixth day I commanded' (30.8); 'and I blessed the seventh day' (32.2) (*OTP*, vol. 2, pp. 146–54).

several times in this narrative in order to indicate that God created seven circles (27.3; cf. 30.3), that there exist seven stars (27.3), and that man was created out of seven components (30.8) with seven properties (30.9). Unlike Gen. 1–2, where creation begins with day one, the author of *2 Enoch* provides a detailed description of creation before the first day. The pre-creation includes the foundation of the lowest and highest things (25.1, 4; 26.3), the light (27.1), seven circles (27.1), and the throne of God (25.4). There is also in *2 Enoch* an interest on the 'eighth day' as the day God appointed to be equivalent to the 'first day' (33.1-2).

The author of *4 Ezra* describes the creation of the world in six days, introducing each day by an explicit indication: 'on the first day' (6.38), 'on the second day' (6.41), 'on the third day' (6.42), 'on the fourth day' (6.45), 'on the fifth day' (6.47), and 'on the sixth day' (6.53) (*OTP*, vol. 1, p. 536). Only the third day of creation has a double time indicator both at the beginning and at the end of the narrative (6.42, 44). The number seven is used to indicate that there is a 'seventh part' of the earth (6.42, 47, 50, 52).[99]

Josephus follows closely the story of creation in Genesis with some variations. Unlike Gen. 1–2, where the identification of each day of creation occurs at the end of the description of what God has created, Josephus puts these chronological identifications at the beginning of each day of creation.[100] Josephus omits the phrase 'and there was evening and

99.   In *4 Ezra* 7.30-31 the number seven is related to the beginning: 'And the world shall be turned back to primeval silence for seven days, as it was at the first beginnings; so that no one shall be left. And after seven days the world, which is not yet awake, shall be roused, and that which is corruptible shall perish' (*OTP*, vol. 2, pp. 537–58). In *1 En.* 93.1-10 there is an eschatological description of seven weeks (or Sabbaths). The author of *1 En.* 93 asserts that at the completion of the seventh week (or Sabbath) the elect would receive a sevenfold instruction concerning his flock. Elsewhere in *1 Enoch* there are also references to 'the second eight week' which is depicted as the 'week of righteousness' (91.12-13). Consider also *T. Levi* 16.1-2 and its indication that for seventy weeks the sacrificial altars will be defiled and the Law will be set aside. All these examples show that 'weeks' and 'days' were often used in Second-Temple Jewish texts not only in creation contexts but also in eschatological contexts. Cf. A. R. Kerr, *The Temple of Jesus' Body: The Temple Theme in the Gospel of John* (JSNTSup, 220; London: Sheffield Academic Press, 2002), p. 70 n. 5.

100.   The only exception is day one. Josephus introduces the creation of day one with 'first day' (πρώτη ἡμέρα) and indicates that Moses called it 'one' (μίαν) (*Ant.* 1.29). According to Feldman, *Judean Antiquities*, p. 10 n. 41, this clarification is required because 'the Jewish day did not end at sunrise (and so it is not possible to understand this clause [Gen. 1.5] as meaning that the evening and the morning formed the first day), and because it is hard to understand how there could be evening before the day on that light was created'. Cf. Philo, *Op. Mund.* 35.

there was morning' found in each day of creation in Gen. 1, and limits himself to say that something was created 'on the second day' (τῇ δευτέρᾳ τῶν ἡμερῶν), 'on the third [day]' (τῇ τρίτη), 'on the fourth [day]' (τῇ τετάρτη), 'on the fifth day' (πέμπτη ἡμέρᾳ), and on 'the sixth day' (τῇ ἕκτη ἡμέρᾳ) (*Ant.* 1.29-32).

Philo also provides explicit time indicators when retelling the Genesis story of creation.[101] He considers that before creation 'the Maker' made first (πρῶτον) an incorporeal heaven and an invisible earth, and next (εἶτα) he made the incorporeal essence of water (*Op. Mund.* 29). Philo follows the sequence of six days of creation found in Genesis but using labels that are slightly different from what it is found in Gen LXX. For the first day of creation, Philo gives an extended comment: 'the first day, which He does not even call "first" (πρώτην), lest it should be reckoned with the others, but naming it "one" (μίαν)' (*Op. Mund.* 15). For the second day of creation, Philo describes what God created and then provides an explicit indication of time: ἡμέραν δευτέραν (*Op. Mund.* 37). Conversely, Philo begins with τῇ τετάρτη ἡμέρᾳ and then gives a description of what God created on the fourth day (*Op. Mund.* 45). The indication of a third day is found in a summary statement (*Op. Mund.* 62), where Philo mentions the third day (τῆς τριάδι) along with the fourth and the fifth (ἡμέρᾳ πέμπτη) days. Philo also devotes a great deal of attention to the number seven (*Op. Mund.* 89–128; cf. *Leg. All.* 1.8-18; *Vit. Mos.* 2.209-211; *Spec. Leg.* 2.58-60).[102] Philo provides expansive comments between each day of creation, often speculating about details that are difficult to interpret in the Genesis account of creation.

It can be concluded that there was some flexibility in the way that Second-Temple texts used the seven-day structure of the Genesis story of creation. There are omissions such as the phrase 'and it came to be evening, and it came to be morning' (Josephus, *Ant.* 1.29-32; Philo,

---

101.   Philo argued that God completed his work of creation in six days because 'six' represents productivity (*Op. Mund.* 13 [Colson and Whitaker, LCL]). Cf. J. D. Worthington, *Creation in Paul and Philo: The Beginning and Before* (WUNT, 2/317; Tübingen: Mohr Siebeck, 2011), pp. 98–115.

102.   In *Fr. Ps.-Gr. Poets* 1, preserved in patristic sources, there is a compilation of verses related to the sacred number seven. Eusebius indicates, 'Both Homer and Hesiod, having taken information from our books, say clearly that it [the number seven] is holy'. Then, Eusebius reproduces some verses attributed to Hesiod and Homer: 'The first, the fourth, and the seventh are holy days'; 'Then, on the seventh day, a holy day returned'; 'It was the seventh day and on it all things were completed'. Eusebius also attributed to Linus this idea: 'The seventh day is counted among primary things and the seventh is perfect' (*OTP*, vol. 2, pp. 823–4).

Op. Mund. 29–89). There are different words to describe each day of creation: e.g. τρίτη ἡμέρᾳ (*Jub.* 2.5), τῇ τρίτη (Josephus, *Ant.* 1.29-32), or τῆς τριάδι (Philo, *Op. Mund.* 62) to refer to the third day of creation rather than the phrase ἡμέρᾳ τρίτη found in Gen. 1.13. There are often long speculations about each day of creation (e.g. Philo, *Op. Mund.* 29–89) or even about what happened before creation (e.g. *2 En.* 30). The location of the time indicators is found always at the end of each day of creation in Gen. 1.5, 8, 13, 19, 23, but those indicators can occur at the beginning or at the end of the narrative of each day in Second-Temple texts (cf. *4 Ezra* 6.38-52; Josephus, *Ant.* 1.29-32; *Jub.* 2.2-16; *2 En.* 30–33). In spite of this flexibility, all these texts surveyed here keep a fairly tight and clear structure of six or seven days that the reader can follow without great difficulties.

As we have seen, some Johannine scholars argue that the sequence of 'days' in GJohn is signalled by τῇ ἐπαύριον (1.29, 35, 43), ἀρχὴν τῶν σημείων (2.11), and δεύτερον σημεῖον (4.54). I have been unable to find evidence that those phrases were used in Second-Temple texts in order to indicate a sequence in the days of creation. Some Johannine scholars have also claimed that the 'third day' mentioned in Jn 2.1 signals the 'first', 'sixth', or 'seventh' day of new creation. Nevertheless, there is no evidence in Second-Temple texts that the phrase 'third day' was used in reference to the first, sixth, or seventh day of creation.[103]

The idea that John has used flexibly the seven days of creation of Gen. 1–2 in order to arrange parts of or his whole Gospel cannot be adequately supported from Second-Temple Jewish texts. There is nothing in those texts like the supposedly subtle way that John is said by some scholars to allude to the seven days of creation.

b. *Early Christian Interpretations*
Here I will look at early Christian interpretations of the life of Jesus in order to determine whether early readers related Jesus' ministry to the days of creation. I will give attention to four authors: Anastasius of Sinai, Barnabas, Victorinus of Pettau, and Theodore of Heraclea.

Anastasius of Sinai (d. ca. 700 C.E.) claims in his *Considerations on the Hexameron I* that there was an early link between the days of creation and Christ and the Church. Anastasius says that this link was made as early as the time of Papias:

---

103.   In some ancient Christian texts the 'third day' is used to indicate that Jesus was raised on the 'third day' (e.g. Mt. 16.21; 17.23; 20.19; 27.64; Lk. 9.22; 18.33; 24.7, 21, 46; 1 Cor. 15.4). Cf. Frey, *Eschatologie*, vol. 2, p. 193 n. 177.

Taking their cue from the great Papias of Hierapolis, who was a disciple of the Bosom-Friend [John], and Clement, from Pantaenus, the priest of the Alexandrians, and Ammonius, the most learned scholar, those ancient and earliest interpreters who agree with each other in understanding the whole 'six days' to refer to Christ and the Church (εἰς Χριστὸν καὶ τὴν ἐκκλησίαν πᾶσαν τὴν ἑξαήμερον νοησάντων).[104]

The 'six days' refers to the six days of creation in Gen. 1.[105] The reference to Papias as he 'who was a disciple of the Bosom-Friend' might be interpreted as if Papias took from John himself (13.23) the idea of relating the six days of creation with Christ and the Church. However, it seems Anastasius has in mind Christian readings of Gen. 1. There is no evidence that he thought that early Christians detected a pattern of six days of new creation in GJohn.

Barnabas relates the days of creation to Christian ideas about the day of the Lord. Reflecting on Gen. 2.2 and Ps. 90.4 (89.4 LXX; cf. 2 Pet. 3.8), Barnabas claimed that the Lord 'will make an end of everything in six thousand years' (15.4), and will rest 'on the seventh day' (15.5 [Lake, LCL]).[106] Based upon Isa. 1.13, Barnabas also claims that there will be a Sabbath where the Lord will give rest to all things 'and make the beginning of an eighth day (ἀρχὴν ἡμέρας ὀγδόης), that is the beginning of another world' (15.8). Barnabas explicitly relates the 'eighth day' to Jesus' resurrection: 'we also celebrate with gladness the eighth day (τὴν ἡμέραν τὴν ὀγδόην) in which Jesus also rose from the dead, and was made manifest, and ascended into Heaven' (15.9). Nevertheless, there is no firm evidence that Barnabas took these ideas exclusively from a reading of GJohn. Before GJohn was written in its final form, 'the first day of the week' was a formula already known to refer to the gathering of the followers of Jesus after his resurrection (1 Cor. 16.2; cf. Acts 20.7; Rev. 1.10).[107] Therefore, the phrases 'first day of the week' (Jn 20.1, 19)

104.   J. B. Lightfoot and J. R. Harmer, *The Apostolic Fathers: Greek Texts and English Translations of Their Writings* (ed. M. W. Holmes; Grand Rapids: Baker, 2nd edn, 1992), p. 579.

105.   Lightfoot and Harmer, *Fathers*, p. 579 n. 23.

106.   Justin Martyr, *Dial.* 41, the ' "first day of the week" (μία τῶν σαββάτων), while it remains the first (πρώτη) of all the days, yet is called the eighth (ὀγδόη), according to the number of all the days of the cycle, and still it remains the first'. Justin relates the precept of circumcision (eight day) to Jesus' resurrection, which took place 'on the first day of the week' (τῇ μιᾷ τῶν σαββάτων ἡμέρᾳ) (*Dial.* 41; cf. J. K. Brown, 'Creation', pp. 283–4; Michaels, *John*, p. 1017 n. 48). See Bobichon, *Justin Martyr*, vol. 1, p. 286; T. B. Falls, *Saint Justin Martyr* (Washington: The Catholic University of America Press, 1977), p. 210.

107.   Brown, *John*, vol. 2, p. 1019; Barrett, *John*, p. 572; Schnackenburg, *John*, p. 331.

and 'eight days later' (20.26) might have 'reminded early readers of their own meetings for worship on the first day of the week'.[108]

Victorinus of Pettau (d. 304 C.E.) finds seven episodes in the life of Jesus: his nativity, his infancy, his boyhood, his youth, his young-manhood, his mature age, and his death.[109] Victorinus also relates the Genesis account of creation to some Christian events. On the first day, 'the Holy Spirit overflowed the Virgin Mary' and Jesus rose from the dead. On the third day, Jesus was incarnated in flesh. On the fifth day, Jesus was circumcised. On the sixth day, Jesus suffered the same day when Adam fell.[110] Since some of these events do not occur in GJohn, it is clear that Victorinus is not finding in this Gospel a sequence of seven days that are related to the Genesis account of creation.[111]

Theodore of Heraclea (d. ca. 351–355 C.E.) sees in Jn 2.1-11 an important instance of creation imagery. He judges that John intended this interpretation. However, there is no evidence that Theodore relates other parts of GJohn to the seven days of creation.

> He convened the wedding on the third day (ἐν τῇ ἡμέρᾳ τῇ τρίτῃ), that is, in the last time of the age (ἐν ἐσχάτοις τοῦ αἰῶνος καιροῖς). For he struck the transgression that was in Adam and again bandaged us on the third day, that is, in the last times (ἐν ἐσχάτοις καιροῖς) when, becoming human

---

108.   Beasley-Murray, *John*, p. 385. Cf. von Wahlde, *John*, vol. 2, p. 868; Carson, *John*, p. 657. Ign. *Magn.* 9.1, asserts that those who used to observe the Sabbath are now living in the observance of the Lord's day (Brown, *John*, vol. 2, p. 1019).

109.   J. Haussleiter (ed.), *Victorini Episcopi Petavionensis Opera* (CSEL, 49; Vienna: F. Tempsky, 1916), p. 4; *ANF*, vol. 7, pp. 341–3. Victorinus also found the number seven elsewhere in Revelation and Acts: seven horns of the Lamb (Rev. 5.6), seven spirits (Rev. 4.5), seven torches (Rev. 1.12), and seven deacons (Acts 6.3) (*ANF*, vol. 7, pp. 342–3). Cf. Quiévreux, 'Jean', p. 148.

110.   Haussleiter, *Victorini*, p. 4. He also explains that the fourth day is called *tetras*, and relates it to the four living creatures (*quattuor animalia*) before God's throne, the four Gospels (*quattuor euangelia*), and the quaternion (*tetradem*) of soldiers who took Jesus as prisoner. The sixth day of creation Victorinus calls *parasceue* because this day is 'the preparation of the kingdom' (*praeparatio scilicet regni*), and relates it to the passion of Jesus. Victorinus also claims that the seventh day represents a true Sabbath still to come that would occur 'in the seventh millenary of years (*septimum miliarium*) when Christ with His elect shall reign' (*ANF*, vol. 7, p. 342). Furthermore, Victorinus links the creation of Adam to Christ, asserting that the nativity of Jesus was the re-creation (*reformauerit*) of Adam 'by means of the week' (*septimanam*).

111.   Victorinus uses GJohn in *On the Creation of the World*, when he quotes Jn 1.1-3 to support his claim that 'the author of the whole creation is Jesus' (*auctori autem totius creaturae istius*) (Haussleiter, *Victorini*, p. 4).

for us he took on the whole fleshly nature that he resurrected in himself from the dead. Therefore, because of this [John] mentions the third as the day when he consecrated the wedding.[112]

In sum, there is evidence that a few ancient Christian readers tended to relate episodes from the life of Jesus to the account of creation, but this they did either through a Christian reading of Genesis or by interpreting several stories of Jesus' ministry found not only in GJohn but elsewhere in the NT. On the other hand, I have been unable to find firm evidence that ancient readers of GJohn detected a seven-day structure related to Gen. 1–2.

IV. Conclusion

There are several proposals about the use of the seven days of creation in GJohn. The suggestion that Jn 1–2 reflects a sequence of six or seven days that intentionally emulates Gen. 1–2 was proposed a long time ago, was later developed by scholars who argued that there are verbal and thematic links between Jn 1–2 and Gen. 1–2, and it is still influential in recent Johannine works. Similarly, some scholars have proposed that the seven days of creation shaped the Johannine arrangement of Jesus' miracles. Here I have offered a comprehensive analysis of the evidence that advocates of these proposals point to for support. The main conclusion is that there is no firm evidence that any such complicated understanding of GJohn would have been intelligible to John's readers. I have been able to determine that it is improbable that John was intending a highly structured literary pattern of six, seven, or eight days that are related to the Genesis account of creation.

By showing that it is unlikely that Johannine readers could be expected to see a sequence of six, seven, or eight days in GJohn that relate to the days of creation, I have reinforced the main contention of this book, which is that John uses limited instances of creation imagery in his Gospel, but has put them in strategic places in order to support his larger Christological concerns. Creation is not the main topic in this Gospel, yet plays a supporting role. By maximizing the influence of Gen. 1–2, some scholars try to highlight the importance of new creation in GJohn; but it also involves a misreading of the place and significance of creation imagery in this Gospel.

---

112. Reuss, *Johannes-Kommentare*, pp. 67–8; Elowsky (ed.), *Scripture*, vol. 4a, p. 89.

Part III

THE PASSION AND RESURRECTION NARRATIVES

In this part I focus on the last section of the Gospel, the passion and resurrection narratives. I will answer the question about the place and significance of creation imagery in Jn 18–21. This Part comprises two separate chapters. In Chapter 6 I will argue that Jn 20.22 is an instance of creation imagery that supports some ideas introduced earlier in the Gospel. In Chapter 7 I will contend against the suggestion that the references to a garden in Jn 18.1, 26; 19.41 and to Jesus as gardener in 20.15 were intended as allusions to the garden of Eden. I will assess critically and extensively the suggestion that Jn 18.1, 26; 19.41; 20.15 are linked to the garden of Eden because this idea is still influential in recent Johannine works. In distinction from several scholars who posit in various ways the importance of creation imagery in Jn 18–21 based on numerous putative allusions to Gen. 1–3, I will argue that it is only in 20.22 that John seems to draw on and creatively deploy a term stemming from Gen. 2.7. The importance of creation imagery in this section of the Gospel is found in the strategic location of Jn 20.22.

A number of scholars have posited many allusions to Gen. 1–3 in Jn 18–21. The basis for most of those suggestions is the observation that John refers to a garden in Jn 18.1, 26; 19.41. The noun 'garden', they claim, alludes to the garden of Eden in the Genesis account of creation and, therefore, warrants many other links between Gen. 1–3 and Jn 18–21. Those suggestions, however, are not convincing when considered in light of GJohn as a whole.[1]

1. For example, the angels in Jn 20.12 recall the cherubim in Gen. 2.24 (J. Suggit, 'Jesus the Gardener: The Atonement in the Fourth Gospel as Re-creation', *Neot* 33 (1999), pp. 161–8 (167); ἰδοὺ ὁ ἄνθρωπος in Jn 19.5 is an allusion to ἰδοὺ Ἀδάμ in Gen. 3.22 (M. D. Litwa, 'Behold Adam: A Reading of John 19:5', *HBT* 32 [2010], pp. 129–43); or ποιέω in Jn 20.30; 21.25 is linked to Gen. 1.1 (D. F. Ford, 'Beginning, Ending and Abundance: Genesis 1:1 and the Gospel of John', in *Leshon Limmudim: Essays on the Language and Literature of the Hebrew Bible* [ed. D. A. Baer and R. P. Gordon; LHBOTS, 593; London: Bloomsbury T&T Clark, 2013], pp. 292–305 [293]). However, Ford recognizes that it 'is…impossible to tell whether or not [John] did intend' this link.

Chapter 6

CREATION IMAGERY IN JOHN 20.22

In this chapter I will provide a thorough assessment of the evidence that supports the claim that John is drawing on the tradition of God's creation of humankind that stems from Gen. 2.7 in his description of Jesus in 20.22. I will argue that the portrayal of Jesus as breathing on the disciples in Jn 20.22 is related to the creation of humans in the Genesis account of creation. John has placed this instance of creation imagery in a strategic place, in the last section of his Gospel and in the middle of the three narratives of Jesus' appearances after his resurrection. John uses this instance of creation imagery in a threefold way. First, John wants to highlight the close association between the risen Lord and the Creator God in order for his readers to grasp the full significance of the portrayal of Jesus as performing two divine activities, the giving of the Spirit and the commissioning of the disciples to forgive and retain sins. Second, John stresses that the universal significance of Jesus and the message about him continues to be effective through the disciples. Jesus' commissioning of his disciples to forgive and retain anyone's sins stems from his authority over creation. Third, John links the Word in creation (1.3, 10) to the risen Jesus (20.22) in order to show that the same agent of creation is the privileged agent of revelation and salvation.

I. Assessment

The verb ἐμφυσάω (Jn 20.22) is a *hapax legomenon* in GJohn. It is not even used anywhere in the rest of the NT.[1] It is striking that John uses this verb in his narrative of Jesus' appearance to his disciples, when

---

1. There is debate about the literary relationship between Jn 20.19-23 and the events of Easter narrated in the Synoptic Gospels. Scholars have related Jn 20.19-23 to Lk. 24.36-43 or Jn 20.21-23 to Mt. 16.19; 18.18; Lk. 24.51 (cf. Acts 2.1-4). The point here, however, is that the description of Jesus breathing is peculiar to GJohn.

presumably λέγω would suffice.[2] The verb ἐμφυσάω is also infrequent in
the LXX. It is used only four times in the aorist indicative (Gen. 2.7; 3
Kgdms 17.21; Job 4.21; Tob. 11.11)[3] and five times in other moods and
tenses (Ezek. 21.36; 37.9; Nah. 2.2; Tob. 6.9; Wis. 15.11).[4] The same
verb form that occurs in Jn 20.22 (ἐνεφύσησεν) is also used in Gen. 2.7; 3
Kgdms 17.21; Tob. 11.11; Job 4.21.[5] However, there is no significant
interpretative link between Jn 20.22 and Tob. 11.11; the link between Jn
20.22 and Job 4.21 is weak; and there is an important difference between
Jn 20.22 and 3 Kgdms 17.21. The healing context found in Tob. 11.11
(cf. 6.9) is absent from Jn 20.22. The verb ἐνεφύσησεν in Job 4.21 is
directly related to God's judgement (cf. Ezek. 21.36), while this verb
in Jn 20.22 is related to the gift of the Holy Spirit. In distinction from
3 Kgdms 17.21, where Elijah breathed on a lad three times and called on
the Lord, Jesus breathes once without calling on or praying to his Father
in Jn 20.22. On the other hand, the similarities and differences between
Gen. 2.7 and Jn 20.22 deserve to be further explored.

John 20.22

καὶ τοῦτο εἰπὼν ἐνεφύσησεν καὶ λέγει αὐτοῖς· λάβετε πνεῦμα ἅγιον·

Genesis 2.7 LXX

καὶ ἔπλασεν ὁ θεὸς τὸν ἄνθρωπον χοῦν ἀπὸ τῆς γῆς καὶ ἐνεφύσησεν εἰς τὸ
πρόσωπον αὐτοῦ πνοὴν ζωῆς, καὶ ἐγένετο ὁ ἄνθρωπος εἰς ψυχὴν ζῶσαν.

2.   John 4.34; 6.20; 13.12-15; 16.19. Cf. T. R. Hatina, 'John 20,22 in Its
Eschatological Context: Promise or Fulfilment?', *Bib* 74 (1993), pp. 196–219 (198).
3.   The verb ἐμφυσάω is used in the longer reading preserved in Sinaiticus but it
does not occur in the shorter text form of Tobit (Vaticanus, Alexandrinus, Venetus,
POxy 1594).
4.   The MT has נפח in Gen. 2.7 and Ezek. 37.9, but has פוח in Ezek. 21.36. In
other texts in which the root נפח is used the LXX has φυσάω (Isa. 54.16) or ἐκφυσάω
(Ezek. 22.21; Hag. 1.9; Mal. 1.13). In the LXX the 'breathing' can cause resurrection
(3 Kgdms 17.21), healing (Tob. 6.9; 11.11), judgement (Job 4.21; Ezek. 21.36), or
life (Gen. 2.7; Ezek. 37.9; Wis. 15.11).
5.   This verb form is infrequent in extant Greek literature outside the biblical
canon and Patristic literature. A search for ἐνεφύσησεν in *TLG* in a period that goes
from the first century B.C.E. to the second century C.E. shows the use of this verb
form only in one 'pagan' author: Philoxenus Alexandrinus, *Fragmenta* 217.16.
Nevertheless, other 'pagan' authors in this same period have used other forms of
ἐμφυσάω: e.g. Dioscorides Pedanius, *De material medica* 1.101.3 (ἐμφυσωμένων);
Posidonius, *Fragmenta* 169.128 (ἐμφυσῶσι); Diodorus Siculos, *Bibliotheca historica*
5.30.3 (ἐμφυσῶσι).

In addition to the obvious use of the same verb (ἐνεφύσησεν),[6] one can also observe a semantic similarity between πνεῦμα and πνοή, a similar syntactical pattern, and common tone in both texts. Both anarthrous nouns (πνεῦμα and πνοή) can convey the general meaning 'wind' (cf. Acts 2.2; Jn 3.8).[7] The structure of both texts has a subject (ὁ Ἰησοῦς, Jn 20.19; ὁ θεός, Gen. 2.7) and the verb ἐνεφύσησεν.[8] In both texts a narrator describes someone breathing once. On the other hand, there are at least three differences between Gen. 2.7 and Jn 20.22. First, ἐνεφύση-σεν does not have a clear object in Jn 20.22,[9] while the narrator in Gen. 2.7 states explicitly that God breathed into the man's face.[10] Second, there are different contexts. In Gen. 2.7 God is creating the man, while in Jn 20.22 Jesus is giving his disciples the Holy Spirit.[11] Third, although the nouns πνεῦμα and πνοή can convey similar meanings, the words are indeed different. In the Genesis account of creation there is a distinction between πνεῦμα (Gen. 1.2) and πνοή (Gen. 2.7). The former is used to indicate that a divine wind (πνεῦμα θεοῦ) was over the water, while the latter is used in the narrative of the creation of the man.[12]

Notwithstanding the third observation made above, there is evidence that the noun πνεῦμα was used instead of πνοή in creation contexts elsewhere in the LXX. The two clearest examples are found in Ezek. 37.9 and Wis. 15.11 (cf. Isa. 42.5; Job 32.8). In the former text the 'spirit' (πνεῦμα) is commanded to blow (ἐμφύσησον) into some corpses in order

6. Symmachus and Theodotion use the cognate ἔπνευσεν. Cf. Wevers, *Notes*, p. 25 n. 18.

7. BDAG, pp. 832, 838; LSJ, pp. 1424–5. Cf. Menken, 'Genesis', p. 91.

8. The MT has יהוה אלהם. The noun אלהם alone is used in Gen. 1.1–2.3, and יהוה אלהם is used in Gen. 2.5, 7, 8, 9, 15, 16, 18, 19, 21, 22. On the other hand, the LXX has ὁ θεός in Gen. 1.1–2.7, but uses κύριος ὁ θεός in Gen. 2.8, 15, 16, 18, 22. Elsewhere in the LXX the verb ἐμφυσάω is used along with several subjects: a young man (Tob. 6.9; 11.11), a prophet (3 Kgdms 17.21), or God himself (Job 4.21; Ezek. 21.36; Wis. 15.11).

9. Only in Tatian, D, and syr[cur] is the object of the verb explicit (αὐτοῖς). Cf. M. M. B. Turner, 'The Concept of Receiving the Spirit in John's Gospel', *VE* 10 (1977), pp. 24–42 (29).

10. Aquila (μυκτῆρσιν) and Symmachus and Theodotion (μυκτῆρας) provide a closer translation of the MT (אף).

11. Cf. M. Wojciechowski, 'Le don de L'Esprit Saint dans Jean 20.22 selon Tg. Gn. 2.7', *NTS* 33 (1987), pp. 289–91 (290).

12. The noun πνεῦμα is used elsewhere in Genesis to describe something related to God (6.3; 41.38) or to creation (6.17; 7.15; 45.27). The LXX has πνοὴν ζωῆς in Gen. 7.22 while the MT has נשמת-רוח חיים.

for them to live (ζωσάτωσαν).[13] In the later text there is a reference to God as the One who infused the man with a 'soul' (τὸν ἐμπνεύσαντα... ψυχὴν) and breathed in a 'living spirit' (ἐμφυσήσαντα πνεῦμα ζωτικόν). Consequently, it is not impossible that in using Gen. 2.7 John preferred πνεῦμα instead of πνοή because the latter served his larger purposes. It is also possible that in using Gen. 2.7 John was, at the same time, taking into account Ezek. 37.9 and Wis. 15.11. However, although both texts (Ezekiel and Wisdom) are used allusively in GJohn,[14] neither Ezek. 37.9 (ἐμφύσησον)[15] nor Wis. 15.11 (ἐμφυσήσαντα) has the verbal form ἐνεφύσησεν found in Jn 20.22 and Gen. 2.7.[16]

The assessment so far would indicate that there might be a link to Gen. 2.7 in Jn 20.22. In order to strengthen this preliminary conclusion, it will be helpful to look at Second-Temple Jewish texts in which Gen. 2.7 has been used and to consider early Christian interpretations of Jn 20.22.[17]

---

13. J. Robson, *Word and Spirit in Ezekiel* (LHBOTS, 447; London: T&T Clark International, 2006), pp. 225–6, 'The two-stage vision of life for the bones [Ezek. 37.9] resonates with the creation account in Gen 2:7... The fact that "breath" in Gen 2:7 is נשרמה should not be seen as significant, since...by the time of the exile, the two words [נשמה and רוח] clearly had overlapping semantic domains.'

14. The editors of NA[28] suggest twenty allusions to Wisdom in GJohn. For a more nuanced statement, see Reim, *Studien*, pp. 193–4, who proposed eight 'probable' allusions, one 'possible' allusion, and more than thirty 'formal parallels'. As for allusions to Ezekiel in GJohn, see Manning, *Echoes*, pp. 100–197.

15. Cursives 130 and 129' (239-306) have εμφυτευσον instead of ἐμφύσησον.

16. Furthermore, there is a significant difference between Ezek. 37.9 and Jn 20.22. While Jesus breathes and then says, 'receive Holy Spirit' in Jn 20.22, the 'spirit' itself is commanded to breath in Ezek. 37.9.

17. There have been a couple of efforts to explain Jn 20.22 in light of Targumic interpretations of Gen. 2.7 and Ezek. 37.1-14. Hatina, 'John 20,22', pp. 217–18, suggests that the Targum of Ezek. 37.14, *Tg. Onq.* Gen. 2.7, and *Tg. Ps.-J* Gen. 2.7 are 'close parallels' to Gen. 2.7. Wojciechowski, 'L'Esprit', p. 291, also relates Jn 20.22 to *Tg. Neof.* Gen. 2.7. Hatina and Wojciechowski observe that in the Targums the 'breath of life' is associated with the gift of speech, and propose that in Jn 20.22 Jesus 'is imparting his words and understanding of eternal life to the disciples' (Hatina, 'John 20,22', pp. 217–18) and that these 'words' should be identified 'avec le don des langues de la Pentecôte' (Wojciechowski, 'L'Esprit', p. 291). Although it is possible that the Targums contain some material that circu- lated during the first century C.E., it is always difficult to discern whether this particular Targumic interpretation of Gen. 2.7 was available to the final editor of GJohn. A problem with Hatina's and Wojciechowski's interpretation is that there are no indications in the context of Jn 20.22 that the Holy Spirit is directly related to speech. Furthermore, Wojciechowski's comment that Jn 20.22 represents 'un geste visible avec une valeur sacramentelle' (p. 291) seems to be anachronistic. Against

a. *Second-Temple Jewish Texts*

The story of God breathing into the man's face (Gen. 2.7) was widely used in extant literature of the Second-Temple period. There are three details in those texts that are relevant to our discussion about Jn 20.22. The first detail is that some ancient authors wrote that God breathed into the man 'spirit' instead of 'breath of life' when he created him. The second detail is that although there is speculation in those texts about what God imparted in the man when he created him, there is no speculation about who performed the act of breathing. In all those texts God himself is portrayed as 'breathing'. The third detail is that the breath of God in the creation of the man is used in most of those texts in order to highlight that the man has a special status in God's creation.

Some texts follow Gen. 2.7 LXX closely by asserting that what God breathed into the man was the 'breath of life' (*Jos. Asen.* 12.1; Theophilus, *Autol.* 2.19; Philo, *Somn.* 1.34; *Plant.* 19; *Leg. All.* 1.31;[18] cf. *4 Ezra* 3.5; Ps. 103.30 LXX), while there are some other texts in which there is speculation about what God put in the man when he created him.[19] God is portrayed as breathing 'spirit' when creating the man in a number of texts. Josephus writes that 'God fashioned man by taking dust from the earth and instilled (ἐνῆκεν) into him spirit (πνεῦμα) and soul (ψυχήν)' (*Ant.* 1.34 [Thackeray, LCL]). In *Apoc. Adam* 2.5 God himself is described as saying that he imparted 'spirit of life for a living soul' in Adam (*OTP*, vol. 1, p. 713; cf. 2 Macc. 7.22-23).

Philo writes that God put 'spirit' in the man when he created him. Philo uses the verb ἐμφυσάω before πνεῦμα ζωῆς when alluding to Gen. 2.7 in *Det. Pot. Ins.* 80 and *Leg. All.* 3.161 (cf. *Rer. Div. Her.* 56). Elsewhere he also explains that the man created by God was made of πνεύματος θείου, and that what God breathed into him was nothing else

Wojciechowski, see also C. Bennema, 'The Giving of the Spirit in John's Gospel – A New Proposal?', *EvQ* 74 (2002), pp. 195–213 (202); M. Turner, *The Holy Spirit and Spiritual Gifts: Then and Now* (Cumbria: Paternoster, 1999), p. 98 n. 22.

18. Elsewhere Philo uses ἐμπνέω (*Plant.* 19; *Leg. All.* 1.32) when referring to Gen. 2.7. Philo, *Leg. All.* 1.36, explains that ἐμφυσάω is equivalent to ἐμπνέω.

19. Some examples are in order: (1) in Sir. 17.7 God is portrayed as filling (ἐμπίμπλημι) the man with understanding and intelligence (ἐπιστήμη, σύνεσις), (2) in r 4Q504 8, 5-6 (cf. 4Q305 II, 2) God is described as giving intelligence and knowledge to the man so that he can rule in Eden, (3) in *Jos. Asen.* 19.11 it is said that Joseph kissed Aseneth three times and gave her 'spirit of life', 'spirit of wisdom', and 'spirit of truth', (4) in Wis. 2.2 the breathing into the man's nostrils is compared to 'smoke' (καπνός), (5) in *Apoc. Adam* 1.5 it is said that 'knowledge' used to breathe within Adam and Eve, and (6) in *2 En.* 65.2 God puts 'reason' in the man.

but πνεῦμα θεῖον (*Op. Mund.* 135; cf. *Plant.* 19, 44).[20] Similarly, Philo explains in *Det. Pot. Ins.* 80 that the essence of life (ἡ ψυχήν οὐσία) is πνεῦμα, and in *Op. Mund.* 134–135 he asserts that God was responsible for putting spirit in the man. In his explanation of the verb ἐμφυσάω in Gen. 2.7 (*Leg. All.* 1.31-42), Philo judges that this verb implies three things: that which inbreathes (God), that which receives (the mind), and that which is inbreathed (the spirit). However, Philo clarifies that Moses 'uses the word "breath" (πνοή) not "spirit" (πνεῦμα) implying a difference between them; for "spirit" is conceived of as connoting strength… while a "breath" is like an air or a peaceful and gentle vapour' (*Leg. All.* 1.42 [Colson and Whitaker, LCL]).

The use of רוח is also frequent in narratives of creation in some Qumran texts. In the non-canonical psalm 4Q381 1, 7 God is described as appointing Adam and Eve to rule on the earth by his spirit (וברוחו). In 1QS III, 18 God is portrayed as putting two spirits (רוחות) in man: a spirit of truth and a spirit of injustice. Elsewhere God is portrayed as creating the spirit of man (לרוח אדם) and fashioning every spirit (כול רוח) and the mighty winds (לרוחות עולם) (1QH[a] IX, 9-15). None of the texts surveyed so far, however, has the phrase 'holy spirit' in a creation context. The only exception that I have been able to find (ורוח קודש)[21] is the paraphrase of Gen. 1–9 preserved in 4Q422 1 I, 7. Nevertheless, the fragmentary state of the text does not allow any clear conclusion to be drawn about the role of this phrase in the creation of the man.

Although there is speculation in Second-Temple Jewish texts about what God put in the man when he created him, all the texts surveyed here agree that the One who performed the act of breathing was God himself.[22] Even Melito, who portrays Jesus taking an active role in the creation of the heavens and the earth and in the formation of the man, does not indicate that Jesus breathed the breath of life (*Pasc.* 104).[23]

---

20. L. Levonian, 'Insufflation', *The Expositor* 22 (1921), pp. 149–54 (151), observed that in Job 33.4 'breath' is explicitly identified with 'spirit' and that both are linked to God. In Job 33.4 Elihu associates the breath of life (Gen. 2.7) with 'divine spirit' (πνεῦμα θεῖον; רוח־אל) and identifies the 'breath' as the 'Almighty's breath' (πνοή παντοκράτορος; נשמת שדי). Cf. *2 Bar.* 23.5, where the Lord's spirit is related to created life.

21. The phrase 'holy spirit' is also used in 1QS 3, 7; 4, 21; 4Q266 II, 12, but there is no creation context in those texts. Cf. É. Puech, 'L'Esprit saint à Qumrân', *SBFLA* 49 (1999), pp. 283–97.

22. In *2 En.* 30.8 God commands 'wisdom' to create man but there is no explicit indication that 'wisdom' breathed into the man the breath of life.

23. J. Fossum, 'Gen 1:26 and 2:7 in Judaism, Samaritanism, and Gnosticism', *JSJ* 16 (1985), pp. 202-39, has demonstrated that in extant early Judaistic texts, God

In many cases the description of God breathing into the man is under-stood to highlight the special status that the man has in God's creation. Philo's point in mentioning the spirit in the creation of the man is that the man is the borderland between mortal and immortal nature (*Op. Mund.* 134–135), having thus a special status (*Somn.* 1.34-35) that allows him to worship the Father (*Somn.* 1.35).[24] Similarly, Philo asserts elsewhere that the spirit given to the man in creation allows him to know God (*Leg. All.* 1.31-42; *Det. Pot. Ins.* 83–85).[25] In some texts found at Qumran the creation of the man is also related to his special status among God's creation. It is said in 4Q381 1, 7 that God appointed the man by his spirit in order for him to have dominion over all creation (cf. r 4Q504 8; 1QS III, 17-18). In 1QH^a XI, 27-31 God is portrayed as creating 'spirit' for the tongue and as imparting the flow of breath on people's lips in order for them to tell about God's glory. Other examples of the use of Gen. 2.7 to highlight the superior status of humans over God's creation are found in early Christian texts (e.g. Theophilus, *Autol.* 2.19; cf. *1 Clem.* 33; Justin, *Dial.* 40). By contrast, there are at least two texts that also relate the 'breath of life' or the 'spirit' to animals (Eccl. 3.20-21) or to the whole of creation (*Jos. Asen.* 12.1).[26]

To summarize thus far, Gen. 2.7 was widely used in extant Second-Temple Jewish texts.[27] It was customary for readers of Gen. 2.7 to judge that God imparted 'spirit' when breathing into the man. Therefore, the suggestion that Jn 20.22 (ἐνεφύσησεν + πνεῦμα ἅγιον) is somehow linked to Gen. 2.7 gains support when considered in light of other texts. In the

alone (without angelic assistance) is portrayed as creating humankind. Only in Samaritanism, Gen. 2.7 could be judged to mean that God had angelic assistance in the creation of humankind.

24. J. R. Levison, *The Spirit in First Century Judaism* (AGJU, 29; Leiden: Brill, 1997), p. 91, has observed that in *Virt.* 217–218 'Gen 2:7 supplies Philo with the exegetical toehold for his construal of Adam's superiority'.

25. Du Rand, 'Creation', p. 45, even suggests that John might have known Philo, *Det. Pot. Ins.* 22, 80, but this is implausible.

26. Furthermore, in 1 Cor. 15.45 Paul omits the detail that God breathed the breath of life into Adam's nostrils. Paul uses Gen. 2.7b in order to make a con-trastive comparison with what the first Adam became. Cf. Worthington, *Creation*, pp. 180–4. There is also a reference to Gen. 2.7 in 1 Tim. 2.13, but there is no mention of the breath of God in this text. Therefore, 1 Tim. 2.13 is of limited value for our study.

27. By contrast, there is no evidence that Ezek. 37.9 was widely used in extant Second-Temple literature, although some verses taken from Ezek. 37 were related to eschatological themes (e.g. Sir. 49.10; 4Q385 2; *Liv. Proph.* 3.12; *Sib. Or.* 4.180-184; Rev. 11.11; Mt. 27.52; Justin, *Dial.* 80; cf. *4 Macc.* 18.17; *1 En.* 90.4-5; 2 Macc. 7.23; *Sib. Or.* 2.224).

next section I will argue that positing creation imagery in Jn 20.22 is not idiosyncratic. Both early and modern readers of Jn 20.22 have linked this Johannine passage to Gen. 2.7.

b. *Christian Interpretations of John 20.22*
John 20.22 is widely used in extant Patristic texts.[28] At least three early church fathers related this Johannine text to Gen. 2.7. Cyril of Alexandria makes a direct connection between Jn 20.22 and Gen. 2.7. Cyril portrays God in Gen. 2.7 as the One who fashioned the man and endowed him with a soul and illuminated him with his own 'Spirit' (*Commentary on John* 12). He portrays Christ as the one through whom God restored humankind to life (*Commentary on John* 12). According to Cyril, Jesus' act in Jn 20.22 shows that Jesus was at the beginning (ἐξ ἀρχῆς) creating the man and is now transforming his disciples into the likeness of their 'Maker' (*Commentary on John* 12).[29] Cyril of Jerusalem also links Jn 20.22 to Gen. 2.7. He judged that Jn 20.22 is the 'second time [Jesus] breathed on man', implying that the first time has to be found in Gen. 2.7 (*Catechetical Lectures* 17.12; *NPNF²*, vol. 7, p. 127). According to Cyril of Jerusalem, this 'second time' was necessary because his first breath was stifled through man's wilful sins. Similarly, Theodore of Mopsuestia links Jn 20.22 to Gen. 2.7 in order to demonstrate that Jesus is the giver of life (*Commentary on John* 7.20-22).[30] Theodore implies that the one who breathed in the beginning is the same one who bestows the Spirit to the disciples in Jn 20.22.

---

28. Some Christian interpreters use Jn 20.22 in order to illustrate the divinity of Jesus (Gregory of Nazianzus, *On Pentecost, Oration* 41.11; Theodore of Mopsuestia, *Commentary on John* 7.20-22; Cyril of Alexandria, *Commentary on John* 12.1). On the other hand, Cyprian sees in Jn 20.22 biblical legitimation for the emerging hierarchy in the early church (*Epistle* 74.16). Cf. J. van Rossum, 'The "Johannine Pentecost": John 20:22 in Modern Exegesis and in Orthodox Theology', *SVTQ* 35 (1991), pp. 149–67 (158–7).

29. P. E. Pusey (ed.), *Sancti Patris Nostri Cyrilli Archiepiscopi Alexandrini in D. Joannis Evangelium* (3 vols.; Brussels: Culture et Civilisation, 1965), vol. 3, p. 135; Cyril of Alexandria, *Commentary on the Gospel according to St. John (IX–XXI)* (trans. T. Randell; LFC, 48; Oxford: Walter Smith, 1885), p. 675.

30. J. M. Vosté, *Theodori Mopsuesteni Commentarius in Evangelium Iohannis Apostoli* (CSCO, 116; Leuven: Peeters, 1940), pp. 354–5; Elowsky (ed.), *Scripture*, vol. 4b, pp. 361–2. Extant Greek fragments of Theodore's commentary do not have the reference to the creation of the man. Cf. G. Kalantzis, *Theodore of Mopsuestia Commentary on the Gospel of John* (ECS, 7; Strathfield, Australia: St Paulus, 2004), pp. 143–4.

Modern readers of Jn 20.22 commonly relate this verse to Gen. 2.7. They offer a number of explanations of the relationship between the two texts. For instance, some interpreters think that Jn 20.22 is an allusion,[31] or a parallel,[32] or a reminiscence[33] of Gen. 2.7. Some scholars also relate Jn 20.22 to both Gen. 2.7 and Ezek. 37.9, or even to Wis. 15.11.[34] Only a few doubt that Jn 20.22 is somehow linked to Gen. 2.7.[35]

In light of the evidence assessed here, I suggest that John is drawing on the tradition of God's creation of humankind that stems from Gen. 2.7. The facts that there is the same rare verb in the same form in Jn 20.22 and that it is very prominent in Second-Temple Jewish texts (discussing Gen. 2.7) make it likely that John is evoking the creation of the man. Although Gen. 2.7 does not have the noun 'spirit', there is firm evidence that ancient readers of Gen. 2.7 easily related the breath of God in creation to the noun 'spirit' (e.g. Ezek. 37.9; Wis. 15.11; Josephus, *Ant.* 1.34; *Apoc. Adam* 2.5; Philo, *Det. Pot. Ins.* 80; 1QS III, 18).

II. The Significance of John 20.22

Here I attempt to show how Jn 20.22 functions as an instance of creation imagery within its literary context (Jn 20) and in light of GJohn as a whole. I will argue that this instance of creation imagery occupies a strategic place in GJohn and supports some ideas introduced earlier in the Gospel. More precisely, the portrayal of Jesus in Jn 20.22 occurs in the broader Johannine context of Jesus' close association with his Father that gives him authority to perform divine activities such as the giving of the Spirit and the sending of the disciples in order to forgive sins. Through his disciples, the universal significance of Jesus and the message about him continues to be effective. By performing an act that resembles that of the Creator God in Gen. 2.7, John is linking the Word as the agent of creation (1.3, 10) with the risen Jesus as the Father's privileged agent of revelation and salvation.

31. Reim, *Studien*, pp. 98, 100, 222 (*Auspielung*); Weidemann, 'Protology', p. 323.

32. Barrett, *John*, p. 570.

33. F. W. Beare, 'The Risen Jesus Bestows the Spirit: A Study of John 20:19–23', *CJT* 4 (1958), pp. 95–100 (98). Cf. J. I. Cook, 'John 20:19–23 – An Exegesis', *RefR* 21 (1967), pp. 2-10 (8); Brodie, *John*, p. 569.

34. See, for example, Lincoln, *John*, p. 499; Schnackenburg, *John*, p. 325.

35. T. Hägerland, 'The Power of Prophecy: A Septuagintal Echo in John 20:19–23', *CBQ* 71 (2009), pp. 84–103, proposes that Jn 20.19-23 echoes the Balaam cycle of Num. 22–24. However, he does not offer any firm arguments against interpreting Jn 20.22 in relation to Gen. 2.7 (p. 96).

Jesus' appearance to his disciples after his resurrection in Jn 20.19-23 is the second of three narratives about Jesus' appearances in Jn 20. All three narratives (vv. 1-18, 19-23, and 24-29) are closely related, since they take place on the 'first day of the week' (vv. 1, 19, 26), although the third appearance takes place a week later.[36] The first two narratives occur on the same day and the last two narratives take place in the same location.[37] Furthermore, all three appearances use similar terminology to describe the seeing of the Lord (ἑώρακα τὸν κύριον, v. 18; ἰδόντες τὸν κύριον, v. 20; ἑωράκαμεν τὸν κύριον, v. 25).[38] All three narratives are closely linked and can be seen as a literary unit.[39] This literary unit (Jn 20) occupies a strategic place in GJohn because it is located in the last section of the Gospel.

The final section of a Gospel is important because those are the last words the intended reader will read (Jn 20–21).[40] John 20, in particular, is an important unit of material within GJohn because the three resurrection appearances fulfil some promises made by Jesus through his earthly ministry.[41] Jesus assured his disciples that he would not abandon them but would come to them (ἔρχομαι πρὸς ὑμᾶς, 14.18). The three appearances in Jn 20 can be seen as the fulfilment of this promise, since Jesus

36. Schnackenburg, *John*, vol. 3, p. 301; Beasley-Murray, *John*, p. 367.

37. Moloney, *John*, p. 517.

38. Schnackenburg, *John*, vol. 3, p. 321. See also the close similarity between Jn 20.19 and 20.26. Cf. G. W. Most, *Doubting Thomas* (Cambridge, Mass.: Harvard University Press, 2005), pp. 28–9; W. Bonney, *Caused to Believe: The Doubting Thomas Story as the Climax of John's Christological Narrative* (BIS, 62; Leiden: Brill, 2002), pp. 144–5 n. 38.

39. Ignace de la Potterie, 'Genèse de la foi Pascale de'après Jn. 20', *NTS* 30 (1984), pp. 26–49 (26–7); D. A. Lee, 'Partnership in Easter Faith: The Role of Mary Magdalene and Thomas in John 20', *JSNT* 50 (1995), pp. 37–49 (38–9). Although John seems to have used traditional material (cf. Mk 16.14-20; Mt. 28.16-20; Lk. 24.36-49) in the composition of Jn 20, the present form of these narratives seems to be a literary unit. See Moloney, *John*, p. 516; Lindars, *John*, p. 597; Bultmann, *John*, p. 690.

40. M. D. Hooker, *Endings: Invitations to Discipleship* (London: SCM, 2003), pp. 67–81.

41. A number of scholars posit that Jn 21 is a later addition to GJohn. Even if Jn 21 is not regarded as an integral part of GJohn, it is not impossible that the final editor of the whole composition wanted to provide a conclusion (Jn 20) and an epilogue (Jn 21) to his work. The conclusion would provide a suitable end to the story of Jesus (20.30-31), while the epilogue would provide a suitable end to the story of some of the disciples. Cf. F. J. Moloney, 'John 21 and the Johannine Story', in Thatcher and Moore (eds.), *Anatomies of Narrative Criticism*, pp. 237–51.

comes (ἦλθεν ὁ Ἰησοῦς, 20.19; ἔρχεται ὁ Ἰησοῦς, 20.26) to his disciples twice.[42] Jesus also promised that his disciples would see him (ὄψεσθέ με, 16.16) again after a little while. This promise is fulfilled in all three resurrection appearances when Mary and the disciples see the Lord (20.18, 20, 25). John 20 is also important because some themes that occur throughout the Gospel are repeated again in the resurrection appearances. For instance, the themes of 'sin' (e.g. 1.29), 'Spirit' (e.g. 1.33; 3.34), 'peace' (e.g. 14.27), and 'joy' (e.g. 16.20-22) all resurface in Jn 20.20-23.[43] In light of this, Jn 20 is a strategic unit of material within GJohn.

Jesus' actions in his first appearance to his disciples are intended to identify him. His greeting 'peace be with you' (20.19) reminds the reader of Jesus' farewell discourses when he told his disciples 'peace I leave with you; my peace I give to you' (14.27). The one who gave peace to his disciples during his earthly ministry is the same one who is now giving them peace after his resurrection. The narrator's indication that Jesus 'stood among' (ἔστη εἰς τὸ μέσον) his disciples (20.19) and said 'receive the Holy Spirit (πνεῦμα ἅγιον)' (20.22) is easily related to John's claim that 'among you stands one' (μέσος ὑμῶν ἔστηκεν) who baptizes with the 'Holy Spirit (πνεύματι ἁγίῳ)' (1.26, 33). The one introduced by the Baptist in 1.26, 33 is the same risen Jesus who is now giving the Spirit to his disciples. The clearest indication that Jesus' actions in Jn 20.19-23 are intended to identify him is found in v. 20. Jesus shows his hands and his side in order to indicate that the risen Lord and the crucified are one.[44] Although there is no explicit indication in Jn 19 that Jesus' hands were damaged during his crucifixion,[45] John has highlighted that the soldiers pierced his side with a spear (19.34, 37).

42. Bultmann, *John*, p. 691.

43. Lindars, *John*, p. 611; Bultmann, *John*, p. 692; Hoskyns, *Gospel*, vol. 2, pp. 649, 651; Lincoln, *John*, pp. 497, 499; Bonney, *Thomas*, p. 156; Keener, *John*, vol. 2, pp. 1196–7.

44. Bultmann, *John*, p. 691; Schnackenburg, *John*, vol. 3, p. 323; Lincoln, *John*, p. 497; Barrett, *John*, p. 567; Beasley-Murray, *John*, p. 379; Wahlde, *John*, vol. 2, p. 863; Carson, *John*, p. 647; Michaels, *John*, p. 1005; Brown, *John*, vol. 2, p. 1033; S. M. Schneiders, 'The Raising of the New Temple: John 20.19-23 and Johannine Ecclesiology', *NTS* 52 (2006), pp. 337–55 (347). Cf. Beare, 'Spirit', p. 98; R. H. Fuller, 'John 20:19-23', *Int* 32 (1978), pp. 180–4 (183). A different interpretation of Jesus showing his hands in Jn 20.20 is offered by E. C. Still, 'Sent to Be Scarred: John 20:19-23', *ExpTim* 113 (2002), p. 190 n. 1, who suggests that Jesus' act points to the suffering ahead for the disciples.

45. The form of crucifixion varied considerably in the ancient world, but it is likely that the victims were nailed or bound to a stake. Cf. M. Hengel, *Crucifixion in the Ancient World and the Folly of the Message of the Cross* (trans. J. Bowden;

If Jesus' act of showing his hands and side was intended to identify him (20.20), it is reasonable to think that his act of breathing in 20.22 had a similar intention, especially when the close resemblance of the phrases describing these actions is taken into account: καὶ τοῦτο εἰπὼν ἔδειξεν κτλ. (20.20); καὶ τοῦτο εἰπὼν ἐνεφύσησεν κτλ. (20.22).[46] If John is drawing on the tradition of God's creation of humankind that stems from Gen. 2.7 in Jn 20.22, there is a deliberate association of the risen Jesus with the Creator God.[47] John portrays Jesus as performing an act that resembles that of the Creator God.

This suggestion gains support when Jn 20.19-23 is considered in light of the literary relationship of Jn 20 to the Johannine prologue.[48] In the encounter of the risen Jesus with Mary Jesus commands her to go to his 'brothers' and tell them, 'I am ascending to my Father and your Father (τὸν πατέρα μου καὶ πατέρα ὑμῶν), to my God and your God (θεόν μου καὶ θεὸν ὑμῶν)' (20.17). In Jesus' second encounter with his disciples Thomas confesses him as 'My Lord and my God (ὁ κύριός μου καὶ ὁ θεός μου)' (20.28). The first references to the 'Father' and to 'God' in GJohn are found in the prologue. There ὁ λόγος is related closely to 'God', θεὸς ἦν ὁ λόγος (1.1). At the same time, ὁ λόγος made flesh (1.14) is the one who is in the bosom of the Father (τοῦ πατρός) and who has made him known (1.18). Those statements about the relationship of ὁ λόγος with God and the Father bracket clear indications of his active involvement in the creation of the world (1.10) and in the creation of everything that exists (1.3). Similarly, Jesus' statement that he will ascend to the Father (20.17)[49] and Thomas' confession of Jesus as 'Lord and God' (20.28) bracket an action performed by Jesus (20.22) that resembles that of the Creator God in Gen. 2.7.

London: SCM, 1977), pp. 24–32; D. W. Chapman, *Ancient Jewish and Christian Perceptions of Crucifixion* (WUNT, 2/244; Tübingen: Mohr Siebeck, 2008), pp. 41–177.

46. Michaels, *John*, p. 1010; von Wahlde, *John*, vol. 2, p. 857–8; Brown, *John*, vol. 1, p. 1029.

47. Brown, *John*, vol. 2, p. 1037; Manning, *Echoes*, p. 167.

48. Lincoln, *John*, p. 501; Moloney, *John*, p. 516.

49. Some judge that Jn 20.17 indicates that Mary not only recognized Jesus but also worshiped him (cf. Mt. 28.9). See P. Perkins, *Resurrection: New Testament Witness and Contemporary Reflection* (Garden City: Doubleday, 1984), p. 176; Barrett, *John*, p. 307; K. S. O'Brien, 'Written that You May Believe: John 20 and Narrative Rhetoric', *CBQ* 67 (2005), pp. 284–302 (302). However, this interpretation is not the *opinion communis* among Johannine scholars.

Since John seems to relate the risen Jesus with the One who created humankind in the beginning, it is reasonable to conclude that John is intending to portray Jesus in close and unique association with the Creator God. However, this does not mean that John has collapsed the risen Jesus into the Creator God. The close identification of Jesus with God both in Jn 20.22 and in Thomas' confession in Jn 20.28 should be read in light of Jesus' own stated distinction between him and his Father. Jesus himself asserts that he will ascend to his 'Father' and his 'God' (20.17). This combination of a close association between the risen Jesus and God (20.22, 28) and a clear distinction between the risen Jesus and the Father recalls the prologue. There ὁ λόγος is identified with God (θεὸς ἦν ὁ λόγος, 1.1) and described as μονογενὴς θεός (1.18). At the same time, ὁ λόγος is said to exist 'with God' (πρὸς τὸν θεόν, 1.1-2; cf. παρὰ πατρός, 1.14) and 'in the bosom of the Father' (εἰς τὸν κόλπον τοῦ πατρός, 1.18). These statements are to be read as complementary. Just as ὁ λόγος is both 'God' and 'with God', the risen Jesus is both 'God' (20.22, 28) and returning to his Father (20.17). The risen Jesus is fully divine and yet also distinguishable from the Father.[50]

The idea that Jesus' act in Jn 20.22 was intended to highlight his close association with God is further supported by the literary links between Jn 20.19-23 and Jn 14.15-21. In the latter text Jesus promises to his disciples that they will be given τὸ πνεῦμα τῆς ἀληθείας (14.17; cf. 14.16, 26), that he will come to them (ἔρχομαι πρὸς ὑμᾶς, 14.18), and that they will see him (ὑμεῖς θεωρεῖτέ με, 14.19). Then the disciples will be able to know that Jesus is in the Father (ἐγὼ ἐν τῷ πατρί μου, 14.20). This realization will happen ἐν ἐκείνῃ τῇ ἡμέρᾳ (14.20). Similarly, Jesus comes (ἦλθεν ὁ Ἰησοῦς, 20.19) to his disciples in 'that day' (τῇ ἡμέρᾳ ἐκείνῃ, 20.19)[51] and the disciples are able to see the Lord (ἰδόντες τὸν κύριον, 20.20). Jesus then gives them the Holy Spirit (πνεῦμα ἅγιον, 20.22). The Johannine reader who is able to perceive that in 20.22 John

50. Bultmann, *John*, pp. 690–1, suggested that Jesus' ability to come to his disciples even though they were behind closed doors is intended to highlight his divinity. This idea, however, is contested by Michaels, *John*, p. 1008. M. Marquez, 'El Espíritu Santo, principio de la nueva creación, en función de la misión apostólica en Jn 20, 21-22', in *Jalones de la historia de la salvación en el Antiguo y Nuevo Testamento* (SBE, 26; Madrid: Consejo Superior de Investigaciones Científicas, 1969), pp. 121–48 (127), suggested that Jesus' greeting 'peace be with you' should be understood as an implicit indication of Jesus' divinity because in the OT 'peace' was a gift from Yahweh (cf. Beasley-Murray, *John*, p. 379; Brown, *John*, vol. 2, p. 1035). In GJohn 'peace' is consistently related to Jesus, not to his Father (14.27; 16.33; 20.19, 21, 26).

51. Marquez, 'Espíritu', p. 124.

is drawing on the tradition of God's creation of humankind stemming from Gen. 2.7 can conclude that the risen Jesus is with the Father just as ὁ λόγος was with God in the beginning (1.1-2). Jesus' act of breathing would provide the insight that the reader needs in order to relate the risen Lord closely with God.[52]

The close association between Jesus and the Creator God helps the reader to grasp the full significance of Jesus' divine activities. One of those activities is the giving of the Spirit.[53] Immediately after breathing, Jesus says, 'receive the Holy Spirit (πνεῦμα ἅγιον)' (20.22).[54] Throughout GJohn, it is not always clear who will give the Spirit, Jesus or his Father (cf. 3.34).[55] Since the Spirit has descended and remained in Jesus (1.32), he is authorized to baptize with the Holy Spirit (πνεύματι ἁγίῳ, 1.33). Similarly, in Jn 15.26 Jesus asserts that he will send the Paraclete (ὁ παράκλητος), the Spirit of truth (τὸ πνεῦμα τῆς ἀληθείας), from the Father (cf. 16.7). However, in Jn 14 the Father is portrayed as the giver of the Spirit. Jesus will pray and the Father will give the disciples another Advocate (παράκλητος), the Spirit of truth (τὸ πνεῦμα τῆς ἀληθείας) (14.16-17). In the same vein, Jesus asserts in Jn 14.26 that the Father will send the Paraclete (ὁ παράκλητος), the Holy Spirit (τὸ πνεῦμα τὸ ἅγιον),[56] in his name. The reader then expects the Spirit to be given by

52. M. M. Thompson, 'The Breath of Life: John 20:22-23 Once More', in *The Holy Spirit and Christian Origins* (ed. G. N. Stanton, B. W. Longenecker, and S. C. Barton; Grand Rapids: Eerdmans, 2004), pp. 69–78 (71, 77); Manning, *Echoes*, p. 167; G. M. Burge, *The Anointed Community: The Holy Spirit in the Johannine Tradition* (Grand Rapids: Eerdmans, 1987), p. 125. On the other hand, Witherington, *John's Wisdom*, p. 343, claims that Jesus 'is being portrayed as Wisdom and as the giver of wisdom' in Jn 20.22. His claim is unpersuasive because the texts that he uses to support his suggestion are loosely tied to Jn 20.22. In Wis. 7.25 'wisdom' is described as the 'breath of the power of God' and in Prov. 8.30 'wisdom' is portrayed as being in the presence of God. None of these texts describes 'wisdom' as actually performing the act of breathing.

53. Keener, *John*, vol. 2, p. 1205, observes that in 'biblical imagery, only God would baptize in his Spirit' (Isa. 42.1; 44.3; 61.1; 63.11; Ezek. 36.27; 37.14; 39.29; Joel 2.28-29; Hag. 2.5; Zech. 4.6; 12.10).

54. The giving of the Spirit was perhaps anticipated in Jn 20.20. The pierced side of Jesus might refer to Jn 19.37, where Zech. 12.10 is quoted. This OT passage combines 'the one they have pierced' with the outpouring of a 'spirit of grace and supplication'. Cf. Wm. R. Bynum, *The Fourth Gospel and the Scriptures: Illuminating the Form and Meaning of Scriptural Citation in John 19:37* (NovTSup, 144; Leiden: Brill, 2012), p. 183; Kubiś, *Zechariah*, pp. 115–218.

55. D. Mollat, *Études johanniques* (PDD; Paris: Seuil, 1979), p. 158.

56. Weidemann, 'Protology', p. 323 n. 78, claims that 'holy spirit' without the definite article in Jn 20.22 is only 'a gift from Jesus' but does not represent the

Jesus or by his Father or by both of them. In Jn 20.22 the Spirit is given by Jesus immediately after he has performed an act that resembles that of the Creator God.[57]

The other divine activity in Jn 20.22 is Jesus' right to give to his disciples the authority to forgive or retain sins. In Jn 5 Jesus claimed that just as his Father is working until now, he too is working (5.17). Just as the Father has been working since the creation of the world even during the Sabbath, Jesus too is authorized to do the works of the Father. The Jews react by accusing him of making himself equal with God (v. 18). In response, Jesus asserts that he takes part in two divine activities, the giving of life (vv. 21, 24) and the bringing of judgement (vv. 22, 27, 30). In Jn 9 Jesus executes judgement (9.39) by declaring whose sins remain and who has no sin (9.40-41; cf. 8.21, 24).[58] Jesus has this authority to execute judgement because he is the Lamb of God who takes away the sin of the world (1.29; cf. 5.14).[59] His words and works bring judgement to those who see and hear (15.22, 24).[60] Elsewhere Jesus has promised that his disciples will partake in his works (14.12) and he has asserted that the Spirit will convince the world concerning sin because the world does not believe in him (16.8-9; cf. 15.24-27).

In light of this broad context of Johannine thought, the reader can see in Jn 20.22-23 that Jesus is giving to his disciples the authority to be involved in the divine activity he has been performing throughout his

---

fulfilment of the Paraclete promises. Weideman identifies 'the Holy Spirit' promised in Jn 14.16-17, 26 with the Paraclete. However, the use of 'holy' in Jn 1.33; 14.26; 20.22 makes the reader relate all three verses to one another and to identify the 'Holy Spirit' in Jn 20.22 with the 'Holy Spirit' in Jn 1.33; 14.26. Cf. J. Joubert, 'Johannine Metaphors/Symbols Linked to the Paraclete-Spirit and Their Theological Implications', *AcT* 27 (2007), pp. 83-103 (92 n. 20); M. M. Thompson, *The God of the Gospel of John* (Grand Rapids: Eerdmans, 2001), pp. 145–53; Beasley-Murray, *John*, p. 380. The anarthrous phrase 'Holy Spirit' is also used in Acts 2.4 (Brown, *John*, vol. 2, p. 1023).

57. Weidemann, 'Protology', pp. 323–4, argues that Jn 20.22 has to be read as the 'animation' of the disciples on the first day of the week (cf. Mateos and Barreto, *Juan*, pp. 49–50). For Weidemann, the disciples remain in the status of Adam before the breathing of life, being only dust. However, if the 'Spirit' in Jn 20.22 is a reference to the promise of the Holy Spirit elsewhere in GJohn, Jesus is not 'animating' his disciples but certainly giving them the 'Holy Spirit'. Cf. Lindars, *John*, pp. 611–12; Lincoln, *John*, p. 498; Schnackenburg, *John*, vol. 3, p. 325; Brown, *John*, vol. 2, p. 1036; Carson, *John*, p. 650.

58. Brown, *John*, vol. 2, p. 1042.

59. Schnackenburg, *John*, vol. 3, p. 327.

60. Lincoln, *John*, p. 499.

ministry.[61] The link between Jesus' mission and the disciples' commission is the Holy Spirit, whom Jesus breathes by performing an act that resembles that of the Creator God.[62] The power to forgive and retain sins in Jn 20.23 is still a divine activity performed by God himself. This is supported by the fact that the verbs ἀφέωνται and κεκράτηνται are in the passive form (20.23).[63] Both verbs can be taken as divine passives, i.e. God is behind the act of forgiving and retaining sins.[64]

The link between Jesus performing an act that resembles that of the Creator God (20.22) and the sending of the disciples perhaps has a precedent in Jn 9.[65] Jesus identifies himself as the one who has been sent by his Father in order to perform his works (τὰ ἔργα τοῦ πέμψαντός, 9.4). Later he commands the blind man to go and wash in the pool of Siloam, 'which is translated "Sent" (ἀπεσταλμένος)' (9.7). The narrator portrays Jesus performing an unusual action: ταῦτα εἰπὼν ἔπτυσεν χαμαὶ καὶ ἐποίησεν πηλὸν (9.6). Similarly, the narrator portrays Jesus performing an unusual action in Jn 20.22: τοῦτο εἰπὼν ἐνεφύσησεν. This action occurs in a context where Jesus identifies himself as the one sent by his Father (ἀπέσταλκέν με ὁ πατήρ, 20.21) and where he sends his disciples (πέμπω ὑμᾶς, 20.21). It seems that in both cases (Jn 9 and Jn 20) Jesus' authority to act as the sender is based upon his close association with the One who

61. Lightfoot, *John*, p. 333; Bultmann, *John*, p. 693; Beasley-Murray, *John*, p. 383–4; Barrett, *John*, p. 571. Cf. Hoskyns, *Gospel*, vol. 2, p. 650; Lincoln, *John*, p. 499.

62. U. Bechmann, 'Der Lebenshauch Gottes: Die Verwandlungskraft des Geistes Gottes am Beispiel von Ez 37,1-4 und Joh 20,19-23', *BK* 64 (2009), pp. 87–92 (88), suggests that the act of Jesus in Jn 20.22 represents for the disciples the 'power of the word' (*Wortgewalt*) and language ability that grant the disciples the capacity to forgive sins. A similar opinion seems to be held by R. W. Lyon, 'John 20:22, Once More', *AsTJ* 43 (1988), pp. 73–85 (79). Although there is a clear connection between the Spirit and the disciples' ability to forgive sins, the link between Jesus' act in Jn 20.22 and the disciples' language ability seems speculative.

63. The present tense αφιενται (e.g. K N W Majority text) and the future tense αφεθησεται (e.g. א*) are perhaps scribal simplifications. Therefore, the perfect tense ἀφέωνται is the most likely reading (e.g. A D; cf. B*). See Metzger, *Commentary*, p. 219.

64. Brown, *John*, vol. 2, pp. 1024, 1039; Lincoln, *John*, p. 500; Michaels, *John*, p. 1014; Keener, *John*, vol. 2, p. 1206. For the use of the passive form in reference to God in the NT, see BDF §130.

65. Cf. Derrett, 'Miracles', p. 77. Commentators often posit that the reference to Siloam ('sent') in Jn 9.7 is somehow related to the larger Johannine use of the divine sending of Jesus (e.g. Beasley-Murray, *John*, pp. 155–6). Furthermore, early Christian readers of Jn 9.7 often related the miracle to baptism and the giving of the Spirit (Brown, *John*, vol. 1, pp. 380–2).

sent him. John expresses this close relationship between the Son and the Father by portraying Jesus performing acts that resemble those of the Creator God.

Therefore, John intends to portray Jesus in close association with God by using an instance of creation imagery in 20.22 to help readers grasp the full significance of Jesus' divine activities. Now I will attempt to show, in the next several paragraphs, that the use of the tradition of God's creation of humankind stemming from Gen. 2.7 is also intended to assert the universal significance of Jesus' mission through the mission of his disciples.

In the prologue ὁ λόγος has a claim on everything that has been created (1.3, 10). His light shines on every human being (1.9), giving those who receive him the authority to become God's children (1.12). He was actively involved in the creation of the world (ὁ κόσμος, 1.10) and has come as the Lamb of God who takes away the sin of the world (τοῦ κόσμου, 1.29; cf. 4.42). Since he has to return to the Father, the Spirit will carry out Jesus' task by convicting the world (τὸν κόσμον) concerning sin (16.8). Jesus' act of breathing in Jn 20.22 is a reminder of his role in creation and, thus, of his claim on everything that has been created. The universal significance of Jesus' mission will be achieved through the disciples who have received the Spirit in order to forgive and retain sins (20.23).[66] The phrase ἄν τινων (20.23) has no specific restriction in the context and can mean 'anyone' in the broadest possible sense.[67] Since the disciples' mission should be an imitation of Jesus' mission (20.21; cf. 17.18), they should include in their agenda Samaritans (4.39-42), Greeks (12.20; cf. 7.35), and Jews (e.g. 3.1-5).

The possibility of reading 'anyone' in the broadest sense is enhanced when Jesus' commission to his disciples in GJohn is compared with their commissioning in the Synoptic Gospels.[68] In his appearance to his disciples recorded in Lk. 24.47, Jesus is portrayed as saying that 'repentance for the forgiveness of sins will be announced in his name to all nations (πάντα τὰ ἔθνη)'. Similarly, the so-called longer ending of

66. It is not clear in Jn 20.19-23 whether those gathered are the 'twelve' (except Judas) or a larger group of disciples. J. Swetnam, 'Bestowal of the Spirit in the Fourth Gospel', *Bib* 74 (1993), pp. 556–76 (572), restricts the group to the 'twelve', but the evidence in Jn 20.19-23 is far from clear.

67. Brown, *John*, vol. 2, p. 1023, allows the translation 'whose ever sins you forgive'.

68. For a detailed treatment of Jn 20.23 in relation to GLuke and GMatthew, see T. Hägerland, *Jesus and the Forgiveness of Sins: An Aspect of His Prophetic Mission* (SNTSMS, 150; Cambridge: Cambridge University Press, 2012), pp. 75–84.

GMark portrays Jesus as sending his disciples into 'all the world' (τὸν κόσμον ἅπαντα) to preach the Gospel to every creature (πάσῃ τῇ κτίσει, 16.15).[69] In Mt. 28.18-19 the authority given to Jesus in heaven and on earth is linked to the sending of the disciples to make disciples of all nations (πάντα τὰ ἔθνη). Instead of a statement about Jesus' authority 'in heaven and on earth' (Mt. 28.18), John portrays Jesus performing an act that resembles that of the Creator God.[70] This act would indicate his authority over creation. If John knew the traditions behind the Synoptic Gospels, it is reasonable to think that he was aware of the universal character of the disciples' mission after the resurrection.[71]

John 20.22 as an instance of creation imagery helps the reader to understand that (1) the risen Jesus has a unique association with the Creator God that allows him to perform divine activities and (2) that his mission through his disciples has a universal significance. Furthermore, Jn 20.22 is intended to link past reality (creation) with present and future reality (Jesus' giving of the Spirit and the disciples' mission). Commentators often observe that Jesus' act in Jn 20.22 is intended as an act of new creation.[72] In context, this new creation should be related to the giving of life, the divine birth of the disciples, the new task they are charged to perform, and the relationship between purity and the Holy Spirit.[73]

69. Brown, *John*, vol. 2, p. 1029.

70. F. J. A. Hort, *The Christian Ecclesia* (London: Macmillan, 1914), p. 33; Barrett, *John*, p. 568.

71. Cf. A. Loisy, *Le quatrième Évangile* (Paris: Émile Nourry, 2nd edn, 1921), p. 507, 'Mais le Christ johannique n'a pas besoin de dire qu'il envoie ses apôtres à tout l'univers, parce que sa propre mission a toujours été conçue comme universelle, depuis le prologue jusqu'à cette conclusion' (see also Marquez, 'Espíritu', p. 134).

72. Lindars, *John*, p. 611; Hoskyns, *Gospel*, vol. 2, p. 649; Lincoln, *John*, p. 499; Barrett, *John*, p. 570; Beasley-Murray, *John*, pp. 380–1; Moloney, *John*, p. 535; Lightfoot, *John*, p. 333; Brown, *John*, vol. 2, p. 1035; Marquez, 'Espíritu', p. 137; Brodie, *John*, p. 569; Beare, 'Spirit', pp. 98, 100; Cook, 'Exegesis', p. 8; Keener, *John*, vol. 2, p. 1204; T. G. Brown, *Spirit in the Writings of John: Johannine Pneumatology in Social-Scientific Perspective* (JSNTSup, 253; London: T&T Clark International, 2003), p. 111; V. Kesich, 'Resurrection, Ascension, and the Giving of the Spirit', *GOTR* 25 (1980), pp. 249–60.

73. Some scholars have suggested that the new creation implied in Jesus' act in Jn 20.22 is further supported by the reference to the 'first day of the week' in Jn 20.19. Cf. Grinfield, *Cosmos*, p. 45; J. K. Brown, 'Creation', pp. 283–4; Painter, 'Light', pp. 21, 43. However, while there is no explicit indication in Gen. 2.7 that the man was created on the sixth day, the reader can reach this conclusion in light of Gen. 1.26, 31 (cf. Carson, *John*, p. 635).

In the prologue 'life' is related to ὁ λόγος who was in the beginning with God, taking an active role in creation (1.1-4). During his earthly ministry, Jesus claims that life is found in him (e.g. 5.40). At the same time, the Spirit is also associated with life elsewhere in GJohn. Jesus himself asserts that 'the Spirit is the one who gives life (τὸ ζωοποιοῦν)' (6.63). The narrator also identifies the 'streams of living water' in Jn 7.38-39 with the Spirit. Furthermore, Jesus' offer of 'living water' in Jn 4.14 is perhaps best understood as a reference to the Spirit.[74] In light of this, the giving of the Spirit in Jn 20.22 through an act that resembles that of the Creator God implies that the disciples are receiving the life which is associated with both Jesus and the Spirit.[75]

In the prologue the Word who took an active role in the creation of the world (1.3, 10) gives people the right to become God's children (1.12). In his dialogue with Nicodemus Jesus relates the 'birth from above' with the Spirit (3.3-8). Jesus claims that people need to be born of 'water and spirit' and asserts that there are those who are born of the 'Spirit' (3.5-6; cf. 3.8). In light of this, the giving of the Spirit in Jn 20.22 would also imply the divine birth of the disciples (cf. Tit. 3.5).[76] This point is supported by Jesus' previous remark to Mary in Jn 20.17, 'Go to my brothers and tell them, "I am ascending…to your Father"'. After his resurrection, and for the very first time in GJohn, Jesus implies that the disciples are to be seen as children of the Father and his brothers (cf. Jn 15.13-15, where Jesus calls them 'friends').

The new creation of the disciples also implies their participation in a new task.[77] Jesus has anticipated elsewhere in GJohn that his disciples will partake in his mission. In Jn 4.38 Jesus tells his disciples that they have been sent to reap what they did not work for,[78] and in Jn 14.12 Jesus promises that believers will perform greater works than those he has performed.[79] By partaking in the divine work of forgiving sins (Jn 20.22),

---

74. In Jewish tradition 'water' was often associated with 'Spirit'. Cf. S. T. Um, *The Theme of Temple Christology in John's Gospel* (LNTS, 312; London: T&T Clark International, 2006), pp. 166–7.

75. Lincoln, *John*, p. 499; Schnackenburg, *John*, vol. 3, p. 325; Beasley-Murray, *John*, p. 381; von Wahlde, *John*, vol. 2, pp. 856, 862; Michaels, *John*, p. 1010.

76. Dodd, *Interpretation*, p. 227; Brown, *John*, vol. 2, p. 1035, 1037; von Wahlde, *John*, vol. 2, p. 862; Lincoln, *John*, p. 499; Keener, *John*, vol. 2, p. 1204.

77. J. R. Levison, *Filled with the Spirit* (Grand Rapids: Eerdmans, 2009), p. 371.

78. Schnackenburg, *John*, vol. 3, p. 324.

79. Some commentators observe that the 'greater (μείζονα) works' that the disciples will perform (Jn 14.12) might refer to the more extensive significance of the disciples' mission, since they will be able to bring judgement and life to more people in other geographical areas (Lindars, *John*, p. 475; Hoskyns, *Gospel*, vol. 2,

the disciples are actively participating in the new creation of God.[80] Just as Jesus took away the sin of the world (1.29) and brought life and light to his creation (e.g. 11.43-44; 8.12; 9.5), the disciples are now in a position where they will be able to forgive and retain people's sins (20.22).[81] They receive authority over God's creation in order to participate in Jesus' mission.[82] The disciples are able to partake in this divine task because they have received the Holy Spirit (πνεῦμα ἅγιον). In his prayer Jesus relates the sending of the disciples into the world to their sanctification: 'I sent them into the world' (17.18) and 'so that they too may be truly sanctified (ἡγιασμένοι)' (17.19). Although there is no reference to the Spirit in Jn 17, the use of the adjective ἅγιος in reference to the Spirit in Jn 20.22 might indicate that the Holy Spirit is related to the sanctification of those who are sent (cf. 1 Cor. 6.11). If that is correct, the new creation represented in Jn 20.22 also includes the sanctification of the disciples that enables them to carry out Jesus' mission.[83]

III. Conclusion

John uses the portrayal of Jesus performing an act that resembles that of the Creator God in order to support some of the ideas introduced earlier in the prologue and elsewhere in his Gospel. John seems to relate both

p. 538; Barrett, *John*, p. 460; Schnackenburg, *John*, vol. 3, pp. 71–2; Michaels, *John*, p. 780). If this was the meaning intended by John, the language of 'works' is used here (14.12) in order to assert the universal significance of Jesus through his disciples (cf. 4.35-38; 10.16-17; 11.52; 12.20-21; Lightfoot, *John*, p. 276). However, Bultmann, *John*, pp. 610–11, and Beasley-Murray, *John*, p. 255, have rejected this interpretation. For them, 'greater works' means that the disciples' mission will take into account the fullness of Jesus' significance (including his death and resurrection). Others embrace Bultmann's suggestion without rejecting the interpretation given by most commentators (e.g. Lincoln, *John*, p. 392; cf. Carson, *John*, p. 496).

80. Lindars, *John*, p. 611; Beasley-Murray, *John*, p. 380. Cf. M. A. Chevallier, *Souffle de Dieu. Le Saint Esprit dans le Nouveau Testament* (LPT, 54; 3 vols.; Paris: Beauchesne, 1990), vol. 2, p. 433.

81. Stamm, 'Creation', p. 17.

82. As has already been noted earlier, in ancient Jewish texts Gen. 2.7 was often used in order to signal the superior status of the man over God's creation (e.g. Philo, *Somn.* 1.34-35; 4Q381 1, 7).

83. J. Schmitt, 'Simples remarques sur le fragment, Jo., XX, 22-23,' in *Mélanges en l'honneur de Monseigneur Michael Andrieu* (RevScRel; Strasburg: Palais Universitaire, 1956), pp. 415–23 (418, 420, 422); Schnackenburg, *John*, vol. 3, p. 325; Brown, *John*, vol. 2, p. 1036. Von Wahlde, *John*, vol. 1, p. 510, suggests that the cleansing from sin through the Spirit appears in the scene of the footwashing (13.1-20; cf. 15.3).

the Word in creation (1.3-5, 10) and the earthly Jesus who performs the works of the Father even during the Sabbath (5.17, 20, 36) with the risen Jesus who bestows the promised Spirit to his disciples (20.22). Therefore, Jesus is to be regarded both as the agent of creation and as the agent of revelation and salvation. Since the risen Jesus performs an act that resembles that of the Creator God, the reader can understand that he has a claim over the whole of God's creation (cf. 1.3, 10). As a result, the mission of the disciples should be regarded as universal in scope. The forgiveness of sins is available to the world God created in the beginning, through the work of those who have been empowered with the Spirit.

Chapter 7

THE GARDEN OF EDEN AND JESUS'
PASSION AND RESURRECTION

In the previous chapter I suggested that John draws on the tradition of God's creation of humankind that stems from Gen. 2.7 in Jn 20.22. The importance of this instance of creation imagery is found in its strategic location in the middle of the three resurrection appearances in Jn 20. In the present chapter I offer a critical assessment of the claim that Jn 18.1, 26; 19.41, and Jn 20.15 are allusions to the garden of Eden. First, I will argue that Mary's identification of Jesus as the gardener in Jn 20.15 was not intended as a link to Adam or God in the garden of Eden. Second, I will contend that the suggested link between Jn 18.1, 26; 19.41 and the garden of Eden is not persuasive. This chapter then supports my main argument that the importance of creation imagery in the Johannine passion and resurrection narratives is found in the strategic location of Jn 20.22.

I. The Gardener (John 20.15)

Scholars who relate the reference to a gardener in Jn 20.15 (ὁ κηπουρός) to the Genesis account of creation draw at least two conclusions. On the one hand, some scholars claim that John intended to portray the risen Jesus as the new Adam. Jeannine Brown, for example, asserts, 'it is very likely' that 'Jesus *is* the gardener [in Jn 20.15], and this implicit message connects Jesus to that first gardener, Adam'.[1] On the other hand, some other scholars maintain that John intended to portray the risen Jesus as

---

1. J. K. Brown, 'Creation', p. 281, her emphasis. Cf. Mateos and Barreto, *Juan*, p. 52; Suggit, 'Gardener', p. 167; F. Manns, *L'Evangile de Jean à la lumière du Judaïsme* (SBF, 33; Jerusalem: Franciscan Printing Press, 1991), pp. 426–8; Cothenet, 'L'arrière-plan', p. 48; H. C. Waetjen, *The Gospel of the Beloved Disciple: A Work in Two Editions* (London: T&T Clark International, 2005), pp. 414–20; N. Wyatt, '"Supposing Him to Be the Gardener" (John 20,15): A Study of the Paradise Motif in John', *ZNW* 81 (1990), pp. 21–38; D. M. Stanley, 'The Passion according to John', *Worship* 33 (1959), pp. 210–30 (213).

the Creator God himself in the garden of Eden. Mary Coloe, for instance, claims that as God is the One who planted and cultivated the garden of Eden in Gen. 2.9, so too Jesus 'returns to Mary as the Divine Gardener walking in the garden of his creation'.[2] Other scholars also relate Jn 20.15 to the Genesis account of creation without indicating clearly whether this suggested link implies an Adam Christology or the portrayal of Jesus as the Creator God.[3] The main problem with the suggestion that ὁ κηπουρός in Jn 20.15 alludes to Adam or God in Gen. 1–3 is the lack of similar vocabulary. The noun κηπουρός is never used in the LXX or the rest of the NT. Furthermore, neither God nor Adam is ever identified explicitly as gardener (using κηπουρός) in the LXX. God is portrayed as the One who planted (ἐφύτευσεν) an orchard in Eden (Gen. 2.8), and Adam is depicted as the one who tilled and kept (ἐργάζεσθαι καὶ φυλάσσειν) the garden (Gen. 2.15).[4] However, neither of them is called gardener in Gen. 1–3. One even searches in vain for references to κηπουρός in extant Greek Second-Temple Jewish texts. The only explicit reference to 'gardeners' that I have been able to find in Second-Temple Jewish texts occurs in 4Q530 II, 7. There, a person who has had a dream recounts that he saw gardeners (גננ[ג]) who were watering in his dream.[5] Nevertheless, this reference to gardeners is not used in a creation context.

Other Second-Temple Jewish texts follow the Genesis account of creation and portray Adam as tilling and keeping the garden (Philo, *Leg. All.* 1.53; 4Q423 2, 1-2). A few texts speculate about this portrayal of Adam. Philo, for example, considers that the 'moulded man' received the command of tilling and warding the garden, but the man created after God's image devoted himself to cultivate virtue (*Leg. All.* 1.54-55; cf. *Quaest. in Gen.* 1.14). Second-Temple Jewish texts also follow the portrayal of God as planting the garden of Eden.[6] God planted (r 4Q504 8, 6;

2. Coloe, 'Creation', p. 8. Cf. Hoskyns, 'Genesis', p. 215; F. Blanquart, *Le premier jour. Étude sur Jean 20* (LD, 146; Paris: Cerf, 1992), p. 66; Moore, 'Creation', p. 43.

3. C. Koch, ' "Es war aber an dem Ort ein Garten" (Joh 19,41): Der Garten als bedeutsames Erzählmotiv in den Johanneischen Passions- und Auferstehungstexten', in *Im Geist und in der Wahrheit: Studien zum Johannesevangelium und zur Offenbarung des Johannes sowie andere Beiträge* (ed. K. Huber and B. Repschinski; NTAbh, 52; Münster: Aschendorff, 2008), pp. 229–38; Lightfoot, *John*, p. 322.

4. The noun 'gardener' is not used in Gen. 1–3 MT. The MT has ויטע יהוה אלהים, 'the Lord God planted' (Gen. 2.8), and לעבדה ולשמרה, 'to till it and keep it' (Gen. 2.15).

5. García-Martínez and Tigchelaar (eds.), *Scrolls*, pp. 1062–3.

6. A speaker in 1QH^a XVI, 5–XVII, 36 is depicted as tending a garden in a context where creation imagery is in view. Cf. J. A. Hughes, *Scriptural Allusions and Exegesis in the Hodayot* (STDJ, 59; Leiden: Brill, 2006), pp. 150–9.

Josephus, *Ant.* 1.37; cf. *1 En.* 25.4-7) or created (*2 Bar.* 4.3) the garden on the third day (*Jub.* 2.7) or before the earth was created (*4 Ezra* 3.6). Theophilus even refers to the garden of Eden as 'plantation planted by God' (*Autol.* 2.24, φυτερία ὑπὸ θεοῦ πεφυτευμένη).[7] A few texts speculate about this portrayal of God as the One who planted Eden. In *3 Bar.* 4.8, for instance, it is said that God used angelic assistance to plant the garden.

It is not possible to show from Second-Temple Jewish texts that Adam or God was referred to explicitly as gardener.[8] Therefore, it is doubtful that John's intended Jewish audience would have related easily Jn 20.15 to Adam or God in the Genesis story of creation. Not even Gentile readers of GJohn would have straightforwardly related Jn 20.15 to God, because there is no evidence that the noun κηπουρός was applied to a creator 'god' in ancient pagan literature. A search for κηπουρός in *TLG* in a period that goes from the second century B.C.E. to the second century C.E. shows that this noun was never used in relation to a creator 'god'. The noun is used several times in reference to people.[9]

Joachim Shaper suggests that, 'Adam, in Genesis 2–3 is the royal "gardener" of Eden, and John 19.38b-42 implicitly sees Adam as the prefiguration of Christ, the royal κηπουρός'.[10] Schaper bases his suggestion on the observation that 'a number of scholars' have pointed out 'that Adam's function in the garden parallels that of Near Eastern monarchs in relation to their palace gardens'.[11] Nevertheless, he recognizes that 'evidence of the concept of the king as gardener in the Hebrew Bible is inconclusive'.[12] Since Schaper does not provide evidence that Adam was regarded as king and gardener in Second-Temple Jewish texts,[13] and

7. Theophilus thought that the Word (ὁ λόγος) took the role of God and conversed with Adam in paradise (παράδεισος) (*Autol.* 2.22). Cf. R. M. Grant, *Theophilus of Antioch: Ad Autolycum* (Oxford: Clarendon, 1970), p. 63.

8. God is referred to as ὁ φυτουργός, 'the planter', in Philo, *Conf. Ling.* 196, in a context where creation imagery is not in view. God is also called 'great Planter (φυτουργός)' in Philo, *Plant.* 2. Cf. Num. 24.6; *4 Macc.* 1.29.

9. For example, Plutarch, *Fac.* 927.B4; Diodorus Siculus, *Bibliotheca historica* 1.59.3; Epictetus, *Dissertationes ab Arriano digestae* 3.24.44.

10. J. Schaper, 'The Messiah in the Garden: John 19.38-41, (Royal) Gardens, and Messianic Concepts', in *Paradise in Antiquity: Jewish and Christian Views* (ed. M. Bockmuehl and G. G. Stroumsa; Cambridge: Cambridge University Press, 2010), pp. 17–27 (26).

11. Schaper, 'Messiah', p. 18.

12. Schaper, 'Messiah', p. 18.

13. Schaper only refers to an article by R. S. Evyasaf, 'Hellenistic and Roman Approaches to Gardens in the Eastern Mediterranean: Judaea as a Case Study', in *The Archaeology of Crop Fields and Gardens: Proceedings of the 1st Conference*

since the evidence of the concept of the king as gardener in the Hebrew Bible is inconclusive, one doubts that John intended to portray Jesus as Adam in Jn 20.15.

Although it is implausible that the Johannine intended audience may have related Jn 20.15 to Adam or God in the garden of Eden, at least one Christian from the fourth century C.E. made this connection. Jerome comments that Mary was indeed mistaken when she thought the risen Jesus to be the gardener. Jerome concludes, 'the very error had its prototype' because Jesus is the gardener of his paradise (*Homily* 87).[14] However, there is no clear evidence to conclude whether Jerome understood this 'prototype' to have been intended by John or one that Christian readers are able to draw due to divine illumination.

But even if Jerome thought that this reading was intended by John, his suggestion is implausible in light of Johannine theology. In Jn 15.1 Jesus tells his disciples that his Father is the 'vinedresser' (ὁ γεωργός). However, it is difficult to link this passage to Jn 20.15 and to argue that the reference to Jesus as gardener was intended as an instance of creation imagery because the nouns used are different (ὁ κηπουρός and ὁ γεωργός) and because there is not a creation context in Jn 15.1.[15]

Proponents of a link between Jn 20.15 and the garden of Eden have also argued that Mary's mistake in Jn 20.15 is an instance of misunderstanding that should be interpreted beyond the literal meaning.[16] In other words, although Mary was wrong when identifying the risen Jesus as the

on *Crop Fields and Gardens Archaeology. Barcelona (Spain), 1–3 June 2006* (ed. J. P. Morel, J. T. Juan, and J. C. Matamala; Bari, Italy: Edipuglia, 2006), pp. 203–4.

14. M. L. Ewald, *The Homilies of Saint Jerome (Homilies 60–96)* (FC, 57; Washington: The Catholic University of America Press, 1966), p. 220. It could be argued that Gregory the Great links Jn 20.15 to Genesis. Gregory suggests that Jesus was the 'spiritual' gardener, since he planted in Mary the seeds of virtue in her heart (*Forty Gospel Homilies* 25 [PL, vol. 76, pp. 1187–96]). According to Gregory, Mary was capable of acknowledging her creator.

15. It is likely that the reference to the Father as 'vinedresser' goes back to biblical imagery about Israel as God's vineyard (Ps. 80.8-18; Isa. 5.1-7; Ezek. 15.1-8; 17.5-8; 19.10-14), according to Michaels, *John*, p. 801; Lincoln, *John*, p. 402.

16. Some scholars have contended that a connection between Jn 20.15 and Gen. 2–3 is possible because GJohn is a symbolic text (e.g. Manns, *L'Evangile*, p. 401; M. Rosik, 'Discovering the Secrets of God's Gardens. Resurrection as New Creation [Gen 2:4b–3:24; Jn 20:1-18]', *SBFLA* 58 [2008], pp. 81–98 [81]; Zimmermann, 'Garden', pp. 223–8; cf. Schaper, 'Messiah', p. 27). Therefore, Jn 20.15 is an example of irony (e.g. Coloe, 'Creation', p. 8), misunderstanding (e.g. J. K. Brown, 'Creation', pp. 280–1; Köstenberger, *Theology*, p. 352), or double-meaning (e.g. Hoskyns, 'Genesis', pp. 214–15; Moore, 'Creation', pp. 1–2, 13, 59) that indicates that Mary was not wrong but right.

gardener, her words should have symbolic meaning because John wanted to portray Jesus as the gardener of Eden.[17] Indeed, GJohn is a highly symbolic book in which misunderstanding and irony seem to play an important role in conveying meaning.[18] Therefore, it is worth asking whether Jn 20.15 as an instance of misunderstanding supports a link to Gen. 1–3.

Herbert Leroy has identified several instances of misunderstanding in GJohn.[19] Most of those instances have a clear explanation, whether by Jesus himself or by the narrator, of that which seems to be misunderstanding. For example, Jesus was talking about his body when referring to the destruction of the temple (Jn 2.21); Jesus' departure means that he is from above (8.23); the freedom that Jesus offers is freedom from sins (8.34-36); Abraham could see Jesus because he existed before Abraham (8.58). In other cases the misunderstanding is clarified, but the clarification is still difficult to grasp for the characters in the narrative. For instance, to be born again means to be born of water and spirit (3.5); the water that Jesus gives is 'living water' (4.10); the bread from God is Jesus' body (6.51); those who believe in him will never see death (8.51-53). In all those cases, a consideration of GJohn as a whole helps the reader to grasp the intended meaning. To be born of water and spirit is related to the experience of believing in Jesus and receiving his Spirit. Living water means the eternal life that Jesus offers. To eat Jesus could

---

17. Moore, 'Creation', p. 13, has observed that the verb δοκέω is used in Jn 20.15 and in Jn 5.39, 45; 11.13, 31, 56; 13.29; 16.2 (cf. Hoskyns, 'Genesis', pp. 214–15). Moore concludes that John is using 'the verb as a rhetorical device, a further example of his employment of lexical and conceptual *amphibologia* [double-meaning and double-reference]'. In other words, Mary was wrong but the 'discerning reader… recognise[s]…that Jesus is indeed the Gardener, the Creator-God' (Moore, 'Creation', p. 13). Nevertheless, the use of misunderstanding in Jn 5.45; 11.13, 31, 56; 13.29; 16.2 does not support Moore's conclusion. In those cases, people think they are right but the context clarifies that they are indeed wrong. For instance, in Jn 11.13 the disciples think (δοκέω) that Lazarus is sleeping, but they are wrong, Jesus tells them plainly that Lazarus is dead (11.14). If we follow this pattern, Mary thinks (δοκέω) that Jesus is the gardener, but the most natural conclusion is that she is wrong, not that her misunderstanding has symbolic meaning.

18. Cf. Koester, *Symbolism*; P. D. Duke, *Irony in the Fourth Gospel* (Atlanta: John Knox, 1953); G. McRae, 'Theology and Irony in the Fourth Gospel', in *The Gospel of John as Literature: An Anthology of Twentieth-Century Perspectives* (ed. M. W. G. Stibbe; NTTS, 17; Leiden: Brill, 1993), pp. 103–13.

19. H. Leroy, *Rätsel und Missverständniss: Ein Beitrag zur Formgeschichte des Johannesevangelium* (BBB; Bonn: Hanstein, 1968), pp. 49–155. See Jn 2.19-22; 3.3-5; 4.10-15, 31-34; 6.32-34, 51-53; 7.33-36; 8.21-22, 31-33, 51-53, 56-58 (cf. 21.23).

be associated with receiving him as the one sent by the Father. Those who believe will experience resurrection. Therefore, it is safe to conclude that when John uses misunderstanding the reader can find explicit clarification of the intended meaning whether in the immediate context or in light of GJohn as a whole.[20]

If John were using misunderstanding in 20.15 in order to convey further meaning, one should expect that the narrator or one of the characters in the narrative would clarify that Jesus is indeed 'the Gardener'. However, there are no clues in the context that could direct the reader towards that conclusion. On the contrary, the context has already shown that Mary was wrong when thinking that Jesus' body was taken away (20.13). Similarly, she should be wrong again when thinking that Jesus is the gardener because she 'did not know that it was Jesus' (20.15). For all those reasons, it is dubious that John intended to relate Jesus in Jn 20.15 with God or Adam in the garden of Eden.[21]

II. The Two Gardens (John 18.1, 26; 19.41)

John refers to two distinguishable gardens in his narrative of Jesus' passion and resurrection. The first garden (κῆπος, 18.1; τῷ κήπῳ, 18.26) is geographically located 'across the wadi of the Kidron' (18.1).[22] John indicates that Jesus often met with his disciples there (18.2; cf. Lk. 22.39).[23] The second garden (κῆπος and τῷ κήπῳ, 19.41) was located

---

20. Cf. Meeks, *Moses*, p. 63; Thatcher, 'Anatomies', pp. 9–10.

21. Mary took the risen Jesus for a gardener because he was buried in a garden (Jn 19.41). Cf. Lindars, *John*, p. 605. Another explanation could be that the text has apologetic overtones. The Jewish allegation that Jesus was 'the gardener abstracted' is found in Tertullian, *Spect.* 30. It is possible that Tertullian is preserving an early tradition. During Tertullian's time, some Jews used the figure of Jesus as gardener in their anti-Christian polemic but without any link to Adam or God in Eden. Cf. Tertullian, *Les Spectacles (De spectaculis)* (ed. M. Turcan; SC, 332; Paris: Cerf, 1986), pp. 323–7; W. Horbury, 'Tertullian on the Jews in the Light of *De spectaculis* XXX. 5-6', *JTS* 23 (1972), pp. 455–9.

22. Some commentators suggest that the backdrop of this geographical identification might be 2 Kgdms 15.23 (thus, e.g. Lincoln, *John*, p. 442).

23. It is not clear whether the betrayal took place inside the garden. The noun 'place' and the adverb 'there' in Jn 18.2 refer to Jn 18.1, either to the 'garden' or to the larger place located 'across the wadi of the Kidron'. The question asked by Malcus' relative in Jn 18.26 ('Did not I see you with him in the garden?') may imply that Jesus met Judas and the soldiers inside the garden. However, there is an evident contrast between Jesus entering and going out (εἰσῆλθεν, ἐξῆλθεν) the garden in Jn 18.1, 4, although the verb ἐξῆλθεν lacks an explicit object. The idea suggested by

where Jesus was crucified, in 'the place of the skull' or 'Golgotha' (19.17-18; cf. Mt. 27.33; Mk 15.22; Lk. 23.33).[24]

A number of scholars relate these Johannine gardens to the garden of Eden in Gen. 2–3, claiming that John intended to link Jn 18.1, 26; and 19.41 to the Genesis story of creation in order to portray Jesus as the one who opens the way back to Paradise that was lost because of Adam's sin. Edwin Hoskyns, for instance, claimed that in Jn 18.1, 26; and 19.41 'once again the Garden of Eden is open to men'.[25] In the same way, Anthony Moore argues that John wanted his readers to understand Jesus' resurrection 'in some sense as the restoration of Paradise, the reconciliation between God and humanity'.[26] Some scholars even claim that both GJohn and the book of Revelation end in the same way, with an 'eschatological consummation of what began in the garden of Eden'.[27] Other scholars suggest that Jesus' resurrection was parallel to creation in Gen. 1–3.[28]

According to a few minuscule manuscripts of the tenth and fifteenth centuries C.E., the reading κῆπος in found in Gen. 2.8 (minuscule 344′=344+127) and Gen. 3.1 (Aquila, minuscule 135) in reference to the garden of Eden.[29] Aquila's translation was finished around 140 C.E. One of the characteristics of this translation is its fidelity to the Hebrew text:

J. Taylor, 'The Garden of Gethsemane, Not the Place of Jesus' Arrest', *BAR* 21 (1995), pp. 26–35, that Jesus went outside a cave located inside the garden is intriguing but not probable, as von Wahlde, *John*, vol. 2, p. 745, has argued.

24. Schaper, 'Messiah', p. 22, supposes that both gardens are identical but recognizes that 'this is impossible to demonstrate'. He argues that 'an educated Jewish or Christian reader of the Gospel of John' will have understood that the scene before Jesus' arrest in Jn 18 is reminiscent 'of the tombs of Manasseh and Amon' in 2 Kgs 21.18, 26 and 'the mention of the tomb of David' in Neh. 3.16 (p. 24). In the same way, Manns, *L'Evangile*, p. 426, suggests that both gardens form a totality because 'Ils sont traversés par un torrent qui évoque le fleuve de Gen 2, 10'. However, it seems to me that John does make a distinction between the two gardens.

25. Hoskyns, 'Genesis', p. 215; Hoskyns, *Gospel*, vol. 2, p. 604. Cf. Blanquart, *Jour*, pp. 65–6; Manns, *L'Evangile*, p. 429; P. Robinson, 'Gethsemane: The Synoptic and the Johannine Viewpoints', *CQR* 167 (1966), pp. 4-11 (5); C. H. Giblin, 'Confrontations in John 18,1-27', *Bib* 65 (1984), pp. 210–32 (218).

26. Moore, 'Creation', p. 2; cf. p. 64. Cf. Koch, 'Garten', pp. 236–8.

27. Köstenberger, *Theology*, p. 352. Cf. Suggit, 'Gardener', p. 167; Rosik, 'Gardens', p. 85; Robinson, 'Gethsemane', p. 6.

28. Charlesworth, *Serpent*, p. 401; C. Grappe, 'Du sanctuaire au jardin: Jésus, nouveau et veritable Temple dans le quatrième évangile', in Dettwiler and Poplutz (eds.), *Studien*, pp. 185–96 (291–3).

29. F. Field, *Origenis Hexaplorum quae supersunt* (Oxford: E Typographeo Clarendoniano, 1875), pp. 13, 16.

'Aquila expresses the same Hebrew words with the same Greek words'.[30] This can be illustrated by his use of κῆπος. Aquila translates גן (MT) in Gen. 3.1; Jer. 38.12; Ezek. 31.8 and גנג in Isa. 1.29, 30 consistently using κῆπος in each case.[31] On the other hand, the LXX uses παράδεισος in Gen. 2.8, 15; Ezek. 31.8, and Isa. 1.30, but κῆπος in Isa. 1.29 and ξύλον ἔγκαρπον in Jer. 38.12.

Theodotion also uses the noun κῆπος in Gen. 3.1 (κήπου) in reference to the garden of Eden, according to the seventh-century C.E. uncial M. Some scholars suggest that the sixth column in Origen's Hexapla attributed to Theodotion is based on a proto-Theodotion recension because there are Theodotionic readings in documents that are much earlier than the historical Theodotion as described by Patristic sources.[32] Some scholars even suggest that proto-Theodotion should be identified with the so-called καίγε revision, tentatively dated as early as the first century B.C.E.[33]

It is indeed possible that the reading κῆπος in Gen. 2–3 circulated during John's time. However, it is impossible to know whether he had access to such a reading. Extant evidence only allows us to assert that the great majority of extant Greek manuscripts of Gen. 2–3 use παράδεισος in reference to the garden of Eden instead of κῆπος.[34] Elsewhere in the LXX, the garden of Eden is also referred to by using the noun παράδεισος (Isa. 51.3; Ezek. 28.13; 31.8, 9; Joel 2.3; *Pss. Sol.* 14.3)[35] with one exception, Ezek. 36.35 (κῆπος).[36] However, more than ten manuscripts of

30. N. Fernández-Marcos, *The Septuagint in Context: Introduction to the Greek Versions of the Bible* (trans. W. G. E. Watson; Leiden: Brill, 2000), p. 116.

31. 'To a very large extent the Hebrew text used by the translator [Aquila] is proved to be the same as the *textus receptus*, at least in respect of the consonantal text' (Fernández-Marcos, *Septuagint*, p. 117).

32. Fernández-Marcos, *Septuagint*, p. 144.

33. E. Tov, *Textual Criticism of the Hebrew Bible* (Minneapolis: Fortress, 3rd rev. and expanded edn, 2012), p. 143.

34. The noun παράδεισος is used in Gen. 2.8, 9, 10, 15, 16; 3.1, 2, 3, 8, 10, 23, 24. The phrase גן־עדן in the MT is translated as either ὁ παράδεισος τῆς τρυφῆς (3.23, 24) or ὁ παράδεισος (2.15) in the LXX. Cf. Philo, *Plant.* 38, 'Eden means luxuriance' ('Εδέμ ἑρμηνεύεται...τρυφή)' (Colson and Whitaker, LCL) and Theophilus, *Autol.* 2.24, 'the Hebrew word Eden means delight ('Εδέμ...ἑβραϊστί τὸ εἰρημένον ἑρμηνεύεται τρυφή)'. See Théophile D'Antioche, *Trois Livres à Autolycus* (SC, 20; Paris: Cerf, 1948), pp. 158–9.

35. R. B. Wright, *The Psalms of Solomon: A Critical Edition of the Greek Text* (JCTCRS, 1; London: T&T Clark International, 2007), p. 154.

36. A full list of examples of the re-use of the garden of Eden in the OT appears in T. Stordalen, *Echoes of Eden: Genesis 2–3 and Symbolism of the Eden Garden in Biblical Hebrew Literature* (CBET, 25; Leuven: Peeters, 2000), pp. 305–454.

the Lucianic recension (*L''*) and Theodoret of Cyrrhus have παράδεισος instead of κῆπος in Ezek. 36.35.[37]

Additionally, the noun κῆπος is used in reference to the garden of Eden in Aquila and Theodotion in Isa. 51.3; Ezek. 28.13;[38] 31.8.[39] All these readings are preserved in one single manuscript of the ninth or tenth century C.E. (minuscule 86), except Aquila Isa. 51.3 that is found in an addition to Origen's text.[40] On the other hand, the LXX has παράδεισος in Isa. 51.3; Ezek. 28.13; 31.8, 9; Joel 2.3; *Pss. Sol.* 14.3.

During John's time, the garden of Eden was referred to by using the noun παράδεισος both in Gen. 2–3 LXX and elsewhere in the LXX. However, there is evidence that the alternative reading κῆπος was used once in Ezek. 36.35, elsewhere in the LXX in five manuscripts that preserve readings of Aquila and Theodotion (86 135 344' M), and in one addition to Origen's text (Isa. 51.3). Nevertheless, even if John knew the reading κῆπος in Gen. 2.8; 3.1; Isa. 51.3; Ezek. 28.13; 31.8; 36.35, a direct link between Jn 18.1, 26; 19.41 and the garden of Eden is not straightforward, because the noun κῆπος is used in various ways in the LXX.

The noun κῆπος is commonplace in the LXX. It is also used in Lk. 13.19. It can refer to a literal garden where plants grow (Deut. 11.10; 3 Kgdms 20.2 [1 Kgs 21.2 MT]; Amos 4.9; 9.14; Jer. 36.28 [29.28 MT]; Ep. Jer. 1.70; Sus. 1.58; Lk. 13.19).[41] It is also used symbolically in order to depict a woman (Song 4.12, 15, 16; 5.1; 6.2; 8.13),[42] human mind (Sir. 24.31), restored people (Isa. 58.11),[43] or God himself (Isa. 61.11). There is ample evidence in the LXX that κῆπος is used in relation to kings. Some kings used to have gardens (4 Kgdms 25.4 [2 Kgs 25.4]; Est. 7.7-8;[44]

---

37. Manuscript 544 adds παραδεισου to the phrase κῆπος τρυφῆς.

38. The original reading of minuscule 86 was κηπος instead of κηπου.

39. However, according to Chrysostom, Theodotion has ως παραδεισον. Cf. Isa. 51.3 Symmachus, which has ως παραδεισον.

40. This reading is explicitly marked as an addition to Origen's text in conformity with the Hebrew. According to Chrysostom, however, Aquila and Symmachus have ως τρυφεριαν instead of ως κηπον.

41. The MT has either גן (Deut. 11.10; 1 Kgs 21.2) or גנה (Amos 4.9; 9.14; Jer. 29.28).

42. For the use of the Song of Songs in GJohn, see McWhirter, *Bridegroom*, pp. 79–122. Cf. S. M. Schneiders, 'John 20:11–18: The Encounter of the Easter Jesus with Mary Magdalene—A Transformative Feminist Reading', in *"What is John?" Readers and Readings of the Fourth Gospel* (ed. F. Segovia; SBLSymS, 3; Atlanta: Scholars Press, 1996), pp. 155–68 (161); Koch, 'Garten', p. 234.

43. In Jer. 31.12 MT restored people are related to a well-watered garden. Nevertheless, Jer. 38.12 LXX has 'fruitful tree' instead of 'garden'.

44. The noun 'garden' is omitted in Est. 7.7 Alpha-text.

Jer. 52.7). Even the son of David is portrayed as making gardens in Eccl. 2.5. Since gardens were places for the burial of kings (4 Kgdms 21.18 [2 Kgs 21.18]; 21.26 [2 Kgs 21.26]; 2 Esd. 13.16 [Neh. 3.16]; 13.26 [Neh. 3.26]),[45] they were regarded as places of worship (Isa. 65.3; cf. 1.29; 66.17).

The use of κῆπος in Jn 18.1, 26; 19.41 does not necessarily mean that John is intending a link to the garden of Eden. He could use this noun in a literal sense in order to denote that the events narrated in Jn 18.1, 26; 19.41 took place in a garden.[46] Nevertheless, it is legitimate to ask whether John wanted to convey further meaning when he used κῆπος in Jn 18.1, 26; 19.41 by relating those verses to the OT. If that were the case, he would have the options mentioned above: (1) royal overtones, (2) a woman, (3) God himself, (4) restored people, (5) human mind, and (6) the garden of Eden. In light of the Johannine narratives of Jesus' passion and resurrection, it seems that the most likely candidate is the royal overtone associated with κῆπος. The kingship of Jesus is an important motif in GJohn (e.g. 1.49; 12.13; 18.33, 36-39; 19.12, 14).[47] Prior to his crucifixion, Jesus was portrayed as a king (18.33-39; 19.12-14), and after his death he was buried in a garden (19.41). The other ideas associated with κῆπος in the LXX hardly resemble Jn 18.1, 26; 19.41. However, if there are uses of the garden of Eden in Second-Temple Jewish texts that resemble what scholars propose is going on in Jn 18.1, 26; 19.41, one would be inclined to entertain the possibility of a link between those texts and Gen. 2–3.

a. *Interpretative Traditions*
There is evidence that the garden of Eden attracted a good deal of attention in Second-Temple Jewish texts.[48] Some Greek Second-Temple

---

45. The noun 'garden' is absent from Neh. 3.16, 26 MT.

46. Von Wahlde, *John*, vol. 2, p. 850, 'the fact that the tomb was in a garden may be a simple factual comment... Certainly, its accuracy is confirmed by the earlier Johannine description of the burial locale and by Josephus' identification of a gate into the city at this point as the "Garden Gate" [*War* 5.146]'.

47. M. Hengel, 'Reich Christi, Reich Gottes und Weltreich im Johannesevangelium', in *Königsherrschaft Gottes und himmlischer Kult im Judentum, Urchristentum und in der hellenischen Welt* (ed. M. Hengel and A. M. Schwemer; Tübingen: J. C. B. Mohr, 1991), pp. 163–84; Meeks, *Moses*.

48. Bockmuehl and Stroumsa (eds.), *Paradise*; Schmid and Riedweg (eds.), *Beyond Eden*; Stordalen, *Eden*; P. T. Lanfer, 'Allusion to and Expansion of the Tree of Life and Garden of Eden in Biblical and Pseudepigraphal Literature', in Evans and Zacharias (eds.), *Early Christian Literature*, pp. 96–108; G. P. Luttikhuizen

Jewish texts use the noun παράδεισος in reference to the garden of Eden (Rev. 2.7; Josephus, *Ant.* 1.37; Philo, *Leg. All.* 1.56-57, 59-62; *Cher.* 1, 11, 20; *Migr. Abr.* 37; *Plant.* 32, 34, 40, 46; Theophilus, *Autol.* 2.20-21; cf. Justin, *Dial.* 86; Philo, *Congr.* 171; Lk. 23.43; 2 Cor. 12.4). Only Josephus uses κῆπος in reference to the garden of Eden in *Ant.* 1.38, 45, 51.[49] The noun κῆπος was also used in different ways in extant Greek Second-Temple Jewish texts: (1) a literal garden (*T. Naph.* 5.8;[50] Josephus, *War* 5.107, 410; Philo, *Leg. Gai.* 351; cf. 4Q271 2 4; 11Q19 XXXVII, 2), or (2) a garden associated with a king (Josephus, *Ant.* 11.265; Philo, *Leg. Gai.* 181; cf. Josephus, *Ant.* 19.8).[51]

Elsewhere in Second-Temple Jewish texts, the garden of Eden was a fertile source for speculation. It was regarded as a sacred place (*Jub.* 4.26; cf. *1 En.* 25.4-7), the dwelling of the Lord (*Jub.* 8.19; cf. *LAE* 22.4),[52] or a place for the future dwelling of the elect (*1 En.* 60.8; 42.3; *T. Levi* 18.10-11; *T. Dan* 5.12; *Odes* 20.7; cf. *4 Ezra* 8.52). One idea found in *LAE* 38–40 is perhaps relevant to our discussion. After his death, Adam is clothed with cloths of linen and silk brought from the third heaven, and his body is poured with oil, according to the Greek version of *LAE* 38–40.[53] His burial in paradise and the preparation of his body would be similar to that of Jesus in a garden in Jn 19.38-41. This would give support to the idea that Jesus is portrayed as Adam in John's passion narrative.

(ed.), *Paradise Interpreted: Representations of Biblical Paradise in Judaism and Christianity* (TBN, 2; Leiden: Brill, 1999).

49. It is striking that those who posit a link to the garden of Eden in Jn 18.1, 26; 19.41 do not notice the use of κῆπος in Josephus. For example, Rosik, 'Gardens', pp. 81–98; Köstenberger, *Theology*, p. 352; cf. Moore, 'Creation', p. 96.

50. De Jonge, *Testaments*, p. 119, καί εἶδον ὅτι ἤμην ἐν κήποις. However, some manuscripts have παρεκεῖ, ἐν κύποις or ἐν παραδείσῳ instead of ἐν κήποις. Cf. R. H. Charles, *The Greek Versions of the Testaments of the Twelve Patriarchs* (Oxford: Clarendon, 1908), p. 152, who thought that παρεκεῖ is a corruption of ἐν παραδείσῳ.

51. Elsewhere Josephus refers to the place of a king's garden using the nouns παράδεισος (*Ant.* 10.46) and κῆπος (*Ant.* 9.227). M. Baillet, J. T. Milik, and R. de Vaux, *Les "petites grottes" de Qumrân* (DJD, 3; Oxford: Clarendon, 1962), p. 246, felt tempted to make a comparison between Zadok's garden in 3Q15 and Jn 19.41, 'Il est tentant d'appliquer ce sens au 'jardin' (κῆπος) de Jean 19⁴¹'.

52. By contrast, see Philo, *Plant.* 32–33, who argued that the garden of Eden is not for God to dwell.

53. The noun used to describe the 'paradise' in this text is παράδεισος. Cf. J. Tromp, *The Life of Adam and Eve in Greek: A Critical Edition* (PVTG, 6; Leiden: Brill, 2005), p. 168. This noun is also used elsewhere in *LAE*; e.g. 1.1; 17.1; 28.4; 37.5; 40.7.

Nevertheless, it is difficult to see *LAE* 38–40 as a precedent for Jn 19.41. There are serious doubts about the non-Christian provenance of the description of Adam's burial in *LAE* and uncertainty about the date and origin of the text of *LAE*. At least, the Greek version of Adam's death in *LAE* 31–37 is believed to have received 'its present form from a Christian redactor-author'.[54] Furthermore, the triangular seal in Adam's grave in *LAE* 42.1 seems to come from a Christian hand (cf. Mt. 27.66) because this practice is unparalleled in antiquity.[55] Therefore, it is reasonable to suspect that a Christian hand also influenced the account given in *LAE* 38–40.[56] Johannes Tromp even suggests that *LAE* 38.4 should be deleted.[57] As for the date of *LAE*, it is possible to date it anywhere between 100 and 600 C.E., with some scholars preferring a date between the second and the fourth centuries.[58]

Even if *LAE* 38–39 is taken as predating GJohn, it is difficult to make a direct link between Jesus' burial in GJohn and Adam's burial in *LAE* 38–39. If the hand behind *LAE* had portrayed Adam alone as buried in a garden, the link between Jn 19.41 and *LAE* would be clearer. However, Abel and Eve were also buried in paradise according to *LAE* 40.6-7; 42.5–43.1. Furthermore, John gives a reason why Jesus was buried in a garden: 'because it was the Jewish day of preparation and the tomb was nearby' (Jn 19.42; cf. v. 40). This specific detail given by the narrator is hardly an invitation to the intended reader to look for a symbolic meaning.

54. M. de Jonge and J. Tromp, *The Life of Adam and Eve and Related Literature* (GsAP; Sheffield: Sheffield Academic Press, 1997), p. 74. Cf. R. Nir, 'The Struggle between the "Image of God" and Satan in the *Greek Life of Adam and Eve*', *SJT* 61 (2008), pp. 327–39. Nir observes that the struggle with Satan is found in Cyril of Jerusalem, *Procatechesis* 16; *The Martyrdom of Perpetua and Felicitas* 4; Athanasius, *Vit. Ant.* 66; *T. Levi* 18.10-12. Nir also contends that this struggle underlines 'Jesus' symbolic struggle with Judas Iscariot' (p. 334). However, there is no symbolic struggle between Judas and Jesus in GJohn. The soldiers and officers, but not Judas, were carrying weapons in Jn 18.3, but Jesus bans Peter from beginning a struggle with his captors in Jn 18.11.

55. De Jonge and Tromp, *Life*, p. 71. Cf. M. de Jonge, *Pseudepigrapha of the Old Testament as Part of Christian Literature: The Case of the Testaments of the Twelve Patriarchs and the Greek Life of Adam and Eve* (SVTP, 18; Leiden: Brill, 2003), pp. 205–6.

56. See de Jonge and Tromp, *Life*, p. 72, 'It seems that the description of Adam's burial may well be understood in the light of the description of Jesus' burial in the Gospels: their bodies are shrouded and embalmed with fragrances, and their tombs are sealed off'.

57. Tromp, *Critical Edition*, p. 168. Tromp believes that *LAE* 38.4 is a secondary addition already present in the archetype.

58. See de Jonge and Tromp, *Life*, p. 77.

Ruben Zimmermann suggests a connection between temple, the garden of Eden, and sacredness in GJohn in light of Second-Temple Jewish texts. Zimmermann observes that Jesus is seen as the 'new temple' in GJohn, that the temple is connected to garden symbolism in early Judaism, and that the garden is a sacred place in early Judaism (*Jub.* 3.12; 4.26; 8.19). He concludes that Jesus in GJohn 'is identified, in the form of the new temple, with the entire garden of paradise'.[59] Zimmerman also observes that in Jewish tradition, a woman is impure after birth and, therefore, she is not allowed to enter the temple (4Q265 7 II; *Jub.* 3.10, 13).[60] According to those Jewish traditions, if the woman gives birth to a boy, she needs to wait one week before she may again enter the temple; if a woman gives birth to a girl, she needs to wait two weeks before she may again enter the temple. Zimmerman combines both ideas (temple–garden–sacredness–Jesus, and different times of purity for males and females before they may enter again the temple) and suggests that they explain two details in the Johannine narrative. The first detail is Jesus' prohibition to Mary to touch him (20.17). The second detail is Peter and the beloved disciple's entrance to the tomb (20.6-9) and Jesus' invitation to Thomas to put his hand into his side (20.27).

There are at least two problems with Zimmermann's conclusions. First, there is a clear distinction between Jesus and the garden of his burial in GJohn. There is no attempt by John to identify Jesus with the garden because he portrays Mary taking him as the gardener not as the garden. Furthermore, although there is evidence elsewhere in GJohn that Jesus is the new temple (cf. Jn 2.19-22) there are no clear instances of Jesus as the new garden in GJohn. Second, if the garden in Jn 19.41 is sacred, why is Mary permitted to enter it? In light of these considerations, it is improbable that John was intending to relate the risen Jesus to the garden of Eden in Jn 19.41.

Nicolas Wyatt has attempted to find a connection between the garden of Jesus' burial in Jn 19.41 and the garden of Eden using Ugaritic material.[61] Wyatt suggests that royal burials in the OT normally would

59. Zimmermann, 'Garden', p. 235.

60. Zimmermann, 'Garden', pp. 229–33. Cf. F. García-Martínez, *Qumranica Minora II: Thematic Studies on the Dead Sea Scrolls* (ed. E. J. C. Tigchelaar; STDJ, 64; Leiden: Brill, 2007), pp. 71–6.

61. Wyatt, 'Gardener', p. 24. Koch, 'Garten', pp. 231–2, observes that gardens are places associated with kings in Mesopotamia (e.g. Gilgamesh and the Akkadian Legend of Sargon). Rosik, 'Gardens', pp. 82–5, refers to ancient Egyptian and Sumerian texts, the Epic of Gilgamesh and the myth of Adonis in order to establish a broad background to the idea that kings were related to gardens in antiquity. Moore,

take place in a garden identified with the king's garden, which later came to be 'the garden of Eden'.[62] Wyatt refers to KTU 1.5 vi 4-7. However, he admits that the word 'Eden' does not occur there. Instead, he argues that other words cover the semantic field of 'Eden'. In this Ugaritic text 'pleasure' (*n'my*) is called the 'land of pasture', 'delight' (*ysmt*), and the 'steppe by the shore of death'.[63] Wyatt also refers to KTU 1.4 viii 1-9, where the phrase *bet hopšit* ('of the earth') is found in parallelism with 'the nether world'.[64] Wyatt deems that the phrase בבית החפשית in reference to the king's dwelling place in 2 Kgs 15.5 MT may be a euphemism for or an allusion to a 'grave'.[65]

The only place in the OT where a king is related to the garden of Eden is Ezek. 28.13. It is said there that the king of Tyre was in Eden, the garden of God.[66] However, there is no indication there or elsewhere in the OT that the garden of Eden was a place of burial for kings. Similarly, there is no clear evidence (apart from *LAE* 38–39) in Second-Temple Jewish texts that the garden of Eden was a place of burial for kings. Since the Ugaritic material itself is far from John's milieu, it would have been very difficult for Johannine intended readers to see in the reference to Jesus' burial a link to the garden of Eden. Granted, it is possible that some readers would have seen in the references to a 'garden' in Jn 18.1, 26; 19.41 royal overtones. But it is doubtful that John attempted to convey the idea that those gardens are somehow related to Eden because elsewhere in GJohn the royal motif is not attached to the garden of Eden.

So far, it can be concluded that it is unlikely that John was attempting to relate Jn 18.1, 26; and 19.41 to the garden of Eden. I will support this conclusion by arguing in the next section that although a few church fathers relate Jesus' passion and resurrection to the Genesis account of creation, a link between Jn 18.1, 28; 19.41 and the garden of Eden does not fit into the larger argument of GJohn.

'Creation', p. 98, is even more optimistic when asserting that 'John could have had knowledge of the cult of Adonis' and when thinking that John could be alluding to Plato's garden of Zeus (Plato, *Symp.* 203B).
    62. Wyatt, 'Gardener', p. 30.
    63. Wyatt, 'Gardener', p. 30.
    64. Wyatt, 'Gardener', p. 31.
    65. Wyatt, 'Gardener', p. 31.
    66. H. G. May, 'The King in the Garden of Eden: A Study of Ezekiel 28:12–19', in *Israel's Prophetic Heritage* (ed. B. W. Anderson and W. Harrelson; London: SCM, 1962), pp. 166–76 (169), suggested that Ezek. 28.12-19 'seems to have been based on a story of a royal First Man, an "Adam" who was king'.

b. *Early Christian Interpretations and Thematic Coherence*
Some scholars dealing with the interpretation of Jn 18.1, 26; 19.41 have
made general observations about the patristic readings of those texts.
Ignace de la Potterie, for instance, claimed that 'Les Pères y ont vu [in
18.1, 26; 19.41] une allusion à un autre jardin, le paradis, où a débuté,
par la faute d'Adam et d'Ève, l'histoire du mal dans le monde'.[67] However, de la Potterie did not identify those church fathers who supposedly
make such connection. A more nuanced statement can be achieved when
looking more closely at the patristic evidence.

The earliest Christian readers who made a link between Jesus' passion
and resurrection and the garden of Eden are Cyril of Jerusalem and Cyril
of Alexandria.[68] Both wrote between the fourth and the fifth centuries
C.E. Cyril of Jerusalem comments, '[in] Paradise was the Fall, and in a
Garden was our Salvation' (*Catechetical Lectures* 13.19; *NPNF²*, vol. 7,
p. 87). Then, he combines some phrases taken from Gen. 3.8 and Lk.
23.43, and asserts: 'I am truly astonished at the truth of the types'
(*Catechetical Lectures* 13.19). However, Cyril was not commenting
specifically on the text of GJohn. Elsewhere, Cyril relates Jn 15.1;
Ps. 85.11 (84.12 LXX), and Song 5.1; 4.14 to the Johannine gardens and
concludes that Jesus was 'planted' in the garden of his burial in order for
the curse of Adam to be rooted out (*Catechetical Lectures* 14.11).

In the same way, Cyril of Alexandria suggests that the garden in Jn
18.1 typified the paradise (*Commentary on John* 11). Cyril of Alexandria
thinks that the garden in Jn 18.1 is the place where 'recapitulation' took
place and where 'our return to humanity's ancient condition was
consummated' (*Commentary on John* 11).[69] He also relates Jn 19.41 to
Paradise, 'The writer of the Gospel says that this sepulchre in the garden
was a new one; this fact signifying to us, as it were, by a type and figure,
that Christ's death is the harbinger and pioneer of our entry into
Paradise' (*Commentary on John* 12).[70] Cyril of Alexandria seems to

67. I. de la Potterie, *La Passion de Jésus selon l'Évangile de Jean: Texte et
Esprit* (Paris: Cerf, 1986), p. 50; cf. Brodie, *John*, p. 525; Moloney, *John*, p. 484;
F. Manns, 'Le Symbolisme du Jardin dans le Récit de la Passion selon St Jean',
SBFLA 37 (1987), pp. 53–80 (54–6).

68. Schnackenburg, *John*, p. 442 n. 6, also includes Augustine, Thomas Aquinas,
and Rupert of Deutz. Suggit, 'Gardener', pp. 161–2, observes that the theme of re-
creation is developed in Athanasius, Origen, Clement of Alexandria, and Melito of
Sardis, but without clarifying whether these authors develop their ideas based on
Jn 18.1, 26; 19.41.

69. Cyril of Alexandria, *John*, p. 566.

70. Cyril of Alexandria, *John*, p. 647.

make a distinction, however, between what the writer wrote and what his writing 'means for us'. Furthermore, he deems that his interpretation was by way of 'type and figure' (ἐν τύπῳ καὶ ὑπογραμμῷ).[71]

There is no firm evidence in Cyril of Jerusalem and Cyril of Alexandria that they regarded their readings of Jn 18.1, 26; 19.41 (or the Gospel accounts in general) as Johannine intentional allusions to Gen. 2–3.[72] But even if they thought John intended such links, there are at least two reasons to doubt that John wanted his readers to see in Jn 18.1, 26; 19.41 links to the garden of Eden.

The first reason is the lack of clear instances of the paradise motif elsewhere in GJohn. There is no indication in Jn 1–17 that Jesus' passion and resurrection will bring the restoration of the garden of Eden. On the one hand, there are a number of promises and predictions in Jn 1–17 that are arguably fulfilled with Jesus' passion and resurrection. Some examples are in order. (1) The narrator asserts in Jn 1.12 that to all who believe in 'his name' he has given the right to become God's children. Jesus refers to his Father as the disciples' Father after his resurrection in Jn 20.17. (2) Jesus anticipates his resurrection in Jn 2.20-21. (3) Jesus' prediction of Judas' betrayal in Jn 13.21 is fulfilled in 18.1-11. (4) Jesus' prediction of Peter's denial in Jn 13.38 is fulfilled in 18.17, 25-27. (5) The giving of the Spirit promised in Jn 1.33; 14.16-17; 16.13 is fulfilled in Jn 20.22. On the other hand, there are no clear promises or predictions of the restoration of paradise in Jn 1–17. Although it is not impossible that John is introducing a novel idea in Jn 18.1, 26; 19.41, it is highly unlikely because the idea of Eden restored is not consonant with John's overall argument.

The second reason is the Johannine use of scene-locations in the description of Jesus' passion and resurrection. Some scholars have argued that the noun 'garden' in Jn 18.1, 26; 19.41 should have symbolic meaning because John refers to this place four times.[73] However, John also refers several times to other locations in his description of Jesus' passion and resurrection without attaching symbolic meaning to those places. John refers to the place of Jesus' interrogation four times (18.28, 33; 19.9). He also identifies as a tomb the place of Jesus burial eleven times (19.41, 42; 20.1, 2, 3, 4, 6, 8; 20.11). It is doubtful that John was

71. Pusey (ed.), *Cyrilli*, p. 105.
72. Other extant early Christian readings of those Johannine passages do not make a link to the garden of Eden. Cf. *Gos. Pet.* 6.24; Theodore of Mopsuestia, *Commentary on John* 7.
73. Suggit, 'Gardener', p. 166; Moore, 'Creation', p. 73; Quiévreux, 'Structure', p. 137; Schaper, 'Messiah', p. 22.

attaching symbolic meaning to those two places.[74] Therefore, it is also doubtful that John wanted to attach symbolic meaning to the scene-locations in Jn 18.1, 26, and 19.41.

III. Conclusion

A number of scholars have suggested that Jn 18.1, 26; 19.41; and 20.15 are examples of creation imagery that John linked to Gen. 2–3. These putative connections allow them to propose that John intended to depict subtly the restoration of paradise in the scenes of Jesus' passion and resurrection and that John attempted to portray Jesus as the new Adam or the Creator God. These supposed links also allow those scholars to posit a number of other parallels between Jn 18–21 and Gen. 2–3. They conclude then that creation imagery plays a prominent role in the Johannine passion and resurrection narratives because there is a good number of links to the garden of Eden. However, the suggested links between Jn 18.1, 26; 19.41; 20.15 and the garden of Eden do not bear up under critical scrutiny.[75] By showing that these Johannine passages are unlikely to have been intended as creation imagery, I have been able to support the argument advocated in this book, namely, that GJohn has a limited (albeit significant) number of instances of creation imagery strategically located in his Gospel.

---

74. Other locations mentioned in Jn 18–20 are the high priest's courtyard (18.15-16), the Stone Pavement or 'Gabbatha' (19.13), and the place of the skull or 'Golgotha' (19.17).

75. Some Johannine commentators have also doubted that Jn 18.1, 26; 19.41; 20.15 are instances of creation imagery: J. H. Bernard, *A Critical and Exegetical Commentary on the Gospel according to St. John* (2 vols.; Edinburgh: T. & T. Clark, 1928), vol. 2, p. 666; Brown, *John*, vol. 2, pp. 806–7, 943, 990; Bultmann, *John*, pp. 638, 680, 686; Barrett, *John*, pp. 517–18, 560, 564; Haenchen, *John 2*, pp. 164, 169, 196, 225; Lindars, *John*, pp. 539, 594, 605; Schnackenburg, *John*, vol. 3, pp. 222, 298, 316–17; Carson, *John*, pp. 576, 630–1, 641; Michaels, *John*, pp. 886–7, 984, 998–9; von Wahlde, *John*, vol. 2, p. 832; J. Lieu, 'Scripture and the Feminine in John', in *A Feminist Companion to the Hebrew Bible in the New Testament* (ed. A. Brenner; FCB, 10; Sheffield: Sheffield Academic Press, 1996), pp. 225–40 (237).

CONCLUSION

In this study I have argued that GJohn has a more limited number of instances of creation imagery than some scholars have claimed, but I have also shown how John has deployed these instances carefully and prominently, with intended significance. His creation imagery does not consist of numerous allusions to Gen. 1–3, nor is it found in a putative creation-like structure of the text. Rather, it consists of a few instances located at strategic points in the Gospel. I have been able to make the case for these select instances of creation imagery in GJohn, while I have ruled out a number of other suggested allusions to, or echoes of, Gen. 1–3.

The prologue occupies a strategic place in GJohn because the opening section of a Gospel is programmatic in signalling the way that readers should engage the rest of the narrative. John has placed in his prologue a clear reference to the creation of the world (1.10), and he has drawn on and creatively deployed terms and images stemming from Gen. 1–2 (Jn 1.1-5) and other creation discourses by using the noun ὁ λόγος (Jn 1.1; cf. 1.14). Similarly, Jesus' prayer in Jn 17 is a strategic unit of material in GJohn because it closes Jesus' farewell speeches and because it is the last unit before the narratives of Jesus' passion and resurrection. There are two references to the foundation of the world in Jn 17 (in vv. 5, 24).

John uses less explicit instances of creation imagery in his description of Jesus' earthly ministry (1.19–17.4). Jesus' claims that he performs the works of his Father in John 5.20, 36; 9.3-4; 17.4 are reminiscent of Gen. 2.1-3, and they can be related to Jewish discussions about God's rest after creation. Those instances are also strategically located because John uses them in the only two Sabbath controversies recorded in the Gospel (Jn 5 and 9) and also in Jesus' prayer (Jn 17). I have also proposed that the portrayal of Jesus performing two distinctive miraculous actions in Jn 6.19 and 9.6 can be seen as possible instances of creation imagery. Jesus walking on the sea in Jn 6.16-21 is another story that occupies an important place in John's narrative because it seems to interrupt the natural flow between the miraculous provision of food (vv. 1-15) and the discourse about the bread of life (vv. 25-40). Its location might have called readers' attention to this particular story. Similarly, the story of

Jesus healing a man born blind by using mud is strategically located in Jn 9, a unit of material that describes the next of Jesus' miracles after a long section of dialogues and discourses (Jn 7–8).

John uses even fewer instances of creation imagery in his narratives of Jesus' passion and resurrection. As I have shown, his portrayal of Jesus performing an act that resembles that of the Creator God in Jn 20.22 is likely the only instance of creation imagery in Jn 18–21. However, this instance is meaningful because it is located at the end of the Gospel (Jn 20–21) and in the middle of John's three narratives of the appearances of Jesus to his disciples after his resurrection (20.10-29).

Although these limited instances of creation imagery are used in varying contexts, I have argued that they function collectively in a threefold way. First, John uses them to portray Jesus in close association with his Father, existing apart from and prior to the created order in a relationship that legitimizes his participation in divine activities. Second, John uses creation imagery to assert the primal and universal significance of Jesus and the message about him, and to privilege him over other important figures in the story of Israel. Finally, John uses creation imagery to link past reality with present and future reality, portraying Jesus as the agent of creation who is also to be regarded as the privileged agent of revelation and salvation.

Contrary to some proposals, I have found no firm evidence to support the views that John uses creation imagery in order to portray Jesus as the new Adam or as the one who opens the way back to the garden of Eden. These topics are not consonant with John's overall narrative. Rather than introducing such topics, the creation imagery in GJohn is used to support some of the claims first made in the prologue (1.1-18). Reflections on the findings of this book may inform our understanding of the overall message of GJohn and may contribute to debated issues in the interpretation of this text. In the following sections I will describe five larger areas that require continued research: (1) the universal significance of Jesus, (2) the dualism of the Gospel, (3) Johannine Christology, (4) the composition of the text of the Gospel, and (5) the use of the Old Testament in GJohn.

I. The Universal Significance of Jesus

An influential trend within Johannine scholarship is the attempt to characterize the 'community' that produced the final form of GJohn as sectarian. The group of believers who created this text is seen as operating with a high degree of isolation and segregation from their environment, and GJohn is seen as intended to reinforce the sharp delineation between this 'group' and the world. Therefore, it is argued by some that this Gospel and the hero portrayed there were intended to be meaningful only to those who were already part of this isolated community.[1] This perspective, however, has been subjected to critique. For example, it has been disputed whether the designation 'sect' is helpful at all when trying to characterize the putative community behind the Gospel.[2]

A clearer characterization of the group or groups associated with GJohn should take into account the way that creation imagery has been deployed in order to shape the message of the text. John includes in his Gospel several assertions about the distinction between the followers of Jesus and the 'world' (e.g. 14.17; 15.18-19; 17.14, 16). Nevertheless, at the same time, there are clear instances of creation imagery that John uses to assert the universal significance of Jesus and the message about him. Jesus has a claim on everything that has been created because everything has been made through the Word (1.3). His light gives light to every human being (1.9). The possibility of becoming children of God is open to all who want to receive him, through whom the world was created (1.10-12). The rejection of the Word is contrasted with the universal openness of him to all who want to believe in his name (1.12). Even John's selection of words that are part of several cultural milieus (e.g. Logos, light, life) might indicate an effort to explain the significance of Jesus to a wider audience, beyond those who are already part of the group or groups responsible for this Gospel.[3] The universal significance

1. W. A. Meeks, 'The Man from Heaven in Johannine Sectarianism', *JBL* 91 (1972), pp. 44–72; J. Clark-Soles, *Scripture Cannot Be Broken: The Social Function of the Use of Scripture in the Fourth Gospel* (Boston: Brill, 2003). Cf. M. de Jonge, 'Christology, Controversy and Community in the Gospel of John', in *Christology, Controversy and Community* (ed. D. G. Horrell and C. M. Tuckett; NovTSup, 99; Leiden: Brill, 2000), pp. 209–29 (226).
2. K. S. Fuglseth, *Johannine Sectarianism in Perspective: A Sociological, Historical, and Comparative Analysis of Temple and Social Relationships in the Gospel of John, Philo, and Qumran* (NovTSup, 119; Leiden: Brill, 2005), pp. 21–8.
3. C. W. Quimby, *John: The Universal Gospel* (New York: Macmillan, 1947), pp. 57–62, argued that John 'universalized the Gospel message' by '*recasting Jewish terms* into the broadest meanings of human experience' (p. 57, his emphasis). However, it seems to me that John used terms that were meaningful to a non-Jewish audience, but without detaching them from their Jewish milieu. For other instances in GJohn where a 'universal perspective' can be detected, see C. H. Williams, '"He Saw His Glory and Spoke About Him": The Testimony of Isaiah and Johannine Christology', in *Honouring the Past and Shaping the Future: Religious and Biblical Studies in Wales* (ed. R. Pope; Leominster: Gracewing, 2003), pp. 53–80 (54–5), and M. L. Coloe, 'Gentiles in the Gospel of John: Narrative Possibilities – John

of Jesus can also be seen in his discourse following his claim that he performs the works of his Father even on the Sabbath (5.17-20; cf. Gen. 2.1-2). The divine work of judgement that Jesus performs will result in 'all people' honouring the Father and the Son (5.23). This is because the Father shows the Son everything that he does (5.20) and the Father has given the Son all judgement (5.22).

The mission of those who are followers of Jesus in GJohn is grounded in the universal significance that is attached to Jesus through creation imagery. Jesus has received authority over all humanity to reveal God and to bestow life (17.2-3). Jesus will achieve this by the testimony of the unity of the disciples. Through that testimony, the world can believe that the Father sent Jesus. Since knowing the Father through the Son is what ultimately provides eternal life, the disciples' testimony will give God's creation (the world) the opportunity to establish a proper relationship with its Creator (17.5, 24). Similarly, by performing an act that resembles that of the Creator God (20.22), Jesus entrusts his disciples with the authority to forgive or retain anyone's sins. Jesus' act of breathing in 20.22 is a reminder of his role in creation (as laid out in the Johannine prologue) and thus of his claim on everything that has been created.

The universal significance of Jesus and the message about him signalled by creation imagery in GJohn should be included in any proper delineation of the putative group or groups associated with this text. A possible area of further research could be a comparison between creation imagery in GJohn and the book of Revelation and Pauline literature in order to see whether John's use of this imagery places his theology alongside that of other foundational texts of the early Christian movement.[4] Such a study could cast some light onto the larger question of the unity and diversity of the theology reflected in the several books that are part of the NT and could also aid in answering the question about the putative 'theological isolation' of the group or groups related to GJohn.[5]

12.12-43', in *Attitudes to Gentiles in Ancient Judaism and Early Christianity* (ed. D. C. Sim and J. S. McLaren; LNTS, 499; London: Bloomsbury T&T Clark, 2013), pp. 209–23.

4. There are a number of studies dealing with creation imagery in Revelation and Pauline literature but I have been unable to find a comparative study between those NT texts and GJohn. T. R. Jackson, *New Creation in Paul's Letters: A Study of the Historical and Social Setting of a Pauline Concept* (WUNT, 2/272; Tübingen: Mohr Siebeck, 2010); M. B. Stephens, *Annihilation or Renewal? The Meaning and Function of New Creation in the Book of Revelation* (WUNT, 2/307; Tübingen: Mohr Siebeck, 2011).

5. Scholars have already compared some aspects of Johannine theology to other NT texts. Cf. F. J. Matera, 'Christ in the Theologies of Paul and John: A Study in the

II. Johannine Dualism

Some scholars have highlighted dualistic features in Johannine language and have concluded that John attempted to portray Jesus as a 'stranger' from heaven. They have argued in various ways that Johannine forms of speech serve to emphasize Jesus' foreignness to the people of this world.[6] The dualistic language of the text has led a number of scholars to view the Gospel as a semi-gnostic work. Rudolf Bultmann represents the classic expression of this position. He asserted that 'The Gnostic view of the world starts out from a strict cosmic dualism' and he concludes that John 'uses the language current in Gnostic circles to give expression to the Christian understanding of faith'.[7] However, the discovery and study of the Qumran scrolls has 'destroyed the credibility of these gnostic theories',[8] and more recent studies have shown that there is not a strict

---

Diverse Unity of New Testament Theology', *ThSt* 67 (2006), pp. 237–56; M. Harding, 'Kyrios Christos: Johannine and Pauline Perspectives on the Christ Event', and C. G. Kruse, 'Paul and John: Two Witnesses, One Gospel', in *Paul and the Gospels: Christologies, Conflicts and Convergences* (ed. M. F. Bird and J. Willitts; LNTS, 411; London: T&T Clark International, 2011), pp. 169–96, and pp. 197–219, respectively; C. W. Skinner, 'Virtue in the New Testament: The Legacies of Paul and John in Comparative Perspective', in *Unity and Diversity in the Gospels and Paul* (ed. C. W. Skinner and K. R. Iverson; SBLECL, 7; Atlanta: Society of Biblical Literature, 2012), pp. 301–24.

6. Meeks, 'Sectarianism', pp. 57, 60; cf. the collection of articles in M. de Jonge, *Jesus: Stranger from Heaven and Son of God; Jesus Christ and the Christians in Johannine Perspective* (ed. J. E. Steely; SBLSBS, 11; Missoula: Scholars Press, 1977), and K. B. Larsen, *Recognizing the Stranger: Recognition Scenes in the Gospel of John* (BIS, 93; Leiden: Brill, 2008).

7. Bultmann, *John*, pp. 7, 9.

8. Hengel, 'Old Testament', p. 24. Cf. J. H. Charlesworth, 'The Fourth Evangelist and the Dead Sea Scrolls: Assessing Trends over Nearly Sixty Years', in *John, Qumran, and the Dead Sea Scrolls: Sixty Years of Discovery and Debate* (ed. M. L. Coloe and T. Thatcher; SBLEJL, 32; Atlanta: Society of Biblical Literature, 2011), pp. 161–82; J. Frey, 'Different Patterns of Dualistic Thought in the Qumran Library: Reflections on their Background and History', in *Legal Texts and Legal Issues: Proceedings of the Second Meeting of the International Organization for Qumran Studies* (ed. M. J. Bernstein, F. García-Martínez, and J. Jampen; STDJ, 23; Leiden: Brill, 1997), pp. 275–335; D. E. Aune, 'Dualism in the Fourth Gospel and the Dead Sea Scrolls: A Reassessment of the Problem', in Aune, Seland, and Ulrichsen (eds.), *Neotestamentica et Philonica*, pp. 281–303. Others have observed that dualistic elements in GJohn are related to a Jewish background that is not restricted to Qumran material: R. Bauckham, 'Qumran and the Fourth Gospel: Is There a Connection?', in *The Scrolls and the Scriptures: Qumran Fifty Years After* (ed. S. E. Porter and C. A. Evans; JSPSup, 26; Sheffield: Sheffield Academic Press, 1997),

cosmic dualism within GJohn.[9] I refer here to the study of the love motif in GJohn by Enno Edzard Popkes.[10] Contrary to previous arguments, Popkes demonstrates that 'the dualistic elements in John do not form a coherent interpretative framework in which all the other themes…must be interpreted' and argues that 'there is no longer…a strict "dualism" within the Fourth Gospel'.[11]

My investigation concurs with Popkes' larger conclusion. Since Jesus is so closely related with the Creator God, there is no such thing as a strict dualism in the Gospel. Jesus is not a 'stranger' who comes into foreign territory with his incarnation (Jn 1.11). Instead, the reader who has perceived the strategic role of creation imagery in the Gospel (especially in the prologue) knows that Jesus comes to the world that has been his possession from the beginning. He gave life and light to the world in creation and is now authorized to bring revelation, salvation, and judgement to the world he created. He is able to restore the sight of a man born blind by performing an act that resembles that of the Creator God (9.6). Jesus was also able to use a form of divine self-proclamation while performing another act that resembles that of the Creator God who walked on the sea as on dry ground (6.19; cf. Job 9.8). Furthermore, Jesus sends his disciples into the world that he created in the beginning so that the world can receive forgiveness of sins (20.22; cf. Gen. 2.7). Although there is darkness, sin, opposition, death, falsehood, and dis-unity in the world, God engages his creation through his Son (and through the Spirit) in order to bring light, forgiveness, faith, life, truth, unity, and ultimately a proper relationship with him.[12]

pp. 267–79; J. Frey, 'Critical Issues in the Investigation of the Scrolls and the New Testament', in *The Oxford Handbook of the Dead Sea Scrolls* (ed. T. H. Lim and J. J. Collins; Oxford: Oxford University Press, 2010), pp. 517–45 (536–8).

9.   Others have even challenged the appropriateness of the designation 'dualism' to describe the thought of GJohn. See S. C. Barton, 'Johannine Dualism and Contemporary Pluralism', in Bauckham and Mosser (eds.), *Gospel of John*, pp. 3-18.

10.   E. E. Popkes, *Die Theologie der Liebe Gottes in den johanneischen Schriften: Zur Semantik der Liebe und zum Motivkreis des Dualismus* (WUNT, 2/197; Tübingen: Mohr Siebeck, 2005). Cf. J. Painter, 'The Point of John's Christology: Christology, Conflict and Community in John', in Horell and Tuckett (eds.), *Christology*, pp. 231–52 (239).

11.   J. Frey, 'Love-Relations in the Fourth Gospel: Establishing a Semantic Network', in Van Belle, Labahn, and Maritz (eds.), *Repetitions*, pp. 171–98 (173–4), in reference to Popkes' thesis. See also Barton, 'Dualism', p. 14.

12.   C. R. Koester, *The Word of Life: A Theology of John's Gospel* (Grand Rapids: Eerdmans, 2008), pp. 13–14.

The recognition that Jesus is portrayed both as existing prior to the created order (1.1-3; 5.20, 36; 6.19; 9.3-6; 17.5, 24) and as the owner of this world where the drama of salvation takes place can prompt further research into the meaning of the designation 'the ruler of this world' (12.31; 14.30; 16.11; cf. *T. Sol.* 2.9; 3.5-6; 6.1; *Mart. Isa.* 1.3; 2.4; 10.29).[13] Why does John refer to the devil as the ruler of this world if it is evident that Jesus had a claim over the whole of creation since the beginning?[14]

III. Christology in GJohn

This study of creation imagery in GJohn may contribute to our understanding of John's Christology. There is some question about how John intended his audience to perceive the Jesus he presented in his Gospel. In particular, scholars debate whether John's Christology is 'high' (divine) or 'low' (human), or whether a tension between 'high' and 'low' Christology is inherent in John's thinking.[15] It seems that the final form of GJohn was hardly intended to convince its readers of a 'low' Christology. John presupposes that Jesus was a man and does not present a defence of this assumption.[16]

13. Ashton, *Understanding*, p. 396. Cf. Koester, *Symbolism*, p. 171.

14. As a point of departure to discuss this question, see J. L. Kovacs, '"Now Shall the Ruler of This World Be Driven Out": Jesus' Death as Cosmic Battle in John 12:20–36', *JBL* 114 (1995), pp. 227–47; A. F. Segal, 'Ruler of This World: Attitudes about Mediator Figures and the Importance of Sociology for Self-Definition', in *Aspects of Judaism in the Graeco-Roman Period* (ed. E. P. Sanders, A. I. Baumgarten, and A. Mendelson; JCSD, 2; London: SCM, 1981), pp. 245–68, 403–13.

15. M. J. J. Menken, 'The Christology of the Fourth Gospel: A Survey of Recent Research', in *From Jesus to John* (ed. M. C. de Boer; JSNTSup, 84; Sheffield: Sheffield Academic Press, 1993), pp. 292–320 (304–6, 316, 320); P. N. Anderson, *The Christology of the Fourth Gospel: Its Unity and Disunity in the Light of John 6* (WUNT, 2/78; Tübingen: J. C. B. Mohr [Paul Siebeck], 1996), pp. 4–7, 12, 19–20, 24–5, 30–1; M. C. de Boer, *Johannine Perspectives on the Death of Jesus* (CBET, 17; Kampen: Kok-Pharos, 1996), pp. 311–15. Cf. A. C. Sundberg, 'Christology in the Fourth Gospel', *BibRes* 21 (1976), pp. 29–37 (37), 'two christologies are at work in the Fourth Gospel. One is the older...christology of the subordinate agent of God... The other is a new christology in which the Son has reached his majority and has been granted like rank, position and power with the Father that, perhaps, should be called binitarian theology rather than christology.'

16. M. M. Thompson, *The Humanity of Jesus in the Fourth Gospel* (Philadelphia: Fortress, 1988), pp. 51–2, 121–2; H. Weder, '*Deus Incarnatus*: On the Hermeneutics of Christology in the Johannine Writings' (trans. D. W. Scott), in Culpepper and Black (eds.), *Exploring the Gospel of John*, pp. 327–45 (332–6).

I suggest that those responsible for the final form of GJohn have used creation imagery in order to influence the reader's final judgement about the identity of Jesus. John shares information with his readers about the role of Jesus in creation (1.1-5, 10; 17.5, 24) that is not readily available to characters in the narrative. John also portrays Jesus as performing acts that resemble those of the Creator God when he is alone with his disciples on a stormy sea at night (6.16-19) or behind locked doors (20.19-22), or when privately healing a man born blind (9.1-6).

In all the places where creation imagery is used in GJohn, it is intended to help readers grasp the full significance of Jesus. Some instances are located in contexts where the unity between Jesus and God is explicit. The most obvious example is Jn 17.4-5, 24. Those instances of creation imagery are in a unit of material (Jn 17) where strong assertions about the unity between the Son and the Father are made (vv. 21-23). Similarly, the claims in Jn 5.20, 36; 9.3-4 that Jesus performs the works of God resurface later in contexts where Jesus' unity with his Father is stated explicitly. The Jews ask Jesus to tell them plainly whether he is the Christ (10.24). In reply, Jesus asserts that the works that he performs speak for him, and that the Jews should believe that he and the Father are one (10.30). Jesus also claims that he is the Son of God (10.36) and then immediately uses the works that he performs as evidence that 'the Father is in me, and I in the Father' (10.38). Likewise, Philip asks Jesus to show them the Father and Jesus replies by using the works that he performs as evidence to support his claim that he is in the Father and the Father is in him (14.10-11).

All of the other instances of creation imagery in GJohn as well are used to help readers grasp the full significance of Jesus more broadly in the narrative. For example, the account of Jesus' first encounter with people during his earthly ministry in Jn 1 includes references to him as 'the Lamb of God' (1.29, 36), 'the Son of God' (1.34, 49), 'Rabbi' (1.38, 49), 'Messiah' (1.41), 'the one Moses wrote about in the Law' (1.45), 'Jesus of Nazareth, the son of Joseph' (1.45), and the 'King of Israel' (1.49). However, the reader knows that this Jesus existed with God before creation and took an active role in the creation of the world (1.1-5, 10). The 'Christology' reflected in all the attributions found in Jn 1.29-49 is more fully understood in light of the claim that the Word was with God in the beginning, bringing into existence all that has been created.

For those who were fed by Jesus close to the Sea of Galilee (6.1-15, 26), it was difficult to understand Jesus' claims. Some of them were ready to believe that he was 'the Prophet who is to come into the world' (6.14). Some wanted to make him king (6.15). However, the reader can grasp the full significance of Jesus' claims and actions in light of Jn 6.19.

The one who offers bread from heaven is the same one who has been portrayed as performing an act that resembles that of the Creator God, walking on the sea (6.19).

The story of the man born blind in Jn 9 is another example of how creation imagery is used in GJohn in order to help readers grasp the full significance of Jesus. The Pharisees who interrogate the formerly blind man think that Jesus is a 'sinner' (9.24) and someone who is not from God (9.16). On the other hand, the formerly blind man believes that he has been cured by a prophet (9.17). The Pharisees and the formerly blind man are trying to discern the identity of the one who performed such a miracle. The reader, however, has received additional information about the identity of this miracle worker. Jesus is made to say in the opening verses of Jn 9 that he performs the works of God (9.3-4) and that he is the light of the world (9.5). Jesus is also portrayed as performing an act that resembles that of the Creator God when he uses mud to restore the sight of the blind man (9.6). Jesus' claims and actions in Jn 9.3-6 influence the way that readers should engage the rest of the narrative in which the identity of Jesus is discussed.[17]

Recent research on early Christology has concluded that the first Christians included Jesus in the work of creation because this was a distinctive divine activity (e.g. 1 Cor. 8.6; Col. 1.15-16; Heb. 1.2-3, 10-12; Rev. 3.14).[18] My work concurs with this overall conclusion. Since God alone was the sole Creator in ancient Judaism,[19] the portrayal of Jesus as existing before creation (Jn 17.5, 24), taking an active role in creation (Jn 1.1-3, 10), and performing acts that resemble those of the Creator God during his earthly ministry (Jn 5.20, 36; 6.19; 9.3-4, 6; 20.22) would indicate John's attempt to articulate Christology.[20] Therefore, parts of this Gospel may be understood as John's reflections on the Creator God in light of the events of Jesus' resurrection and the giving of the Spirit. If that is the case, then this Gospel might have been an invitation to its readers to join in those theological reflections.

17. The portrayal of Jesus using creation imagery coheres with the larger presentation of Jesus found elsewhere in GJohn. The use of the 'I Am' sayings and the link between Jesus and God's glory and name all amounts to 'a distinctively Johannine portrait of Jesus in which his divine significance is programmatically presented', as has been persuasively argued by L. W. Hurtado, *Lord Jesus Christ: Devotion to Jesus in Earliest Christianity* (Grand Rapids: Eerdmans, 2003), p. 392. Cf. Anderson, *Christology*, pp. 20 n. 7, 266.

18. Hurtado, *Lord*, p. 36; R. Bauckham, *God Crucified: Monotheism and Christology in the New Testament* (Carlisle: Paternoster, 1998), p. 36.

19. Bauckham, *Monotheism*, p. 36.

20. Weder, '*Deus Incarnatus*', p. 331; Bauckham, *Monotheism*, p. 36.

IV. The Composition of GJohn

Extant material evidence of GJohn comes from papyri dated to the second and third centuries. Some phrases, words, and letters from the Johannine passion narrative are attested in two papyri dated to the second century: Papyrus[52] (Jn 18.31-33, 37-38) and Papyrus[90] (18.36-40; 19.1-7).[21] Much more evidence is found in the third century. There is scholarly consensus that Papyrus[45] (4.51, 54; 5.21, 24; 10.7-25; 10.30–11.10, 18-36, 42-57), Papyrus[75] (1.1–11.45, 48-57; 12.3–13.10), and Papyrus[95] (14.8–15.10) come from the third century, and newly published Papyrus[106] (1.29-35, 40-46), Papyrus[107] (17.1-2, 11), Papyrus[108] (17.23-24; 18.1-5), Papyrus[109] (21.18-20, 23-25), Papyrus[119] (1.21-28, 38-44), and Papyrus[121] (19.17-18, 25-26) have also been dated to that century. Additionally, there is Papyrus[66], a manuscript dated to around 200 C.E. which contains the whole of the Gospel of John, except 6.12-34; 14.27-28, 31; 15.1, 27; 16.1, 5, 8-9; 20.21, 24; 21.10-25.[22]

Although extant material evidence of the text of GJohn takes us back only to the second century, many scholars have attempted to trace the putative stages of composition of this text all the way from Jesus' own teachings during the third decade of the first century to the final form of the Gospel at the end of that century. The basis for this is found in what some scholars have called Johannine *aporias*. These are perceived cracks and joins at various points in the final form of GJohn (e.g. Jn 5–6 and 14.31–15.1)[23] that are indicative of several strata in the composition of the text.[24] The final Gospel then is seen as a 'multilayered work, in

21. C. H. Roberts, *An Unpublished Fragment of the Fourth Gospel in the John Rylands Library* (Manchester: The Manchester University Press, 1935); A. K. Bowman et al. (eds.), *The Oxyrhynchus Papyri* (GRM, 70; London: Egypt Exploration Society, 1983), pp. 3–8. The traditional dating of Papyrus[52] has been challenged by B. Nongbri, 'The Use and Abuse of $\mathfrak{P}$[52]: Papyrological Pitfalls in the Dating of the Fourth Gospel', *HTR* 98 (2005), pp. 23–48.

22. V. Martin, *Papyrus Bodmer II: Évangile de Jean, chap. 1–14* (Cologny: Bibliotheca Bodmeriana, 1956), and idem, *Papyrus Bodmer II: Supplément, Évangile de Jean, chap. 14–21* (Cologny: Bibliotheca Bodmeriana, 1958); V. Martin and J. W. B. Barns, *Papyrus Bodmer II: Supplément, Évangile de Jean, chap. 14–21, nouvelle edition augmentée et corrigée* (Cologny: Bibliotheca Bodmeriana, 1962). The date of Papyrus[66] has also been challenged by B. Nongbri, 'The Limits of Palaeographic Dating of Literary Papyri: Some Observations on the Date and Provenance of P. Bodmer II (P66)', *MH* 71 (2014), pp. 1–35.

23. E. Schwartz, *Aporien im vierten Evangelium* (NKGWG, 1, 2, 4; Berlin: Weidmannsche Buchhandlung, 1907–1908), vol. 1, pp. 342–72; vol. 2, pp. 115–88; vol. 4, pp. 497–560.

24. J. L. Martyn, *The Gospel of John and Christian History: Essays for Interpreters* (New York: Paulist, 1978), p. 90.

which texts from various stages of the community's history have been preserved alongside one another'.[25]

The most recent and thorough proposal about stages of composition in GJohn is found in the three-volume commentary by U. von Wahlde.[26] He suggests that GJohn 'has gone through a series of three editions at the hands of three different individuals'.[27] The first edition is related to a Jewish Christian community that existed around 55–65 C.E. It was a complete narrative of the ministry of Jesus including all the miracles recorded in GJohn, his passion, death, and resurrection.[28] The Christ-ology reflected in this early stage was a 'traditional Jewish one focusing on an identification of Jesus as greater than Moses'.[29]

The second edition took place when the community underwent the trauma of separation from its parent Judaism around 60–65 C.E. The community's 'high' Christology (Jesus has been sent by the Father, does the work of the Father, and is the Son of God) resulted in exclusion from the synagogue.[30] Finally, a third hand made an intervention around 90–95 C.E. in order to relate the Johannine tradition to other sectors of early Christianity, especially those associated with Peter.[31] The Christology of the third hand is 'even more exalted…than the second author had done', and includes notions of pre-existence and Jesus' use of 'I am' state-ments.[32]

My analysis of creation imagery in GJohn has found that passages such as 1.1-5, 10; 5.20, 36; 6.16-21; 9.3-4; 17.4-5, 24; 20.22 are intended to portray Jesus in close association with his Father, existing apart from and prior to the created order. Some could take these findings to imply that instances of creation imagery are evidence of later redaction because they support the 'high' Christology characteristic of the putative third edition of the text.

However, this should not be the case. It is remarkable that instances of creation imagery are found in all three stages of composition sug-gested by von Wahlde. He considers that the first editor was responsible for 6.19-21 (except v. 17b), that the second editorial hand introduced 5.20 ('greater works than these'), 36; 9.3; 17.4; 20.22, and that some-one responsible for the final shape of GJohn introduced 17.5, 24 and

25. Ashton, *Understanding*, p. 29.
26. Von Wahlde, *John*.
27. Von Wahlde, *John*, vol. 1, p. 1.
28. Von Wahlde, *John*, vol. 1, p. 50.
29. Von Wahlde, *John*, vol. 1, p. 51.
30. Von Wahlde, *John*, vol. 1, p. 51.
31. Von Wahlde, *John*, vol. 1, pp. 5, 53.
32. Von Wahlde, *John*, vol. 1, p. 233.

incorporated theology (1.1-5, 10) that supports his own thought.[33] The close and unique association between Jesus and his Father is not restricted to the latest stage in the composition of the Gospel.

Additionally, one should take into account that recent research on Christology in earliest Christianity has put forward the idea that 'high' Christology is not necessarily late. On the contrary, 'high' Christology is found in the earliest manifestations of faith in Jesus.[34] If my analysis of creation imagery in GJohn proves persuasive, theories about the composition of GJohn that relate 'high' Christology to late redactional activity will have to be reconsidered.

V. John's Use of the Old Testament

John seems to use creation imagery in order to assert the primal significance of Jesus and to privilege him over other important figures in the story of Israel. However, this hardly means that John disregards the OT or the figures portrayed there. John has used the OT in a positive way in order to shape his presentation of Jesus as existing with God before creation and performing acts that resemble those of the Creator God. Jesus is greater than Moses, Abraham, and John the Baptist, but he is not in competition with them.[35] On the contrary, Moses (5.45-47), Abraham (8.58), John the Baptist (1.15), and the Scriptures as a whole (5.39)[36] are witnesses to him who was with God in the beginning. This represents an important innovation if we take into account how OT texts were used in Second-Temple Judaism. In those traditions OT texts were seen primarily as witnesses to God and his dealings with his people and with his creation.[37] In GJohn, it seems, the OT is primarily a witness to Jesus.

---

33. Von Wahlde, *John*, vol. 1, pp. 18, 239, 256–7, 277–8, 429, 716–17, 738, 858.

34. Hurtado, *Lord*, p. 2, suggests that 'an exalted significance of Jesus appears astonishingly early in Christian circles' and affirms, 'Well within the first couple decades of the Christian movement (i.e. ca. 30–50 C.E.) Jesus was…associated with God in striking ways'.

35. M. D. Hooker, 'Creative Conflict: The Torah and Christology', in Horrell and Tuckett (eds.), *Christology*, pp. 117–36 (136); Menken, 'Observations', pp. 155, 159–66; Myers, *Characterizing Jesus*, p. 184.

36. See J. Beutler, 'The Use of "Scripture" in the Gospel of John', in Culpepper and Black (eds.), *Exploring the Gospel of John*, pp. 147–62.

37. For a recent treatment of biblical interpretation in Judaism of the Second-Temple period, see the collection of articles in G. A. Anderson, R. A. Clements, and D. Satran (eds.), *New Approaches to the Study of Biblical Interpretation in Judaism of the Second Temple Period and in Early Christianity* (Proceedings of the Eleventh International Symposium of the Orion Center for the Study of the Dead Sea

This study on the use of creation imagery in GJohn has also confirmed scholars' perception of the use of the OT in GJohn as 'allusive'. That is, John prefers oblique references to OT texts rather than direct quotations.[38] But, once one recognizes the 'allusiveness' of GJohn, there is a temptation to find hidden echoes or allusions where they may not exist. I have provided numerous examples of this throughout this investigation. It is necessary, therefore, to exercise clear and rigorous exegetical controls over the oblique references that occur to one as a reader. Here I have offered critical assessment of several putative allusions to Gen. 1–3 in GJohn. However, further research is needed in order to validate or eliminate numerous other suggested allusions to OT books in this Gospel.

Scrolls and Associated Literature, Jointly Sponsored by the Hebrew University Center for the Study of Christianity, 9–11 January, 2007; STDJ, 106; Leiden: Brill, 2013).

38. J. Lieu, 'How John Writes', in Bockmuehl and Hagner (eds.), *The Written Gospel*, pp. 171–83 (175); Cothenet, 'L'arrière-plan', pp. 48–9; C. H. Williams, 'The Testimony of Isaiah and Johannine Christology', in *"As Those Who Are Taught": The Interpretation of Isaiah from the LXX to the SBL* (ed. C. Mathews McGinnis and P. K. Tull; SBLSymS, 27; Atlanta: Society of Biblical Literature, 2006), pp. 107–24 (107); C. H. Williams, 'Inspecting an Aerial Photograph of John's Engagement with Sources', in Thatcher (ed.), *What We Have Heard*, pp. 83–5 (85).

BIBLIOGRAPHY

I. Primary Sources and Reference Works

Abegg, Jr., M. G., J. E. Bowley, and E. M. Cook (eds.), *The Dead Sea Scrolls Concordance* (3 vols.; Leiden: Brill, 2003–2010).

Abegg, Jr., M. G., P. Flint, and E. Ulrich, *The Dead Sea Scrolls Bible* (Edinburgh: T. & T. Clarke, 1999).

Aland, B., K. Aland, J. Karavidopoulos, C. M. Martini, and B. M. Metzger (eds.), *Novum Testamentum Graece* (Stuttgart: Deutsche Bibelgesellschaft, 28th rev. edn, 2012).

Baillet, M., J. T. Milik, and R. de Vaux, *Les "petites grottes" de Qumrân* (DJD, 3; Oxford: Clarendon, 1962).

Bensly, R. L., *The Fourth Book of Ezra* (TS, 3/2; Cambridge: Cambridge University Press, 1895).

Berthelot, K., T. Legrand, and A. Paul, *La Bibliothèque de Qumrân: Torah. Genèse* (vol. 1; Paris: Cerf, 2008).

Black, M., *Apocalypsis Henochii Graece* (PVTG, 3; Leiden: Brill, 1970).

Bobichon, P., *Justin Martyr: Dialogue avec Tryphon. Édition critique, traduction et commentaire* (Paradosis, 47; 2 vols.; Fribourg: Academic Press Fribourg, 2003).

Borgen, P., K. Fuglseth, and R. Skarsten, *The Philo Index: A Complete Greek Word Index to the Writings of Philo of Alexandria Lemmatised & Computer–Generated* (UniSt, 25; Trondheim: University of Trondheim, 1997).

Bowman, A. K., et al. (eds.), *The Oxyrhynchus Papyri* (GRM, 70; London: Egypt Exploration Society, 1983).

Braude, W. G., *The Midrash on Psalms* (YJS, 13; 2 vols.; New Haven: Yale University Press, 1959).

—*Pesikta Rabbati: Discourses for Feasts, Fasts, and Special Sabbaths* (YJS, 18; 2 vols.; New Haven: Yale University Press, 1968).

Charles, R. H., *The Greek Versions of the Testaments of the Twelve Patriarchs* (Oxford: Clarendon, 1908).

Coles, R. A., et al. (eds.), *The Oxyrhynchus Papyri* (GRM, 51; London: Egypt Exploration Society, 1970).

Colson, F. H., and G. H. Whitaker, trans., *Philo* (LCL; 10 vols.; Cambridge, Mass.: Harvard University Press, 1929–1962).

Corderio, B., *Catena Patrum Graecorum in Sanctum Ioannem ex Antiquissimo Graeco Codice Ms. Nunc Primum in Lucem Edita* (Belgium: Ex Officina Plantiniana Balthasaris Moreti, 1630).

Cramer, J. A. (ed.), *Catenae Graecorum Patrum in Novum Testamentum* (8 vols.; Oxford: E Typographeo Academico, 1838–1844).

Cyril of Alexandria, *Commentary on the Gospel according to St. John (IX–XXI)* (trans. T. Randell; LFC, 48; Oxford: Walter Smith, 1885).

Delamarter, S., *A Scripture Index to Charlesworth's The Old Testament Pseudepigrapha* (London: Sheffield Academic Press, 2002).

Denis, A. M., *Concordance grecque des pseudépigraphes d'Ancien Testament* (Louvain: Université catholique de Louvain, 1987).

—*Fragmenta pseudepigraphorum quae supersunt Graeca* (PVTG, 3; Leiden: Brill, 1970).

Elliott, J. K., *The Apocryphal New Testament: A Collection of Apocryphal Christian Literature in an English Translation* (Oxford: Clarendon, 1993).

Elowsky, J. C. (ed.), *Ancient Christian Commentary on Scripture* (vols. 4a–4b; Downers Grove, Ill.: InterVarsity, 2006–2007).

Ewald, M. L., *The Homilies of Saint Jerome (Homilies 60–96)* (FC, 57; Washington: The Catholic University of America Press, 1966).

Falls, T. B., *Saint Justin Martyr* (Washington: The Catholic University of America Press, 1977).

Feldman, L. H., *Judean Antiquities 1–4: Translation and Commentary* (Leiden: Brill, 2000).

Field, F., *Origenis Hexaplorum quae supersunt* (Oxford: E Typographeo Clarendoniano, 1875).

Freedman, H., and M. Simon, *Midrash Rabbah: Leviticus* (London: Soncino, 1939).

García-Martínez, F., and E. J. C. Tigchelaar (eds.), *The Dead Sea Scrolls Study Edition* (Leiden: Brill, 1999).

Grant, R. M., *Theophilus of Antioch: Ad Autolycum* (Oxford: Clarendon, 1970).

Harrington, D. J. (ed.), *Pseudo-Philon: Les Antiquités bibliques* (SC, 229; 2 vols.; Paris: Cerf, 1976).

Haussleiter, J. (ed.), *Victorini Episcopi Petavionensis Opera* (CSEL, 49; Vienna: F. Tempsky, 1916).

Holladay, C. R., *Fragments from Hellenistic Jewish Authors* (SBLTT, 20, 30, 39, 40; 4 vols.; Atlanta: Scholars Press, 1983–1996).

Jonge, M. de, *The Testaments of the Twelve Patriarchs: A Critical Edition of the Greek Text* (PVTG, 1/2; Leiden: Brill, 1978).

Kalantzis, G., *Theodore of Mopsuestia Commentary on the Gospel of John* (ECS, 7; Strathfield, Australia: St Paulus, 2004).

Keble, J., *Five Books of s. Irenaeus: Against Heresies* (Oxford: James Parker, 1872).

Lange, A., and M. Weigold, *Biblical Quotations and Allusions in Second Temple Jewish Literature* (JAJSup, 5; Göttingen: Vandenhoeck & Ruprecht, 2011).

Lightfoot, J. B., and J. R. Harmer, *The Apostolic Fathers: Greek Texts and English Translations of Their Writings* (ed. M. W. Holmes; Grand Rapids: Baker, 2nd edn, 1992).

Malatesta, E., *St. John's Gospel 1920–1965: A Cumulative and Classified Bibliography of Books and Periodical Literature on the Fourth Gospel* (AnBib, 32; Rome: Pontificio Istituto Biblico, 1967).

Martin, V., *Papyrus Bodmer II: Évangile de Jean, chap. 1–14* (Cologny: Bibliotheca Bodmeriana, 1956).

—*Papyrus Bodmer II: Supplément, Évangile de Jean, chap. 14–21* (Cologny: Bibliotheca Bodmeriana, 1958).

Martin, V., and J. W. B. Barns, *Papyrus Bodmer II: Supplément, Évangile de Jean, chap. 14–21, nouvelle edition augmentée et corrigée* (Cologny: Bibliotheca Bodmeriana, 1962).

McCarthy, C., *Saint Ephrem's Commentary on Tatian's Diatessaron: An English Translation of Chester Beatty Syriac MS 709* (JSSSup, 2; Oxford: Oxford University Press, 1993).

McLean, B. H., *Citations and Allusions to Jewish Scripture in Early Christian and Jewish Writings through 180 C.E.* (Lewiston, New York: Edwin Mellen, 1992).

Mozley, J. H., 'The Vitae Adae', *JTS* 30 (1929), pp. 121–49.

Neusner, J., *Pesiqta deRab Kahana: An Analytical Translation* (BJS, 123; 2 vols.; Atlanta: Scholars Press, 1987).

Pusey, P. E. (ed.), *Sancti Patris Nostri Cyrilli Archiepiscopi Alexandrini in D. Joannis Evangelium* (3 vols.; Brussels: Culture et Civilisation, 1965).

Rahlfs, A., and R. Hanhart (eds.), *Septuaginta* (Stuttgart: Deutsche Bibelgesellschaft, rev. edn, 2006).

Rea, J. R. (ed.), *The Oxyrhynchus Papyri* (GRM, 83; London: Egypt Exploration Society, 1996).

Rengstorf, K. H., *A Complete Concordance to Flavius Josephus* (4 vols.; Leiden: Brill, 1973–1983).

Reuss, J., *Johannes-Kommentare aus der griechischen Kirche* (TUGAL, 89; Berlin: Akademie Verlag, 1966).

Roberts, C. H., *An Unpublished Fragment of the Fourth Gospel in the John Rylands Library* (Manchester: The Manchester University Press, 1935).

Rousseau, A., L. Doutreleau, and C. Mercier, *Irénée de Lyon: Contre les Hérésies* (SC, 153; 2 vols.; Paris: Cerf, 1969).

Schmidt, C., and W. Schubart, *ΠΡΑΞΕΙΣ ΠΑΥΛΟΥ: Acta Pauli nach dem Papyrus der Hamburger Staats und Universität-Bibliothek* (Glückstadt: J. J. Augustin, 1936).

Stevenson, A. (ed.), *Oxford Dictionary of English* (New York: Oxford University Press, 3rd edn, 2010).

Tertullian, *Les Spectacles (De spectaculis)* (ed. M. Turcan; SC, 332; Paris: Cerf, 1986).

Thackeray, H. St. J., et al., trans., *Josephus* (LCL; 10 vols.; Cambridge, Mass.: Harvard University Press, 1926–1965).

Théophile D'Antioche, *Trois Livres à Autolycus* (SC, 20; Paris: Cerf, 1948).

Tromp, J., *The Assumption of Moses: A Critical Edition with Commentary* (SVTP, 10; Leiden: Brill, 1993).

—*The Life of Adam and Eve in Greek: A Critical Edition* (PVTG, 6; Leiden: Brill, 2005).

Ulrich, E. (ed.), *The Biblical Qumran Scrolls: Transcriptions and Textual Variants* (VTSup, 134; Leiden: Brill, 2010).

Van Belle, G., *Johannine Bibliography 1966–1985: A Cumulative Bibliography on the Fourth Gospel* (BETL, 82; Leuven: Leuven University Press, 1988).

Vosté, J. M., *Theodori Mopsuesteni Commentarius in Evangelium Iohannis Apostoli* (CSCO, 116; Leuven: Peeters, 1940).

Wright, R. B., *The Psalms of Solomon: A Critical Edition of the Greek Text* (JCTCRS, 1; London: T&T Clark International, 2007).

II. Other Sources

Abbott, E. A., *Johannine Grammar* (London: Adam & Charles Black, 1906).

—*Johannine Vocabulary: A Comparison of the Words of the Fourth Gospel with Those of the Three* (London: Adam & Charles Black, 1905).

Aland, K., 'Eine Untersuchung zu Joh 1:3. 4. Über die Bedeutung eines Punktes', *ZNW* 59 (1968), pp. 174–209.

Allison, Jr., D. C., *The Intertextual Jesus: Scripture in Q* (Harrisburg: Trinity University Press, 2000).

—*The New Moses: A Matthean Typology* (Edinburgh: T. & T. Clark, 1993).

Allo, E. B., *L'évangile spirituel de Jean* (Paris: Cerf, 1944).

Anderson, G. A., R. A. Clements, and D. Satran (eds.), *New Approaches to the Study of Biblical Interpretation in Judaism of the Second Temple Period and in Early Christianity* (Proceedings of the Eleventh International Symposium of the Orion Center for the Study of the Dead Sea Scrolls and Associated Literature, Jointly Sponsored by the Hebrew University Center for the Study of Christianity, 9–11 January, 2007; STDJ, 106; Leiden: Brill, 2013).

Anderson, P. N., *The Christology of the Fourth Gospel: Its Unity and Disunity in the Light of John 6* (WUNT, 2/78; Tübingen: J. C. B. Mohr [Paul Siebeck], 1996).

Appold, M. L., *The Oneness Motif in the Fourth Gospel: Motif Analysis and Exegetical Probe into the Theology of John* (WUNT, 2/1; Tübingen: J. C. B. Mohr, 1976).

Ashton, J., 'Second Thoughts on the Fourth Gospel', in Thatcher (ed.), *What We Have Heard*, pp. 1–18.

—*Understanding the Fourth Gospel* (Oxford: Oxford University Press, 2nd edn, 2007).

Asiedu-Peprah, M., *Johannine Sabbath Conflicts as Juridical Controversy* (WUNT, 2/132; Tübingen: J. C. B. Mohr, 2001).

Aune, D. E., 'Dualism in the Fourth Gospel and the Dead Sea Scrolls: A Reassessment of the Problem', in Aune, Seland, and Ulrichsen (eds.), *Neotestamentica et Philonica*, pp. 281–303.

Aune, D. E., T. Seland, and J. H. Ulrichsen (eds.), *Neotestamentica et Philonica: Studies in Honor of Peder Borgen* (NovTSup, 106; Leiden: Brill, 2003).

Bacon, B. W., 'After Six Days: A New Clue for Gospel Critics', *HTR* 8 (1915), pp. 94–120.

Ballard, J. M., 'The Translation of John xvii. 5', *ExpTim* 47 (1935–1936), p. 284.

Barrett, C. K., *The Gospel according to St John* (London: SPCK, 2nd edn, 1978).

Barrosse, T., 'The Seven Days of the New Creation in St. John's Gospel', *CBQ* 21 (1959), pp. 507–16.

Barton, S. C., 'Johannine Dualism and Contemporary Pluralism', in Bauckham and Mosser (eds.), *Gospel of John*, pp. 3–18.

Bauckham, R., *God Crucified: Monotheism and Christology in the New Testament* (Carlisle: Paternoster, 1998).

—'Qumran and the Fourth Gospel: Is There a Connection?', in *The Scrolls and the Scriptures: Qumran Fifty Years After* (ed. S. E. Porter and C. A. Evans; JSPSup, 26; Sheffield: Sheffield Academic Press, 1997), pp. 267–79.

—'The Relevance of Extra-Canonical Jewish Texts to New Testament Study', in *Hearing the New Testament: Strategies for Interpretation* (ed. J. B. Green; Grand Rapids: Eerdmans, 1995), pp. 90–108.

Bauckham, R., and C. Mosser (eds.), *The Gospel of John and Christian Theology* (Grand Rapids: Eerdmans, 2008).

Baumgarten, O. et al., *Die Schriften des Neuen Testaments* (ed. J. Weiss; 4 vols.; Göttingen: Vandenhoeck & Ruprecht, 3rd edn, 1918).

Beare, F. W., 'The Risen Jesus Bestows the Spirit: A Study of John 20:19–23', *CJT* 4 (1958), pp. 95–100.

Beasley-Murray, G. R., *John* (WBC, 36; Waco, Tex.: Word, 1987).

Bechmann, U., 'Der Lebenshauch Gottes: Die Verwandlungskraft des Geistes Gottes am Beispiel von Ez 37,1-4 und Joh 20,19-23', *BK* 64 (2009), pp. 87–92.

Beetham, C. A., *Echoes of Scripture in the Letter of Paul to the Colossians* (BIS, 96; Leiden: Brill, 2008).

Bennema, C., 'The Giving of the Spirit in John's Gospel – A New Proposal?', *EvQ* 74 (2002), pp. 195–213.

Ben-Porat, Z., 'The Poetics of Literary Allusion', *PTL* 1 (1976), pp. 105–28.

Berg, W., *Die Rezeption alttestamentlicher Motive im Neuen Testament – dargestellt an den Seewandelerzählungen* (HSTE, 1; Freiburg: HochschulVerlag, 1979).

Bernard, J. H., *A Critical and Exegetical Commentary on the Gospel according to St. John* (2 vols.; Edinburgh: T. & T. Clark, 1928).

Beutler, J., 'The Use of "Scripture" in the Gospel of John', in Culpepper and Black (eds.), *Exploring the Gospel of John*, pp. 147–62.

Bird, M. F,. and J. Willitts (eds.), *Paul and the Gospels: Christologies, Conflicts and Convergences* (LNTS, 411; London: T&T Clark International, 2011).

Bissell, E. C., 'The "Protevangelium" and the Eighth Psalm', *JBL* 6 (1886), pp. 64–8.

Blanquart, F., *Le premier jour. Étude sur Jean 20* (LD, 146; Paris: Cerf, 1992).

Bockmuehl, M., and D. A. Hagner (eds.), *The Writen Gospel* (Cambridge: Cambridge University Press, 2005).

Bockmuehl, M., and G. G. Stroumsa (eds.), *Paradise in Antiquity: Jewish and Christian Views* (Cambridge: Cambridge University Press, 2010).

Boer, M. C. de, *Johannine Perspectives on the Death of Jesus* (CBET, 17; Kampen: Kok-Pharos, 1996).

Boismard, M.-É., 'Critique textuelle et citations patristiques', *RB* 57 (1950), pp. 388–408.

—*Du baptême à Cana (Jean 1,19–2,11)* (Paris: Cerf, 1956).

—'L'évangile à quatre dimensions', *LumVie* 1 (1951), pp. 93–114.

—*Moïse ou Jésus: Essai de Christologie Johannique* (BETL, 84; Leuven: Leuven University Press, 1988).

—*Le Prologue de Saint Jean* (LD, 11; Paris: Cerf, 1953).

Boismard, M.-É., and A. Lamouille, *L'évangile de Jean. Commentaire* (SQEF, 3; Paris: Cerf, 1977).

—*Un évangile pré-johannique* (EBib, 17–18, 24–25, 28–29; Paris: Gabalda, 1996).

Bonney, W., *Caused to Believe: The Doubting Thomas Story as the Climax of John's Christological Narrative* (BIS, 62; Leiden: Brill, 2002).

Borgen, P., 'Creation, Logos and the Son: Observations on John 1:1-18 and 5:17-18', *ExAud* 3 (1987), pp. 88–97.

—*Early Christianity and Hellenistic Judaism* (Edinburgh: T. & T. Clark, 1996).

—*Logos Was the True Light and Other Essays on the Gospel of John* (Trondheim: Tapir, 1983).

—*Philo, John and Paul: New Perspectives on Judaism and Early Christianity* (BJS, 131; Atlanta: Scholars Press, 1987).

Braum, F. M., 'L'arrière-fond du quatrième Évangile', in *L'Évangile de Jean: Études et Problèmes* (RechBib, 3; Louvain: Desclée De Brouwer, 1958), pp. 179–96.

Brayford, S., *Genesis* (SCS; Leiden: Brill, 2007).

Brodie, T. L., *The Gospel according to John: A Literary and Theological Commentary* (New York: Oxford University Press, 1993).

Brown, J. K., 'Creation's Renewal in the Gospel of John', *CBQ* 72 (2010), pp. 275–90.

Brown, R. E., *The Gospel according to John* (AB, 29–29a; 2 vols.; Garden City: Doubleday, 1966–1970).

Brown, T. G., *Spirit in the Writings of John: Johannine Pneumatology in Social-Scientific Perspective* (JSNTSup, 253; London: T&T Clark International, 2003).

Brown, W. P., *Structure, Role, and Ideology in the Hebrew and Greek Texts of Genesis 1:1–2:3* (SBLDS, 132; Atlanta: Scholars Press, 1993).

Brunson, A. C., *Psalm 118 in the Gospel of John: An Intertextual Study on the New Exodus Pattern in the Theology of John* (WUNT, 2/158; Tübingen: Mohr Siebeck, 2003).

Bultmann, R., *The Gospel of John: A Commentary* (trans. G. R. Beasley-Murray, R. W. N. Hoare, and J. K. Riches; Philadelphia: Westminster, 1971).

Burer, M. H., *Divine Sabbath Work* (BBRSup, 5; Winona Lake: Eisenbrauns, 2012).

Burge, G. M., *The Anointed Community: The Holy Spirit in the Johannine Tradition* (Grand Rapids: Eerdmans, 1987).

Burkholder, B. J., 'Considering the Possibility of a Theological Corruption in Joh 1,18 in Light of Its Early Reception', *ZNW* 103 (2012), pp. 64–83.

Bussche, H. Van den, 'La structure de Jean I-XII', in *L'Évangile de Jean: Études et Problèmes* (RechBib, 3; Bruges: Desclée De Brouwer, 1958), pp. 61–109.

Bynum, Wm. R., *The Fourth Gospel and the Scriptures: Illuminating the Form and Meaning of Scriptural Citation in John 19:37* (NovTSup, 144; Leiden: Brill, 2012).

Carmichael, C. M., *The Story of Creation: Its Origins and Its Interpretation in Philo and the Fourth Gospel* (Ithaca: Cornell University Press, 1996).

Carson, D. A., *The Gospel according to John* (Grand Rapids: Eerdmans, 1991).

Chapa, J., 'The Early Text of John', in *The Early Text of the New Testament* (ed. C. E. Hill and M. J. Kruger; Oxford: Oxford University Press, 2012), pp. 140–56.

Chapman, D. W., *Ancient Jewish and Christian Perceptions of Crucifixion* (WUNT, 2/244; Tübingen: Mohr Siebeck, 2008).

Charlesworth, J. H., 'The Fourth Evangelist and the Dead Sea Scrolls: Assessing Trends over Nearly Sixty Years', in *John, Qumran, and the Dead Sea Scrolls: Sixty Years of Discovery and Debate* (ed. M. L. Coloe and T. Thatcher; SBLEJL, 32; Atlanta: Society of Biblical Literature, 2011), pp. 161–82.

—*The Good and Evil Serpent: How a Universal Symbol Became Christianized* (ABRL; New Heaven: Yale University Press, 2010).

Chevallier, M. A., *Souffle de Dieu. Le Saint Esprit dans le Nouveau Testament* (LPT, 26, 54, 55; 3 vols.; Paris: Beauchesne, 1978–1991).

Cimosa, M. 'La traduzione greca dei Settanta nel Vangelo di Giovanni', *BeO* 39 (1997), pp. 41–55.

Clark-Soles, J., *Scripture Cannot Be Broken: The Social Function of the Use of Scripture in the Fourth Gospel* (Boston: Brill, 2003).

Claussen, C., 'Turning Water to Wine: Re-reading the Miracle at the Wedding in Cana', in *Jesus Research: An International Perspective* (ed. J. H. Charlesworth and P. Pokorný; Grand Rapids: Eerdmans, 2009), pp. 73–97.

Coloe, M. L., 'Gentiles in the Gospel of John: Narrative Possibilities – John 12.12-43', in *Attitudes to Gentiles in Ancient Judaism and Early Christianity* (ed. D. C. Sim and J. S. McLaren; LNTS, 499; London: Bloomsbury T&T Clark, 2013), pp. 209–23.

—*God Dwells with Us: Temple Symbolism in the Fourth Gospel* (Collegeville: Liturgical, 2001).

—'The Structure of the Johannine Prologue and Genesis 1', *ABR* 45 (1997), pp. 40–55.

—'Theological Reflexions on Creation in the Gospel of John', *Pacifica* 24 (2011), pp. 1–12.

Cook, J. I., 'John 20:19–23 – An Exegesis', *RefR* 21 (1967), pp. 2–10.

Cothenet, É., 'L'arrière-plan vétéro-testamentaire du IVᵉ Évangile', in *Origine et postérité de L'évangile de Jean* (LD, 143; Paris: Cerf, 1990), pp. 43–69.

Cullmann, O., 'The Theological Content of the Prologue of John in Its Present Form', in Fortna and Gaventa (eds.), *The Conversation Continues*, pp. 295–8.

Culpepper, R. A., *Anatomy of the Fourth Gospel: A Study in Literary Design* (Philadelphia: Fortress, 1983).

—'Cognition in John: The Johannine Signs as Recognition Scenes', *PRSt* 35 (2008), pp. 251–60.

—*John, the Son of Zebedee: The Life of a Legend* (Edinburgh: T. & T. Clark, 2000).

Culpepper, R. A., and C. C. Black (eds.), *Exploring the Gospel of John: In Honor of D. Moody Smith* (Louisville: Westminster John Knox, 1996).

Dahms, J. V., 'The Johannine Use of Monogenēs Reconsidered', *NTS* 29 (1983), pp. 222–32.

Daise, M. A., 'Biblical Creation Motifs in the Qumran Hodayot', in *The Dead Sea Scrolls Fifty Years after their Discovery* (ed. L. H. Schiffman, E. Tov, and J. C. VanderKam; Jerusalem: Israel Exploration Society, 2000), pp. 293–305.

—*Feasts in John: Jewish Festivals and Jesus' "Hour" in the Fourth Gospel* (WUNT, 2/229; Tübingen: Mohr Siebeck, 2007).

Daly-Denton, M., *David in the Fourth Gospel: The Johannine Reception of the Psalms* (AGJU, 47; Leiden: Brill, 2000).

Davies, W. D., 'Reflexions on Aspects of the Jewish Background of the Gospel of John', in Culpepper and Black (eds.), *Exploring the Gospel of John*, pp. 41–64.

De Ausejo, S., '¿Es un himno a Cristo el prólogo de San Juan? Los himnos cristológicos de la Iglesia primitiva y el prólogo del IV Evangelio', *EstBíb* 15 (1956), pp. 381–427.

Derrett, J. D. M., 'John 9:6 Read with Isaiah 6:10; 20:9', *EvQ* 66 (1994), pp. 251–4.

—'Miracles, Pools, and Sight: John 9,1-41; Genesis 2,6-7; Isaiah 6,10; 30,20, 35,5-7', *BeO* 36 (1994), pp. 71–85.

—'Τί ἐργάζῃ; (Jn 6,30): An Unrecognized Allusion to Is 45,9', *ZNW* 84 (1993), pp. 142–44.

Dettwiler, A., and U. Poplutz (eds.), *Studien zu Matthäus und Johannes / Études sur Matthieu et Jean* (ATANT, 97; Zurich: Theologischer Verlag, 2009).

Dodd, C. H., *Historical Tradition in the Fourth Gospel* (Cambridge: Cambridge University Press, 1963).

—*The Interpretation of the Fourth Gospel* (Cambridge: Cambridge University Press, 1953).

Doering, L., *Schabbat: Sabbathalacha und –praxis im antiken Judentum und Urchristentum* (TSAJ, 78; Tübingen: J. C. B. Mohr [Paul Siebeck], 1999).

Droge, A. J., 'Sabbath Work/Sabbath Rest: Genesis, Thomas, John', *HR* 47 (2007–2008), pp. 112–41.

Duke, P. D., *Irony in the Fourth Gospel* (Atlanta: John Knox, 1953).

Dunn, J. D. G., *Christology in the Making: A New Testament Inquiry into the Origins of the Doctrine of the Incarnation* (London: SCM, 1980).

Du Rand, J. A., 'The Creation Motif in the Fourth Gospel: Perspectives on Its Narratological Function within a Judaistic Background', in Van Belle, van der Watt, and Maritz (eds.), *Theology and Christology*, pp. 21–46.

Edwards, J. C., *The Ransom Logion in Mark and Matthew: Its Reception and Its Significance for the Study of the Gospels* (WUNT, 2/327; Tübingen: Mohr Siebeck, 2012).

Edwards, M., *John* (Oxford: Blackwell, 2004).

Ehrman, B., *The Orthodox Corruption of Scripture* (New York: Oxford University Press, 1993).

Endo, M., *Creation and Christology: A Study on the Johannine Prologue in the Light of Early Jewish Creation Accounts* (WUNT, 2/149; Tübingen: Mohr Siebeck, 2002).

Engberg-Pedersen, T., '*Logos* and *Pneuma* in the Fourth Gospel', in *Greco-Roman Culture and the New Testament* (ed. D. E. Aune and F. E. Brenk; NovTSup, 143; Leiden: Brill, 2012), pp. 27–48.

Ensor, P. W., *Jesus and His 'Works': The Johannine Sayings in Historical Perspective* (WUNT, 2/85; Tübingen: J. C. B. Mohr, 1996).

Evans, C. A., *Word and Glory: On the Exegetical and Theological Background of John's Prologue* (JSNTSup, 89; Sheffield: Sheffield Academic Press, 1993).

Evans, C. A., and J. A. Sanders (eds.), *Paul and the Scriptures of Israel* (JSNTSup, 83; SScEJC, 1; Sheffield: JSOT Press, 1992).

Evans, C. A., and H. D. Zacharias (eds.), *Early Christian Literature and Intertextuality* (LNTS, 392; New York: T&T Clark International, 2009).

Evyasaf, R. S., 'Hellenistic and Roman Approaches to Gardens in the Eastern Mediterranean: Judaea as a Case Study', in *The Archaeology of Crop Fields and Gardens: Proceedings of the 1st Conference on Crop Fields and Gardens Archaeology. Barcelona (Spain), 1–3 June 2006* (ed. J. P. Morel, J. T. Juan, and J. C. Matamala; Bari, Italy: Edipuglia, 2006), p. 203–4.

Fernández-Marcos, N., *The Septuagint in Context: Introduction to the Greek Versions of the Bible* (trans. W. G. E. Watson; Leiden: Brill, 2000).

Fernández-Marcos, N., and A. Sáenz-Badillos, *Anotaciones críticas al texto griego del Génesis y estudio de sus grupos textuales* (TSt, 12; Madrid: Consejo Superior de Investigaciones Científicas, 1972).

Feuillet, A., 'Les *Ego eimi* christologiques du quatrième Évangile (à suivre)', *RSR* 54 (1966), pp. 5–22.

Ford, D. F., 'Beginning, Ending and Abundance: Genesis 1:1 and the Gospel of John', in *Leshon Limmudim: Essays on the Language and Literature of the Hebrew Bible* (ed. D. A. Baer and R. P. Gordon; LHBOTS, 593; London: Bloomsbury T&T Clark, 2013), pp. 292–305.

Fortna, R. T., and B. R. Gaventa (eds.), *The Conversation Continues: Studies in Paul & John in Honor of J. Louis Martyn* (Nashville: Abingdon, 1990).

Fossum, J., 'Gen 1:26 and 2:7 in Judaism, Samaritanism, and Gnosticis', *JSJ* 16 (1985), pp. 202–39.

—*The Image of the Invisible God: Essays on the Influence of Jewish Mysticism on Early Christology* (NTOA, 30; Göttingen: Vandenhoeck & Ruprecht, 1995).

Franke, A. H., *Das alte Testament bei Johannes. Ein Beitrag zur Erklärung und Beurtheilung der johanneischen Schriften* (Göttingen: Vandenhoeck & Ruprecht, 1885).

Frayer-Griggs, D., 'Spittle, Clay, and Creation in John 9:6 and Some Dead Sea Scrolls', *JBL* 132 (2013), pp. 659–70.

Frediksen, P., *From Jesus to Christ: The Origins of the New Testament Images of Jesus* (New Heaven: Yale University Press, 1988).

Freed, E. D., *Old Testament Quotations in the Gospel of John* (NovTSup, 11; Leiden: Brill, 1965).

Frey, J., 'Critical Issues in the Investigation of the Scrolls and the New Testament', in *The Oxford Handbook of the Dead Sea Scrolls* (ed. T. H. Lim and J. J. Collins; Oxford: Oxford University Press, 2010), pp. 517–45.

—'"…dass sie meine Herrlichkeit schauen" (Joh 17.24) Zu Hintergrund, Sinn und Funktion der johanneischen Rede von der δόξα Jesu', *NTS* 54 (2008), pp. 375–97.

—*Die johanneische Eschatologie* (WUNT, 96, 110, 117; 3 vols.; Tübingen: Mohr Siebeck, 1997–2000).

—'Different Patterns of Dualistic Thought in the Qumran Library: Reflections on their Background and History', in *Legal Texts and Legal Issues: Proceedings of the Second Meeting of the International Organization for Qumran Studies* (ed. M. J. Bernstein, F. García-Martínez, and J. Jampen; STDJ, 23; Leiden: Brill, 1997), pp. 275–335.

—'Love-Relations in the Fourth Gospel: Establishing a Semantic Network', in Van Belle, Labahn, and Maritz (eds.), *Repetitions*, pp. 171–98.

Fuglseth, K. S., *Johannine Sectarianism in Perspective: A Sociological, Historical, and Comparative Analysis of Temple and Social Relationships in the Gospel of John, Philo, and Qumran* (NovTSup, 119; Leiden: Brill, 2005).

Fuller, R. H., 'John 20:19-23', *Int* 32 (1978), pp. 180–4.

Gamble, H. Y., *Books and Readers in the Early Church: A History of Early Christian Texts* (New Heaven: Yale University Press, 1995).

García-Martínez, F., 'Creation in the Dead Sea Scrolls', in van Kooten (ed.), *The Creation of Heaven and Earth*, pp. 53–70.

—*Qumranica Minora II: Thematic Studies on the Dead Sea Scrolls* (ed. E. J. C. Tigchelaar; STDJ, 64; Leiden: Brill, 2007).

García-Moreno, A., *Temas teológicos del Evangelio de Juan: La creación* (Madrid: Rialp, 2007).

Giblin, C. H., 'Confrontations in John 18,1-27', *Bib* 65 (1984), pp. 210–32.

—'The Miraculous Crossing of the Sea (Jn 6,16-21)', *NTS* 28 (1983), pp. 96–103.

Giere, S. D., *A New Glimpse of Day One: Intertextuality, History of Interpretation, and Genesis 1.1–5* (Berlin: W. de Gruyter, 2009).

Girard, M., 'La composition structurelle des sept « signes » dans le quatrième évangile', *SR* 9 (1980), pp. 315–24.

—'La structure heptapartite du quatrième évangile', *SR* 5 (1975–1976), pp. 350–9.

Glasson, T. F., *Moses in the Fourth Gospel* (SBT; London: SCM, 1963).

Goettmann, J., *Saint Jean: Évangile de la Nouvelle Genèse* (Paris: Cerf, 1982).

Goff, M., 'Genesis 1–3 and Conceptions of Humankind in 4QInstruction, Philo and Paul', in Evans and Zacharias (eds.), *Early Christian Literature*, pp. 114–19.

Gordley, M. E., 'Creation Imagery in Qumran Hymns and Prayers', *JJS* 59 (2008), pp. 252–72.

Goulder, M. D., 'Exegesis of Genesis 1–3 in the New Testament', *JJS* 43 (1992), pp. 226–9.

Grappe, C., 'Du sanctuaire au jardin: Jésus, nouveau et veritable Temple dans le quatrième évangile', in Dettwiler and Poplutz (eds.), *Studien*, pp. 185–96.

Grassi, J. A., 'The Role of Jesus' Mother in John's Gospel: A Reappraisal', *CBQ* 48 (1986), pp. 67–80.

Grigsby, B., 'The Reworking of the Lake-Walking Account in the Johannine Tradition', *ExpTim* 100 (1989), pp. 295–7.

Grinfield, E. W., *The Christian Cosmos: The Son of God the Revealed Creator* (London: Seeley, Jackson & Halliday, 1857).

Grob, F., *Faire l'oeuvre de Dieu: Christologie et éthique dans L'Evangile de Jean* (Paris: Presses Universitaires de France, 1986).

Guilding, A., *The Fourth Gospel and Jewish Worship: A Study of the Relation of St. John's Gospel to the Ancient Jewish Lectionary System* (Oxford: Clarendon, 1960).

Haenchen, E., *John 1* (trans. R. W. Funk; Hermeneia; Philadelphia: Fortress, 1984).

—*John 2* (trans. R. W. Funk; Hermeneia; Philadelphia: Fortress, 1984).

—'Probleme des johanneischen "Prologs"', *ZTK* 60 (1963), pp. 305–34.

Hägerland, T., *Jesus and the Forgiveness of Sins: An Aspect of His Prophetic Mission* (SNTSMS, 150; Cambridge: Cambridge University Press, 2012).

—'The Power of Prophecy: A Septuagintal Echo in John 20:19–23', *CBQ* 71 (2009), pp. 84–103.

Hakola, R., *Identity Matters: John, the Jews and Jewishness* (NovTSup, 118; Leiden: Brill, 2005).

Hambly, W. F., 'Creation and Gospel: A Brief Comparison of Genesis 1,1–2,4 and John 1,1–2,12', in *Studia Evangelica* (ed. F. L. Cross; TUGAL, 103; Berlin: Akademie Verlag, 1968), pp. 69–74.

Hanson, A. T., *The Prophetic Gospel: A Study of John and the Old Testament* (Edinburgh: T. & T. Clark, 1991).

Harding, M., 'Kyrios Christos: Johannine and Pauline Perspectives on the Christ Event', in Bird and Willitts (eds.), *Paul*, pp. 169–96.

Harl, M., *La Bible d'Alexandrie: La Genèse* (Paris: Cerf, 2nd edn, 1986).

Harnack, A. von, *Das 'Wir' in den Johanneischen Schriften* (SPAW; Berlin: Akademie der Wissenschaften, 1923).

Harris, E., *Prologue and Gospel: The Theology of the Fourth Evangelist* (JSNTSup, 107; Sheffield: Sheffield Academic Press, 1994).

Hatina, T. R., 'John 20,22 in Its Eschatological Context: Promise or Fulfilment?', *Bib* 74 (1993), pp. 196–219.

Hays, R. B., 'Can the Gospels Teach Us How to Read the Old Testament?', *ProEccl* 11 (2002), pp. 402–18.

—*The Conversion of the Imagination: Paul as Interpreter of Israel's Scripture* (Grand Rapids: Eerdmans, 2005).

—*Echoes of Scripture in the Letters of Paul* (New Heaven: Yale University Press, 1989).

Heath, J., '"Some Were Saying, 'He is Good'" (John 7.12b): "Good" Christology in John's Gospel?', *NTS* 56 (2010), pp. 513–35.

Heil, J. P., *Jesus Walking on the Sea: Meaning and Gospel Functions of Mt. 14:22-23, Mark 6:45-52 and John 6:15b-21* (AnBib, 87; Rome: Biblical Institute, 1981).

Hengel, M., *Crucifixion in the Ancient World and the Folly of the Message of the Cross* (trans. J. Bowden; London: SCM, 1977).

—'Eye-Witness Memory and the Writing of the Gospels', in Bockmuehl and Hagner (eds.), *The Written Gospel*, pp. 70–96.

—'The Old Testament in the Fourth Gospel', *HBT* 12 (1990), pp. 19–41.

—'The Prologue of the Gospel of John as the Gateway to Christological Truth', in Bauckham and Mosser (eds.), *Gospel of John*, pp. 265–94.

—'Reich Christi, Reich Gottes und Weltreich im Johannesevangelium', in *Königsherrschaft Gottes und himmlischer Kult im Judentum, Urchristentum und in der hellenischen Welt* (ed. M. Hengel and A. M. Schwemer; Tübingen: J. C. B. Mohr, 1991), pp. 163–84.

Hill, C. E., *The Johannine Corpus in the Early Church* (Oxford: Oxford University Press, 2004).

Hirsch, E., *Das vierte Evangelium: in seiner ursprünglichen Gestalt* (Tübingen: J. C. B. Mohr, 1936).

Hofius, O., 'Struktur und Gedankengang des Logos-Hymnus in Joh 1,1–18', in *Johannestudien: Untersuchungen zur Theologie des vierten Evangeliums* (ed. O. Hofius and H. C. Kammler; WUNT, 88; Tübingen: Mohr Siebeck, 1996), pp. 1–23.

Holleran, J. W. 'Seeing the Light: A Narrative Reading of John 9. I', *ETL* 69 (1993), pp. 5–26.

—'Seeing the Light: A Narrative Reading of John 9. II', *ETL* 69 (1993), pp. 354–82.

Hooker, M. D., 'Creative Conflict: The Torah and Christology', in Horrell and Tuckett (eds.), *Christology*, pp. 117–36.

—*Endings: Invitations to Discipleship* (London: SCM, 2003).

—'The Johannine Prologue and the Messianic Secret', *NTS* 21 (1974), pp. 40–58.

Horbury, W., 'Tertullian on the Jews in the Light of *De spectaculis* XXX. 5-6', *JTS* 23 (1972), pp. 455–9.

Horrell, D. G., and C. M. Tuckett (eds.), *Christology, Controversy and Community* (NovTSup, 99; Leiden: Brill, 2000).

Hort, F. J. A., *The Christian Ecclesia* (London: MacMillan, 1914).

Hoskyns, E. C., *The Fourth Gospel* (ed. F. N. Davey; 2 vols.; London: Faber & Faber, 1940).

—'Genesis I—III and St John's Gospel', *JTS* 21 (1920), pp. 210–18.

Hübner, H., *Vetus Testamentum in Novo* (2 vols.; Göttingen: Vandenhoeck & Ruprecht, 1997–2003).

Hughes, J. A., *Scriptural Allusions and Exegesis in the Hodayot* (STDJ, 59; Leiden: Brill, 2006).

Hühn, E., *Die alttestamentlichen Citate und Reminiscenzen im Neuen Testamente* (Tübingen: J. C. B. Mohr, 1900).

Hunt, S. A., 'The Roman Soldiers at Jesus' Arrest: "You Are Dust, and to Dust You Shall Return"', in Hunt, Tolmie, and Zimmermann (eds.), *Character Studies in the Fourth Gospel*, pp. 554–67.

Hunt, S. A., D. F. Tolmie, and R. Zimmermann (eds.), *Character Studies in the Fourth Gospel: Narrative Approaches to Seventy Figures in John* (WUNT, 1/314; Tübingen: Mohr Siebeck, 2013).

Hurtado, L. W., *Lord Jesus Christ: Devotion to Jesus in Earliest Christianity* (Grand Rapids: Eerdmans, 2003).

Hylen, S., *Allusion and Meaning in John 6* (BZNW, 137; Berlin: W. de Gruyter, 2005).

Jackson, T. R., *New Creation in Paul's Letters: A Study of the Historical and Social Setting of a Pauline Concept* (WUNT, 2/272; Tübingen: Mohr Siebeck, 2010).

Jacobsen, A. C., 'The Importance of Genesis 1–3 in the Theology of Irenaeus', *ZAC* 8 (2004), pp. 299–316.

Jeannière, A., '«En arkhê ên o logos». Note sur des problèmes de traduction', *RSR* 83 (1995), pp. 241–7.

Jonge, H. J. de, 'The Use of the Old Testament in Scripture Readings in Early Christian Assemblies', in *The Scriptures of Israel in Jewish and Christian Tradition* (ed. B. J. Koet, S. Moyise, and J. Verheyden; NovTSup, 148; Leiden: Brill, 2013), pp. 377–92.

Jonge, M. de, 'Christology, Controversy and Community in the Gospel of John', in Horrell and Tuckett (eds.), *Christology*, pp. 209–29.

—*Jesus: Stranger from Heaven and Son of God; Jesus Christ and the Christians in Johannine Perspective* (ed. J. E. Steely; SBLSBS, 11; Missoula: Scholars Press, 1977).

—*Pseudepigrapha of the Old Testament as Part of Christian Literature: The Case of the Testaments of the Twelve Patriarchs and the Greek Life of Adam and Eve* (SVTP, 18; Leiden: Brill, 2003).

—'Signs and Works in the Fourth Gospel', in *Miscellanea Neotestamentica* (ed. T. Baarda, A. F. I. Klijn, and W. C. van Unnik; NovTSup, 48; Leiden: Brill, 1978), pp. 107–26.

Jonge, M. de, and J. Tromp, *The Life of Adam and Eve and Related Literature* (GsAP; Sheffield: Sheffield Academic Press, 1997).

Joubert, J., 'Johannine Metaphors/Symbols Linked to the Paraclete-Spirit and Their Theological Implications', *AcT* 27 (2007), pp. 83–103.

Käsemann, E., *New Testament Questions of Today* (trans. W. J. Montague; London: SCM, 1969).

—*The Testament of Jesus: A Study of the Gospel of John in the Light of Chapter 17* (trans. G. Krodel; NTL; London: SCM, 1968).

Keener, C. S., *The Gospel of John: A Commentary* (2 vols.; Peabody: Hendrickson, 2003).

Kerr, A. R., *The Temple of Jesus' Body: The Temple Theme in the Gospel of John* (JSNTSup, 220; London: Sheffield Academic Press, 2002).

Kesich, V., 'Resurrection, Ascension, and the Giving of the Spirit', *GOTR* 25 (1980), pp. 249–60.

Koch, C., '"Es war aber an dem Ort ein Garten" (Joh 19,41): Der Garten als bedeutsames Erzählmotiv in den Johanneischen Passions- und Auferstehungstexten', in *Im Geist und in der Wahrheit: Studien zum Johannesevangelium und zur Offenbarung des Johannes sowie andere Beiträge* (ed. K. Huber and B. Repschinski; NTAbh, 52; Münster: Aschendorff, 2008), pp. 229–38.

—'Geschaffen, um Gott zu sehen. Die Heilung des Blindgeborenen als „Schöpfungsereignis" in Joh 9,1-38', in *Horizonte biblischer Texte* (ed. A. Vonach and G. Fischer; OBO, 196; Göttingen: Vandenhoeck & Ruprecht, 2003), pp. 195–222.

Koester, C. R., *Symbolism in the Fourth Gospel: Meaning, Mystery, Community* (Minneapolis: Fortress, 2nd edn, 2003).

—*The Word of Life: A Theology of John's Gospel* (Grand Rapids: Eerdmans, 2008).

Kooten, G. H. van, '"The True Light which Enlightens Everyone" (*John* 1:9): John, *Genesis*, the Platonic Notion of the "True, Noetic Light", and the Allegory of the Cave in Plato's *Republic*', in van Kooten (ed.), *The Creation of Heaven and Earth*, pp. 149–94.

Kooten, G. H. van (ed.), *The Creation of Heaven and Earth: Re-interpretations of Genesis I in the Context of Judaism, Ancient Philosophy, Christianity, and Modern Physics* (TBN, 8; Leiden: Brill, 2005).

Köstenberger, A. J., 'The Seventh Johannine Sign: A Study in John's Christology', *BBR* 5 (1995), pp. 87–103.

—*A Theology of John's Gospel and Letters: The Word, the Christ, the Son of God* (BTNT; Grand Rapids: Zondervan, 2009).

Kovacs, J. L., '"Now Shall the Ruler of This World Be Driven Out": Jesus' Death as Cosmic Battle in John 12:20–36', *JBL* 114 (1995), pp. 227–47.

Krans, J., B. J. Lietaert Peerbolte, P. B. Smit, and A. Zwiep (eds.), *Paul, John, and Apocalyptic Eschatology* (NovTSup, 149; Leiden: Brill, 2013).

Kruse, C. G., 'Paul and John: Two Witnesses, One Gospel', in Bird and Willitts (eds.), *Paul*, pp. 197–219.

Kubiś, A., *The Book of Zechariah in the Gospel of John* (EBib, 64; Pendé, France: Gabalda, 2012).

Kurz, W. S., 'Intertextual Permutations of the Genesis Word in the Johannine Prologues', in *Early Christian Interpretation of the Scriptures of Israel: Investigations and Proposals* (ed. C. A. Evans and J. A. Sanders; JSNTSup, 148; Sheffield: Sheffield Academic Press, 1997), pp. 179–90.

Labahn, M., *Offenbarung in Zeichen und Wort: Untersuchungen zur Vorgeschichte von Joh 6,1–25a und seiner Rezeption in der Brotrede* (WUNT, 2/117; Tübingen: Mohr Siebeck, 2000).

Lamarche, P., 'Le Prologue de Jean', *RSR* 52 (1964), pp. 497–537.

Lanfer, P. T., 'Allusion to and Expansion of the Tree of Life and Garden of Eden in Biblical and Pseudepigraphal Literature', in Evans and Zacharias (eds.), *Early Christian Literature*, pp. 96–108.

Larsen, K. B., *Recognizing the Stranger: Recognition Scenes in the Gospel of John* (BIS, 93; Leiden: Brill, 2008).

Laurentin, A., '*We'attah – Kai nun.* Formule caractéristique des textes juridiques et liturgiques (à propos de Jean 17,5)', *Bib* 45 (1964), pp. 413–32.

Lausberg, H., *Der Vers J 1,19 des Johannes-Evangeliums (im Rahmen des ‚redaktionellen Kapitels' J 1,19 – 2,11). Rhetorische Befunde zu Form und Sinn des Textes* (NAWG, 2; Göttingen: Vandenhoeck & Ruprecht, 1987).

—*Der Vers J 1,27 des Johannes-Evangeliums: Rhetorische Befunde zu Form und Sinn des Texts* (NAWG, 6; Göttingen: Vandenhoeck & Ruprecht, 1984).

—*Die Verse J 2,10-11 des Johannes-Evangeliums. Rhetorische Befunde zu Form und Sinn des Texts* (NAWG, 3; Göttingen: Vandenhoeck & Ruprecht, 1986).

Le Donne, A., and T. Thatcher (eds.), *The Fourth Gospel in First-Century Media Culture* (LNTS, 426; London: T&T Clark International, 2011).

Lee, D. A., 'Partnership in Easter Faith: The Role of Mary Magdalene and Thomas in John 20', *JSNT* 50 (1995), pp. 37–49.

Léon-Dufour, X., *Lecture de l'Évangile selon Jean* (4 vols.; Paris: Seuil, 1988–1996).

Leroy, H., *Rätsel und Missverständniss: Ein Beitrag zur Formgeschichte des Johannes-evangelium* (BBB; Bonn: Hanstein, 1968).

Levison, J. R., *Filled with the Spirit* (Grand Rapids: Eerdmans, 2009).

—*The Spirit in First Century Judaism* (AGJU, 29; Leiden: Brill, 1997).

Levonian, L., 'Insufflation', *The Expositor* 22 (1921), pp. 149–54.

Lieu, J., 'How John Writes', in Bockmuehl and Hagner (eds.), *The Written Gospel*, pp. 171–83.

—'Scripture and the Feminine in John', in *A Feminist Companion to the Hebrew Bible in the New Testament* (ed. A. Brenner; FCB, 10; Sheffield: Sheffield Academic Press, 1996), pp. 225–40.

Lightfoot, R. H., *St. John's Gospel: A Commentary* (Oxford: Clarendon, 1956).

Lincoln, A. T., *The Gospel according to Saint John* (BNTC; London: Continuum, 2005).

Lindars, B., *The Gospel of John* (NCB; London: Oliphants, 1972).

Lindeskog, G., *Studien zum neutestamentlichen Schöpfungsgedanken* (UUÅ, 11; Uppsala: Lundequist, 1952).

Little, E., *Echoes of the Old Testament in the Wine at Cana in Galilee (John 2:1-11) and the Multiplication of the Loaves and Fish (6:1-15): Towards an Appreciation* (CahRB, 41; Paris: Gabalda, 1998).

Litwa, M. D., 'Behold Adam: A Reading of John 19:5', *HBT* 32 (2010), pp. 129–43.

Lohmeyer, E., 'Über Aufbau und Gliederung des vierten Evangeliums', *ZNW* 27 (1928), pp. 11–36.

Loisy, A., *Le quatrième Évangile* (Paris: Émile Nourry, 2nd edn, 1921).

Löning, K., and E. Zenger, *Als Anfang schuf Gott: Biblische Schöpfungstheologien* (Düsseldorf: Patmos, 1997).

Loos, H. van der, *The Miracles of Jesus* (NovTSup, 9; Leiden: Brill, 1965).

Lund, N. W., 'The Influence of Chiasmus upon the Structure of the Gospels', *ATR* 13 (1931), pp. 41–6.

Luttikhuizen, G. P. (ed.), *Paradise Interpreted: Representations of Biblical Paradise in Judaism and Christianity* (TBN, 2; Leiden: Brill, 1999).

Luzárraga, J., 'Presentación de Jesús a la luz del A.T. en el Evangelio de Juan', *EstEcl* 51 (1976), pp. 497–520.

Lyon, R. W., 'John 20:22, Once More', *AsTJ* 43 (1988), pp. 73–85.

Madden, P. J., *Jesus' Walking on the Sea: An Investigation of the Origin of the Narrative Account* (BZAW, 81; Berlin: W. de Gruyter, 1997).

Malbon, E. S., 'Ending at the Beginning: A Response', *Semeia* 52 (1990), pp. 175–84.

Malina, B. J., and R. L. Rohrbaugh, *Social-Science Commentary on the Gospel of John* (Minneapolis: Fortress, 1998).

Manning, Jr., G. T., *Echoes of a Prophet: The Use of Ezekiel in the Gospel of John and in Literature of the Second Temple Period* (JSNTSup, 270; London: T&T Clark International, 2004).

Manns, F., *L'Evangile de Jean à la lumière du Judaïsme* (SBF, 33; Jerusalem: Franciscan Printing Press, 1991).

—'Le Symbolisme du Jardin dans le Récit de la Passion selon St Jean', *SBFLA* 37 (1987), pp. 53–80.

Marconi, G., 'La vista del cieco. Struttura di Gv 9,1-41', *Greg* 79 (1998), pp. 625–43.

Marquez, M., 'El Espíritu Santo, principio de la nueva creación, en función de la misión apostólica en Jn 20, 21-22', in *Jalones de la historia de la salvación en el Antiguo y Nuevo Testamento* (SBE, 26; Madrid: Consejo Superior de Investigaciones Científicas, 1969), pp. 121–48.

Marsh, J., *The Gospel of St John* (Harmondsworth: Penguin, 1968).

Martin, F. (ed.), *Narrative Parallels to the New Testament* (SBLRBS, 22; Atlanta: Scholars Press, 1988).

Martyn, J. L., *The Gospel of John and Christian History: Essays for Interpreters* (New York: Paulist, 1978).

—*History and Theology in the Fourth Gospel* (Louisville: John Knox, 3rd edn, 2003).

Mateos, J., and J. Barreto, *El Evangelio de Juan: Análisis lingüístico y comentario exegético* (Madrid: Cristiandad, 3rd edn, 1992).

—*Vocabulario Teológico del Evangelio de Juan* (Madrid: Cristiandad, 1980).

Matera, F. J., 'Christ in the Theologies of Paul and John: A Study in the Diverse Unity of New Testament Theology', *ThSt* 67 (2006), pp. 237–56.

May, H. G., 'The King in the Garden of Eden: A Study of Ezekiel 28:12–19', in *Israel's Prophetic Heritage* (ed. B. W. Anderson and W. Harrelson; London: SCM, 1962), pp. 166–76.

McDonough, S. M., *Christ as Creator: Origins of a New Testament Doctrine* (Oxford: Oxford University Press, 2009).

McHugh, J. F., *A Critical and Exegetical Commentary on John 1–4* (ed. G. N. Stanton; London: T&T Clark International, 2009).

McRae, G., 'Theology and Irony in the Fourth Gospel', in *The Gospel of John as Literature: An Anthology of Twentieth-Century Perspectives* (ed. M. W. G. Stibbe; NTTS, 17; Leiden: Brill, 1993), pp. 103–13.

McWhirter, J., *The Bridegroom Messiah and the People of God: Marriage in the Fourth Gospel* (New York: Cambridge University Press, 2006).

Meeks, W. A., 'Equal to God', in Fortna and Gaventa (eds.), *The Conversation Continues*, pp. 309–21.

—'The Man from Heaven in Johannine Sectarianism', *JBL* 91 (1972), pp. 44–72.

—*The Prophet-King: Moses Traditions and the Johannine Christology* (NovTSup, 14; Leiden: Brill, 1967).

Menken, M. J. J., '"Born of God" or "Begotten by God"? A Translation Problem in the Johannine Writings', *NovT* 51 (2009), pp. 352–68.

—'The Christology of the Fourth Gospel: A Survey of Recent Research', in *From Jesus to John* (ed. M. C. de Boer; JSNTSup, 84; Sheffield: Sheffield Academic Press, 1993), pp. 292–320.

—'Genesis in John's Gospel and 1 John', in *Genesis in the New Testament* (ed. M. J. J. Menken and S. Moyise; LNTS, 466; London: Bloomsbury T&T Clark, 2012), pp. 83–98.

—*Numerical Literary Techniques in John: The Fourth Evangelist's Use of Numbers of Words and Syllables* (NovTSup, 55; Leiden: Brill, 1985).

—'Observations on the Significance of the Old Testament in the Fourth Gospel', in Van Belle, van der Watt, and Maritz (eds.), *Theology and Christology*, pp. 155–75.

—*Old Testament Quotations in the Fourth Gospel: Studies in Textual Form* (CBET, 15; Kampen: Pharos, 1996).

—'What Authority Does the Fourth Evangelist Claim for His Book?', in Krans et al. (eds.), *Paul, John*, pp. 186–202.

Metzger, B. M., *A Textual Commentary on the Greek New Testament* (Stuttgart: United Bible Societies, 2nd edn, 1994).

Michaels, J. R., *The Gospel of John* (NICNT; Grand Rapids: Eerdmans, 2010).

Mihalios, S., *The Danielic Eschatological Hour in the Johannine Literature* (LNTS, 436; London: T&T Clark International, 2011).

Miller, Ed. L., '"In the Beginning": A Christological Transparency', *NTS* 45 (1999), pp. 587–92.

—*Salvation-History in the Prologue of John: The Significance of John 1:3/4* (Leiden: Brill, 1989).

Minear, P. S., *Christians and the New Creation: Genesis Motifs in the New Testament* (Louisville: Westminster John Knox, 1994).

—'John 17:1-11', *Int* 32 (1978), pp. 175–9.

—'Logos Affiliations in Johannine Thought', in *Christology in Dialogue* (ed. R. F. Berkey and S. A. Edwards; Cleveland: Pilgrim, 1993), pp. 142–56.

—'The Promise of Life in the Gospel of John', *TTod* 49 (1993), pp. 485–99.

Mollat, D., *Études johanniques* (PDD; Paris: Seuil, 1979).

Moloney, F. J., *Glory Not Dishonor: Reading John 13–21* (Eugene, Ore.: Wipf & Stock, 2004).

—*The Gospel of John* (SP, 4; Collegeville: Liturgical, 1998).

—'The Gospel of John: The "End" of Scripture', *Int* 63 (2009), pp. 356–66.

—'John 21 and the Johannine Story', in Thatcher and Moore (eds.), *Anatomies of Narrative Criticism*, pp. 237–51.

Moody, D., 'God's Only Son: The Translation of John 3:16 in the Revised Standard Version', *JBL* 72 (1953), pp. 213–19.

Moore, A. M., *Signs of Salvation: The Theme of Creation in John's Gospel* (Cambridge: James Clark, 2013).

—'The Theme of Creation in the Fourth Gospel' (Ph.D. diss., University of Leeds, 2010).

Morgenthaler, R., *Statistik des neutestamentlichen Wortschatzes* (Zurich: Gotthelf Verlag, 3rd edn, 1992).

Most, G. W., *Doubting Thomas* (Cambridge, Mass.: Harvard University Press, 2005).

Moyise, S., 'Intertextuality and Biblical Studies: A Review', *VerEc* 23 (2002), pp. 418–31.

Muñoz-León, D., 'El Pentateuco en San Juan', in *Entrar en lo Antiguo: Acerca de la relación entre Antiguo y Nuevo Testamento* (ed. I. Carbajosa and L. Sánchez-Narravo; PD, 16; Madrid: Facultad de Teología San Dámaso, 2007), pp. 107–66.

Myers, A. D., *Characterizing Jesus: A Rhetorical Analysis on the Fourth Gospel's Use of Scripture in Its Presentation of Jesus* (LNTS, 458; London: T&T Clark International, 2012).

Neirynck, F., *Jean et les Synoptiques: Examen critique de l'exégèse de M.-É Boismard* (BETL, 49; Leuven: Leuven University Press, 1979).

Nicholls, R., *Walking on the Water: Reading MT 14:22-23 in the Light of Its Wirkungsgeschichte* (Leiden: Brill, 2008).

Nicklas, T., *Ablösung und Verstrickung: 'Juden' und Jüngergestalten als Charaktere der erzählten Welt des Johannesevangeliums und ihre Wirkung auf den impliziten Leser* (RST, 60; Frankfurt: Peter Lang, 2002).

Nir, R., 'The Struggle between the "Image of God" and Satan in the *Greek Life of Adam and Eve*', *SJT* 61 (2008), pp. 327–39.

Nolland, J., *The Gospel of Matthew: A Commentary on the Greek Text* (NIGTC; Grand Rapids: Eerdmans, 2005).

—'The Thought in John 1:3c-4', *TynBul* 62 (2011), pp. 295–312.

Nongbri, B., 'The Limits of Palaeographic Dating of Literary Papyri: Some Observations on the Date and Provenance of P. Bodmer II (P66)', *MH* 71 (2014), pp. 1–35.

—'The Use and Abuse of 𝔓⁵²: Papyrological Pitfalls in the Dating of the Fourth Gospel', *HTR* 98 (2005), pp. 23–48.

O'Brien, K. S., 'Written that You May Believe: John 20 and Narrative Rhetoric', *CBQ* 67 (2005), pp. 284–302.

O'Day, G. R., 'John 6:15-21: Jesus Walking on Water as Narrative Embodiment of Johannine Christology', in *Critical Readings of John 6* (ed. R. Alan Culpepper; Leiden: Brill, 1997), pp. 149–59.

Odeberg, H., *The Fourth Gospel: Interpreted in Its Relation to Contemporaneous Religious Currents in Palestine and the Hellenistic-Oriental World* (Uppsala: Almquist & Wiksell, 1929).

Omodeo, A., *La Mistica giovannea: saggio critico con nuova traduzione dei testi* (CS; Bari, Italy: Gius, Laterza & Figli, 1930).

Opatrný, D., 'The Figure of a Blind Man in the Light of the Papyrological Evidence', *Bib* 91 (2010), pp. 583–94.

Pagels, E., *The Johannine Gospel in Gnostic Exegesis: Heracleon's Commentary on John* (SBLMS, 17; Nashville: Abingdon, 1973).

Painter, J., 'Earth Made Whole: John's Rereading of Genesis', in *Word, Theology, and Community in John* (ed. J. Painter, R. A. Culpepper, and F. F. Segovia; St. Louis, Miss.: Chalice, 2002), pp. 65–84.

—'Inclined to God: The Quest for Eternal Life—Bultmannian Hermeneutics and Theology of the Fourth Gospel', in Culpepper and Black (eds.), *Exploring the Gospel of John*, pp. 346–68.

—'John 9 and the Interpretation of the Fourth Gospel', *JSNT* 28 (1986), pp. 31–61.

—'"The Light Shines in the Darkness...": Creation, Incarnation, and Resurrection in John', in *The Resurrection of Jesus in the Gospel of John* (ed. C. R. Koester and R. Bieringer; Tübingen: Mohr Siebeck, 2008), pp. 21–46.

—'The Point of John's Christology: Christology, Conflict and Community in John', in Horrell and Tuckett (eds.), *Christology*, pp. 231–52.

—'Rereading Genesis in the Prologue of John?', in Aune, Seland, and Ulrichsen (eds.), *Neotestamentica et Philonica*, pp. 179–201.

—'The Signs of the Messiah and the Quest for Eternal Life', in Thatcher (ed.), *What We Have Heard*, pp. 233–56.

Palmer, S., 'Repetition and the Art of Reading: καὶ τῇ ἡμέρᾳ τῇ τρίτῃ, "On the Third Day" in John's Gospel', in Van Belle, Labahn, and Maritz (eds.), *Repetitions*, pp. 403–17.

Pancaro, S., *The Law in the Fourth Gospel* (NovTSup, 42; Leiden: Brill, 1975).

Pendrick, G., 'ΜΟΝΟΓΕΝΗΣ', *NTS* 41 (1995), pp. 587–600.

Perkins, P., *Resurrection: New Testament Witness and Contemporary Reflection* (Garden City: Doubleday, 1984).

Phillips, P. M., *The Prologue of the Fourth Gospel: A Sequential Reading* (LNTS, 294; London: T&T Clark International, 2006).

Phillips, T. E., '"The Third Fifth Day?" John 2:1 in Context', *ExpTim* 115 (2004), pp. 328–31.

Phythian-Adams, W. J., 'The New Creation in St. John', *CQR* 144 (1947), pp. 52–75.
Poirier, J. C., '"Day and Night" and the Punctuation of John 9.3', *NTS* 42 (1996), pp. 288–94.
—'"Day and Night" and the Sabbath Controversy of John 9', *FN* 19 (2006), pp. 113–19.
Pollard, T. E., 'Cosmology and the Prologue of the Fourth Gospel', *VC* 12 (1958), pp. 147–53.
Popkes, E. E., *Die Theologie der Liebe Gottes in den johanneischen Schriften: Zur Semantik der Liebe und zum Motivkreis des Dualismus* (WUNT, 2/197; Tübingen: Mohr Siebeck, 2005).
Porter, S. E., 'Allusions and Echoes', in *As It Is Written: Studying Paul's Use of Scripture* (ed. S. E. Porter and C. D. Stanley; SBLSymS, 50; Atlanta: Society of Biblical Literature, 2008), pp. 29–40.
Potterie, I. de la, 'L'emploi dynamique de εἰς dans Saint Jean et ses incidences théologiques', *Bib* 43 (1962), pp. 366–87.
—'Genèse de la foi Pascale de'après Jn. 20', *NTS* 30 (1984), pp. 26–49.
—*La Passion de Jésus selon l'Évangile de Jean: Texte et Esprit* (Paris: Cerf, 1986).
—*La Vérité dans Saint Jean* (AnBib, 73–74; 2 vols.; Rome: Biblical Institute Press, 1977).
Puech, É., 'L'Esprit saint à Qumrân', *SBFLA* 49 (1999), pp. 283–97.
Quiévreux, F., 'La structure symbolique de l'Évangile de Saint Jean', *RHPR* 33 (1953), pp. 123–65.
Quimby, C. W., *John: The Universal Gospel* (New York: Macmillan, 1947).
Rae, M., 'The Testimony of Works in the Christology of John's Gospel', in Bauckham and Mosser (eds.), *Gospel of John*, pp. 295–310.
Rasimus, T. (ed.), *The Legacy of John: Second-Century Reception of the Fourth Gospel* (NovTSup, 132; Leiden: Brill, 2010).
Reim, G., *Studien zum alttestamentlichen Hintergrund des Johannesevangeliums* (SNTSMS, 22; Cambridge: Cambridge University Press, 1974).
Revell, C. N., and S. A. Hunt, 'The Co-Crucified Men: Shadows by His Cross', in Hunt, Tolmie, and Zimmermann (eds.), *Character Studies in the Fourth Gospel*, pp. 607–17.
Robinson, J. A. T., 'The "Others" of John 4,38: A Test of Exegetical Method', *SE* 1 (1959), pp. 510–15.
—*The Priority of John* (London: SCM, 1985).
Robinson, P., 'Gethsemane: The Synoptic and the Johannine Viewpoints', *CQR* 167 (1966), pp. 4–11.
Robson, J., *Word and Spirit in Ezekiel* (LHBOTS, 447; London: T&T Clark International, 2006).
Ronning, J., *The Jewish Targums and John's Logos Theology* (Peabody: Hendrickson, 2010).
Rosik, M., 'Discovering the Secrets of God's Gardens. Resurrection as New Creation (Gen 2:4b–3:24; Jn 20:1-18)', *SBFLA* 58 (2008), pp. 81–98.
Rossum, J. van, 'The "Johannine Pentecost": John 20:22 in Modern Exegesis and in Orthodox Theology', *SVTQ* 35 (1991), pp. 149–67.
Runia, D. T., Review of C. M. Carmichael, *The Story of Creation: Its Origins and Its Interpretation in Philo and the Fourth Gospel*, *RevBL* 1 (1999), pp. 299–301.

Rutten, J. T. A. G. M. van, 'The Creation of Man and Woman in Early Jewish Literature', in *The Creation of Man and Woman: Interpretations of the Biblical Narratives in Jewish and Christian Traditions* (ed. G. P. Luttikhuizen; TBN, 3; Leiden: Brill, 2000), pp. 34–62.

Saxby, H., 'The Time-Scheme in the Gospel of John', *ExpTim* 104 (1992), pp. 9–13.

Schaper, J., 'The Messiah in the Garden: John 19.38-41, (Royal) Gardens, and Messianic Concepts', in *Paradise in Antiquity: Jewish and Christian Views* (ed. M. Bockmuehl and G. G. Stroumsa; Cambridge: Cambridge University Press, 2010), pp. 17–27.

Schmid, K., and C. Riedweg (eds.), *Beyond Eden: The Biblical Story of Paradise (Genesis 2–3) and Its Reception History* (FAT, 2/34; Tübingen: Mohr Siebeck, 2008).

Schmitt, J., 'Simples remarques sur le fragment, Jo., XX, 22-23', in *Mélanges en l'honneur de Monseigneur Michael Andrieu* (RevScRel; Strasburg: Palais Universitaire, 1956), pp. 415–23.

Schnackenburg, R., *The Gospel according to St John* (trans. K. Smyth; HTKNT; 3 vols.; London: Burns & Oates, 1968–1982).

Schneiders, S. M., 'John 20:11–18: The Encounter of the Easter Jesus with Mary Magdalene—A Transformative Feminist Reading', in *"What is John?" Readers and Readings of the Fourth Gospel* (ed. F. Segovia; SBLSymS, 3; Atlanta: Scholars Press, 1996), pp. 155–68.

—'The Raising of the New Temple: John 20.19-23 and Johannine Ecclesiology', *NTS* 52 (2006), pp. 337–55.

Schnelle, U., *Theology of the New Testament* (trans. M. E. Boring; Grand Rapids: Baker Academic, 2009).

Schuchard, B. G., *Scripture within Scripture: The Interrelationship of Form and Function in the Explicit Old Testament Citations in the Gospel of John* (SBLDS, 133; Atlanta: Scholars Press, 1992).

Schwartz, E., *Aporien im vierten Evangelium* (NKGWG, 1, 2, 4; Berlin: Weidmannsche Buchhandlung, 1907–1908), vol. 1, pp. 342–72; vol. 2, pp. 115–88; vol. 4, pp. 497–560.

Schwarz, G., 'Gen 1 1 2 2a und John 1 1a.3a – ein Vergleich', *ZNW* 73 (1982), pp. 136–7.

Schweizer, E., *The Holy Spirit* (trans. R. H. Fuller and I. Fuller; Philadelphia: Fortress, 1980).

Segal, A. F., 'Ruler of This World: Attitudes about Mediator Figures and the Importance of Sociology for Self-Definition', in *Aspects of Judaism in the Graeco-Roman Period* (ed. E. P. Sanders, A. I. Baumgarten, and A. Mendelson; JCSD, 2; London: SCM, 1981), pp. 245–68, 403–13.

Skehan, P. W., 'The Date of the Last Supper', *CBQ* 20 (1958), pp. 192–9.

Skinner, C. W., 'Virtue in the New Testament: The Legacies of Paul and John in Comparative Perspective', in *Unity and Diversity in the Gospels and Paul* (ed. C. W. Skinner and K. R. Iverson; SBLECL, 7; Atlanta: Society of Biblical Literature, 2012), pp. 301–24.

Smith, D. A., *Revisiting the Empty Tomb: The Early History of Easter* (Minneapolis: Fortress, 2010).

Sosa Siliezar, C. R., 'La creación en el Evangelio de Juan: Una revisión bibliográfica de autores anglófonos', *ScrTh* 45 (2013), pp. 445–63.

Spencer, W. H., 'John ix.3', *ExpTim* 55 (1944), p. 110.

Spieckermann, H., 'Is God's Creation Good? From Hesiodos to Plato and from the Creation Narratives (Genesis 1–3) to Ben Sira', in Schmid and Riedweg (eds.), *Beyond Eden*, pp. 79–94.

Staley, J. L., *The Print's First Kiss: A Rhetorical Investigation of the Implied Reader in the Fourth Gospel* (SBLDS, 82; Atlanta: Scholars Press, 1988).

—'Stumbling in the Dark, Reaching for the Light: Reading Characters in John 5 and 9', *Semeia* 53 (1991), pp. 55–80.

Stamm, R. T., 'Creation and Revelation in the Gospel of John', in *Search the Scripture: New Testament Studies in Honor of Raymond T. Stamm* (ed. J. M. Myers; Leiden: Brill, 1969), pp. 13–32.

Stanley, C. D., *Arguing with Scripture: The Rhetoric of Quotation in the Letters of Paul* (London: T&T Clark International, 2004).

Stanley, D. M., 'The Passion according to John', *Worship* 33 (1959), pp. 210–30.

Stauffer, E., *Jesus and His Story* (trans. D. M. Barton; London: SCM, 1960).

Stephens, M. B., *Annihilation or Renewal? The Meaning and Function of New Creation in the Book of Revelation* (WUNT, 2/307; Tübingen: Mohr Siebeck, 2011).

Stibbe, M. W. G., *John* (Sheffield: JSOT Press, 1993).

Still, E. C., 'Sent to Be Scarred: John 20:19-23', *ExpTim* 113 (2002), p. 190.

Stordalen, T., *Echoes of Eden: Genesis 2–3 and Symbolism of the Eden Garden in Biblical Hebrew Literature* (CBET, 25; Leuven: Peeters, 2000).

Straub, E., 'Alles ist durch ihn geworden. Die Erschaffung des Lebens in der Sabbatheilung Joh 5,1-18', in Dettwiler and Poplutz (eds.), *Studien*, pp. 157–67.

Strauss, D. F., *The Life of Jesus Critically Examined* (trans. G. Eliot; London: Swan Sonnenschein, 1898).

Suggit, J., 'Jesus the Gardener: The Atonement in the Fourth Gospel as Re-creation', *Neot* 33 (1999), pp. 161–8.

Sundberg, A. C., 'Christology in the Fourth Gospel', *BibRes* 21 (1976), pp. 29–37.

Swart, G., 'Aristobulus' Interpretation of LXX Sabbath Texts as an Interpretative Key to John 5:1-18', *JSem* 18 (2009), pp. 569–82.

Swetnam, J., 'Bestowal of the Spirit in the Fourth Gospel', *Bib* 74 (1993), pp. 556–76.

Taylor, J., 'The Garden of Gethsemane, Not the Place of Jesus' Arrest', *BAR* 21 (1995), pp. 26–35.

Temple, S., 'The Two Signs in the Fourth Gospel', *JBL* 81 (1962), pp. 169–74.

Terian, A., 'Creation in Johannine Theology', in *Good News in History: Essays in Honor of Bo Reicke* (ed. Ed. L. Miller; Atlanta: Scholars Press, 1993), pp. 45–61.

Thatcher, T., 'Anatomies of the Fourth Gospel: Past, Present, and Future Probes', in Thatcher and Moore (eds.), *Anatomies of Narrative Criticism*, pp. 1–37.

—'The Riddle of the Baptist and the Genesis of the Prologue: John 1.1-18 in Oral/Aural Media Culture', in Le Donne and Thatcher (eds.), *Media Culture*, pp. 29–48.

Thatcher, T. (ed.), *What We Have Heard from the Beginning: The Past, Present, and Future of Johannine Studies* (Waco, Tex.: Baylor University Press, 2007).

Thatcher, T., and S. D. Moore (eds.), *Anatomies of Narrative Criticism: The Past, Present, and Futures of the Fourth Gospel as Literature* (SBLRBS, 55; Atlanta: Society of Biblical Literature, 2008).

Thompson, M., *Clothed with Christ: The Example and Teaching of Jesus in Romans 12.1–15.13* (JSNTSup, 59; Sheffield: JSOT Press, 1991).

Thompson, M. M., 'The Breath of Life: John 20:22-23 Once More', in *The Holy Spirit and Christian Origins* (ed. G. N. Stanton, B. W. Longenecker, and S. C. Barton; Grand Rapids: Eerdmans, 2004), pp. 69–78.

—*The God of the Gospel of John* (Grand Rapids: Eerdmans, 2001).

—*The Humanity of Jesus in the Fourth Gospel* (Philadelphia: Fortress, 1988).

Tilborg, S. van, 'Cosmological Implications of Johannine Christology', in Van Belle, van der Watt, and Maritz (eds.), *Theology and Christology*, pp. 483–502.

Tov, E., 'The Septuagint', in *Mikra: Text, Translation, Reading and Interpretation of the Hebrew Bible in Ancient Judaism and Early Christianity* (ed. M. J. Mulder; CRINT, 2; Philadelphia: Fortress, 1988), pp. 161–88.

—*Textual Criticism of the Hebrew Bible* (Minneapolis: Fortress, 3rd rev. and expanded edn, 2012).

Trudinger, P., '"On the Third Day There Was a Wedding at Cana": Reflexions on St John 2, 1-12', *DRev* 104 (1986), pp. 41–3.

—'The Seven Days of the New Creation in St. John's Gospel: Some Further Reflections', *EvQ* 44 (1972), pp. 154–9.

Turner, M. M. B., 'The Concept of Receiving the Spirit in John's Gospel', *VE* 10 (1977), pp. 24–42.

—*The Holy Spirit and Spiritual Gifts: Then and Now* (Cumbria: Paternoster, 1999).

Turpie, D. M., *The Old Testament in the New: A Contribution to Biblical Criticism and Interpretation* (London: Williams and Norgate, 1868).

Um, S. T., *The Theme of Temple Christology in John's Gospel* (LNTS, 312; London: T&T Clark International, 2006).

Van Belle, G., *Les parenthèses dans l'évangile de Jean: Aperçu historique et classification, texte grec de Jean* (Leuven: Leuven University Press, 1985).

—'Tradition, Exegetical Formation, and the Leuven Hypothesis', in Thatcher (ed.), *What We Have Heard*, pp. 325–37.

Van Belle, G., J. G. van der Watt, and P. Maritz (eds.), *Theology and Christology in the Fourth Gospel* (BETL, 184; Leuven: Leuven University Press, 2005).

Van Belle, G., M. Labahn, and P. Maritz (eds.), *Repetitions and Variations in the Fourth Gospel: Style, Text, Interpretation* (BETL, 223; Leuven: Peeters, 2009).

Vanhoye, A., 'L'œuvre du Christ, don du Père (Jn 5,36 et 17,4)', *RSR* 48 (1960), pp. 377–419.

Voortman, T. C., 'Understanding the Fourth Gospel from the Perspective of the Creation Theme' (D.Litt. et Phil. diss., Rand Afrikaans University, 1998).

Waaler, E., *The Shema and The First Commandment in First Corinthians: An Intertextual Approach to Paul's Re-reading of Deuteronomy* (WUNT, 2/253; Tübingen: Mohr Siebeck, 2008).

Waetjen, H. C., *The Gospel of the Beloved Disciple: A Work in Two Editions* (London: T&T Clark International, 2005).

Wahlde, U. C. von, 'Faith and Works in Jn VI 28-29. Exegesis or Eisegesis?', *NovT* 22 (1980), pp. 304–15.

—*The Gospel and Letters of John* (ECC; 3 vols.; Grand Rapids: Eerdmans, 2010).

Watt, J. van der, '"Working the Works of God": Identity and Behaviour in the Gospel of John', in Krans et al. (eds.), *Paul, John*, pp. 135–50.

Weder, H., '*Deus Incarnatus*: On the Hermeneutics of Christology in the Johannine Writings' (trans. D. W. Scott), in Culpepper and Black (eds.), *Exploring the Gospel of John*, pp. 327–45.

Weidemann, H. U., 'The Victory of Protology over Eschatology? Creation in the Gospel of John', in *Theologies of Creation in Early Judaism and Ancient Christianity* (ed. T. Nicklas and K. Zamfir; DCLS, 6; Berlin: W. de Gruyter, 2010), pp. 299–334.

Weiss, H., 'The Sabbath in the Fourth Gospel', *JBL* 110 (1991), pp. 311–21.

Weiss, J. (ed.), *Die Schriften des Neuen Testaments* (4 vols.; Göttingen: Vandenhoeck & Ruprecht, 3d ed., 1918).

Wevers, J. W., *Notes on the Greek Text of Genesis* (SBLSCS, 35; Atlanta: Scholars Press, 1993).

Williams, C. H., 'Abraham as a Figure of Memory in John 8.31-59', in Le Donne and Thatcher (eds.), *Media Culture*, pp. 205–22.

—'The Gospel of John', in *The Oxford Handbook of the Reception History of the Bible* (ed. M. Lieb, E. Mason, J. Roberts, and C. Rowland; Oxford: Oxford University Press, 2011), pp. 104–17.

—'"He Saw His Glory and Spoke About Him": The Testimony of Isaiah and Johannine Christology', in *Honouring the Past and Shaping the Future: Religious and Biblical Studies in Wales* (ed. R. Pope; Leominster: Gracewing, 2003), pp. 53–80.

—*I am He: The Interpretation of 'Anî Hû' in Jewish and Early Christian Literature* (WUNT, 2/113; Tübingen: Mohr Siebeck, 2000).

—'"I Am" or "I Am He"? Self-Declaratory Pronouncements in the Fourth Gospel and Rabbinic Tradition', in *Jesus in Johannine Tradition* (ed. R. T. Fortna and T. Thatcher; Louisville: Westminster John Knox, 2001), pp. 343–52.

—'Inspecting an Aerial Photograph of John's Engagement with Sources', in Thatcher (ed.), *What We Have Heard*, pp. 83–5.

—'Interpretations of the Identity and Role of Jesus', in *The Biblical World* (ed. J. Barton; vol. 2; London: Routledge, 2002), pp. 332–54.

—'Isaiah in John's Gospel', in *Isaiah in the New Testament* (ed. S. Moyise and M. J. J. Menken; London: T&T Clark International, 2005), pp. 101–16.

—'John and the Rabbis Revisited', in *Engaging with C. H. Dodd on the Gospel of John: Sixty Years of Tradition and Interpretation* (ed. T. Thatcher and C. H. Williams; Cambridge: Cambridge University Press, 2013), pp. 107–25.

—Review of C. M. Carmichael, *The Story of Creation: Its Origins and Its Interpretation in Philo and the Fourth Gospel; JTS* 49 (1998), pp. 531–2.

—'The Testimony of Isaiah and Johannine Christology', in *"As Those Who Are Taught": The Interpretation of Isaiah from the LXX to the SBL* (ed. C. Mathews McGinnis and P. K. Tull; SBLSymS, 27; Atlanta: Society of Biblical Literature, 2006), pp. 107–24.

Williams, P. J., 'Not the Prologue of John', *JSNT* 33 (2011), pp. 375–86.

Winter, P., 'ΜΟΝΟΓΕΝΗΣ ΠΑΡΑ ΠΑΤΡΟΣ', *ZRGG* 5 (1953), pp. 335–63.

Witherington, B., *John's Wisdom: A Commentary on the Fourth Gospel* (Cambridge: Lutterworth, 1995).

Witkamp, L. Th., 'Some Specific Johannine Features in John 6.1-21', *JSNT* 40 (1990), pp. 43–60.

Wojciechowski, M., 'Le don de L'Esprit Saint dans Jean 20.22 selon Tg. Gn. 2.7', *NTS* 33 (1987), pp. 289–91.

Wold, B. G., *Women, Men, and Angels: The Qumran Wisdom Document* Musar leMevin *and Its Allusions to Genesis Creation Traditions* (WUNT, 2/201; Tübingen: Mohr Siebeck, 2005).

Worthington, J. D., *Creation in Paul and Philo: The Beginning and Before* (WUNT, 2/317; Tübingen: Mohr Siebeck, 2011).

Wright IV, W. M., *Rhetoric and Theology: Figural Reading of John 9* (BZAW, 165; Berlin: W. de Gruyter, 2009).

Wyatt, N., '"Supposing Him to Be the Gardener" (John 20,15). A Study of the Paradise Motif in John', *ZNW* 81 (1990), pp. 21–38.

Yarbro-Collins, A., 'Rulers, Divine Men, and Walking on the Water (Mark 6:45-52)', in *Religious Propaganda and Missionary Competition in the New Testament World* (ed. L. Bormann, K. del Tredici, and A. Standhartinger; NovTSup, 74; Leiden: Brill, 1994), pp. 207–27.

Zeilinger, F., *Die sieben Zeichenhandlungen Jesu im Johannesevangelium* (Stuttgart: Kohlhammer, 2011).

Zimmermann, R., 'Symbolic Communication between John and His Reader: The Garden Symbolism in John 19–20', in Thatcher and Moore (eds.), *Anatomies of Narrative Criticism*, pp. 221–35.

Zumstein, J,. 'Intratextuality and Intertextuality in the Gospel of John' (trans. M. Gray), in Thatcher and Moore (eds.), *Anatomies of Narrative Criticism*, pp. 121–35.

INDEX OF AUTHORS

May, H. G. 187
McCarthy, C. 82, 117
McDonough, S. M. 9, 41, 63, 113, 114
McHugh, J. F. 33–6, 43–7, 49, 52, 54, 55, 74
McLean, B. H. 17, 18
McRae, G. 83, 178
McWhirter, J. 11, 13, 16, 17, 19, 20, 182
Meeks, W. A. 88, 110, 179, 183, 193, 195
Menken, M. J. J. 14, 16, 19, 31, 44, 51, 61, 83, 123–5, 155, 197, 202
Mercier, C. 82, 117
Metzger, B. M. 46, 76, 125, 168
Michaels, J. R. 25, 32, 33, 36, 41, 44, 46–9, 51, 52, 54, 59, 64, 74, 85, 87, 88, 91–3, 95–102, 105, 114, 119, 121, 127, 133, 135, 138, 140, 147, 163–5, 168, 171, 172, 177, 190
Mihalios, S. 11, 16, 74
Milik, J. T. 184
Miller, Ed. L. 35
Minear, P. S. 5, 6, 28, 61, 83, 84, 90, 113
Mollat, D. 166
Moloney, F. J. 37, 44, 45, 49, 50, 52, 60, 62, 79, 85, 88, 89, 92, 94, 95, 97, 101, 119, 120, 133, 134, 137, 138, 140, 162, 164, 170, 188
Moody, D. 51
Moore, A. M. 7, 8, 127, 131, 132, 135–40, 175, 177, 178, 180, 184, 186, 187, 189
Morgenthaler, R. 73
Most, G. W. 162
Moyise, S. 14
Mozley, J. H. 116
Muñoz-León, D. 141
Myers, A. D. 16, 202

Neirynck, F. 126
Neusner, J. 101
Nicholls, R. 105
Nicklas, T. 93
Nir, R. 185
Nolland, J. 46, 86
Nongbri, B. 200

O'Brien, K. S. 164
O'Day, G. R. 110, 112, 113
Odeberg, H. 81
Omodeo, A. 123
Opatrný, D. 115

Pagels, E. 19
Painter, J. 8, 9, 41, 49, 83, 90, 93, 95, 113, 120, 131, 170, 196
Palmer, S. 135
Pancaro, S. 78
Paul, A. 15
Pendrick, G. 51
Perkins, P. 164
Phillips, P. M. 33, 41, 43–6, 48, 50–2
Phillips, T. E. 126
Phythian-Adams, W. J. 3
Poirier, J. C. 93
Pollard, T. E. 35
Popkes, E. E. 196
Porter, S. E. 13
Potterie, I. de la 35, 44, 83, 112, 162, 188
Puech, É. 158
Pusey, P. E. 160, 189

Quiévreux, F. 124, 128, 131, 141, 189
Quimby, C. W. 193

Rae, M. 90, 95, 131, 132, 136
Rasimus, T. 19
Rea, J. R. 15
Reim, G. 30, 31, 33, 84, 100, 105, 116, 156, 161
Rengstorf, K. H. 18, 115
Reuss, J. 19, 149
Revell, C. N. 21
Roberts, C. H. 200
Robinson, J. A. T. 96, 124, 125, 141
Robinson, P. 180
Robson, J. 156
Rohrbaugh, R. L. 114
Ronning, J. 5
Rosik, M. 177, 180, 184, 186
Rossum, J. van 160
Rousseau, A. 82, 117
Runia, D. T. 131
Rutten, J. T. A. G. M. van 15

Sáenz-Badillos, A. 34, 35, 38, 39, 72
Sanders, J. A. 11
Satran, D. 202, 203
Saxby, H. 100, 124, 125, 127, 131, 133
Schaper, J. 176, 177, 180, 189
Schmidt, C. 108
Schmitt, J. 172